Shaping Phonology

Shaping Phonology

EDITED BY DIANE BRENTARI AND
JACKSON L. LEE

The University of Chicago Press   Chicago and London

The University of Chicago Press, Chicago 60637
The University of Chicago Press, Ltd., London

For more information, contact the University of Chicago Press, 1427 E. 60th St., Chicago, IL 60637.
Published 2018
Printed in the United States of America

27 26 25 24 23 22 21 20 19 18 1 2 3 4 5

ISBN-13: 978-0-226-56245-2 (cloth)
ISBN-13: 978-0-226-56259-9 (e-book)
DOI: https://doi.org/10.7208/chicago/9780226562599.001.0001

Library of Congress Cataloging-in-Publication Data

Names: Brentari, Diane, editor. | Lee, Jackson L., editor.
Title: Shaping phonology / edited by Diane Brentari and Jackson L. Lee.
Description: Chicago ; London : The University of Chicago Press, 2018. | Includes bibliographical references and index.
Identifiers: LCCN 2017051657 | ISBN 9780226562452 (cloth : alk. paper) | ISBN 9780226562599 (e-book)
Subjects: LCSH: Grammar, Comparative and general—Phonology. | Autosegmental theory (Linguistics) | Computational linguistics—Methodology. | Computational learning theory.
Classification: LCC P217.3.S53 2018 | DDC 414—dc23
LC record available at https://lccn.loc.gov/2017051657

♾ This paper meets the requirements of ANSI/NISO Z39.48-1992 (Permanence of Paper).

Contents

Preface

Within the last forty years, the field of phonology has undergone several important theoretical shifts with regard to phonological representation that have now become part of standard practice in the field. The two shifts that will be taken up in this volume have some properties in common: (1) both have had the effect of taking phonological analysis "off the page," which made it necessary to think of phonology in multidimensional space; and (2) John Goldsmith has been a major force in bringing about these changes. Part 1 of this volume has to do with a radical elaboration of the abstract domains (or units of analysis) that come under the purview of phonology, along with a more multidimensional approach to considering their role in the system. Autosegmental phonology (Goldsmith 1976) and feature geometry (Clements 1985; Sagey 1986) demonstrated this multidimensionality of phonological representation. The second radical shift, which occurred in the mid-1990s, has to do with machine learning and the computational techniques that phonologists had begun using to analyze large amounts of data. The empiricist view to linguistics (Goldsmith 2015) makes us rethink what doing linguistics really means. With the ability to employ computational tools that allow for the analysis of larger and larger data sets, the field has shifted from being satisfied to look for key examples that demonstrate a particular generalization to striving for statistical generalizations across large corpora of relevant data.

This volume includes fourteen chapters that follow these two shifts from the perspective of one protagonist responsible for making them a part of our fundamental phonologist's tool kit. That protagonist is John Goldsmith.

John Goldsmith is a household name in linguistic circles, particularly in phonology, but not exclusively so. Most associate him with the creation of autosegmental phonology in 1976. But autosegmental phonology was like a pebble thrown into a pond—it created waves of innovation in the field that lasted for decades. The paradigm shift that occurred as a result of autosegmental phonology meant that phonological representations were no longer considered bundles of features that could be organized on a two-dimensional surface, but instead those representations were units similar to molecules in which submolecular units were in *n*-dimensional space. In essence, Goldsmith and the colleagues he worked with at the time, many of whom are represented in this volume, freed us from the notion that phonological analysis provided generalizations over types of notations on cards and in notebooks and allowed us to see more clearly that our results pertained to mental representations that could have *n*-dimensions in a way that was similar to that which occurs in other branches of natural science. The study of these various new dimensions of phonological representation—the autosegment, the syllable, and other prosodic units—has been at the top of the agenda of the field for several decades. The contributions in part 1 address domains both smaller and larger than the segment. Until the late 1970s, the segment and the distinctive feature were still considered the primary units of phonological analysis.

In addition to new representational units, the field began to open up to new tools of analysis in the early 1990s, and Goldsmith was a protagonist in this charge as well. In his presentations, seminars, and editorial projects, he was adamant in encouraging students and colleagues not to rely on examples from previous works, which were often cited but seldom verified, but rather to seek out fresh sources of data to confirm the generalizations that are often taken for granted. This started with Goldsmith's work on the topics of the syllable and sonority (e.g., Goldsmith and Larson 1990), but quickly expanded to include new areas of linguistic inquiry in phonology and morphology. The availability of large corpora made it increasingly possible to state generalizations as statistical probabilities rather than as absolutes based on a small set of elicited examples. Parallel to the use of large data sets is the evolving understanding of what the goal of linguistic theory is in light of machine learning, visualization, and other computational tools that have been brought into the picture. The contributions in part 2 address profound insights to be gained by looking at the patterns in large sets of data.

These insights challenge what we know about certain well-studied phenomena, such as French liaison, and show us that sometimes the facts about them that we think are very clear are actually more complex and nuanced than we had previously thought.

This volume is organized around these two developments in the field of phonological theory. Chapters 1 and 2, by John Coleman and William Leben, respectively, are concerned with the historical roots of autosegmental phonology. They examine the links that autosegmental phonology has to the history of the field more generally, including a few nuggets of historiographical interest, and outline the role of tone, accent, and syllable structure, which are elements of the prosodic system that were major interests of autosegmental phonology from the very start. Chapters 3 and 4, by Larry Hyman and David Odden, are specific case studies of two Bantu languages—Lusoga and Logoori—within autosegmental phonology. These contributions showcase the theory's methodological strength in capturing complex interactions between the morphological structure on the one hand and tones, syllables, and words as phonological units on the other hand.

Chapters 5 through 9 are analyses that are extensions of autosegmental phonology, addressing its specific implications on theories of phonological representation. Robert Ladd (chapter 5) discusses issues about the autosegment itself and how the field has obscured some of its most important implications in recent years. Diane Brentari (chapter 6) outlines the impact of autosegmental tiers on sign language phonology. Bert Vaux and Bridget Samuels (chapter 7) address how autosegmental phonology fits into our understanding of underlying representations, abstractness, and opacity within the prosodic system, and Caroline Wiltshire (chapter 8) discusses the usefulness of a dual role for sonority in syllabification, with examples ranging across alternations in native language use, loanword adaptations, and second language acquisition. Mark Liberman (chapter 9) concludes part 1 as a kind of bridge between the two parts of the book, carefully examining the difference between symbolic (phonological) and signal (phonetic) accounts of two widely discussed examples of allophony, and arguing that signal-based accounts (purely phonetic ones) should be taken more seriously as a null hypothesis when considering the efficacy of the range of symbolic (phonological) accounts. Such phonetic-based analyses have only been feasible recently with the sorts of corpus work and computational tools that are used in part 2.

Chapters 10 through 14 all employ large sets of data in answering questions about phonology and morphology, and they utilize the computational methods that Goldsmith has favored in more recent years (e.g., Goldsmith 2001, 2015). Jackson Lee (chapter 10) captures the motivation of this approach most directly and argues that a research program on unsupervised learning of linguistic structure, such as Goldsmith's, achieves a goal of linguistic theory that Chomsky (1957) thought was unreasonable—that is, it is an instantiation of the discovery procedure itself. James Kirby and Morgan Sonderegger (chapter 11) reflect on the interpretation of experimental results with respect to statistical power using a wealth of data on incomplete neutralization. Khalil Iskarous and Louis Goldstein (chapter 12) examine how local computation results in global and typologically well-defined patterns of metrical structure. Bernard Laks, Basilio Calderone, and Chiara Celata (chapter 13) take a data-intensive perspective on French liaison and discuss the variability of this seemingly well-studied phenomenon. Aris Xanthos (chapter 14) describes an algorithm for the unsupervised learning of nonconcatenative, root-and-pattern morphology, with competitive results compared to similar systems.

These contributions speak to the two specific shifts in theoretical focus that are associated with Goldsmith, but even more than that, they capture an important principle that we all strive for as we have been conversing with John over the years, about any topic in linguistics: namely, freely challenging basic assumptions about our field in order to make notable breakthroughs. We believe all of the contributions follow that principle, one that also clearly underlies Goldsmith's own work.

A comment about the cover of this book is in order. The Calder mobile *Four Boomerangs* (circa 1949) represents the change that occurred as the result of the multidimensionality of Goldsmith's autosegmental theory. Colored forms are released from the two-dimensional page in the Calder mobile, just as phonological representations were released from two-dimensional space in autosegmental phonology. We hope that as you read the contributions of this volume you will gain a new appreciation for the immense impact that our inspiring colleague and friend John Goldsmith has had on the way we do the work of phonology today.

Diane Brentari and Jackson L. Lee

References

Chomsky, Noam. 1957. *Syntactic Structures*. Berlin: Mouton.

Clements, G. Nick. 1985. The geometry of phonological features. *Phonology Yearbook* 2:225–252.

Goldsmith, John A. 1976. Autosegmental phonology. PhD diss., Massachusetts Institute of Technology. Bloomington: Indiana University Linguistics Club. http://people.cs.uchicago.edu/~jagoldsm/Papers/dissertation.pdf. Published by Garland Press, New York [1979].

———. 2001. Unsupervised learning of the morphology of a natural language. *Computational Linguistics* 27:153–198.

———. 2015. Towards a new empiricism for linguistics. In *Empiricism and Language Learnability*, ed. Nick Chater et al., 58–105. Oxford: Oxford University Press.

Goldsmith, John, and Gary Larson. 1990. Local modeling and syllabification. *Chicago Linguistic Society* 26, no. 2: 129–142.

Sagey, Elizabeth. 1986. The representation of features and relations in non-linear phonology. PhD diss., Massachusetts Institute of Technology.

PART ONE

Autosegmental Phonology

A. History

ONE

The Secret History of Prosodic and Autosegmental Phonology

JOHN COLEMAN

1.1. Autosegmental Phonology, 1971–1976

The Sound Pattern of English left prosody on the "to do" list as an item for future work (Chomsky and Halle 1968: 329). One problem for such an unshakably segmental formalism was almost immediately evident: although in some languages prosodic features such as tone may be squeezed into a segmental formalism, there are many cases in which "segmental tone features cannot explain and can only awkwardly characterize the operation of tone," such as floating tones, contour tones, word games that manipulate tone independently of segments, and so on (Leben 1973: 25). Some aspects of prosody just are not segmental, by which I mean they are not simply attributes of consonants and vowels, but they relate to other kinds of phonological units. Leben (1973: 42–43) attacked such problems within the framework of generative phonology (as it was then), arguing that, in some languages, tone and nasality were better analyzed as if they were features of morphemes on a separate level of representation from segments:

We may picture the phonological specification of Mende *kenya* in the following way, where the segmental features are designated schematically as F_1, F_2, . . . , F_n and their values are assigned arbitrarily, and where the suprasegmental feature [H] stands for "high-toned":

(22) *kenya*

a. Matrix 1:

F_1	+	−	+	−	+
F_2	−	+	−	+	−
⋮					
F_n	+	+	+	+	+

b. Matrix 2:

H	+	−

c. Other morpheme features

Leben (1973: 44) went on to define how the tonal morpheme gets mapped onto the segments, from which it is initially independent; for this he introduced a more parsimonious notation in which the originally separate tonal morpheme is written as an initial superscript, and tone features mapped onto segments are written on a second line beneath the vowels and consonants:

(24) TONE MAPPING (Mende)

a. If the number of level tones in the pattern is equal to or less than the number of vowels in the word possessing the pattern, put the first tone on the first vowel, the second on the second, and so on; any remaining vowels receive a copy of the last tone in the pattern.

E.g. ^{LHL}nikili becomes nikili
L HL

^{H}pɛlɛ becomes pɛlɛ and then pɛlɛ
H HH

b. If the number of level tones in the pattern is greater than the number of vowels in the word possessing the pattern, put the first tone on the first vowel, the second on the second, and so on; remaining tones are expressed as a sequence on the last vowel available.

E.g. ^{HL}mbu becomes mbu
HL

^{LHL}nyaha becomes nyaha
L HL

This idea of *tone mapping* as a mechanism for assigning suprasegmental features to segments was also used by Williams (1971), though Williams and Leben proposed—in the lexicon, at least—separate tonal and segmental tiers, with rules that map the suprasegmental tones onto segments, thus maintaining a rigidly segmental output.

Leben's thesis is dated September 1973. In November 1973, a critical response by Goldsmith (1973) gets rid of this tone mapping operation:

> I will suggest that the two tiers—the phonemic and the tonemic—remain separate throughout the segmental derivation. In place of a tone-mapping rule which merges the two tiers into one, I suggest a correspondence rule. . . .
>
> What I would like to suggest to replace a rule of Tone Mapping is a two-tiered approach which retains the two sequences of segments, tonemic and phonemic. . . . First I should say that I consider the arguments for suprasegmental tone to be not only interesting but persuasive. The arguments that tones become segmental are, however, very poor. Rather than to say that the toneme becomes mapped into a tone feature on the phonemic segment, I suggest that a correspondence be formally set up between successive tonemes in the tonemic sequence and successive syllabic segments in the phonemic. . . .
>
> There are two alternative and equivalent representations for this system. The first is a graphic one showing the system as literally two-tiered, representing the correspondences with lines. Thus CV̀CV̂ would be represented:

```
C V C V .
  |   /\
  L   HL
```

Goldsmith's, Leben's, and Williams's proposals helped to bring suprasegmental phenomena into the arena of generative phonology, providing formalizations that then yielded further insights such as the parallel treatments of subsegmental structure: contour tones on short vowels and contour segments such as short diphthongs and affricates. Goldsmith saw that this theory of representation of tone—autosegmental phonology—immediately found application to a variety of quite distinct and not obviously suprasegmental phenomena, such as short diphthongs, contour segments, gemination, vowel harmony, and nonconcatenative morphology.

A notation for *complex segments* utilizing multicolumn matrices of distinctive features had been proposed by Hoard (1967) and taken up by

Campbell (1974), Anderson (1976), and a few others. For the affricate *č*, Campbell (1974: 60) wrote:

$$\begin{bmatrix} -\text{anterior} & +\text{strident} \\ +\text{coronal} & +\text{continuant} \\ -\text{continuant} & \end{bmatrix}$$

for the labialized labial p^w:

$$\begin{bmatrix} +\text{ant} & +\text{round} \\ -\text{cor} & \\ -\text{cont} & \end{bmatrix}$$

and for the palatalized "palatal" $\check{s}^y$:

$$\begin{bmatrix} -\text{ant} & \\ +\text{cor} & +\text{high} \\ +\text{cont} & \end{bmatrix}$$

In such examples, the brackets are intended to delimit a single segment, each containing an earlier part (features in the left-hand column) and a later part (features in the right-hand column). Anderson (1976: 335), in a paper that is primarily concerned with the representation of prenasalized and postnasalized consonants, discussed contour tones in similar terms, though he did not explicitly present a complex segment representation for them: "When systems of contour tones are considered in the most general case, and particularly in a number of languages of Africa, it can be seen that tone specifications must in fact have a domain smaller than a single segment. . . . Contour tones can occur distinctively on single-mora or short vowels; thus it must be the case that a tone specification in such a case describes only a proper subpart of a single segmental unit."

Goldsmith (1976: 21) presented a possible instantiation of how the complex segment formalism could be used for contour tones on a single segment:

Or one could attempt an equally radical revision of the notion of segment with the introduction of a notation as in (8).

(8)

$$\left[\begin{array}{cc} \multicolumn{2}{c}{+\text{syllabic}} \\ \multicolumn{2}{c}{+\text{CP}} \\ \multicolumn{2}{c}{-\text{High}} \\ \multicolumn{2}{c}{-\text{round}} \\ \begin{bmatrix}+\text{Highpitch}\\ -\text{Lowpitch}\end{bmatrix} & \begin{bmatrix}-\text{Highpitch}\\ +\text{Lowpitch}\end{bmatrix} \\ \text{A}\qquad\qquad\text{A} & \text{B}\qquad\qquad\text{B} \end{array}\right]$$

Although the logic of the possibility is clear, this has something of the look of a straw man; for example, no specific citation is given, nor is there one in a manuscript antecedent of this paragraph (Goldsmith 1974: 3):

Some people have suggested breaking up the segment into two parts, and specifying tone features for each half—the first half H, the second L. All the other features of the segment don't get split up, but just belong to the whole segment. This is usually written something like:

$$\left[\begin{array}{c} +\text{syllabic} \\ +\text{high} \\ \text{etc} \\ [+\text{high tone}][+\text{low tone}] \end{array}\right] \stackrel{?}{=} \text{Falling Vowel}$$

With the arrival of autosegmental phonology, complex segment notation persisted for only a short time. The argument was won: the explanatory potential of autosegmental phonology was so far reaching that forty years later, autosegmental representation remains at the heart of the phonology syllabus (e.g., Gussenhoven and Jacobs 2011). Of course, autosegmental phonology did not arise in a vacuum: as Goldsmith knows and has written about himself, he built upon a wide range of earlier work on prosodic features, such as Zellig Harris's *long components* (Harris 1944) and J. R. Firth's *Prosodic Analysis* (Palmer 1970). In the remainder of this chapter, I shall try to draw together some perhaps surprising historiographical marginalia on prosodic thinking in the works of our intellectual predecessors. Rather than proceeding strictly chronologically, I shall examine some key periods. In section 1.2, I consider the traditional descriptive approach to prosody in (mainly) the 1920s and 1930s. Then in section 1.3, I trace how J. R. Firth's more phonological-theoretical approach to prosodic phenomena arose in the wake of (post)-Saussurean linguistics, and in particular the importance of Prague School thinking to the shaping of Firthian phonology.

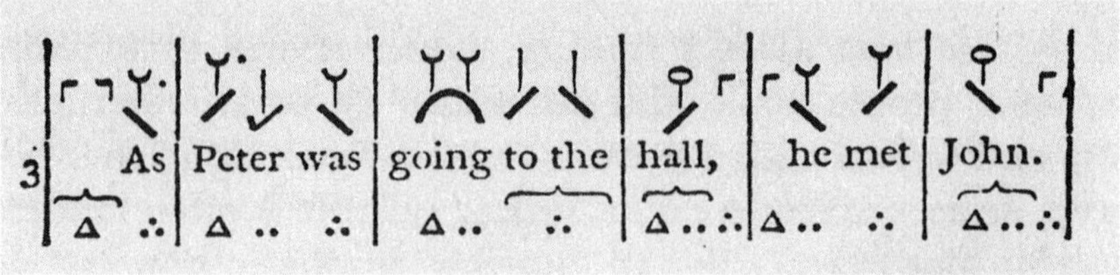

1.1 Suprasegmental notation of pitch movements, rhythm, and loudness. (From Steele 1775.)

1.2. Tone and Intonation in London, 1920s–1930s

The idea or intuition that suprasegmental units such as tone behave as if they were on a different tier or level from the vowels and consonants and their features has been a common conception for hundreds of years. Steele (1775), for example, gave numerous transcriptions of the intonation and rhythm of speech, such as figure 1.1.

Even at the start of the twentieth century, the treatment of certain aspects of speech—such as tone, intonation, loudness, accentuation, and stress—were recognized as being somewhat problematic for a strictly segmental approach to phonology, as such features are often produced on different time scales from, and have linguistic functions independent of, the "phoneme-sized units," vowels, and consonants.

The problems of analysis presented by suprasegmental features were keenly felt in Daniel Jones's Department of Phonetics at University College, London. At that time, Great Britain had the largest empire the world has ever known, governing massive populations speaking a huge range of languages, in Africa, the Middle East, the Indian Empire (including modern-day Pakistan, India, Bangladesh, and Burma), Malaysia, and Hong Kong. Consequently, linguistic analysis, documentation, and training (of civil servants, for instance) in a wide range of indigenous languages was necessary. Furthermore, international students from across the empire came to Britain—and to London and Oxford, especially—providing linguists such as Jones, Firth, and their colleagues with no shortage of data from African and Oriental languages.

Jones (1918: 137) gave numerous examples of two kinds of intonation transcriptions—linear and musical—with phonemic transcriptions on a separate line (e.g., figure 1.2). An earlier, longer work (Jones 1909) drew the linear pitch traces on a musical stave. The fine detail of these transcriptions is no conceit: even though it must have been

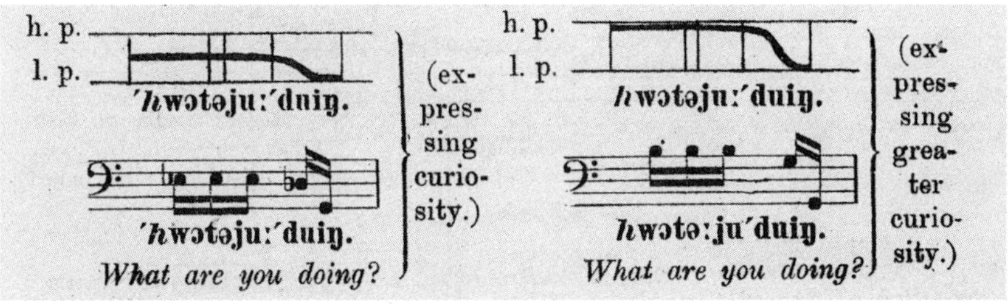

1.2 Suprasegmental representations of English intonation. (From Jones 1918.)

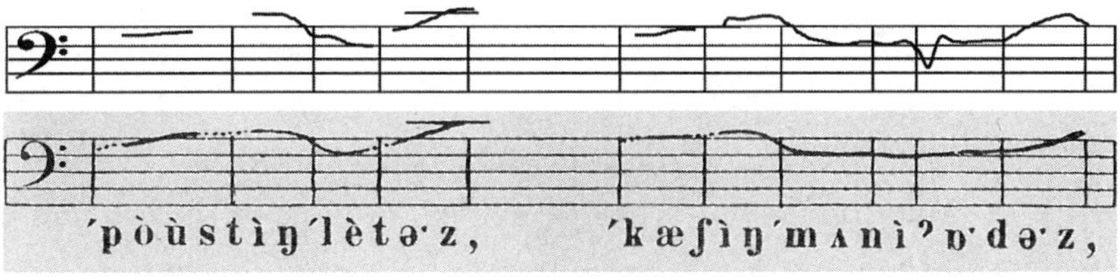

1.3 *Top,* Automatically measured f_0 curve (in semitones) for a randomly selected phrase. *Bottom,* Daniel Jones's version. (Reproduced with permission from Ashby 2015: fig. 7.)

a slow and onerous procedure to make them by listening to gramophone recordings, one word or short phrase at a time, Jones had "perfect pitch" perception. Ashby (2015) presented a comparison of Jones's pitch diagrams with f_0 analyzed from the original recordings, demonstrating an extraordinary accuracy in Jones's impressionistic transcription (figure 1.3). In Ashby's comparison figure, the measured plot is time-warped at the bar-lines by simple linear extension or compression for comparability with Jones's version, but the pitch in semitones is not manipulated at all.

Phonetic pitch records are not, however, phonological representations. The abstraction over many particular instances to a small number of tune types is seen in later editions of Jones's (1918/1932) *An Outline of English Phonetics,* in which he follows two of his students, Armstrong and Ward (1926), in recognizing two intonational tunes in English: Tune 1 (early peak, slowly descending to a final brisk fall), and Tune 2 (early peak, similar to Tune 1 to begin with, but ending on a low rise). Jones (1932: 279) noted: "These tunes may be spread over a large number of syllables, or they may be compressed into smaller spaces. . . . When the tunes are applied to small groups of syllables or to the extreme case of

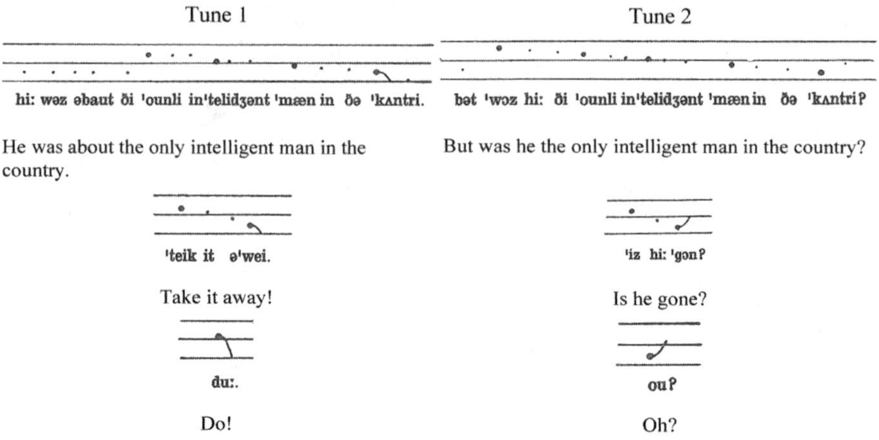

1.4 Illustrations of the "two tunes" of English intonation, according to Jones (1932).

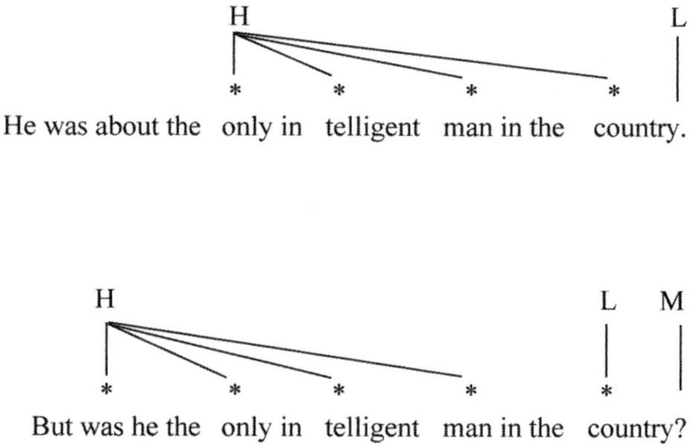

1.5 Jones's "two tunes" represented in the manner of Goldsmith (1978).

monosyllables, several of these features disappear." See figure 1.4 for an example.

In terms similar to those of Goldsmith (1978), we might represent Tune 1 in autosegmental notation as H* M* L (or following Pierrehumbert 1981, as perhaps H* L%, with the final fall being from a downstepped H*), and Tune 2 as H* L* M (or H* L*+H%), as in figure 1.5.

The idea of parallel representations for segments and tones, as well as conventions for mapping a shorter sequence of tones onto a possibly longer sequence of syllables already had some currency in descriptive linguistics, especially in relation to African tone languages. Westermann and Ward (1933: chap. 24) provided an extraordinarily modern treatment of tone, including the following remarks:

"The tones of a language must be considered in relation to syllables" (141).

"Every syllable not provided with a tone mark has the tone of the last syllable which *has* a tone mark [i.e., left-to-right spreading]" (145).

"In any diacritic method of marking tones, the number of marks required is one less than the number of essential tones, since one can be left unmarked: the mid tone is the one usually chosen to be left unmarked" (146).

"Vowel elision is extremely common in African languages and its influence on tones must be considered. . . . We find that generally speaking the tone of the elided vowel is not dropped entirely, but is often combined with that of the vowel which is retained, and forms a new tone. This new tone keeps some characteristic of both tones. This if the vowel in one of two neighbouring syllables bearing the tones high–low is elided, the resulting syllable has a falling tone" (149).

Ida Ward had moved from Jones's University College, London Phonetics Department to the University of London School of Oriental and African Studies (SOAS) in 1932, becoming head of the African Department in 1937. Many of the departments at SOAS were organized on a geographical basis, and so linguists were engaged there for their expertise in the relevant language areas. After J. R. Firth's migration to SOAS in 1938, and the establishment of the Department of Linguistics and Phonetics in 1940, other key figures of the "Firthian school" were recruited for their expertise in specific language areas. Eugénie Henderson, Lecturer in Phonetics from 1942, for South-East Asian languages such as Thai, Lao, and Cambodian; Jack Carnochan (also Lecturer in Phonetics from 1945) for West African languages such as Hausa, Igbo, and Yoruba; and Keith Sprigg (appointed in 1947) for Tibetan. Firth's own primary language focus was Indian languages—including, given the British organization of the Indian Empire—Burmese.

In many of those Asian languages, lexical tone is often characterized by particular phonatory and/or durational features, as well as pitch patterns; sometimes, the phonatory characteristics may be more reliable or salient cues to a word's lexical tone than its pitch movements. For example, Firth (1933) described Burmese Toneme I (which has slightly falling pitch) as having "vowels of medium length" and creaky voice, when in open or nasal-final syllables, and "very short 'bright' vowels" if closed with a glottal stop. Toneme II has a low level tone, a "gradual ending," and breathy voice. Toneme III also has breathy voice and a "fade-out" ending, but is falling, so in this respect it is distinguished from

Toneme III by a different pitch movement. Firth and Rogers (1937) described Hunanese tone 1 as "Long—longer than 3. Normal voice quality. Sometimes ends with slight creak." Tone 2 is "Long—often longer than 1. Voice quality breathy, hollow, 'chesty' with slight initial friction." Though they also note the different pitch movements associated with these tones, they transcribe the tonal distinctions with letters that owe more to their associated phonation, length, and vowel qualities than pitch: tone 1 is marked with syllable-final **y** or **w**, depending on the front or back quality of the vowel; tone 2, being breathy, is marked with **h**; tone 5, being long but not so breathy, is marked by vowel doubling, and tone 4, being short, is marked by single letter vowel spellings.

Sprigg (1955: 125) stated that in Lhasa Tibetan, which has only a two-term contrast, the exponents that have been used as

> criteria for setting up the Tonal system are of four orders:–
>
> A. features of pitch.
> B. features of duration of vowel.
> C. word-initial features.
> D. features of voice quality.

For example, Tone One is associated with word-initial voicelessness, whereas Tone Two is associated with word-initial voicing, and may have greater duration and more peripheral vowel qualities. Such a view of tone, which does not privilege pitch, may seem odd to readers of modern phonological handbooks, but it is quite consistent with the traditional Chinese view of tone: for example, the Middle Chinese *rù* (entering) tone is still marked by short vowels checked by final glottalized stops in modern Cantonese. Another striking example is afforded by Vietnamese, which alongside higher and lower level tones, and higher and lower rising tones, also has higher versus lower rising tones with a glottal stop *voice break* that divides the rising vowel into two vocalic portions, as in [baʔá] 'residue', [bàʔak] 'silver', in which [aʔá] and [àʔa] are minimally contrastive, single phonological vowels: higher rising /ã/ and lower rising /ã/, respectively.

1.3. Origins of Firthian Phonology, 1922–1937

J. R. Firth's *prosodic analysis* is often contrasted with phonemic phonology by reference to its emphasis on long-domain prosodic features, such as tone, intonation, and vowel harmony. But this is only half of the story: Firthian phonology has *two* characteristics that distinguish it from phonemic phonology. One is its willingness to accept *any* feature of articulation as potentially having suprasegmental characteristics or functions, according to the pattern of the language in question, not just the conventional suprasegmental features of tone, intonation, and stress; such prosodies may serve to signal the extent and boundaries of linguistic units such as words, phrases, and utterances. Many works illustrate this plainly enough, and its similarities to autosegmental phonology have often been discussed. The second respect in which Firthian prosodic phonology diverged from phonemic phonology, which at that stage was still debated and rather ill-defined, was in its insistence that phonological units and systems of opposition in different parts of a language (e.g., nouns vs. verbs) and in different positions in a word or utterance (e.g., word-initially vs. medially vs. finally) were *incommensurable*—the *polysystemic* approach first hinted at in Firth (1936b: 177–180):

> It may be practically convenient to think of a language as having a sound system, or phonetic structure as a whole, but this is little more than a sum of all the possible alternances of sounds in all contexts. . . .
>
> It is only in certain general contexts that all forty alternances or substitutions [of the Hindi consonant inventory] are possible, e.g., medially or intervocalically, so that I should hesitate to make any general statement about the function or value of any one term in the language as a whole apart from a more or less determined context. . . .
>
> Nasals and nasalization in the Sanskritic languages raise fundamental questions of phonetic and phonological theory. . . . In initial position [in Marathi], only two nasal consonants can be used, **n** and **m**.

The localization of phonological features to specific positions in structure leads almost naturally to the concept of *prosodic hierarchy,* which is familiar to us from modern work in nonlinear phonology. Its first expressions, however, can be found in the Firthian literature, such as figure 1.6, one of several examples of hierarchical prosodic analysis in Henderson (1949).

Firth's emphasis on language as a polysystemic "system of systems" at every level of description is strongly influenced by the Saussurean school. In the early 1920s, when Firth was professor of English in Lahore, before he moved to London, he wrote to Otto Jespersen asking for advice about where to go in Europe to see the best examples of teaching English using the then-new phonetic methods of instruction. Jespersen extended

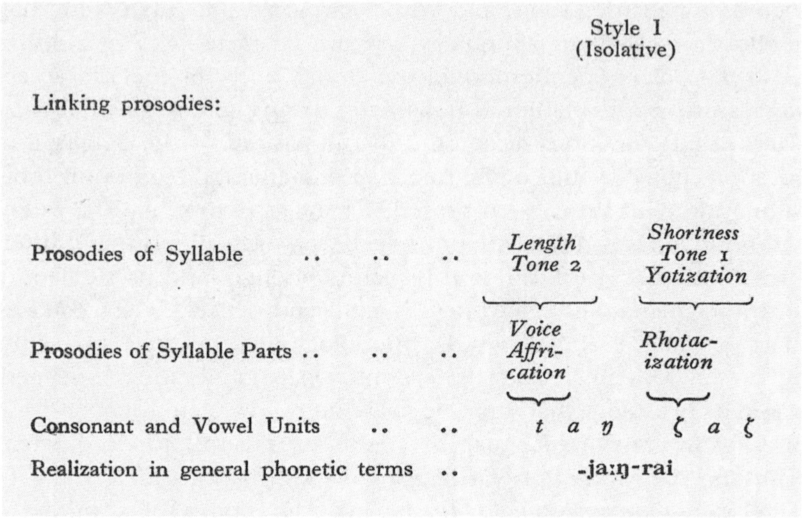

1.6 Example of hierarchical prosodic structure. (From Henderson 1949: 200.)

Firth a welcome to Copenhagen, but said: "You mention Marburg, but probably you are not aware of the death of Viëtor; I do not know who is his successor, and probably there will not be much for you there. I should think that Berlin will be better, or perhaps Hamburg with its new university and with the fully equipped experimental phonetical laboratory directed by Calzia."[1]

In March 1924, Firth was given permission and funds from the high commissioner for India to travel to Europe to study methods of teaching English phonetics. He proposed and was given permission in April to go to Switzerland. A notebook belonging either to Eugénie Henderson or to Elizabeth Uldall, now in the Firthian Phonology Archive at the University of York, records among some brief biographical notes about Firth that he went to Geneva and studied with Bally, Saussure's successor.

The question as to whether similar sounds in different positions in a word should or should not be analyzed as the same or different phonological units was very much in contention at that time. The appendix to the introduction, "Principles of Phonology," to Bally and Sechehaye's edition of Saussure's *Course*, contains a careful discussion of syllable-initial (*explosive*) versus syllable-final (*implosive*) consonants. Firth's view that they are distinct sounds in distinct positions is consistent with Saussure's view, as given by Bally and Sechehaye in Saussure ([1915] 1974: 53):

The table of [French] phonemes must therefore be redoubled, except for *a*, and the following list of irreducible units set up:

$\overset{>}{\text{p}}$ $\overset{<}{\text{p}}$, etc.
$\overset{>}{\text{f}}$ $\overset{<}{\text{f}}$, etc.
$\overset{>}{\text{m}}$ $\overset{<}{\text{m}}$, etc.
$\overset{>}{\text{r}}$ $\overset{<}{\text{r}}$, etc.
$\overset{>}{\text{i}}$ $\overset{<}{\text{y}}$, etc.
$\overset{>}{\text{e}}$ $\overset{<}{\text{e}}$, etc.
a.

Twaddell (1935) expressed a similarly polysystemic conception, *microphonemes*, which Trubetzkoy rather ridiculed in a letter of May 17, 1935, to Roman Jakobson: "In principle [Twaddell] operates with our definition of the phoneme as TERME D'OPPOSITION, but draws an absurd conclusion: since in a given position only some, rather than all, phonemes are opposed, a special system has to be set up for each position (my TEILSYSTEME!), but these systems are allegedly incompatible (it is not clear why); consequently, a unified system of phonemes does not exist in a language" (Trubetzkoy 1975: 334–335; Trubetzkoy 2001: 246).

According to the testimony of Abercrombie (1980), it seems likely that the prosodic aspect of Firth's view of phonology crystalized at the 1935 International Congress of Phonetic Sciences in London, specifically because of a paper given by Uldall on the function of the glottal stop in Danish, and a keynote paper by Trubetzkoy (1936), "Die phonologischen Grenzsignale." In this paper, Trubetzkoy explained how certain phonetic features, by being tied to particular linguistic contexts, may serve to cue the limits of those linguistic units. A conventionally suprasegmental example is stress in languages with fixed stress placement. If stress always falls on the first, last, or penultimate syllable of a word, it indicates to the listener the location of the word boundary. Another example—perhaps a more striking one—concerns vowel harmony in Turkic languages. As Trubetzkoy presented it: "In Kazan' Tatar, Bashkir, Kazakh, and many other Turkic languages, where each word contains either fronter or backer vowels, all the consonants (except *j*) are velarized in the back vowel words, and palatalized in the front vowel words. So when a palatalized consonant is found next to a velarized consonant, that is a sign that a word boundary lies between them" (Trubetzkoy 1936: 46–47).[2] Though vowel harmony is now a standard of phonology courses, it was at the time an exotic novelty, and something of a problem to the then-emerging phonemic theory as it appears to involve correlations between distinct segments that form a discontinuous sequence.

Sitting with Firth during various sessions of the congress was David Abercrombie, then a postgraduate student of Jones's, with whom Firth was friendly. In a private conversation and a letter dated October 17, 1991, from David Abercrombie to his former student John Kelly, Abercrombie recounted that he sat with Firth during the phonology session on the afternoon of July 22, 1935, when Trubetzkoy, Hjelmslev, and Uldall gave their papers. Abercrombie recalled that Firth had fallen completely silent after Trubetzkoy's paper, which was uncharacteristic for him, and usually a sign that he was impressed. It is noteworthy that among the many examples of positional variation of sounds given by Trubetzkoy, he mentions two details from Tamil:

> As examples of aphonematic boundary markers, the aspirated **k**, **p**, **t** in Tamil may be cited: these voiceless aspirated plosives are not independent phonemes in Tamil, rather only a word-initial pronunciation characteristic of those phonemes which in other contexts are produced as voiced plosives (following nasals) or as unaspirated tenues (following liquids) or as fricatives **x**, **ƀ**, **ð** (following vowels).
>
> NEGATIVE PHONEMATIC integrative markers are for example . . . in Tamil the retroflex consonants (except **ɳ**, which may not occur word-internally). . . . A negative aphonematic integrative marker is for example the Tamil **x**, which only occurs between vowels inside a word, while **k** does not occur in this position, so that **x** and **k** are not two distinct phonemes, but two variants of the same phoneme. (Trubetzkoy 1936: 46–47)

He almost certainly got these examples from Firth, either from Firth (1934) or from a personal communication, for this was not their first contact; they already knew each other a little. In 1934, Trubetzkoy traveled to London to deliver three lectures on the North Caucasian languages at the School of Slavonic Studies, where Roman Jakobson's brother Sergius Yakobson was working (Trubetzkoy 1975: 297–298). In May 1934, Trubetzkoy sent Jakobson an amusing report of the state of linguistics in England:

> I did not see any linguists there in the strict sense of the word. It seems they do not exist at all. There are people who are curious almost like children (in a half-sporting, Anglo-Saxon way) about language phenomena and see them as an entertainment. Most frequently they are interested in becoming polyglots. There are quite a few such

people, but it seems there are no real linguists. Phonology succeeds exactly because it is seen as something odd: everybody is very amused that in some language two totally different sounds are perceived as one phoneme. It does not go any deeper. A certain Firth seemed to me the most serious of all. But his brochure on the notion of "function" in linguistics shows that he has no understanding of general issues. (Trubetzkoy 1975: letter 130)[3]

On May 17, 1935, Trubetzkoy wrote to Jakobson: "Among Firth's works in addition to his brochure reviewed by Mathesius in Sl. a. Sl. [*Slovo a Slovesnost'*], others well deserving attention are his description of the phonological system of Tamil, the project of a Latin alphabet for Burma and his last article on usage and combination of sounds in English (Isachenko has all three)" (Trubetzkoy 1975: letter 142). Trubetzkoy (1935), a brochure prepared for the International Congress of Phonetic Sciences as part of the Prague School's propaganda drive, cited Firth (1933, on Burmese) as well as the example of [x] as a "negative aphonematic boundary signal" of word-internal position in Tamil. Its "prefatory remarks" even recommend Firth's sketch of Tamil as a model of phonological description.

Trubetzkoy was fabulously knowledgeable about all sorts of languages, especially Caucasian and other languages of the Russian Empire. But where did he get the data for his Turkic example from?

On April 6, 1929, Jakobson wrote to Trubetzkoy:

Another question is to know whether it is appropriate to put on the same plan the correlation "prepalatal–postpalatal vowel quality" and the disjunctive distinctions. I can see in Turkish, for example, two vocalic systems, one of palatalisation and one of length with four phonological elements in each. . . . The modification I propose [to one of the theses proposed in the manuscript of Trubetzkoy (1929)] is particularly important when one is dealing with languages with vowel harmony, which relates to the word, as in Turkish, or to the syllable, as in Proto-Slavic. (Trubetzkoy 1975, letter 44, n. 11)

Trubetzkoy replied on April 16:

As for the Turkish languages, you may be right: in those, at least, where the consonants are soft in words with a front vowel and velarised when there is a back vowel, as is the case in Kazan Tatar, one can effectively speak of a four-vowel system, which presents itself as

o	a	
u	y	[i.e., ɨ – JC]

in a velarized consonantal environment and as

ö ä
ü i

in the opposite environment. Unfortunately, we don't know which Turkish languages are concerned. An experimental study on palatalisation and duration of consonants has not been done except for Tatar (by Šaraf), and the descriptive grammars say nothing about the hard or soft character of consonants. (Trubetzkoy 1975, letter 44)

The study of Kazan' Tatar referred to here is Šaraf (1927), "Palatograms of the Sounds of Tatar Compared to Russian," published (in Russian) in the *Journal of the Tatar Scientific Society*, Kazan'. The date of publication is after the foundation of the Tatar Soviet Socialist Republic in May 1920, by which time Trubetzkoy was in Vienna. It is interesting that he nevertheless managed to obtain a copy. Ironically, the palatograms presented in Šaraf's paper do not strongly support the claims made about coarticulatory palatalization in Trubetzkoy's letters or his 1935 conference paper. In the lower half of figure 1.7, the dashed line is much higher on the figure than the solid line/shaded area, which means that the area of contact between the tongue dorsum and palate in [g^j] and [k^j] is much more anterior in Russian than in Tatar, whereas the contact regions for Tatar [g^j] and [k^j] are hardly any different from those for nonpalatalized [g] and [k] given in the upper half of the figure.

In spite of this, Trubetzkoy was not wrong: clear evidence that velar consonants in front vowel harmony environments may be more advanced in Turkish was later given by Waterson (1956). Trubetzkoy (1936) listed two other Turkic varieties with similar behavior, however: Bashkir and Kazakh; I have not found his source for Bashkir, though for Kazakh he elsewhere cited Radloff (1882).

The effect of Trubetzkoy's (1935) London congress paper on Firth's emergent thinking is revealed to some extent by comparison of his two papers on Burmese—Firth (1933), written before the congress, and Firth (1936a), written after it. The approach of the latter is more explicitly prosodic in its view of phonology: "Another feature of the *Alphabetum* which deserves notice is the classification of the different types of syllable to be met with in this so-called monosyllabic language. It seems to me more enlightening than a mere catalogue of so-called individual sounds" (Firth 1936a: 530).

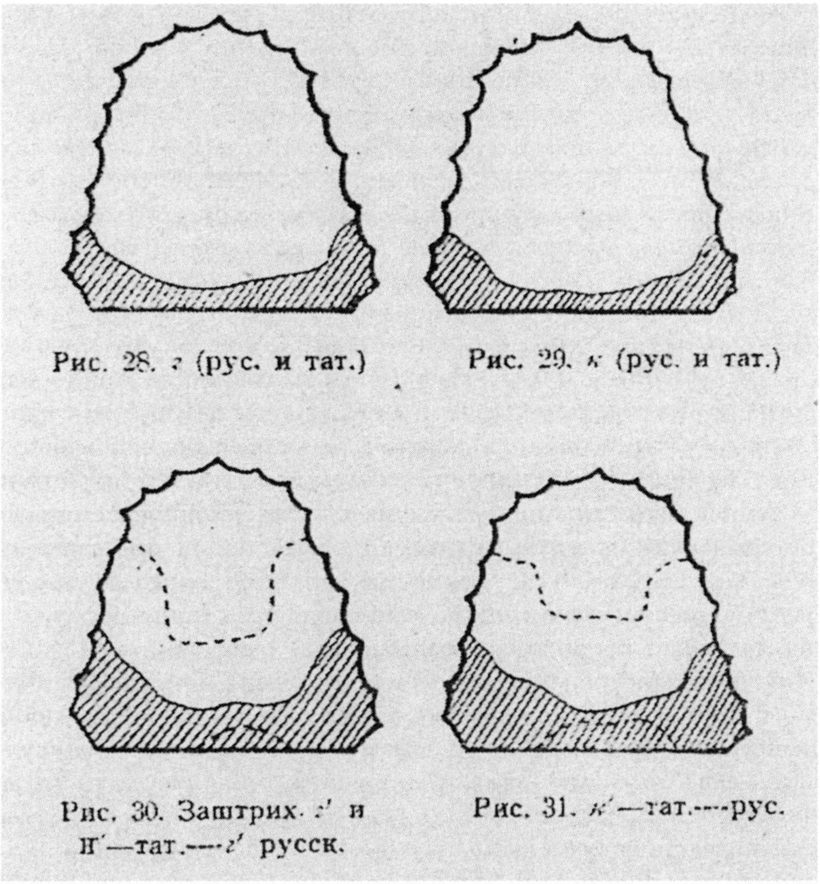

1.7 *Top,* Palatograms of nonpalatalized [g] (*left*) and [k] (*right*) in Russian and Tatar. *Bottom,* Palatograms of palatalized [g^j] (*left*) and [k^j] (*right*) in Tatar (*shaded area* below the *solid line*) and Russian (*area* below the *dashed line*). (From Šaraf 1927.)

As illustration of this point, Firth enumerates:

- the distinction between the short sharply checked syllables and the long breathy ones
- those syllables which begin with aspirated consonants, as well as the breathy ones which fade out
- diphthong-syllables
- those which begin with a yotized consonant group and those beginning with a labio-velarized group: e.g., **py, phy, my, hmy, ly, hly,** etc., against **pw, phw, mw, hmw, lw, hlw,** etc.

He also implies that place of articulation may be prosodic, or at least not limited to an individual segment, in suggesting that "the homorganic nasal on-glides to the voiced stops are noticed, which we may represent by **˜k, ˜p, ˜t,** etc., in the Indian way" (Firth 1936a: 525).

The prosodic contrast between "yotized" versus velarized *syllables* appears again in Firth and Rogers (1937). Innovatively, the different tones of Hunan Chinese are marked not by tone-graphs, but by differences in the *correlative attributes* of the vowels: their voice quality, register, and nasality. For Firthians, tone is not just a matter of pitch movements. Firth (1948a) again listed "the dark or clear qualities of the syllables" as prosodic features of the word in colloquial Cairene Arabic, prosodic ə (as in centering diphthongs, "intrusive" *r*, and "linking" *r*) in English, and glottality, such as [ʔ] in vowel-initial words in English or German and Danish *stød*.

For Firth, his students, and followers, pretty much any phonetic feature or contrast that may serve to distinguish one word from another in a phonematic fashion may, in some language or another, also function prosodically, meaning either that it "spreads out" across a suprasegmental domain, or that it is associated with some particular prosodic position, such as syllable-final or word-initial. Apart from tone, length, breath, aspiration, yotization, velarization, and place of articulation, the Firthian literature provides examples of prosodic function of retroflexion (Allen 1951), voicing (Carnochan 1957), nasality (Robins 1953; Bendor-Samuel 1960), the openness or closeness of vowels in vowel harmony (e.g., Palmer 1956), and lip-rounding in vowel harmony systems such as Turkish (Waterson 1956).

Firthian phonologists by tradition focused on the specific patterns and systems of particular languages, and indeed specific subsystems of individual languages, such as nouns, verbs, monosyllables, loanwords, and so on, resisting any attempt to enumerate or systematize a grand scheme of prosodic universals or cross-linguistic patterns. In this respect, they were rather unlike the generative linguists, in focusing on externally observable aspects of language rather than its cognitive aspects, and they were quite opposed to the universalizing quest of Jakobson, Greenberg, or Chomsky. It came as a considerable surprise, therefore, when I came across a quite general chart of prosodies in the J. R. Firth papers in the SOAS archives (table 1.1).[4] It is evident that Firth had originally intended this table to appear at the end of Firth (1948b); it is introduced by a page of typewritten text which is, until the final sentence, identical to the penultimate paragraph of that paper: "Even on general grounds, quite apart from the showings of palatography, a simple grouping of types of articulation has proved useful in phonology. A number of tentative suggestions

Table 1.1 Grouping and modification articulations

	Articulation Types	~~General Symbol~~ General Articulation Groups	Modifications	General Prosodic Types	General Phonematic Types	Coupled prosodies
Within the buccal cavity	Front Mouth (pre-buccal)	Dental y Alveolar r Palatal l	y-modification palatalization r-modification rhotacization l-modification s-modification	y	t, d, (n), ʈ, ɖ, ɳ, θ, ð, s, z, r, etc.	
	Back Mouth (post-buccal)	velar (w) uvular (l) faucal	w-modification, velarization l-modification	w	k, g, (ŋ) q, x, ɣ, ʀ, etc.	
Outside the buccal cavity	Labials (extra-buccal)	w Labial Labio Dental	w-modification Labialization		m, p, b w, f, v etc.	
	Naso- pharyngals (supra-buccal)	Nasal ɱ ~	ɱ-modification nasalization anuswar	ɱ ~	m n ɳ ŋ	
	Laryngals and Pharyngals (infra-buccal)	h aspirate ʕ* pharyng. ɛ* laryngal ə glottal ˳	h-modification aspiration, breathiness glottal modification glottalization ɛ-modification pharyngalization voice devocalization	h ʕ ɛ ə _	h ʕ ɛ a, etc.	
	All		aspiration plosion	Stress Pause Hiatus Silence	Plosives Ejectives Implosives Ingressives Glottalics	Tones Intonation Shortness Length Gemination Creak

Note: Unpublished table omitted from Firth (1948b). Text in handwriting font represents Firth's handwritten emendations to the typescript.

*Here Firth uses ʕ for IPA [ʔ] and ɛ for IPA [ʕ], possible revisions of the IPA proposed at that time by Arabists (International Phonetic Association 1949: 19; Pullum and Ladusaw 1986: 183, 189).

are set out in Table II [i.e., table 1.1]." In the vocabulary of the time, "general" means cross-linguistic, as in the term *general linguistics*. This table is the closest that Firthian phonology ever came to a comprehensive enumeration of phonological features; its very existence is extraordinary, and the fact that Firth decided not to include it in the published versions of this paper is quite telling.

1.4. Conclusion

Throughout the history of phonological thinking, prosodic aspects of speech have been recognized as being equally important to segmental, lexically contrastive, phonematic properties. Though to some, "prosody" connotes only tone, stress, and intonation, research in the mid-twentieth century showed that a far wider range of phonetic properties, including voice quality, vowel quality, place of articulation, and nasality can have prosodic functions, and that the prosodic or segmental function of a certain sound can vary from language to language. In autosegmental phonology, John Goldsmith gave us the formal means to represent the place in structure, and thereby the prosodic or segmental function, of phonological features in each language or morphophonological context.

Notes

Title note: Much of this is not so much secret as just recherché, as some of the work I discuss is unpublished, or is in languages other than English. But I like the ring and resonances of "secret history."

1. Letter from Jespersen to Firth, October 1, 1922, John Rupert Firth Collection, box 9, London University, School of Oriental and African Studies Archives.
2. Except where cited otherwise, all translations are by me.
3. Translation by Anastassia Loukina.
4. PP MS 75, John Rupert Firth Collection, box 24.

References

Abercrombie, David. 1980. Fifty years: A memoir. *Work in Progress* 13. Reprinted in *Forum Linguisticum* 5, no. 2, and in Abercrombie, David. 1991. *Fifty Years in Phonetics*, 1–11. Edinburgh: Edinburgh University Press.

Allen, W. S. 1951. Some prosodic aspects of retroflexion and aspiration in Sanskrit. *Bulletin of the School of Oriental and African Studies* 13:939–946.

Anderson, Stephen R. 1976. Nasal consonants and the internal structure of segments. *Language* 52:326–344.

Armstrong, Lilias, and Ida Ward. 1926. *Handbook of English Intonation.* Cambridge: Heffer.

Ashby, Michael. 2015. Experimental phonetics at University College London before World War I. In *First International Workshop on the History of Speech Communication Research (HSCR 2015), Dresden, Germany; September 4–5, 2015*, ed. R. Hoffmann and J. Trouvain, 118–127. Studientexte zur Sprachkommunikation 79. Dresden, Germany: TUD-Press.

Bendor-Samuel, John T. 1960. Some problems of segmentation in the phonological analysis of Terena. *Word* 16:348–355.

Campbell, Lyle. 1974. Phonological features: Problems and proposals. *Language* 50:52–65.

Carnochan, Jack. 1957. Gemination in Hausa. In *Studies in Linguistic Analysis: Special Volume of the Philological Society*, ed. J. R. Firth, 149–181. Oxford: Basil Blackwell.

Chomsky, Noam, and Morris Halle. 1968. *The Sound Pattern of English.* New York: Harper and Row.

Firth, J. R. 1933. Notes on the transcription of Burmese. *Bulletin of the School of Oriental Studies* 7:137–140.

———. 1934. A short outline of Tamil pronunciation. Appendix to A. H. Arden, *A Progressive Grammar of Common Tamil*, 4th rev. ed. Madras: Christian Literature Society for India.

———. 1936a. Alphabets and phonology in India and Burma. *Bulletin of the School of Oriental Studies* 8:517–546.

———. 1936b. Phonological features of some Indian languages. In *Proceedings of the Second International Congress of Phonetic Sciences: Held at University College, London*, ed. Daniel Jones and D. B. Fry, 76–182. Cambridge: Cambridge University Press.

———. 1948a. Sounds and prosodies. *Transactions of the Philological Society* 47:127–152.

———. 1948b. Word-palatograms and articulation. *Bulletin of the School of Oriental and African Studies* 12:857–864.

Firth, J. R., and B. B. Rogers. 1937. The structure of the Chinese monosyllable in a Hunanese dialect (Changsha). *Bulletin of the School of Oriental Studies* 8:1055–1074.

Goldsmith, John A. 1973. Tonemic structure. Unpublished manuscript.

———. 1974. An autosegmental tonology of a fragment of Igbo. Preliminary draft II. Unpublished manuscript.

———. 1976. Autosegmental phonology. PhD dissertation, Massachusetts Institute of Technology. Bloomington: Indiana University Linguistics Club.

http://people.cs.uchicago.edu/~jagoldsm/Papers/dissertation.pdf. Published by Garland Press, New York [1979].

———. 1978. English as a tone language. *Communication and Cognition* 11:453–476. Reprinted in *Phonology in the 1980s*, ed. D. Goyvaerts, 287–308. Ghent: Story-Scientia [1981].

Gussenhoven, Carlos, and Haike Jacobs. 2011. *Understanding Phonology*. London: Arnold.

Harris, Zellig S. 1944. Simultaneous components in phonology. *Language* 20:181–205.

Henderson, Eugénie J. A. 1949. Prosodies in Siamese: A study in synthesis. *Asia Major*, n.s., 1:189–215.

Hoard, James A. 1967. On the foundations of phonological theory. PhD dissertation, University of Washington.

International Phonetic Association. 1949. *The Principles of the International Phonetic Association*. London: International Phonetic Association.

Jones, Daniel. 1909. *Intonation Curves*. Leipzig: Teubner.

———. 1918. *An Outline of English Phonetics*. Leipzig: Teubner.

———. 1932. *An Outline of English Phonetics*. 3rd ed. Leipzig: Teubner.

Leben, William R. 1973. Suprasegmental phonology. PhD dissertation, Massachusetts Institute of Technology.

Palmer, Frank R. 1956. Openness in Tigre: A problem in prosodic statement. *Bulletin of the School of Oriental and African Studies* 18:561–577.

———, ed. 1970. *Prosodic Analysis*. London: Oxford University Press.

Pierrehumbert, Janet B. 1981. *The Phonology and Phonetics of English Intonation*. Bloomington: Indiana University Linguistics Club.

Pullum, Geoffrey K., and William A. Ladusaw. 1986. *Phonetic Symbol Guid*e. Chicago: University of Chicago Press.

Radloff, W. 1882. *Phonetik der Nördlichen Türksprachen*. Leipzig: Teubner.

Robins, R. H. 1953. The phonology of the nasalized verbal forms in Sundanese. *Bulletin of the School of Oriental and African Studies* 15:138–145.

Šaraf, G. 1927. Paljatogramy zvukov tatarskogo jazyka sravnitel'no s russkim [Palatograms of the sounds of Tatar compared to Russian]. *Vestnik Naučnogo obščestva tatarovedenija* [Journal of the Tatar Scientific Society] 7:65–102.

Saussure, Ferdinand de. (1915) 1974. *Course in General Linguistics*. Rev. ed. Translated by Wade Baskin. London: Fontana.

Sprigg, R. K. 1955. The tonal system of Tibetan (Lhasa dialect) and the nominal phrase. *Bulletin of the School of Oriental and African Studies* 17, no. 1: 133–153.

Steele, Joshua. 1775. *An Essay towards Establishing the Melody and Measure of Speech, to Be Expressed and Perpetuated by Peculiar Symbols*. London.

Trubetzkoy, N. S. 1929. Zur allgemeinen Theorie der phonologischen Vokalsysteme. *Mélanges linguistiques dédiés au premier congrès des philologues slaves. Travaux du Cercle Linguistique de Prague* 1:39–67.

———. 1935. *Anleitung zu phonologischen Beschreibungen*. Edition du Cercle Linguistique de Prague. English translation by L. A. Murray (1968) as *Introduction to the Principles of Phonological Descriptions*. The Hague: Martinus Nijhoff.

———. 1936. Die phonologischen Grenzsignale. In *Proceedings of the Second International Congress of Phonetic Sciences: Held at University College, London*, ed. Daniel Jones and D. B. Fry, 45–49. Cambridge: Cambridge University Press.

———. 1975. *N. S. Trubetzkoy's Letters and Notes*, prepared for publication by Roman Jakobson. The Hague: Mouton. Translated into French by Patrick Sériot (2006) as *Correspondance avec Roman Jakobson et autres écrits*. Lausanne: Editions Payot. Some parts in Trubetzkoy (2001).

———. 2001. *Studies in General Linguistics and Language Structure*. Translated by Marvin Taylor and Anatoly Liberman. Durham, NC: Duke University Press.

Twadell, W. F. 1935. *On Defining the Phoneme*. Baltimore: Waverly Press.

Waterson, Natalie. 1956. Some aspects of the phonology of the nominal forms of the Turkish word. *Bulletin of the School of Oriental and African Studies* 18:578–591.

Westermann, D., and Ida C. Ward. 1933. *Practical Phonetics for Students of African Languages*. London: Oxford University Press.

Williams, Edwin S. 1971 [1976]. Underlying tone in Margi and Igbo. *Linguistic Inquiry* 7:463–484.

TWO

A Brief History of Autosegmental Phonology with Special Reference to Its Founder

WILLIAM R. LEBEN

Studying the source of our ideas is the surest way to conceptual liberation, a state we always strive for (and occasionally we get somewhere close to it). This is counter-intuitive, but it is very true. . . . In order make progress, we need to step back and peel back the genealogy of our ideas, so that we understand what those assumptions are. JOHN GOLDSMITH, "THEORY, KERNELS, DATA, METHODS," CHICAGO LINGUISTIC SOCIETY, 2012

2.1. Generative Phonology Prior to 1976

At the time John Goldsmith wrote his dissertation, the dominant paradigm in generative phonology followed Chomsky and Halle's (1968) *The Sound Pattern of English* (*SPE*). The descriptive capabilities of the framework were so great and so welcome that phonologists around that time devoted much of their attention to exploring its ins and outs. This often took the form of either applying or extending the *SPE* model to languages other than English or revising the *SPE* analysis of English, which was reasonably exhaustive but left ample room for alternative analyses. Within a few years of the publication date of *SPE*, Morris Halle published two major reanalyses of *SPE* stress rules, Halle and Keyser (1971) and Halle (1973).

The *SPE* model served as an excellent descriptive tool but not as a very adequate explanatory one because the framework was relatively unconstrained. The capacity of a totally explicit theory to embody significant claims about formal and substantive universals of languages was widely recognized among generativists but remained to be realized in practice. A phonological rule could change or add any number of features or even a whole segment in the most implausible environments, and phonological rules applied linearly in cycles, with essentially no constraints on how rule application was ordered within a given cycle.

Taming this Wild West situation was one of the first items of business in generative phonology, giving rise to attempts to constrain the power of phonological theory. Kiparsky (1968) pulled lessons from diachrony to motivate constraints on the abstractness of underlying representations, and Anderson (1969) put together generalizations from far-flung languages of the world to suggest constraints on their ordering and then, in Anderson (1974), on their format as well.

Another line of attack was to examine phenomena that got short shrift in *SPE*. Among these was lexical tone—understandably enough, since lexical tone is lacking in English. McCawley (1968) looked at the phonological component of a grammar of Japanese and memorably accounted for accent reduction in Japanese word and phrasal phonology by adapting *SPE*'s innovative conventions on stress reduction. This was quite a coup for McCawley and for the *SPE* theory, given the considerable typological differences thought to exist at the time between the accentual systems of English and Japanese. Woo (1969) looked into the features of tone, and one of her lasting contributions was to show that tone and stress are not reflexes of an abstract feature (accent). Her arguments cited a range of tonal languages, beginning with Chinese, whose lexical entries are fully tonal, and extending to Bambara and Serbo-Croatian, which have more limited lexical tonal specifications. Woo also found that with only level tone distinctive features, representing these features on vowels and the occasional sonorant consonant, one could account for the distribution of contour tones in several languages if contours were made up of level tones sequences, with each tone in the sequence represented on a separate vowel (or sometimes sonorant consonant). This was possible in the cases she described, as long as one allowed for a few additional factors, including stress and neighboring consonants, to bring about contouring in tone production.

In Leben (1973) I argued against Woo's (1969) claim that tone was phonologically represented on vowels, citing, among other things, cases of distinctive contour tones, which typically are broken down into sequences of level tones yet can be found on phonologically short CV syllables.

Some earlier generative work tried adapting segment-based distinctive features to tone by positing abstract segments to carry leftover tone features after all of the vowels or sonorants in the neighborhood had already been used up. For example, Schachter and Fromkin's (1968) landmark generative phonology of Akan (Kwa, Ghana) describes a high tone unassociated with a tone-bearing unit (TBU) as [+seg, +tone, ØF]. The Akan rule that absorbs such a tone, whether low or high, into an adjacent tone on either side is expressed as follows by Schachter and Fromkin (1968: 114):

$$\left\{\begin{matrix} \begin{bmatrix}\alpha\text{Tone}\\ \beta\text{F}\end{bmatrix}\begin{bmatrix}\gamma\text{Tone}\\ \varnothing\text{F}\end{bmatrix} \\ \begin{bmatrix}\alpha\text{Tone}\\ \varnothing\text{F}\end{bmatrix}\begin{bmatrix}\gamma\text{Tone}\\ \beta\text{F}\end{bmatrix}\end{matrix}\right\} \rightarrow \left\{\begin{matrix} \begin{bmatrix}+\text{Tone}\\ \beta\text{F}\end{bmatrix} & \text{(where } \alpha \text{ or } \gamma = +) \\ \begin{bmatrix}-\text{Tone}\\ \beta\text{F}\end{bmatrix} & \text{(where } \alpha \text{ and } \gamma = -)\end{matrix}\right\}$$

(where [βF] indicates that segmental features are present and [ØF] indicates that no segmental features are present)

What this rule is describing is highly common and natural in tone languages, yet as we see, the fit with the existing formalism is very poor. In Leben (1973) I began with this observation and similar cases where representing tone as a feature on segments failed to bring out its true character. What was needed was an underlying representation of tone that was better fitted to its typical behavior. The solution, drawn from Firthian prosodic analysis (see section 2.3), was to represent tones phonologically on domains larger than the segment—syllables and morphemes. That seemed plausible enough, but what was still needed was a working mechanism to incorporate that insight. That was boldly supplied by Goldsmith (1976): separate autosegmental tiers of representation for tones and segments, linked by association lines subject to a variety of rules and conventions, many of them plausibly universal. Since then, autosegmental phonology has played a role in one way or another in virtually all generative descriptive and theoretical work that has followed.

2.2. Early Results in Autosegmental Phonology

The autosegmental framework was quickly and widely adopted, thanks to the many analytic puzzles it elegantly solved. Even more important was its success at making transparent some common patterns of operation in tone languages. With two independent tiers—for tones and segments—and simple rules and conventions for associating them, the new framework offered a graphic tool for visualizing and expressing such basic tonal operations as mapping, spreading, and delinking. What is more, autosegmental phonology, simply by virtue of its geometry, explained the common fact that a tone remains even when the TBU bearing it has been deleted.

It was not just that rules of linking and spreading became easy to formulate. These simple rules interacted in different ways in different languages, expressing patterns that might be language-particular but using mechanisms that were universal. A striking example is Tonga (Bantu, Zambia), ingeniously analyzed by Meeussen (1963), but in a way that left the impression that it was highly idiosyncratic.

Note how tone behaves in the following typical simple present-tense verb forms. High tone is marked with an acute accent, and low tone is unmarked.

(1)	a.	tu - la - lang - a 'we Pres. look at FV'	tu - la - bon - a 'we Pres. see FV'	tu - la - ba - bon - a 'we Pres. them see FV'
	b.	ba - la - lang - a 'they Pres. look at FV'	ba - lá - bon - a 'they Pres. see FV'	ba - lá - ba - bon - a 'they Pres. them see FV'
	c.	tu - la - mu - lang - a 'we Pres. 3sg look at FV'	tu - la - mu - bon - a 'we Pres. 3sg see FV'	tu - la - ba - bon - a 'we Pres. them see FV'
	d.	ba - la - mu - lang - a 'they Pres. 3sg look at FV'	ba - lá - mú - bon - a 'they Pres. 3sg see FV'	ba - lá - ba - bon - a 'they Pres. them see FV'

Meeussen (1963) interpreted Tonga's underlying tones not as high (H) and low (L), which change a lot from form to form, but in terms of abstract tone markers he called neutral (N) and determinant (D), realized as follows:

(2) D = L
N = H / D __ D
N = L elsewhere

In (1), the determinants are *bon* 'see' and *ba* 'they'. A nagging aspect of Meeussen's solution is that it is based on abstract entities instead of phonological elements—suggesting the null hypothesis that tonal systems can differ from one another in unlimited ways. McCawley (1973) rectified the theoretical problem by reformulating Meeussen's analysis with underlying high and low tones. The trade-off was that for language-particular diacritics, McCawley substituted language-particular rule ordering, but rule order was widely held to differ from one language to another. Still, the reanalysis, as Goldsmith (1976: 142) commented, is quite arbitrary—a verdict McCawley himself might well have agreed with, since at the end of his article, McCawley pointed to the possibility of a revision based on accent.

According to Goldsmith, that very possibility was explored in Cohen (1974) and developed further in Goldsmith (1976: 142–148; 1984b). Determinant tones in Meeussen's (1963) analysis, appearing on morphemes such as *bon* 'see' or *ba* 'they', were reinterpreted by Goldsmith as accented, marked by an asterisk, and these accented morphemes match up with the accented tone, *L*, as in these examples:

```
(3)  (see [1c], column 2)   (see [1c], column 3)   (see [1d], column 3)
                  *                 *     *           *     *    *
     tu - la - mu - bon - a    tu - lá - ba - bon - a    ba - lá - ba - bon - a
```

In the two columns on the right, *ba* and *bon* are adjacent accented syllables. By a common rule of Eastern Bantu, of two adjacent accents, the second is deleted. (Equivalently in a tone-based analysis, as we will see, of two adjacent high tones, the second is deleted.) Goldsmith (1984a) dubbed this Meeussen's rule; it deletes the second accent from the string in the right-hand column.

```
(4)  (see [1c], column 2)   (see [1c], column 3)
                  *                 *                 *     *
     tu - la - mu - bon - a    tu - lá - ba - bon - a    ba - lá - ba - bon - a
```

This set of accents yields the right surface tones if we postulate a melody $H\overset{*}{L}$ for each accented morpheme. This melody is added in (5):

(5)

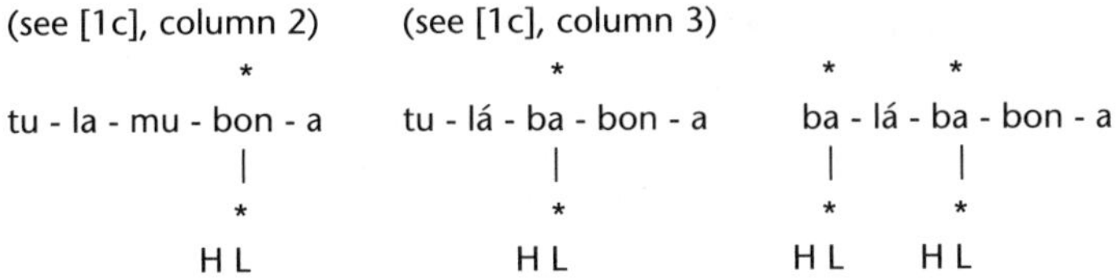

The well-formedness condition, one of the key innovations of autosegmental phonology, requires that any TBU be associated with a tone and that any tone be associated with some TBU. This derives (6) from (5):

(6)

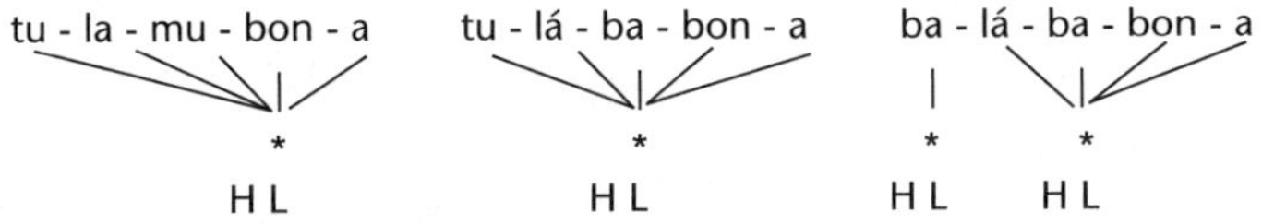

In the right-hand column of (6) the leftmost tone, H, has not been associated, because only one tone is associated to a single TBU. This stray tone is erased by an independent convention.

Pulleyblank (1986) sought to establish that Goldsmith's accents are actually tones underlyingly and reinterpreted Goldsmith's asterisk as a linked high tone.[1] Pulleyblank further revised the autosegmental model in line with new underspecification theory by removing the requirement that tone spreading be automatic under the well-formedness condition, leaving the application or not of spreading to language-particular rules.

In the revised Tonga analysis, a linked high tone spreads to any string of toneless TBUs immediately to the left. Later rules delink the rightmost TBU from any multiply linked H sequence and delete a high tone associated with the string-initial TBU. Pulleyblank's analysis also diverges from Goldsmith's by positing that low is the default tone in Tonga. Some sample derivations, leaving off the final step, where default L is assigned to toneless TBU, follow. For more, see Pulleyblank (1986: 164–185).

(7) Tonga indicative present affirmative strong tense (Pulleyblank 1986: 169–170)

'they see him/her'	'we see them'	'they see them'
bà lá bòn à	tù là bà bòn à	bà lá bà bòn à

Underlying representations

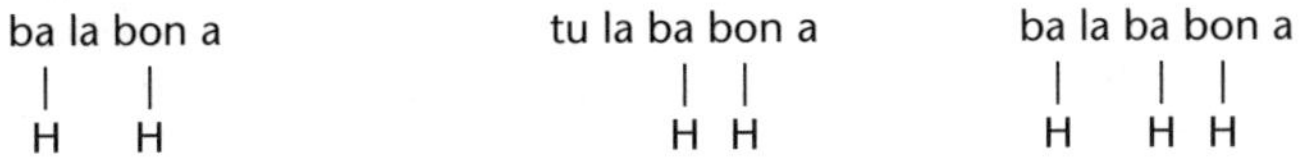

Meeussen's rule, deleting the second of two adjacent H*'s*

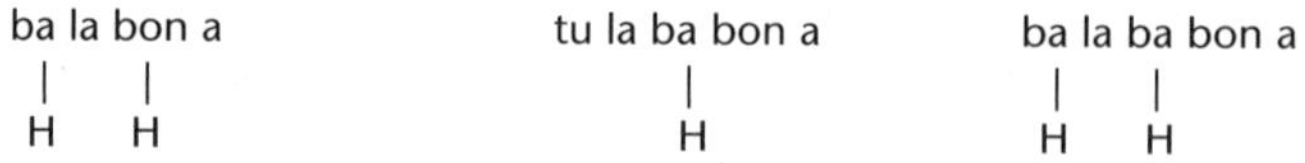

Tone spreading

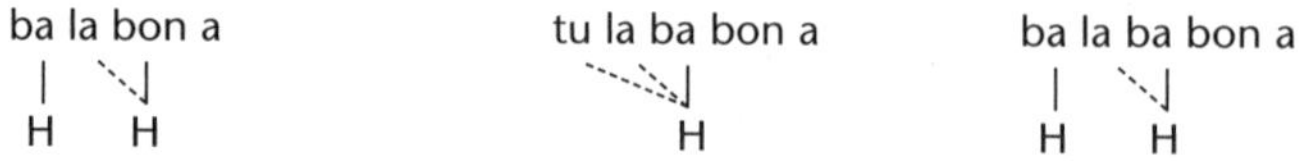

Rightmost high tone delinking

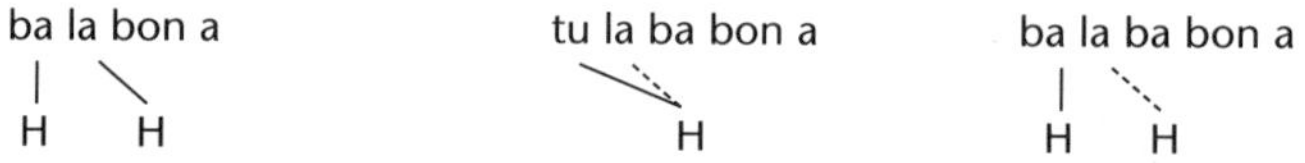

Initial high tone deletion

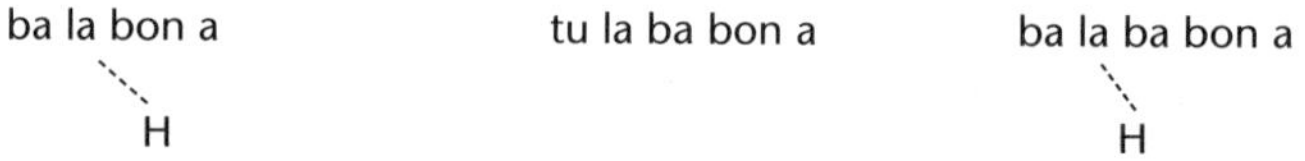

Next, default low insertion assigns a low tone to each TBU not linked to a high tone in the final step of (7). Pulleyblank was interested in eliminating abstract accent marks in principle in favor of tones. Another feature of this reanalysis is that it answers an objection raised by Hyman and Katamba (1993:42). Their point was that Goldsmith's (1976, 1984b) choice of underlying accent for Tonga analysis was inconsistent with his choice in Goldsmith (1985a) of underlying tone in the structurally similar case of Sukuma (with tones reversed). Under Pulleyblank's reanalysis, Tonga and Sukuma now are treated in the same fashion—both have tones, not accents, in their underlying forms.[2] We return to accent in section 2.5.

2.3. Where Did Autosegmental Phonology Come From?

Goldsmith and Laks (2010: 17) situated autosegmental phonology on a line extending back to Bloch, Harris, and Hockett, who all challenged Saussure's purely linear view of phonological representation.[3] Beyond this, Goldsmith and Laks said, autosegmental phonology "laid out as a research project for phonologists the discovery of a consistent geometry for phonological representations that would allow for considerable simplification of the conception of phonological rule and even of abstractness."

Autosegmental phonology also has roots in the work of Firth (1948) and his followers. Goldsmith (1992: 154) indicated that "the Firthian approach encouraged investigators to notice respects in which a tone pattern was a property of an entire word," though he found Firthian treatments of tone, at least in African languages, "a good deal less insightful than its treatment of other prosodic effects." His reasons for that judgment, it turns out, also express the essence of the autosegmental concept:

> But tone is not like nasalization, even when the nasalization is as grammaticized as Bendor-Samuel showed that it is in Terena, where the first-person singular is marked by a prosody of nasalization (Bendor-Samuel, 1960). For in tone systems, it is necessary to come to grips with a kind of internal segmentation within the tonal melody or envelope. As we have come to see in the last ten or fifteen years, this autonomous segmentation of tone, and other prosodic levels, is an important characteristic of African tone systems, and autosegmental analyses specifically differ from their Firthian counterparts in insisting on segmentation of a uniform sort on each tier. Indeed, this is the central idea of autosegmental phonology: that the effects impressionistically called "suprasegmental" are still just as SEGMENTAL as anything else, in the sense that they consist of linear sequences of more basic units which can be treated analytically. (Goldsmith 1992: 154)

Thus, tonal autosegments are essentially segments represented on a separate tier. So are nasal and other autosegments, but tonal autosegments tend to be freer to combine into melodies.

Autosegmental phonology, cast within the framework of generative phonology, also departs from earlier traditions by being in principle totally explicit. A generative analysis must satisfy formal criteria that enable a given analysis to be judged against others. In the earlier structuralist and Firthian traditions, the criteria were less clear.

In contrast to the highly critical attacks by Chomsky (1964) and others of that era, Goldsmith (2008: 37) offered his view of "an intellectual continuity from the work of Sapir and Bloomfield, through that of Wells and Harris, to that of Chomsky [and] Halle."

2.4. Advances under Autosegmental Phonology

The greater explicitness and transparency of generative theory paid off in descriptive successes, in turn attracting many followers. Earlier approaches to phonology, particularly by the American structuralists, were shown to lead to descriptively incorrect, sometimes absurd results.[4] Early generative analyses captured exciting new generalizations while making defects in a given analysis easier to spot. For example, as sketched in section 2.1, Schachter and Fromkin's (1968) analysis of Twi, though rigorous and illuminating, was clearly hampered by inadequate machinery for expressing the behavior of tone. Autosegmental phonology changed that.

Autosegmental phonology also changed a lot more, and quickly, leading within a decade to major revisions in views of metrical prominence, syllable structure, and the organization of distinctive features. This exciting period has been covered in many surveys, including Anderson (1985), Goldsmith (1990), Goldsmith and Noske (2006), and Leben (2011). Several other surveys focused on autosegmental theories of tone, accent, and intonation: Yip (2002), Gussenhoven (2004), and Ladd (2008). Early in this period of sweeping change, Goldsmith (1981) showed that the change from [s] to [h] in dialects of Spanish could be made to seem eminently natural by extending the autosegmental framework to what he called subsegmentals. Another extension of the framework—multiple autosegmental vowel tiers—was Goldsmith's (1985b) remedy for problems noted by Anderson (1980) for the autosegmental analysis of vowel harmony. But as in his thesis, most of Goldsmith's attention in his autosegmental work went to tone and accent.

2.5. Goldsmith's Continuing Contributions to Autosegmental Phonology

In the 1980s and early 1990s, Goldsmith produced about a dozen analyses and surveys of tone and accent in Bantu. For Goldsmith (1984a, 1984b) and Clements and Goldsmith (1984), the division in Bantu between tone languages and accentual ones is marked by Meeussen's rule, which applies in the accentual languages but not the purely tonal ones.[5] This is echoed by Downing (2004), even though in her view Meeussen's rule applies to tones, not accents. She noted that by removing all but the first in a sequence of high tones (which Goldsmith interpreted as accents), Meeussen's rule gives rise to culminative accent in languages where it applies. While linguists differ on the place of pitch accent in a typology of prosodic systems,[6] the class of "Bantu accentual languages" is much narrower and forms a natural class, defined by a set of shared features that distinguish them from nonaccentual Bantu languages.[7] Thus, connecting tonal typology in Bantu with the application of Meeussen's rule is an interesting and testable synchronic and diachronic proposition.[8]

Another facet of Meeussen's rule explored by Goldsmith is the possibility of casting it in terms of accent clash resolution. Goldsmith (1987) proposesd this for Kintandu, a member of the Kikongo cluster of languages (Democratic Republic of the Congo). A similar idea was pursued by Bickmore (1992) for Kinyambo (Tanzania), where Bickmore found the stress-like phenomena lapse and clash avoidance, and where tone is assigned to the metrical grid by virtually the last rule of the phonology.[9]

What exactly is accent, though? This is one of the basic questions raised by Goldsmith's work on Bantu. Many linguists have tried to identify accent with a more substantive phonological feature. Liberman (1975) endowed English intonational tunes with hierarchical metrical structure as a way to align tunes with texts, while Goldsmith (1978)—an article written around the same time as Liberman's but published later—posited the simple asterisk for the same purpose. In current intonational studies deriving from Pierrehumbert (1980) and Beckman and Pierrehumbert (1986), it is this asterisk that distinguishes a "pitch accent" from other tones and accents. This is the case in the Tones and Break Indices transcription system (Beckman and Ayers-Elam 1997), and it has always been true in Goldsmith's work as well, where accent is the abstract device attracting certain tones to certain TBUs.[10]

In systems with contrastive lexical tone or accent, accent can sometimes be identified phonologically as a linked tone in an underlying representation. We saw this in Pulleyblank's (1986) reanalysis of Tonga, and Hyman (1989) advocated this generally for the Bantu languages that have been called accentual. Incidentally, one might ask whether privative tones[11]—tone features with just one value, as motivated by Goldsmith and Sabimana (1986) for Kirundi—could be identified as accents, but an argument against this from Hyman (2011) is that certain languages—Hyman's example is Haya—demonstrably have privative tones underlyingly yet are fully tonal at the surface. This is precisely the sort of situation McCawley (1970) first drew attention to.

Another approach, not just for Bantu but for languages at large, interprets accent as the strong node of a metrical foot, and indeed cases have surfaced in which metrical position can explain a variety of phonetic and phonological effects. The earliest example is Rice (1987) for Slave (Athabaskan, Northwest Territories). More recent studies aligning tone with metrical structure that is motivated independently on phonetic grounds are Pearce (2006, 2007) and Green (2010). However, in many other cases to date, metrical structure has been posited without justification, either to account for register effects (Huang [1980] 1985; Clements 1983) or as an abstract counting or positioning device (Sietsema 1989; Bamba 1991).

Hyman (1989: 115), in his survey of the ways accent and metrical structure had been used in Bantu tone studies, found that "Bantu is marked by accents of different kinds, e.g. those used to predict segmental properties, tonal properties, juncture, rhythmic or intonational effects, etc. The conclusion to be drawn is that if all of these things are (metrically) accent, then Bantu languages must allow for multiple (and usually conflicting) metrical representations." He observed tellingly that "there have been no segmental correlates to the alternating H tones reported in Bantu" (1989: 129). In his brief paper, Hyman sketched how Goldsmith's asterisks can be reinterpreted as underlying tones in several languages, but only time will tell how this will play out in fuller analyses of more languages and what generalizations will be gained or lost in the process.[12] Whatever the outcome, Goldsmith's asterisk, abstract though it is, is different in character from Meeussen's diacritic features neutral and determinant seen in section 2.1. Neutral and determinant, which Meeussen posited for Tonga as well as for two other Bantu languages, Bangubangu (Democratic Republic of the Congo) (Meeussen 1954) and Luganda (Uganda) (Meeussen 1954, 1974), were inherently diacritics, defined ad hoc for each language, and in fact their definitions actually differ across the three languages in which Meeussen used them. Accent, on the other hand, can be associated with cross-linguistic properties, especially culminativity and phonetic prominence.[13]

2.6. Autosegmental Phonology and Constraint-Based Theories

Phonological theory has changed drastically over the last two decades, with constraint-based approaches dominating the field. In principle, the autosegmental architecture does not require the application of rules per se, as we can see from Myers (1997) and Zoll (2003). Indeed, the well-formedness condition is itself nothing but an early set of phonological constraints, and Goldsmith himself in works from 1989, 1991, and 1993 presented a model of harmonic phonology where constraints play a wider role than they had previously. Still, in a 2002 paper, Goldsmith showed the need for intermediate representations in Mituku and motivated an intrasyllabic version of Meeussen's rule as an autosegmental rule.

Such proposals do not alter our notions about autosegmental representation, but other constraint-based approaches would certainly have this effect. Three I will mention here are optimal domains theory (ODT), headed span theory, and ABC+Q theory (Agreement by Correspondence theory [ABC] plus its representational component, Q theory).

For many decades, globality has been a concern in certain tonal systems, primarily in Bantu.[14] With this in mind, Cassimjee (1998) and Cassimjee and Kisseberth 1998, 2001) specifically design an alternative that builds global reference directly into phonological representations, as illustrated here:

(8) a. *ODT representation* (spreading case)
x (x̲́ x́ x́) x
b. *ODT representation* (shifting case)
x (x̲ x x́) x

Compare these to the corresponding standard autosegmental structures:

(9) a. spreading b. shifting

```
a. spreading          b. shifting
   x x x > x x x         x x x > x x x
   |       |\ \          |           |
   H       H             H           H
```

Referring to the standard autosegmental structures, in (9a) a linked tone spreads to the two TBUs on its right, while in (9b), the linked tone, after spreading to the two TBUs on its right, is delinked from all but the rightmost position. Both operations are widely attested in tone languages. What is interesting is that in the Southern Bantu languages that Cassimjee and Kisseberth (1998) described, it is important to know for a given surface tonal configuration such as the ones on the right side of the arrow in (9a) and (9b) what their underlying source was.

That information is precisely what is built into the ODT structures in (8a) and (8b). The underline on the first *x* in the parenthesized expression (x̲́ x́ x́) of (8a) indicates that this *x* was underlying high-toned, while the acute accents on each *x* in the same expression indicate the surface tones. The parentheses enclosing this group are the equivalent of multiple linking in autosegmental representations: all three high-toned *x*'s are, in effect, linked to a single H, with the underlined H serving as the head of the domain, in a sense related to the headedness of metrical feet. Thus the ODT representation (8a) conflates the derivational sequence in (9a) into a single structure. The same is true of the corresponding representations in (8b) and (9b). ODT takes two steps away from autosegmental phonology by explicitly ruling out floating features

(Cassimjee and Kisseberth 1998: 60) and the distinction between singly and multiply linked autosegments (Cassimjee and Kisseberth 1998: 56).

ODT has yet to be widely explored per se, but a related proposal for headed autosegmental spans was made by McCarthy (2004). A span is an exhaustive string of adjacent feature-bearing units with the same value for any distinctive feature. For example, the three-TBU sequences associated with H in this representation

(10) 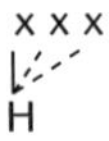

count as a span and would need to be marked either left-headed or right-headed. The advantage, according to McCarthy, is that this would make it possible to account for directionality effects in non-rule-based frameworks by means of constraints on location of the head segment of a span. See McCarthy (2004: 11–12) for an example and Key (2007) for a demonstration covering some of the same phenomena as ODT, by showing how headed spans work in Bantu tonology.

A more radical alternative to autosegmental representation has recently been advanced by Inkelas and Shih (2013) and Shih and Inkelas (2014a, 2014b). Their Q theory divides each segment into three quanta, permitting a three-tone sequence such as LHL, for example, to be expressed on a single TBU, which is analyzed into a quantized sequence $a_1a_2a_3$, yielding what can be represented informally as $\grave{a}_1\acute{a}_2\grave{a}_3$. This approach, they argue, captures both the unity of contours and the separability of the individual components. Furthermore, using agreement by correspondence (Hansson 2001, Rose and Walker 2004), they can account naturally for consonant-tone interactions and possibly also vowel harmony and autosegmental spreading.[15]

Autosegmental representation grew out of the need—recognized decades earlier—to represent phonological features on distinct tiers of representation. McCarthy (2004) mentioned that if autosegmental spans have heads, they still can be represented in the familiar multitier style, though this makes for a very cumbersome appearance, especially in an optimality theory tableau. The underlining of TBUs in ODT also serves as an extension of autosegmental theory, not a turning away from it. Q theory, on the other hand, is an entirely different theory of how features spread, shift, and float.[16] Thanks to four decades of results in autosegmental phonology, it should be straightforward to judge how these competing approaches measure up.

Notes

I am grateful to Larry Hyman for his valuable suggestions.

1. This follows the position taken for Japanese by Poser (1984), who reinterprets the accent mark in earlier analyses as a high tone.
2. For more on competing analyses of Tonga tone, see Hyman (2001: 252).
3. The references, I believe, are to Bloch (1948), Harris (1944), Hockett (1947), and Saussure (1916).
4. Halle (1962) and Chomsky (1964) are among the most highly charged and highly influential essays on the merits of the generative approach over its predecessors. Still, several of the next generation of generativists, including John Goldsmith, John McCarthy, and Nick Clements, explicitly traced the roots of the autosegmental approach back to the American structuralists and to the Firthians. See Encrevé (2000) for a summary, including this quote from McCarthy (1981: 414): "In view of apparent similarities between many of the notions of autosegmental phonology and Harris's long components, we could reasonably expect the theory developed here to have been prefigured somewhat by earlier work. In fact there exists a fairly detailed account of Biblical and Modern Hebrew in terms of the theory of long components."
5. Goldsmith (1982: 50): "What rule do all, or most, of the accentual Bantu languages share? The answer is Meeussen's Rule (or its mirror-image, as in Rimi and Sukuma)."
6. Hyman (2006) argued that the term "pitch accent languages" covers a highly diverse set of languages in between the well-defined poles of stress languages versus tone languages. Non-Bantu languages from Hyman (2006: 34) that could be grouped among "pitch accent" systems because they combine tone and accent include Ma'ya, Usarufa, Fasu, Serbo-Croatian, Swedish-Norwegian, and Ayutla Mixtec.
7. See Downing (2011: sec. 2) for a list of distinguishing characteristics of Bantu accentual systems.
8. Philipson (1998) in fact tested this proposition and found it wanting. He argued, among other things, that Meeussen's rule is not attested in many of the languages called accentual and that culminativity can and did develop independently of Meeussen's rule.
9. Bickmore (1992) also posited multiple prominence levels as a way to account for the varying degrees to which an accented syllable affects or is affected by the accent of a neighboring syllable. In closely related Haya, Hyman (1993) pointed to problems with the grid-based analysis that seem to favor a strictly tonal approach.
10. For intonation, see Goldsmith (1978) and for tone, see Goldsmith (1987, 1988).

11. See Goldsmith (1985b, 1990) on privative autosegments for consonants and vowels.
12. Also, there are several variants of the accent model, including metrical trees and grids. For general discussion, see Goldsmith (1990). For a grid-based analysis of Meeussen's rule, see Goldsmith (1984a).
13. The notions culminativity and phonetic prominence need to be tightened. In Goldsmith's (1976, 1984b) Tonga analysis, accent is not culminative, as we see in the multiply accented cases in (3) to (6) in section 2.2. Note, too, that accent's phonetic prominence in Goldsmith's Tonga analysis consists solely in its realization as a pitch obtrusion. But the particular pitch obtrusion for Tonga, an accented low tone preceded by high tone, is Tonga-specific, not unlike Meeussen's definitions of determinant and neutral.
14. For this problem in Bangubangu, see McCawley (1974). For Luganda, see Hyman (1982) and Hyman and Katamba (1993, 2010). For Kinande, see Hyman and Valinande (1985).
15. But see Steriade (2014) for alternatives.
16. A question unanswered in the headed span approach, attributed by McCarthy (2004) to Lee Bickmore, is the status of floating features. The same question arises in ODT and ABC+Q.

References

Anderson, Stephen R. 1969. West Scandinavian vowel systems and the ordering of phonological rules. PhD dissertation, Massachusetts Institute of Technology.

———. 1974. *The Organization of Phonology*. New York: Academic Press.

———. 1980. Problems and perspectives in the description of vowel harmony. In *Issues in Vowel Harmony: Proceedings of the CUNY Linguistics Conference on Vowel Harmony, May 14, 1977*, ed. R. Vago, 1–48. Amsterdam: John Benjamins.

———. 1985. *Phonology in the Twentieth Century: Theories of Rules and Theories of Representations*. Chicago: University of Chicago Press.

Bamba, M. 1991. Sur la relation entre ton et accent. PhD dissertation, Université du Québec à Montréal.

Beckman, Mary E., and Gayle Ayers-Elam. 1997. Guidelines for ToBI labelling. The Ohio State University. http://www.ling.ohio-state.edu/research/phonetics/E_ToBI/.

Beckman, Mary E., and Janet B. Pierrehumbert. 1986. Intonational structure in Japanese and English. *Phonology Yearbook* 3:255–309.

Bendor-Samuel, J. T. 1960. Some problems of segmentation in the phonological analysis of Terena. *Word* 16:348–355. Reprinted in *Prosodic Analysis*, ed. F. R. Palmer, 214–221. London: Oxford University Press, 1970.

Bickmore, Lee S. 1992. Multiple phonemic stress levels in Kinyambo. *Phonology* 9:155–198.

Bloch, Bernard. 1948. A set of postulates for phonemic analysis. *Language* 24:3–46.

Cassimjee, Farida. 1998. *IsiXhosa Tonology: An Optimal Domains Theory Analysis.* Munich: Lincom Europa.

Cassimjee, Farida, and Charles W. Kisseberth. 1998. Optimal domains theory and Bantu tonology: A case study from Isixhosa and Shingazidja. In *Theoretical Aspects of Bantu Tone,* ed. Larry Hyman and Charles Kisseberth, 33–132. Stanford, CA: CSLI.

———. 2001. Zulu tonology and its relation to other Nguni languages. In *Proceedings of the Symposium on Cross-Linguistic Studies of Tonal Phenomena, Tonogenesis, Japanese Accentology, and Other Topics,* ed. Shigeki Kaji, 327–359. Tokyo: Tokyo University of Foreign Studies.

Chomsky, Noam. 1964. Current issues in linguistic theory. In *The Structure of Language,* ed. Jerry A. Fodor and Jerrold J. Katz, 50–118. Upper Saddle River, NJ: Prentice-Hall.

Chomsky, Noam, and Morris Halle. 1968. *Sound Pattern of English.* New York: Harper & Row.

Clements, G. Nick. 1983. The hierarchical representation of tone features. In *Current Approaches to African Linguistics,* vol. 1, ed. Ivan R. Dihoff, 145–176. Dordrecht: Foris Publications.

Clements, G. Nick, and John Goldsmith. 1984. Autosegmental studies in Bantu tone: Introduction. In *Autosegmental Studies in Bantu Tone,* ed. G. Nick Clements and John Goldsmith, 1–17. Dordrecht: Foris Publications.

Cohen, Michael. 1974. Topics in Tonga tone. Unpublished paper, Massachusetts Institute of Technology.

Downing, Laura J. 2004. What African languages tell us about accent typology. *ZAS Papers in Linguistics* 37:101–136.

———. 2011. Bantu tone. In *The Blackwell Companion to Phonology,* ed. Marc van Oostendorp et al., vol. 5, chap. 114. New York: Wiley.

Encrevé, Pierre. 2000. The old and the new: Some remarks on phonology and its history. *Folia Linguistica* 34:57–84.

Firth, J. R. 1948. Sounds and prosodies. In *Prosodic Analysis,* ed. F. R. Palmer, 1–26. London: Oxford University Press, 1970.

Goldsmith, John. 1976. Autosegmental phonology. PhD dissertation, Massachusetts Institute of Technology. Bloomington: Indiana University Linguistics Club. http://people.cs.uchicago.edu/~jagoldsm/Papers/dissertation.pdf. Published by Garland Press, New York [1979].

———. 1978. English as a tone language. *Communication and Cognition* 11, no. 3–4: 453–476. Reprinted in *Phonology in the 1980s,* ed. D. Goyvaerts, 287–308. Ghent: Story-Scientia [1981].

———. 1981. Subsegmentals in Spanish phonology: An autosegmental approach. In *Linguistic Symposium on Romance Languages* ed. D. Napoli, 1–16. Washington, DC: Georgetown University Press.

———. 1982. Accent systems. In *The Structure of Phonological Representations (Part 1)*, ed. Harry van der Hulst and Norval Smith, 47–63. Dordrecht: Foris Publications.

———. 1984a. Meeussen's rule.In *Language Sound Structure*, ed. Mark Aronoff and Richard T. Oehrle, 245–259. Cambridge, MA: MIT Press.

———. 1984b. Tone and accent in Tonga. In *Autosegmental Studies in Bantu Tone*, ed. G. Nick Clements and John Goldsmith, 19–51. Dordrecht: Foris Publications.

———. 1985a. On tone in Sukuma. In Goyvaerts 1985, 167–187.

———. 1985b. Vowel harmony in Khalkha Mongolian, Yaka, Hungarian and Finnish. *Phonology Yearbook* 2:253–275.

———. 1987. Tone and accent and getting the two together. In *Proceedings of the Thirteenth Annual Meeting of the Berkeley Linguistics Society*, ed. Jon Aske, Natasha Beery, Laura Michaelis, and Hana Filip, 88–104. Berkeley, CA: Berkeley Linguistics Society.

———. 1988. Prosodic trends in the Bantu languages. In *Autosegmental Studies on Pitch Accent*, ed. Harry van der Hulst and Norval Smith, 81–93. Dordrecht: Foris Publications.

———. 1989. Autosegmental licensing, inalterability, and harmonic rule application. In *Papers from the 25th Meeting of the Chicago Linguistic Society*, 145–156. Chicago: Chicago Linguistic Society.

———. 1990. *Autosegmental and Metrical Phonology*. Oxford: Blackwell.

———. 1991. Phonology as an intelligent system. In *Bridges between Psychology and Linguistics: A Swarthmore Festschrift for Lila Gleitman*, ed. Donna Jo Napoli and Judy Kegl, 247–267. Mahwah, NJ: Lawrence Erlbaum.

———. 1992. A note on the genealogy of research traditions in modern phonology. *Journal of Linguistics* 28, no. 1: 149–163.

———. 1993a. Harmonic phonology. In Goldsmith 1993b, 21–60.

———, ed. 1993b. *The Last Phonological Rule: Reflections on Constraints and Derivations*. Chicago: University of Chicago Press.

———. 2002. Tone in Mituku: How a floating tone nailed down an intermediate level. *Phonetics, Phonology, and Cognition* 3:80.

———. 2008. Generative phonology in the late 1940s. *Phonology* 25:37–59.

———. 2012. Theory, kernels, data, methods. In *Proceedings from the Annual Meeting of the Chicago Linguistic Society* 48, no. 1, 263–277. Chicago: Chicago Linguistic Society. http://people.cs.uchicago.edu/~jagoldsm/Papers/cls2010.pdf.

Goldsmith, John A., and Bernard Laks. 2012. Generative phonology: Its origins, its principles, and its successors. In *The Cambridge History of Linguistics*. Cambridge: Cambridge University Press. http://hum.uchicago.edu/~jagoldsm/Papers/GenerativePhonology.pdf.

Goldsmith, John A., and Manuela Noske. 2006. Autosegmental phonology and underspecification theory. In *History of the Language Sciences*, ed. S. Auroux,

K. Koerner, H.-J. Niederehe, and K. Versteegh, vol. 3, 2280–2291. Berlin: Walter de Gruyter.

Goldsmith, John A., and Firmard Sabimana. 1986. The Kirundi verb. In *Modèles en tonologie*, ed. Francis Jouannet, 19–62. Paris: Editions du CNRS.

Goyvaerts, Didier L., ed. 1985. *African Linguistics: Essays in Memory of MWK Semikenke*. Amsterdam: Benjamins.

Green, Christopher R. 2010. Prosodic phonology in Bamana (Bambara): Syllable complexity, metrical structure, and tone. PhD dissertation, Indiana University.

Gussenhoven, Carlos. 2004. *The Phonology of Tone and Intonation*. Cambridge: Cambridge University Press.

Halle, Morris. 1962. Phonology in generative grammar. *Word* 18:54–72.

———. 1973. Stress rules in English: A new version. *Linguistic Inquiry* 4:451–464.

Halle, Morris, and Samuel Jay Keyser. 1971. *English Stress: Its Form, Its Growth, and Its Role in Verse*. New York: Harper & Row.

Hansson, Gunnar Ólafur. 2001. Theoretical and typological issues in consonant harmony. PhD dissertation, University of California, Berkeley.

Harris, Zellig. 1944. Simultaneous components in phonology. *Language* 20:181–205.

Hockett, Charles. 1947. Componential analysis of Sierra Popoluca. *International Journal of American Linguistics* 13:259–267.

Huang, C. T. James. [1980] 1985. The autosegmental and metrical nature of tone terracing. In Goyvaerts 1985, 209–238.

Hyman, Larry M. 1982. Globality and the accentual analysis of Luganda tone. *Journal of Linguistic Research* 2:1–40.

———. 1989. Accent in Bantu: An appraisal. *Studies in the Linguistic Sciences* 19, no. 2: 111–128.

———. 1993. Problems in rule ordering in phonology: Two Bantu test cases. In Goldsmith 1993b, 195–222.

———. 2001. Privative tone in Bantu. In *Crosslinguistic Studies of Tonal Phenomena: Tonogenesis, Japanese Accentology, and Other Topics*, ed. Shigeki Kaji, 237–257. Tokyo: Institute for the Study of Languages and Cultures of Asia and Africa, Tokyo University of Foreign Studies.

———. 2006. Word-prosodic typology. *Phonology* 23:225–257.

———. 2011. Tone: Is it different? In *The Handbook of Phonological Theory*, 2nd ed., ed. John Goldsmith, Jason Riggle, and Alan Yu, 197–239. Oxford: Wiley-Blackwell.

Hyman, Larry M., and Francis X. Katamba. 1993. A new approach to tone in Luganda. *Language* 69:34–67.

———. 2010. Tone, syntax, and prosodic domains in Luganda. In *Papers from the Workshop on Bantu Relative Clauses*, ed. Laura J. Downing et al., special issue, *ZAS Papers in Linguistics, Berlin* 53:69–98.

Hyman, Larry M., and Nzama Valinande, 1985. Globality in the Kinande tone system. In Goyvaerts 1985, 239–260.

Inkelas, Sharon, and Stephanie S. Shih. 2013. Contour segments and tones in (sub)segmental agreement by correspondence. Paper presented at the 21st Manchester Phonology Meeting, May 23–25, 2013, University of Manchester, UK.

Key, Michael. 2007. Headed spans and Bantu tonology. In *Papers in Optimality Theory*, vol. 3, ed. Leah Bateman, Michael O'Keefe, Ehren Reilly, and Adam Werle, 187–207. University of Massachusetts Occasional Papers in Linguistics 32. Amherst, MA: GLSA.

Kiparsky, Paul. 1968. How abstract is phonology? Mimeo. Bloomington: Indiana University Linguistics Club.

Ladd, D. Robert. 2008. *Intonational Phonology*, 2nd ed. Cambridge: Cambridge University Press.

Leben, William R. 1973. Suprasegmental phonology. PhD dissertation, Massachusetts Institute of Technology. [Published, New York: Garland Press, 1980.]

———. 2011. Autosegments. In *Blackwell Companion to Phonology*, ed. Marc van Oostendorp et al., vol. 2, chap. 14. New York: Wiley.

Liberman, Mark. 1975. The intonational system of English. PhD dissertation, Massachusetts Institute of Technology.

McCarthy, John J. 1981. A prosodic theory of nonconcatenative morphology. *Linguistic inquiry* 12:373–418.

———. 2004. Headed spans and autosegmental spreading. Rutgers Optimality Archive 685. http://roa.rutgers.edu/files/685-0904/685-MCCARTHY-0-0.PDF.

McCawley, James D. 1968. *The Phonological Component of a Grammar of Japanese*. The Hague: Mouton.

———. 1970. Some tonal systems that come close to being pitch accent systems but don't quite make it. In *Proceedings of the Sixth Regional Meeting of the Chicago Linguistic Society*, 526–532. Chicago: Chicago Linguistic Society.

———. 1973. Some Tonga tone rules. In *A Festschrift for Morris Halle*, ed. Stephen R. Anderson and Paul Kiparsky, 140–152. New York: Holt, Rinehart and Winston.

———. 1974. Global rules and Bangubangu tone. In *Issues in Phonological Theory*, ed. Michael Kenstowicz and Charles W. Kissebeth, 160–168. The Hague: Mouton.

Meeussen, A. E. 1954. *Linguistische schets van het Bangubangu*. Vol. 5. Brussels: Koninklijk Museum van Belgisch-Kongo.

———. 1963. Morphophonology of the Tonga verb. *Journal of African Languages* 2:72–92.

———. 1974. A note on global rules in Bangubangu tone. *Studies in African Linguistics* 5:95.

Myers, Scott. 1997. OCP effects in optimality theory. *Natural Language and Linguistic Theory* 15:847–892.

Pearce, Mary. 2006. The interaction between metrical structure and tone in Kera. *Phonology* 23:259–286.

———. 2007. Iambicity in Kera. In *Selected Proceedings of the 37th Annual Conference on African Linguistics*. Somerville, MA: Cascadilla Proceedings Project.

Philippson, Gérard. 1998. Tone reduction vs. metrical attraction in the evolution of Eastern Bantu tone systems. In *Theoretical Aspects of Bantu Tone*, ed. Larry M. Hyman and Charles W. Kisseberth, 315–329. Stanford, CA: CSLI.

Pierrehumbert, Janet B. 1980. The phonology and phonetics of English intonation. PhD dissertation, Massachusetts Institute of Technology.

Poser, William J. 1984. The phonetics and phonology of tone and intonation in Japanese. PhD dissertation, Massachusetts Institute of Technology.

Pulleyblank, Douglas. 1986. *Tone in Lexical Phonology*. Dordrecht: Reidel.

Rice, Keren. 1987. Metrical structure in a tone language: The foot in Slave (Athapaskan). Parasession on Metrical and Autosegmental Phonology. *Proceedings of the Chicago Linguistic Society* 23:239–252.

Rose, Sharon, and Rachel Walker. 2004. A typology of consonant agreement by correspondence. *Language* 80, no. 3: 475–531.

Saussure, Ferdinand de. 1916. *Course in General Linguistics*. Reprint, New York: Columbia University Press [2011].

Schachter, Paul, and Victoria Fromkin. 1968. A phonology of Akan: Akuapem, Asante, Fante. *UCLA Working Papers in Phonetics* 9.

Shih, Stephanie S., and Sharon Inkelas. 2014a. Revisiting the TBU in an ABC+Q approach to tone. UC Berkeley Phonology Lab Annual Report: ABC↔Conference. berkeley.edu/phonlab/annual_report/documents/2014/annual_report_2014_ABCC.html.

———. 2014b. A subsegmental correspondence approach to contour tone (dis)harmony patterns. In *Proceedings of Phonology 2013*, ed. John Kingston. Washington, DC: Linguistic Society of America. http://journals.linguisticsociety.org/proceedings/index.php/amphonology/article/view/22.

Sietsema, Brian M. 1989. Metrical dependencies in tone assignment. PhD dissertation, Massachusetts Institute of Technology.

Steriade, Donca. 2014. Theories of diphthongs, contour tones and blockers in harmony. UC Berkeley ABC↔Conference Archive. http://www.linguistics.berkeley.edu/phonlab/annual_report/documents/2014/ABCC/Steriade.pdf.

Woo, Nancy Helen. 1969. Prosody and phonology. PhD dissertation, Massachusetts Institute of Technology.

Yip, Moira. 2002. *Tone*. Cambridge Textbooks in Linguistics. Cambridge: Cambridge University Press.

Zoll, Cheryl. 2003. Optimal tone mapping. *Linguistic Inquiry* 34:225–268.

B. Applications to Tone

THREE

The Autosegmental Approach to Tone in Lusoga

LARRY M. HYMAN

3.1. Introduction

One of the major contributions of John Goldsmith's (1976a, 1976b, 1990) autosegmental approach to tone was its application to Bantu. Both in his own work and in the work he coedited, Clements and Goldsmith (1984), a new avenue was opened up to account for the often opaque relationship between underlying versus surface high (H) and low (L) tonal representations. As an alternative to unitary H and L tones, Goldsmith proposed underlying tonal melodies, such as HL, as in Tonga (Goldsmith 1984b), or LH, as in Sukuma (Goldsmith 1985), that required specific mapping, indicated by prelinking or mediated by accents which he specified with asterisks. In a metrical analysis of Kirundi, Goldsmith, and Sabimana (1986) showed that a metrical analysis of alternating privative /H/ versus Ø tone is more insightful than one recognizing "equipollent" /H/ versus /L/. In each case his intuition was that Bantu H and L tones do not behave in an equipollent way as they do in many West African and other tone systems, instead Bantu H and L tones require a more syntagmatic and privative, perhaps accentual interpretation. Thus, beyond having an underlying binary contrast, traceable to Proto-Bantu

(Greenberg 1948), the present-day two-height Bantu tone systems exhibit considerable variation in at least two senses. First, there is the question concerning which of the tonal elements are "phonologically activated" (Clements 2001): only /H/? only /L/? both /H/ and /L/? Second, there is the variation in the phonological rules that the one or two tones undergo. Chief among these are tone spreading, tone shifting, tone anticipation, tone insertion and deletion, contour tone simplification, boundary tone phenomena, and obligatory contour principle (OCP) effects that prohibit sequences of the same tone, such as /H-H/ → H-L or H-Ø. It is these latter processes that provide the evidence for whether a system should be interpreted as equipollent /H/ versus /L/, privative /H/ versus Ø or privative /L/ versus Ø (cf. Stevick 1969; Odden 1995; Hyman 2001, 2007; Kisseberth and Odden 2003; Marlo 2013).

In this chapter I add to the repertory of privative /L/ versus Ø tone systems by addressing some of the tonal properties of Lusoga, the most closely related language to Luganda, on which considerably more tonal research has been done (see Hyman and Katamba 2010 and references cited therein).[1] In the following two sections I will account for the tonal patterns on Lusoga verb infinitives, first diachronically (3.2), then synchronically (3.3) in terms of traditional autosegmental phonology. In section 3.4 I extend the analysis to nouns and noun reduplication and conclude in section 3.5 that John Goldsmith's autosegmental phonology still provides the best tools to express the basic insights as to what is going on in Bantu tone systems.

3.2. A Diachronic Analysis of Lusoga Infinitives

In this section we begin by considering the tones on affirmative infinitives, as these reveal the central properties of the tone system in a rather straightforward way. Since there are several ways to interpret Lusoga tone synchronically, the discussion in this section will account for the data in terms of the historical tonal changes that have taken place since Proto-Luganda-Lusoga. I will therefore start with a synchronic analysis of /H/ versus Ø, which corresponds to Proto-Bantu *H and *L, after which a different analysis will be proposed in section 3.3.

As seen in the two tone patterns in (1), Lusoga is like most Bantu languages in distinguishing two lexical tone patterns in infinitives. As indicated, these tone patterns correspond with *L or *H tone in the protolanguage:[2]

(1)

	*L root		*H root	
1σ	ò-kú-gw-á	'to fall'	ò-kú-ty-à	'to fear'
	ò-kú-mw-á	'to shave'	ò-kú-ly-à	'to eat'
2σ	ò-kú-bál-á	'to count'	ò-kú-bòn-á	'to see'
	ò-kú-lím-á	'to cultivate'	ò-kú-kùb-á	'to beat'
3σ	ò-kú-lágír-á	'to command'	ò-kú-ghùlìr-á	'to hear'
	ò-kú-lúmúk-á	'to run away'	ò-kú-sèkùl-á	'to pound'
4σ	ò-kú-súmúlúl-á	'to untie'	ò-kú-kàlàkát-á	'to scrape'
	ò-kú-kálírír-á	'to grill'	ò-kú-fùkàmír-á	'to kneel'
5σ	ò-kú-lágír-ágán-á	'to command e.o.'	ò-kú-ghùlìr-ágán-á	'to hear e.o.'
	ò-kú-súmúlúl-ír-á	'to untie for (s.o.)'	ò-kú-kàlàkát-ír-á	'to scrape for (s.o.)'
	STEM = H^n		STEM = $L((L)H^n)$	

The forms in (1) are arranged by the number of syllables in the stem, which consists of a verb root, possibly extended by derivational suffixes such as *-agan-* 'reciprocal' and *-ir-* 'applicative', and an inflectional final vowel (FV), here /-a/. As seen, the infinitive is marked with an L tone vowel prefix *ò-* known as the "augment" in Bantu, followed by the H tone noun class 15 prefix *-kú-*. Both it and all subsequent tones are H in the left column (corresponding to Proto-Bantu *L verb roots). In the right column, the first stem syllable drops to L in all cases, and the FV *-á* will be H unless the stem is monosyllabic. It is important to note that the longer verbs require two L tone stem vowels before the remaining vowels are H. I shall refer to this as the two L tone requirement, or 2LTR. The forms in (2) whose first syllable has a long vowel (VV) show that the 2LTR is a property of moras, not syllables:

(2)

2σ	ò-kú-zíík-á	'to bury'	ò-kú-lèèt-á	'to bring'
	ò-kú-túúnd-á	'to sell'	ò-kú-tùùng-á	'to weave'
3σ	ò-kú-súúbír-á	'to hope'	ò-kú-fàànán-á	'to resemble'
	ò-kú-táándík-á	'to begin'	ò-kú-tààmbúl-á	'to walk'
4σ	ò-kú-yáándúlúz-á	'to spread out'	ò-kú-fùùdhúlúlá	'to spit out'
	ò-kú-dóóndólím-á	'to make idle talk'	ò-kú-sààndúkúl-á	'to uncover'

We thus obtain forms such as *ò-kú-fàànán-á* 'to resemble', rather than **ò-kú-fààn àn-á*, where the two L tones would be counting syllables. However, if the first syllable is short and the second long, the whole of the second syllable (and hence three moras) will be affected:

(3)	3σ	ò-kú-támíír-á	'to become drunk'	ò-kú-tègèèr-á	'to know'
		ò-kú-kólóót-á	'to purr'	ò-kú-dàlàànd-á	'to climb'
	4σ	ò-kú-dóbóónkán-á	'to get spoiled'	ò-kú-sèrèèngétá	'to roll down'
		ò-kú-kólóót-ír-á	'to purr for (s.o.)'	ò-kú-mèsùùnkán-á	'to be shiny'

This is because Lusoga does not allow LH rising tone syllables (e.g., **ò-kú-tègèér-á*). Finally, note that when the verb root begins with a vowel, the *-ku-V-* sequence becomes *-kw-VV-*, with the /u/ gliding to [w] and the root-initial vowel undergoing compensatory lengthening, such as /o-ku-ey-a/ → *ò-kw-ééy-á* 'to sweep'. As seen in the forms on the right in (4), where an HL falling tone results, the L of the bimoraic syllable counts in calculating one of the two L tone moras:

(4)	2σ	ò-kw-éèy-á	'to sweep'	ò-kw-éèt-á	'to call'
		ò-kw-íídh-á	'to come'	ò-kw-íìt-á	'to kill'
	3σ	ò-kw-óógér-á	'to speak'	ò-kw-íìnìk-á	'to dip, immerse'
		ò-kw-íígál-á	'to close'	ò-kw-íìngìr-á	'to enter'
	4σ	ò-kw-íídhúkír-á	'to remember'	ò-kw-áàsìmúl-á	'to sneeze'
		ò-kw-áásííkán-á	'to scream'	ò-kw-áàgàànán-á	'to meet, find'

Having established these patterns, we now turn to their interpretation. First, we note that the LH^n pattern of *L verb infinitives is reminiscent of Luganda, which can also realize such infinitives as all L: *ò-kú-bál-á ~ ò-kù-bàl-à* 'to count'. The normal analysis of Luganda is that these surface tones are due to initial %L and (optional) final H% boundary tones. For now, we can assume the same here.[3] Concerning the forms on the right, it is clear that the tone of the *H root is anticipated onto the infinitive prefix, which was historically *L. We thus propose a rule of H tone retraction (HTR) that shifts an H tone to the preceding mora. As a result, if the underlying representation of 'to beat' is /o-ku-kúb-a/, it will become *o-kú-kub-a* by HTR (but see sections 3.3 and 3.4 for more detail and alternatives). That the final H is due to a phrasal H% boundary tone is also justified by the fact that the L of infinitives ending H-L is realized with level rather than falling pitch before pause, in other words, *ò-kú-ty-à°* 'to fear', *ò-kú-lyà°* 'to eat' (where L° represents a level L tone).[4] The historical underlying representations of infinitives are as shown in (5):

(5)		/Ø/ root		/H/ root	
	1σ	ò-kú-gú-á	'to fall'	ò-kú-tì-à°	'to fear'
		%L H%		%L H H%	

2σ	ò-kú-bál-á	'to count'	ò-kú-bòn-á	'to see'
	%L H%		%L H H%	
3σ	ò-kú-lágír-á	'to command'	ò-kú-ghùlìr-á	'to hear'
	%L H%		%L H H%	
4σ	ò-kú-súmúlúl-á	'to untie'	ò-kú-kàlàkát-á	'to scrape'
	%L H%		%L H H%	'to kneel'
5σ	ò-kú-lágír-ágán-á	'to command e.o.'	ò-kú-ghùlìr-ágán-á	'to hear e.o.'
	%L H%		%L H H%	

As seen, I have posited a %L boundary tone that links to the augment vowel *ò-*. In the forms on the left, the final H% tone associates onto all of the preceding moras up to the initial L. In the forms on the right, the H on the initial mora of the root shifts onto the toneless infinitive prefix /-ku-/. The boundary H% links to the final vowel unless the last two syllables of the word end H-L. In this case, H% stays out, but levels the final L to the nonfalling L°: *ò-kú-ty-à°* 'to fear'.[5] Because this nonfalling L° is predictable (e.g., it obligatorily occurs at the end of a declarative, but not an imperative or interrogative sentence), it will not be transcribed except when it is under discussion.

The preceding analysis leaves two open questions. The first concerns the 2TLR: Whenever there is an H to L transition, the L is realized on two moras, unless it cannot be. There is a single L in *ò-kú-ty-à°* 'to fear' since there is only one post-H syllable, and in *ò-kú-kùb-á* 'to beat', where linking of the H% boundary tone overrides the 2LTR. In other words, it is preferable to violate the H-L-L requirement than to leave the H% unassociated. But why should there be such a double L tone requirement that produces forms such as *ò-kú-ghùlìr-á* 'to hear' and *ò-kú-kàlàkát-á* 'to scrape' instead of **ò-kú-ghùlír-á* and **ò-kú-kàlákát-á*? The answer is historical. The output tones are derived diachronically as in (6).

(6)	*stage 1*		*stage 2*		*stage 3*		*stage 4*		*stage 5*
a.	*ó-ku-bón-a	>	o-ku-bón-a	>	-oku-bón-à	>	o-kú-bòn-à	>	ò-kú-bòn-á
	H H		H		H L		H L L		%L H L H%
b.	*ó-ku-ghúlir-a	>	o-ku-ghúlir-a	>	o-ku-ghúlìr-a	>	o-kú-ghùlìr-a	>	ò-kú-ghùlìr-á
	H H		H		H L		H L L		%L H L L %H
c.	*ó-ku-kálakat-a	>	o-ku-kálakat-a	>	o-ku-kálàkat-a	>	o-kú-kàlàkat-a	>	ò-kú-kàlàkát-á
	H H		H		H L		H L L		%L H L L %H
d.	*ó-ku-lim-a	>	o-ku-lim-a	>	o-ku-lim-a	>	o-ku-lim-a	>	ò-kú-lím-á
	H								%L %H

At historical stage 1, the augment /ó-/ is *H as is the first mora of the root in (6a)–(6c). Other moras are phonologically toneless. In stage 2 the deletion of the augment *H is the first change I propose, since it characterizes most of the closely related languages as well. This is followed by a rule of L tone insertion (LTI) after the last H of a word, a process well known from Luganda (Hyman and Katamba 2010: 72). It is in stage 4 that Lusoga parts company with Luganda: H tones are retracted onto the preceding mora, in this case onto the toneless infinitive prefix **-ku-*. I have indicated an overt L tone in its place, much as Hyman and Valinande (1985) originally proposed as an "L tone trace" of /H/ in Kinande.[6] As seen, this produces the double L tone sequence that precedes the final H% boundary tone that, along with initial %L, is assigned in stage 5 to all remaining toneless moras, the H% counting from the end of the word.

One of the arguments for early lowering (here, deletion) of the augment H is that this is a very common change in the closest Bantu languages in the interlacustrine area (but not in Lugwere or Lulamogi [Hyman 2014]). The derivations in (6) confirm this decision and provide a second reason that augment *H>Ø had to be the first change. Had augment lowering been recognized as part of the *H>L change occurring in stage 4, that is, at the stage of general HTR, denecessitating stage 2, we would have expected the derivation of toneless root infinitives such as 'to cultivate' to begin with two L tones:

(7)	*stage 1*		*stage 3*		*stage 4*		*stage 5*
	*ó-ku-lim-a	>	ó-kù-lim-a	>	ò-kù-lim-a	>	*ò-kù-lím-á
	H		H L		L L		L L H%

Instead, as seen in (6d) and previous examples, such infinitives (and other underlyingly toneless words in the language) begin with a single L (cf. *ò-mú-límí* 'farmer').[7] There is in fact clear synchronic evidence that the *H augment still has an underlying /H/, which surfaces whenever there is a preceding toneless proclitic, such as /na/ 'with, and':

(8)								
	a.	/na=ó-ku-lim-a/	>	na=ó-kù-lim-a	>	ná=ò-kù-lim-a	>	n' óò-kù-lím-á
		H		H L		H L L		HL L H%
	b.	/na=ó-ku-bón-a/	>	na=ó-ku-bón-à	>	ná=ò-kú-bòn-à	>	n' óó-kú-bòn-á
		H H		H H L		H L H L L		HH H L H%

In (8a) the /H/ of the augment is preserved after *na*=onto which it is anticipated. With vowel coalescence and final H% assignment, the output is *n'óò-kù-lím-á* 'and to cultivate'. The augment /H/ is also preserved in

(8b), where the root *-bón-* 'see' is also underlyingly /H/. After HTR, vowel coalescence, and H% assignment, we should but do not obtain an initial falling tone (**n'óò-kú-bòn-á*). Instead, the expected L on *n'óò-* is lost by a rule of H tone plateauing (HTP) by which an H-L^n-H sequence becomes all H in the word-level phonology (i.e., preceding assignment of H%). We thus obtain *n'óó-kú-bòn-á* 'and to see'. As in Luganda, HTP is responsible for the generalization that there cannot be an H-L^n-H sequence in a Lusoga word.[8] The corresponding forms without an augment confirm that /na/ does not have an H tone of its own: *nà=kú-bòn-á, nà=kù-lím-á*. We can thus firmly establish that the augment morpheme preserves evidence of its original *H in synchronic Lusoga.[9] What is important is that unlike the augment, other initial Ls from *H are able to assign an H to the final mora of a preceding word.[10] In other words, when initial, the augment behaves as if it were from *L, hence synchronically toneless.

To conclude this subsection we consider the realization of affirmative infinitives with an object marker (OM). Since all OMs have the same tone in Lusoga, it will suffice to illustrate the tone patterns with the same OM throughout, here *-tu-* 'us'. As can be seen in (9), forms containing either a *L or *H root show the same tones: the OM is L, as is the first mora of verb stems of two or more syllables. (One syllable stems take the H% boundary tone.) In other words, the OM+first syllable of the verb stem has the same tonal patterns as the *H verb forms without an OM—although realized one syllable to the left: whereas the forms in (1b) begin with two stem L tones, those in (9) have an L OM followed by one L stem mora.

(9)		*L root		*H root	
	1σ	ò-kú-tù-mwá	'to shave us'	ò-kú-tù-ty-á	'to fear us'
	2σ	ò-kú-tù-bàl-á	'to count us'	ò-kú-tù-bòn-á	'to see us'
	3σ	ò-kú-tù-làgír-á	'to command us'	ò-kú-tù-ghùlír-á	'to hear us'
	4σ	ò-kú-tù-sùmúlúl-á	'to untie us'	ò-kú-tù-kàlákát-á	'to scrape us'
	5σ	ò-kú-tù-sùmúlúl-ír-á	'to untie for us'	ò-kú-tù-kàlákát-ír-á	'to scrape for us'

To account for the H on the prefix *-ku-*, the OM has to have been *H in the infinitive. In the following derivations I start with stage 2, that is, where the augment *H has already been deleted.

(10)	a.	o-ku-tú-lagir-a >		> o-ku-tú-làgir-a >	ò-kú-tù-làgír-á
		H		H L	%L H L L H%
	b.	o-ku-tú-ghúlir-a >	o-ku-tú-ghùlir-a >	>	ò-kú-tù-ghùlír-á
		H H	H L		%L H L L H%

In the case of the *L root form in (10a), the derivation is straightforward: LTI inserts an L after the H of the OM *-tú-* 'us', whose H is then anticipated onto the infinitive prefix *-ku-*, leaving an L tone trace. This produces a double L sequence, allowing the H% boundary tone to link to the final two toneless moras of the word. The derivation in (10b) is similar, the main difference being in the change of a contiguous sequence of H tones to H+L. Known as Meeussen's rule (MR) (Goldsmith 1984a), a change of H-H to H-L attributable to the OCP is quite common in Eastern Bantu languages. As in Luganda, MR must precede LTI, or else the wrong output with too many Ls will obtain, as in (11).

(11)	o-ku-tú-ghúlir-a	>	ò-ku-tú-ghúlìr-a	>	ò-kú-tù-ghùlìr-a	> *ò-kú-tù-ghùlìr-á
	L H H		L H HL		L H L LL	L H L LLH%

Since MR produces H-L sequences, it bleeds LTI, which will apply only after the last H of a word that is not followed by L.

However, when we turn to consider forms with two (ultimately three) OMs, a problem arises:

(12)	a.	o-ku-cí-tú-bal-ir-a	>	ò-kú-cì-tù-bàl-ír-á	'to count it for us'
		H H		%L H L L L H%	
	b.	o-ku-cí-tú-kúb-ir-a	>	ò-kú-cì-tù-kùb-ír-á	'to beat it for us'
		H H H		%L H L L L H%	
	c.	o-ku-cí-mú-tú-ghá-er-a	>	ò-kú-cì-mù-tù-ghè-èr-á	'to give it to him for us'
		H H H H		%L H L L L L H%	

The forms with a *H verb root in (12b) and (12c) work by the rules already discussed: In each case MR applies to all but the first of a sequence of H tones. Thus, H-H-H becomes H-L-L in (12b) and H-H-H-H becomes H-L-L-L in (12c). Since MR has created these Ls, LTI does not apply. The problem, however, is why the toneless verb root /-bal-/ 'count' has an L tone in (12a). According to what we have seen, the application of MR that changes *-cí-tú-* to *-cí-tù-* should have bled LTI. This unexpected L is found only on the root-initial mora. One ad hoc move would be to assume an early copying of the H of an OM onto the first mora of a *L verb root, thereby merging it with *H roots. Both would then correctly undergo MR. Another alternative is to recognize an internal structure to the infinitive (and perhaps other verb forms). The OM+stem constituent is known in Bantu as the macro-stem and excludes any earlier prefixes, including other OMs. In order to avoid the incorrect output seen in (11), LTI must not be operative within the stem level phonology, but rather it comes into play at the macro-stem and word levels. As seen in (13), a cyclic analysis produces the correct outputs in (12a) and (12b):

(13)	a.	*cycle 1:*		[tu-	[bal-ir-a]]	*cycle 1:*		[tu-	[kub-ir-a]]
		(LTI)		H	Ø	(MR)		H	H
					↓				↓
					L				L
	b.	*cycle 2:*	[ci-	[tu-	bal-ir-a]]	*cycle 2:*	[ci-	[tu-	kub-ir-a]]
		(MR)	H	H	L	(MR)	H	H	L
				↓				↓	
				L				L	

As indicated, both LTI and MR apply in the first cycle, but MR must apply first (or, again, we will derive the incorrect output in [11]). Whether this solution turns out to be correct or not, it is important to note that this happens only in the affirmative infinitive. In other parts of the paradigm, a single, prestem OM is toneless. Before moving on to propose a restructured analysis of the Lusoga tonal system, I present a table of the personal OMs to show that they all do show the same tones independent of whether their shape is CV-, N-, or V-:[11]

(14)	*L root	*H root	
1sg	ò-kúù-n-dàgír-á	ò-kúù-m-pùlír-á	'to command/hear me'
2sg	ò-kú-kù-làgír-á	ò-kú-kù-ghùlír-à	'to command/hear you sg.'
3sg	ò-kú-mù-làgír-á	ò-kú-mù-ghùlír-á	'to command/hear him/her'
1pl	ò-kú-tù-làgír-á	ò-kú-tù-ghùlír-á	'to command/hear us'
2pl	ò-kú-bà-làgír-á	ò-kú-bà-ghùlír-á	'to command/hear you pl.'
3pl	ò-kú-bà-làgír-á	ò-kú-bà-ghùlír-á	'to command/hear them'
refl	ò-kw-éè-làgír-á	ò-kw-éè-ghùlír-á	'to command/hear oneself/ oneselves'

With this established we can now evaluate the previous analysis and, as I shall now suggest, adopt another.

3.3. A Synchronic Reanalysis

In the preceding section we started with an underlying contrast between /H/ and Ø and introduced L tones in the course of the derivation. These were seen to originate from four distinct sources (TBU=tone-bearing unit):

(15)	a.	Meeussen's rule (MR):	H-H → H-L
	b.	L tone insertion (LTI):	insert a following L if the last tone of a word is H
	c.	H tone retraction (HTR):	leave a L tone on a TBU whose H has been retracted onto the preceding TBU
	d.	%L boundary tone:	assign an initial %L boundary tone

In contrast, the rules involving the introduction of more H tones were HTP and the assignment of the final H% boundary tone that changes final L-L to L-H and links to a word-final sequence of toneless moras. The question is whether we should not have considered starting with a different underlying tonal contrast. In (16) I enumerate several of the possible underlying analyses of a two-height tone system, illustrated on the last three syllables of *kù-bál-á* '(it is) to count' and *kú-bòn-á* '(it is) to see', where the absence of the augment indicates an abstract zero copula:[12]

(16)	a.	/H/ vs. Ø	:	/ku-bal-a/	/ku-bón-a/
	b.	/H/ vs. /L/	:	/kù-bàl-à/	/kù-bón-à/
	c.	/L/ vs. Ø	:	/ku-bal-a/	/ku-bòn-a/
	d.	/H/ vs. /L/	:	/kú-bál-á/	/kú-bòn-á/

Example (16a) is the privative analysis considered in section 3.2. Example (16b) differs only in proposing non-H moras are /L/ instead of toneless. Both (16a) and (16b) correspond to the historical tones, the choice being whether one thinks Proto-Bantu had a privative system (Stevick 1969) or an equipollent one (Greenberg 1948).[13] In contrast, the two analyses in (16c) and (16d) represent restructurings of the inherited system: (16c) assumes a privative contrast with /L/ as the marked tone, while (16d) keeps an equipollent contrast, but with the historical tones inverted. Either analysis would greatly affect the way that the rules in (15) are expressed—something to which I will return when I further consider (and justify) a /L/ versus Ø analysis in (23) below.

First, however, let us note that the problem with the more historically direct analyses in (16a) and (16b) is that an L tone trace has to be mysteriously left in the place of an /H/ tone that is anticipated onto the preceding TBU. What might be advantageous is an analysis that represents the marked tone as having both an H and L component. There are multiple ways to do this in autosegmental phonology. As seen in (17), this can be done in one of three ways.

(17) a. μ b. μ c. μ

```
(17)  a.  μ        b.  μ        c.   μ
          /\           |             |
          H L          H L         H L
```

Instead of /H/, (17a) treats the marked tone as an /HL/ contour. This approach was adopted for Luganda by Hyman and Katamba (1993) and more recently by Jones (2015) for Luganda, Kinande, and Shi. However, it is not necessary to assume that both tones are underlyingly linked. In the representation in (17b), a linked H is followed by an unlinked L, while in (17c) a linked L is preceded by an unlinked H. To get the tonal retraction of Proto-Bantu *H onto the preceding mora in Lusoga, the following would be needed, assuming that the preceding mora is toneless:

(18) a. If (17a) is adopted, the H of the linked HL would delink from its sponsoring mora and relink to the preceding mora.
b. If (17b) is adopted, the unlinked L would link to the mora and delink the H from its sponsoring mora, which would then relink to the preceding mora.
c. If (17c) is adopted, the unlinked H would link to the preceding mora.

Of the three possibilities, (18c) appears to be the simplest analysis.[14] It is therefore appropriate to consider how the rules that would be required compare to those in the /H, Ø/ and /L, Ø/ analyses, as in (19).

(19) a.	augment lowering:	H→Ø at the left edge of a clitic group
b.	Meeussen's rule (MR):	unlinked H→Ø between two linked Ls (which then "fuse" to avoid an OCP violation)
c.	L tone insertion (LTI):	if the last /L/ of a word is preceded by Ø, spread it onto the next mora
d.	H tone retraction (HTR):	link an unlinked H to the preceding mora
e.	%L boundary tone:	assign an initial %L boundary tone

Although I continue to express each process as a rule, recall that the input-output relations could be derived by ranking of appropriate constraints. In (19a) I have expressed augment lowering as the deletion of its unlinked H. The reason for this is that unlike other would-be initial /^{H}L/ prefixes, such as most subject prefixes, the unlinked H (indicated by ^{H}) is never anticipated onto a preceding word, such as *ò-kú-bòn-à ò-mú-límí* 'to see a farmer', where the verb 'to see' ends L-L (cf. note 10). Thus, the initial unlinked H of the augment would have to be deleted to avoid being assigned to the FV -á of the infinitive. Since H% works differently (see [22a]), as well as word-initial subject markers (see note 10), the most direct analysis, which I shall adopt, is to recognize two tonal allomorphs of the augment morpheme. In the /ᴴL/ analysis, this augment would be toneless (Ø) if word-initial, and /ᴴL/ if preceded by a proclitic. (In the /L/ versus Ø analysis ultimately to be adopted, this allomorph of the augment would be /L/.)[15]

To help us decide whether the marked tone should be /ᴴL/ or /L/, consider what happens if the H of /ᴴL/ attempts to be anticipated onto a mora that itself has an L, that is, in the MR context. As schematized in (20), MR would have to be expressed as the deletion of any unlinked H between linked Ls:

(20) AUG-INF-it-him-us-give-APPL-FV

o- ku- ci- mu- tu- gha- er- a → ò-kú-cì-mù-tù-ghè-èr-á 'to give it to him for us'

%L H L H L H L H L H% → L H L H%

↓ ↓ ↓

Ø Ø Ø

As a result of MR, only the unlinked H of the first OM /-´cì-/ 'it' (class 7) is able to link to the preceding mora, here the toneless infinitive prefix /-ku-/. Also shown in (20) is the spreading of the last L on to the toneless mora of the applicative suffix *-er-*, since Lusoga does not allow LH rising tones. As a result the phrase-final H% boundary tone can only link to the single mora of the last syllable. In the output to the right I show the sequence of Ls fusing as a branching structure so as not to violate the OCP. Accordingly, LTI becomes a rule of L tone spreading (LTS), as in (21).

(21) o- ku- kalakat - a → ò-kú-kàlàkát-á 'to scrape'

H L H L H%

↓

Ø

As shown, the /L/ of /-´kàlakat-/ 'scrape' spreads onto the second mora. This can be interpreted as a response to the 2LTR. The H% boundary tone links to the last two moras that follow. As was seen in (1), shorter verb stems will not be able to exhibit both LTS and linking of H%:

```
(22)  a.   o- ku- bon- a      →   o- ku- bon- a        ò-kú-bòn-á   'to see'
           |    \   |/             |   |    |   ⁞
         H L    H  L               L   H    L   H%
         ↓
         Ø

      b.   o- ku- ti- a       →   ò-kú-ty-à°     'to fear'
           |    \  |/
         H L   H  L  H%
         ↓
         Ø
```

In (22a), the H% boundary tone links to the final vowel /-a/. Since LTI is a word-level rule, the L tone of /-´bòn-/ 'see' first spreads onto the FV in (23a), after which phrase-level H% is assigned to the FV, thereby delinking the L. In (23b), H% cannot link or a LH rising tone would result. Instead, the L of the root /-´tì-/ 'fear' spreads onto the final vowel. The result is a final level L° tone that is prevented from falling to the lowest pitch by the unlinked H% boundary tone.

In considering different approaches, I have been assuming that the analysis that most directly accounts for the facts is the one to be preferred, in other words, the analysis that requires the fewest changes between underlying and output tones. The Goldsmith-type /^{H}L/ versus Ø analysis represents an improvement over the historical /H, Ø/ analysis in section 3.2, which required HTR to both shift the H onto the preceding TBU, as well as introduce an L trace on the TBU of the /H/. In the /^{H}L/ analysis, the L is already linked to the correct output TBU, and the reason for anticipation is encoded in the unlinked property of the /^{H}/. However, MR requires multiple deletions of the /H/, as was seen in (20). Importantly, this can be avoided if we start instead with underlying /L/. If /L, Ø/ were postulated, we would need to reinterpret the earlier rules as follows:

(23)	a.	augment lowering:	the augment would be underlyingly /L/ after a proclitic, elsewhere Ø
	b.	Meeussen's rule (MR):	a sequence of contiguous /L/s fuses as one multilinked L (preceded by an H tone)
	c.	L tone spreading (LTS):	if the last /L/ of a word is preceded by Ø, spread it onto the next mora
	d.	H tone anticipation (HTR):	insert an H tone on a toneless TBU that precedes an L tone mora (or contiguous L moras)
	e.	%L boundary tone:	assign an initial %L boundary tone

As indicated in (23a), the augment would have an /L/ tone allomorph after a proclitic, otherwise the augment would be toneless. Meeussen's rule (23b) now becomes a simple process of L tone fusion to avoid an OCP violation. In (23c), the old LTI rule has been reinterpreted as LTS rule. Example (23d) inserts an H to the TBU that precedes an L or sequence of L tone moras. The result is surprisingly efficient—in fact, I would argue it is superior both to the /H, Ø/ and /^{H}L, Ø/ analyses.

The one minor complication of the /L/ versus Ø approach is the need of a rule of H tone insertion (HTI), which inserts an H before an L (or the first L of a sequence of L tone moras). This is not unprecedented, as tone systems often place requirements on what can precede or follow a specific tone.[16] I thus adopt the /L/ versus Ø analysis in the remainder of this study: In underlying representations toneless moras will continue to be unmarked, for example, /o-ku-bal-a/ 'to count', while /L/ moras will be indicated with a grave accent, such as /o-ku-bòn-a/ 'to see'. An unmarked TBU that immediately precedes the vowel marked with the grave accent is pronounced H by a process of HTI, for example, *o-kú-bòn-a*. As seen in these underlying representations, I will continue to assume that the augment vowel is underlyingly toneless when occurring initially, but /L/ when preceded by a proclitic. With these assumptions, the derivation in (21) can now be greatly simplified, as in (24):

```
(24)   o- ku- ci- mu- tu- gha- er- a    →  ò-kú-cì-mù-tù-ghè-èr-á    'to give it to him for us'
       ⋮   \  |   |   |    |/  ⋮          |  |     \|//          |
      %L   H L   L   L    L    H%         L  H       L           H%
```

As seen, the only rules needed now are the LTS rule to satisfy the 2LTR and the H inserted before the sequence of Ls, which can again be assumed to fuse into a single L autosegment, as to the right of the arrow in (24). In comparison with (21) there is considerable economy in not assuming that every input /L/ has an H before it. While this may seem to be at odds with Goldsmith's melodic approach to Bantu, the autosegmental framework is crucial in this analysis, as will also be seen in the following section.

3.4. A Closer Look at H Tone Plateauing

Here I will further develop HTP to show that Goldsmith's (1976a, 1976b) original idea, that a free (in this case, inserted) H tone will link to as many TBUs as are available, works well in Lusoga. The evidence will come from noun stem reduplication. To appreciate this process, it is necessary, first, to say a few words about the structure of nouns.

As was seen in the case of the infinitive, which is in fact a noun class 15 nominal, the vast majority of Lusoga nouns take an augment vowel and noun class prefix of the shape CV-, V-, or N-. The basic noun classes are exemplified in (25).

(25)	class 1:	ò-mú-límí	'farmer'	class 2:	à-bá-límí	'farmers'
	class 3:	ò-mú-líró	'fire'	class 4:	è-mí-líró	'fires'
	class 5:	è-ì-búgá	'gourd'	class 6:	à-má-búgá	'gourds'
	class 7:	è-cí-tábó	'book'	class 8:	è-bí-tábó	'books'
	class 9:	è-n-dhóvú	'elephant'	class 10:	è-n-dhóvú	'elephants'
	class 11:	ò-lú-súsú	'skin'	class 10:	è-n-súsú	'skins'
	class 12:	à-ká-tíkó	'mushroom'	class 14:	ò-bú-tíkó	'mushrooms'

As seen, the noun classes in (25) form the singular-plural pairs 1/2, 3/4, 5/6, 7/8, 9/10, 11/10, and 12/14.[17] Like the *L root infinitives in (1), all of the preceding nouns are underlyingly toneless (other than the potential for the augment to be /L/ if preceded by a proclitic). When their stems reduplicate, they remain toneless, surfacing with the %L and H% boundary tones:

(26)	a.	ò-mú-límí-límí	'a lousy ol' farmer, not a real farmer'
	b.	è-cí-tábó-tábó	'a lousy ol' book, not a real book'
	c.	à-bú-tíkó-tíkó	'lousy ol' mushrooms, not real mushrooms'

As the glosses indicate, noun stem reduplication is used to express a contemptuous view of the object, which is seen as inadequate, an inferior example of what it should be. Thus, *ò-mú-límí-límí* can be used to refer to someone who farms badly, or who thinks he is a farmer, but is not.

While no tonal issues arise when the nouns are toneless, a quite different story obtains when there is an H to L pitch drop in the word. Such nouns may have one or more Hs and one or more Ls. In addition, the final syllable of a noun can be lexically L or Ø, with final H(s) attributed to the boundary H%, as before. Representative tone patterns are shown in (27) for noun stems of different lengths:

(27)	σ	/L/	:	/o-mu-tì/	→	ò-mú-tì	'tree'
	σ–σ	/L-Ø/	:	/o-mu-kàzi/	→	ò-mú-kàzí	'woman'
		/Ø-L/	:	/e-ki-kopò/	→	è-cí-kópò	'cup'

σ:–σ	/LØ-Ø/	:	/e-ki-wùuka/	→	è-cí-wùùká	'insect'
	/ØL-Ø/	:	/a-ka-saàle/	→	à-ká-sáàlé	'arrow'
	/ØØ-L/	:	/e-ki-deedè/	→	è-cí-déédè	'grasshopper'
σ–σ–σ	/L-Ø-Ø/	:	/o-bu-thùpuzi/	→	ò-bú-thùpùzí	'corruption'
	/Ø-L-Ø/	:	/o-mu-pakàsi/	→	ò-mú-pákàsí	'porter'
	/Ø-Ø-L/	:	/o-mu-vubukà/	→	ò-mú-vúbúkà	'adolescent'

As seen, each pattern has one underlying /L/, preceded by all H tones except the augment, which receives the %L boundary tone. Where possible, the /L/ undergoes LTS onto a following syllable. Finally, the H% boundary tone links to the final syllable unless it ends /L/.

While there are other less common tone patterns, the examples in (27) will serve as input to the reduplication process, exemplified in (28). Again, the meaning is one of disparagement: 'a lousy ol' tree', 'a not very good cup', etc.

(28)	σ	/L/	:	/o-mu-tì/	→	ò-mú-tíí-tì
	σ–σ	/L-Ø/	:	/o-mu-kàzi/	→	ò-mú-kází-kàzí
		/Ø-L/	:	/e-ki-kopò/	→	è-cí-kópó-kópò
	σ:–σ	/LØ-Ø/	:	/e-ki-wùuka/	→	è-cí-wúúká-wùùká
		/ØL-Ø/	:	/a-ka-saàle/	→	à-ká-sáálé-sáàlé
		/ØØ-L/	:	/e-ki-deedè/	→	è-cí-déédé-déédè
	σ–σ–σ	/L-Ø-Ø/	:	/o-bu-thùpuzi/	→	ò-bú-thúpúzí-thùpùzí
		/Ø-L-Ø/	:	/o-mu-pakàsi/	→	ò-mú-pákásí-pákàsí
		/Ø-Ø-L/	:	/o-mu-vubukà/	→	ò-mú-vúbúká-vúbúkà

The observed output tones show that the second stem has the same tones as in the nonreduplicated noun in (27), while the preceding first stem is all H. There are at least three analyses that can account for these facts.

1. We might propose that the first stem is the reduplicant, which does not copy the tones of the base. If the /L/ tone is not copied, then HTI will link the inserted H to the mora that precedes the L(s) and then spread onto all preceding TBUs except the augment. This approach departs, however, from what we know about Bantu noun reduplication in two ways (cf. Mutaka and Hyman 1990: 103 for Kinande): First, we expect the second stem to be the reduplicant. Second, unlike verb stem reduplication, we expect the tones to be copied. It is possible that Lusoga has restructured the inherited system, but since this defection is surprising, let us consider the other two options.

2. We might copy the tone and then fix it up to produce the outputs observed in (28). An example of how this might work is shown in (29).

(29) a. reduplicated input: /o-mu-pakàsi-pakàsi/ 'a lousy ol' porter'
L L

b. H tone insertion: o-mu-pakasi-pakasi
H L H L

c. H tone plateauing: o-mu-pakasi-pakasi
H L

d. Output with %L . . . H% ò-mú-pákásí-pákàsí

As seen, the /L/ is copied in (29a). In (29b), HTI inserts an H before each of the Ls and then spreads to available toneless moras. This is followed by HTP in (29c), which deletes the L occurring between the two Hs, which then fuse into a single multilinked tone. In (29d), %L links to the augment and H% to the last syllable of the noun.

3. While (29) undoubtedly represents the correct historical derivation, the facts can be much more simply accounted for in a third analysis. In (29c), the deletion of the L and the fusion of the Hs by HTP are assumed to be a response to the prohibition against two H to L pitch drops within a word, which is well known from Luganda (McCawley 1970) and already recognized for Lusoga (van der Wal 2004:29). However, the Lusoga facts allow us to dispense with the insertion of two separate H autosegments in (29b). We maintain that the /L/ is copied, as in (29), but the first L undergoes a rule of L deletion:

(30) L tone deletion (LTD) $L \rightarrow \emptyset$ / ___ L

An L tone is deleted when followed by another L tone within the word. Since the rule is stated without reference to TBUs, this process will take place "at a distance," as seen now in (31).

(31) a. reduplicated input: /o-mu-pakàsi-pakàsi/ 'a lousy ol' porter'
L L

b. L tone deletion: o-mu-pakasi-pakasi
L

c. H tone insertion: o-mu-pakasi-pakasi
H L

d. Output with %L . . . H% ò-mú-pákásí-pákàsí

Because the L of the first stem is always deleted, the result will always be as in (31): the first stem will be all H, while the second maintains the same output tones as it would have had when not reduplicated.

It is clear that we can now reject the analysis in (29). However, it needs to be shown why (31) should be preferred over the first proposal, which was to not copy the L tone in the first place. The evidence comes from the behavior of certain enclitics such as /-ò/ 'your sg.' and /-è/ 'his/her', which agree with the preceding noun in noun class. The following examples show how /-è/ affects the nouns in (27).

(32)	σ	/L/	:	/o-mu-tì/	→	ò-mú-tíí=gwè
	σ–σ	/L-Ø/	:	/o-mu-kàzi/	→	ò-mú-kází=wè
		/Ø-L/	:	/e-ki-kopò/	→	è-cí-kópó=cè
	σ:–σ	/LØ-Ø/	:	/e-ki-wùuka/	→	è-cí-wúúká=cè
		/ØL-Ø/	:	/a-ka-saàle/	→	à-ká-sáálé=kè
		/ØØ-L/	:	/e-ki-deedè/	→	è-cí-déédé=cè
	σ–σ–σ	/L-Ø-Ø/	:	/o-bu-thùpuzi/	→	ò-bú-thúpúzí=bwè
		/Ø-L-Ø/	:	/o-mu-pakàsi/	→	ò-mú-pákásí=wè
		/Ø-Ø-L/	:	/o-mu-vubukà/	→	ò-mú-vúbúká=wè

As seen, the different tone patterns merge as all H before 'his/her' (as well as /-ò/ 'your sg.').[18] This is exactly parallel to the all H first stem in (31), with the L of the noun stem being deleted before the /L/ enclitic, as in (33).

(33) a. noun+enclitic input: /o-mu-pakàsi=o-e/ 'his/her porter'
                                      | |
                                      L   L

b. L tone deletion: o-mu-pakasi=we
                                         |
                                         L

c. H tone insertion: o-mu-pakasi=wè
                                         |
                                   H   L

d. Output with %L ò-mú-pákásí-pákàsí

In this case, however, there is no question about starting without a tone, since the noun stems must be entered into the lexicon with different tonal representations. Instead, their /L/ tone is deleted before these enclitics—as, I suggest, also occurs on the first stem of the reduplicated noun.[19] I will now consider the significance of the Lusoga facts in the final section.

3.5. Conclusion

In the preceding sections we have considered different analyses of the basic tonal properties of Lusoga within the context of autosegmental phonology. While I did not opt for the HL melodic approach, the result is still one that the autosegmental approach is best equipped to handle. As was seen, the OCP prohibits successive L tones on the tonal tier, functioning as a conspiracy with different repairs: If the Ls are linked to successive TBUs, they fuse into a single, multilinked L, as in (29c). If there are intervening toneless TBUs, the rule of LTD deletes the first L. That the two L tones can "see" each other at a distance is something explicitly observed in autosegmental representations such as (31a) and (33a), where the two Ls are adjacent on the tonal tier. The result is not inconsequential, as there has been a definite trend of disinterest in, if not active opposition to abstract representations in phonology (cf. the discussion in Hyman 2018). The representational questions raised by the above-mentioned Lusoga facts are thus interesting not only in what they have to contribute to tonal typology, but also from the point view of determining how different phonological representations can differ from their surface outputs. I have suggested that the Lusoga tone system contrasts /L/ versus Ø and that the Hs that are observed on the surface derive either from a rule of HTI or from the final H% boundary tone. The tonal facts presented have been intentionally chosen to make this point, keeping things relatively simple. However, the rest of the tone system, for example, the tonal morphology of the verb and tonal interactions at the phrase level, is consistent with this analysis, with only a few potential tweaks, such as sensitivity to certain grammatical categories. In work in progress, I am now considering the possibility that Lusoga has a true "inverted" tone system with marked, underlying /L/ and default H. Rather than a rule of HTI, the Hs that are observed before an L or sequence of L TBUs might simply be there by a late default spelling rule. This would also affect the H% final boundary tone. In all of the analyses considered herein it was assumed that H% is generally present at the end of a phrase except in questions and imperatives (cf. note 4). If H is a default, then imperatives would require a final L%, and the final Hs in declaratives and citation forms would be default. So far, this reinterpretation requires its own tweaks and, in any case, takes us far beyond the scope of the goal of the present chapter, which I hope has been established: John Goldsmith's basic autosegmental insights, that tones and TBUs are semiautonomous and hence can "see" each other at a distance, have been confirmed in the Lusoga tone system.

Notes

1. The term *Lusoga* refers to several different Bantu speech varieties spoken in Busoga subregion including sometimes Lulamogi, which should instead be recognized as dialectal with Lugwere JE17 (Hyman 2014; Hyman and Merrill 2016). The current study focuses on Lutenga, the standard Lusoga dialect, which has been the subject of considerable recent, especially lexicographic work (Gulere 2009; Nabirye 2009; Nzogi and Diprose 2012). Although I have relied on these resources for confirmation, the data presented in this study are based on the speech of Fr. Fred Jenga, a native of Wairaka (Jinga District).
2. In citing examples, I write *ci* and *ji* (pronounced with alveopalatal affricates) to reflect the pronunciation of my language consultant, rather than *ki* and *gi*, as in standard Lusoga orthography. When not preceded by *m*, *b* stands for [β] and *gh* for voiced velar [ɣ] varying with [ɰ] and sometimes [w], while *th, dh, nh* are dental consonants that contrast with alveolar *t, d, n*.
3. In contexts where the augment vowel is absent (e.g., following a negative verb), the infinitive prefix *ku-* takes the %L tone, for example, *kù-gw-á* 'to fall', *kù-bál-á* 'to count', *kù-lágír-á* 'to command'. The *H tone forms do not realize the %L since *kú-* carries an H tone (anticipated from the verb root): *kú-ty-à* 'to fear', *kú-bòn-á* 'to see', *kú-ghùlìr-á* 'to hear'.
4. Although not further discussed here, the final H% boundary tone is not present in yes-no questions or imperatives. Thus, compare: *è-cí-sàghó* 'bag', *è-cí-kópò*° 'cup' (with H%) versus *gùl-à è-cí-sàghò* 'buy the bag!', *gùl-à è-cí-kópò* 'buy the cup!' (both without H%, the latter falling to L rather than L°). This extends also to hearer-directed epithets, such as *ìwè mú-sìrù* 'you idiot!' (cf. *ò-mú-sìrú* 'stupid person').
5. While this might first appear to be an OCP effect prohibiting *H-H, it is more likely the result of a constraint against a phrase-final H-ꜜH sequence, which may only occur phrase-medially. (ꜜH is a downstepped H.)
6. Stage 4 likely represents a telescoping involving an intermediate HL falling tone stage H-HL-L, as proposed for Ruwund (Nash 1992–1994), a language that subsequently inverted the original Bantu tones to /L/ versus Ø.
7. Synchronically, one could still formulate the double L constraint to be in effect only when there is a preceding H in the output, as when the augment *H is saved by a preceding enclitic (see [8a]).

8. HTP must apply before the assignment of the phrasal H% boundary tone or we would obtain **n'óó-kú-bón-á* instead of the correct *n'óó-kù-bòn-á*. Since HTP is a word-level rule and H% is not assigned until the phrasal phonology, this is not a problem.
9. This H is also presumably responsible for the allomorph *ní*=‘with, and’, which occurs in contexts where an augment is required, but cannot be spelled out by an initial vowel, for example, *y-á-bì-tà mù=cì-tábó ní=mú=cí-kópò* ‘he put them (class 8 *-bi-*) in the book and in the cup’. After a negative verb, where nominals do not take an augment, *na*=occurs instead: *tì-y-á-bì-tà mù=cì-tábó nà=mù=cí-kópò* ‘he didn’t put them in the book and in the cup’.
10. Thus compare *ò-kú-bòn-à à-bá-kàlí* ‘to see women’, where the augment *à-* of ‘women’ fails to raise the final L of ‘to see’ versus à-bá-kàlí bà-sèk-á ‘the women laugh’, where the *H of the subject marker **bá-* shifts its H onto the final syllable of ‘women’.
11. As seen in the examples, the class 2 OM *-ba-* ‘them’ is used also with the meaning ‘you plural’.
12. Compare *mù-límí* ‘s/he’s a farmer’ and *mú-kàzí* ‘she’s a woman’. I leave out consideration a system of /H/ versus /L/ versus Ø with a ternary contrast.
13. Since both /H, L/ and /H, Ø/ Bantu languages are attested today, the question is whether the original system treated the tones as relatively symmetric, both activated in the phonology, or whether the non-H tone was inactive, with L pitch being a default. Discussion of this would take us quite far afield from the intention of this chapter.
14. All three analyses would require an L spreading rule to produce a sequence of two L tones, so this does not distinguish between them. The solution in (17c) resembles the one proposed by Goldsmith (1984b) for Tonga, although without the use of asterisk notation. All of these alternatives can also be tested against other Bantu systems with historical H tone anticipation, for example, Kinande (Mutaka 1994, Jones 2015), Tembo (Kaji 1996), and Totela (Crane 2014).
15. The historical process was undoubtedly the deletion of *H directly, as many languages do not tolerate an H tone vowel at the left edge. When phrase-initial, the Ø allomorph acquires an L tone that can be attributed to the initial %L boundary tone, as shown in (20).
16. Interestingly, the requirement that an L be preceded by an H is identical to the constraint I proposed for Tianjin dialect of Mandarin (Hyman 2007: 17–18). In both languages, an L must be approached from an H pitch level. What this means in Lusoga is that a default L cannot be inserted before an L. The only input /L/ or sequence of /L/s in Lusoga that will not be preceded by an H is the initial %L, which has no TBU preceding it.
17. In addition to (25), there are several derived noun classes used to create diminutives, augmentatives, and locatives. We will not be concerned with these here.
18. The same all H pattern is found on toneless nouns as well: *ò-mú-límí=wè* ‘his/her farmer’, *è-cí-tábó=cè* ‘his/her book’, etc.

19. Having two instances of HTI, one before the /L/ of the noun, one before /-è/ or /-ò/, similar to (29), again seems unnecessarily complex. An allomorphy approach, as advocated by Archangeli and Pulleyblank (2015), seems equivalent, but would require every noun stem to list a second toneless allomorph—in fact, every morpheme, since derived noun stems are polymorphemic. Since LTD is general and predictable, I will assume that the rule of LTD in (30) is the more motivated approach.

References

Archangeli, Diana, and Douglas Pulleyblank. 2015. Tonal allomorphy in Kinande. In *Capturing Phonological Shades*, ed. Lian Hee Wee and Yuchau Hsiao, 76–100. Newcastle upon Tyne: Cambridge Scholars Publishing.

Clements, G. Nick. 2001. Representational economy in constraint-based phonology. In *Distinctive Feature Theory*, ed. T. Alan Hall, 71–146. Berlin: Mouton de Gruyter.

Clements, G. Nick, and John Goldsmith, eds. 1984. *Autosegmental Studies in Bantu Tone*. Dordrecht: Foris Publications.

Crane, Thera. 2014. Melodic tone in Totela TAM. *Africana Linguistica* 20:63–80.

Goldsmith, John. 1976a. Autosegmental phonology. PhD dissertation, Massachusetts Institute of Technology. Bloomington: Indiana University Linguistics Club. http://people.cs.uchicago.edu/~jagoldsm/Papers/dissertation.pdf. Published by Garland Press, New York [1979].

———. 1976b. An overview of autosegmental phonology. *Linguistic Analysis* 2:23–68.

———. 1984a. Meeussen's rule. In *Language Sound Structure*, ed. Mark Aronoff and Richard T. Oehrle, 245–259. Cambridge, MA: MIT Press.

———. 1984b. Tone and accent in Tonga. In *Autosegmental Studies in Bantu Tone*, ed. G. Nick Clements and John Goldsmith, 19–51. Dordrecht: Foris Publications.

———. 1985. On tone in Sukuma. In *African Linguistics: Essays in Memory of M.W.K. Semikenke*, ed. Didier L. Goyvaerts, 167–187. Amsterdam: Benjamins.

———.1990. *Autosegmental and Metrical Phonology*. Oxford: Basil Blackwell.

Goldsmith, John, and Firmard Sabimana. 1986. The Kirundi verb. In *Modèles en tonologie*, ed. Francis Jouannet, 19–62. Paris: Editions du CNRS.

Greenberg, Joseph H. 1948. The tone system of Proto-Bantu. *Word* 4:196–208.

Gulere, Cornelius W. 2009. *Lusoga-English Dictionary*. Kampala, Uganda: Fountain Publishers.

Hyman, Larry M. 2001. Privative tone in Bantu. In *Cross-Linguistic Studies of Tonal Phenomena*, ed. Shigeki Kaji, 237–257. Tokyo: Institute for the Study of Languages and Cultures.

———. 2007. Universals of tone rules: 30 years later. In *Tones and Tunes: Studies in Word and Sentence Prosody*, ed. Tomas Riad and Carlos Gussenhoven, 1–34. Berlin: Mouton de Gruyter.

———. 2014. Tonal melodies in the Lulamogi verb. *Africana Linguistica* 20:163–180.
———. 2018. Why underlying representations? *Journal of Linguistics*, forthcoming.
Hyman, Larry M., and Francis X. Katamba. 1993. A new approach to tone in Luganda. *Language* 69:34–67.
———. 2010. Tone, syntax, and prosodic domains in Luganda. In *Papers from the Workshop on Bantu Relative Clauses*, ed. Laura J. Downing et al., special issue, *ZAS Papers in Linguistics, Berlin* 53:69–98.
Hyman, Larry M., and John Merrill. 2016. Morphology, irregularity, and Bantu frication: The case of Lulamogi. *Mémoires de la Société de Linguistique de Paris* 23:139–157.
Hyman, Larry M., and Nzama Valinande. 1985. Globality in the Kinande tone system. In *African Linguistics*, ed. Didier Goyvaerts, 239–260. Amsterdam: Benjamins.
Jones, Patrick. 2015. Underlying falling tones in three interlacustrine Bantu languages. Paper presented at the 46th Annual Conference on African Linguistics, Eugene, Oregon, March 26–28.
Kaji, Shigeki. 1996. Tone reversal in Tembo (Bantu J.57). *Journal of African Languages and Linguistics* 17:1–26.
Kisseberth, Charles, and David Odden. 2003. Tone. In *The Bantu Langauges*, ed. Derek Nurse and Gérard Philippson, 59–70. London: Routledge.
Marlo, Michael. 2013. Verb tone in Bantu languages: Micro-typological patterns and research methods. *Africana Linguistica* 19:137–234.
McCawley, James D. 1970. Some tonal systems that come close to being pitch accent, but don't quite make it. *Chicago Linguistic Society* 6:526–532.
Mutaka, Ngessimo. 1994. *The Lexical Tonology of Kinande*. Munich: LINCOM.
Mutaka, Ngessimo, and Larry M. Hyman. 1990. Syllables and morpheme integrity in Kinande reduplication. *Phonology* 7:73–119.
Nabirye, Minah. 2009. *Eiwanika ly'Olusoga. Eiwanika ly'aboogezi b'Olusoga n'abo abenda okwega Olusoga* [A Dictionary of Lusoga. For speakers of Lusoga, and for those who would like to learn Lusoga]. Kampala: Menha Publishers.
Nash, Jay A. 1992–1994. Underlying low tones in Ruwund. *Studies in African Linguistics* 23:223–278.
Nzogi, Richard, and Martin Diprose. 2012. *Ekideero ky'oLugwere/Lugwere Dictionary*. Budaka, Uganda: Lugwere Bible Translation and SIL International.
Odden, David. 1995. Tone: African languages. In *The Handbook of Phonological Theory*, ed. John Goldsmith, 444–475. Hoboken, NJ: Blackwell.
Stevick, Earl. 1969. Tone in Bantu. *International Journal of American Linguistics* 35:330–341.
van der Wal, Jenneke. 2004. Lusoga phonology. Master's thesis, Leiden University.

FOUR

Tonal Melodies in the Logoori Verb

DAVID ODDEN

4.1. Introduction

One of the most compelling arguments for decomposing segment sequences into a many-to-many mapping between autonomous tiers, as characterizes autosegmental phonology, is the phenomenon of "tone melody," where constant tone profiles are abstracted from their segmental bearers. Such analyses are given in Goldsmith (1976) for a number of languages, including Etung, Ganda, Tonga, and especially Mende and Tiv where, in the latter case, specific tone patterns—regardless of the number of vowels in the stem—express inflectional tense-aspect distinctions. For example, in Tiv the general past reveals the lexical distinction between high (H) and low (L) verbs where the root contrast is manifested on the first stem syllable (vé$^{!}$ *yé*vèsè 'they flee-past', vé *ngò*hòr̀ 'they accept-past') and L subsequently, habitual 1 augments that contrast with a melodic H on just the second vowel (vé yévésè, vé ngòhór̀), and habitual 3 has H on all noninitial vowels of the stem (vé$^{!}$ yévésé-ń, vé ngòhóró-ń).

This concept of tone melody has been especially useful in the analysis of tone as a part of the inflectional system of Bantu languages: see the essays in Clements and Goldsmith (1984a, 1984b), especially Clements (1984) and Odden (1984) for inflectional patterns in Kikuyu and Shona. More recently, systems of tone modifications as a feature of

Bantu verb inflection are studied in a number of papers in a special issue of *Africana Linguistica*. See Odden and Bickmore (2014) for a general overview of the varying properties of these melodic inflection systems. It appears that in every Bantu language with tone, such tone alternation plays an important role in verb inflection.

The general picture is that each inflectional tense (covering distinctions for time reference, aspect, mood, polarity, clause type, and other properties such as focus) is indicated by some number of conjugational affixes, such as /ti-, -a-, -ra-, -ire, -e/, plus patterns of stem tone change in a fashion reminiscent of inflectional vowel patterning in Semitic. This tone patterning usually involves adding some number of H tones (occasionally L tones) to particular positions in the stem—for example, second syllable, third vowel, penult, last syllable. Independent tone rules often affect the realization of these abstracted tones; for example, in Makua, H tones initially assigned are then subject to tone doubling and other general rules (Cheng and Kisseberth 1979). In Shona (Odden 1984, 2014), a wide range of tense forms add H to the stem, but the realization of that H reflects complications whereby surface adjacent H tones are avoided, so that lexically H verbs leave a toneless syllable between the root-initial H and the melodic H; L verbs assign the H to the second stem vowel but H verbs assign the H to the final vowel. Depending on the length and lexical tone of the verb, the melodic H requires a preceding L, may or may not be realized, and varies in initial position between the final and second stem vowels. The task for the analyst of inflectional tone patterns is to abstract away from these phonotactic complications and discern the underlying content of a given tone pattern and the rules for associating it to the verb: these are the essential factors that have conveyed the notion of "melodic pattern" in the grammar. In some languages, especially those in the western zone, the more interesting variation is in the sequence of tones comprising the underlying melody, but in most languages, representational contrast is minimal—often simply "add an H," and the interest arises from the different ways of initially associating H to a stem. As the data discussed here show, rule content behind tone melodies can be rather complex and representational content can be extremely sparse. In Logoori, differences in what the tones do is more important than the inventory of tonal affixes in defining the concept of melodic pattern.

These systems seem to have evolved historically from a system where final inflectional suffixes may bear distinctive H versus L (the normal situation in Bantu is that only the root-initial syllable bears distinctive H), and the suffixal tone spreads leftward within the stem. In a number of languages, the simpler system has been reanalyzed as involving floating tones not tied to specific suffixal morphemes and often involving direct mapping of tones to particular positions within the stem. See Goldsmith (1987) for analysis of the development of such patterns in the Lacustrine group of Bantu.

Tone patterning as a feature of verb inflection becomes quite complex in the Lacustrine group, and the Luhya language subgroup has proven to be particularly challenging, in terms of expressing the unity of these inflectionally determined tone changes. See Ebarb, Green, and Marlo (2014) for an overview of tone in the Luhya languages. The purpose of the present chapter is to survey the problem of melodic patterns in verb inflections in the Luhya language Logoori.

The tonal system of Logoori has been analyzed previously in Leung (1986, 1991)[1] and, based on that data, is further discussed in Goldsmith (1991). This chapter is based on data elicited from Rose Kamwesa and Editon Mulera, both from South Maragoli in Kenya.

4.2. Basic Tonology

As is typical in Bantu, verbs make a two-way lexical distinction between H and toneless[2] first vowels of the root, and the remaining tones are predictable based on general morphosyntactic properties, mainly tense inflection. These sources of tonal distinction then interact with certain general phonological rules to yield the surface form.[3] The examples in (1) exemplify infinitives of toneless roots and reveal the basic morphology of the infinitive—kʊ 'infin.'–STEM–a 'infl.'.

(1)	kʊ[gw-a]	'to fall'
	kʊ[rɪɪ-a]	'to cry'
	kʊ[rɪɪnd-a]	'to wait'
	kʊ[gavʊr-a]	'to divide'
	kʊ[haandiik-a]	'to write'
	ko[veenzeger-a]	'to belch'

H-toned roots have an H on the first stem vowel, which spreads to the left by a general rule.

(2)	kʊ́[ry-á̱]	'to eat'
	kʊ́[kí̱n-a]	'to play'
	kʊ́[há̱kiz-a]	'to scorch tr.'

kʊ́[ká̱raang-a]	'to fry'
kʊ́[tʊ̱́ng'amiɲ-a]	'to invert'

In Logoori, H spreads unboundedly and variably to the left. If no H (or specified L) precedes an H, that H spreads to the beginning of the utterance as in (3a). When H precedes the H as in (3b), the second H spreads up to that H, and the Hs are separated by a downstep.[4]

(3)	a.	kʊ[gʊra]	'to buy'
		kʊ́[gʊ́rá] máchúunga	'to buy oranges'
	b.	kʊ́[vʊ́gʊra]	'to receive'
		kʊ́[vʊ́ꜜgʊ́rá] máchúunga	'to receive oranges'

There are contexts where surface non-H syllables systematically resist leftward spreading of H—for example mweene máchúunga 'owner of oranges', na va[zá̱ázá̱mé] 'they will taste'—a limitation that crucially enters into the analysis of melodic tones.

Fall and level H contrast in a limited way. Falling tone only appears on a long syllable and does not precede the penult except on the subject prefix syllable of a few tenses. In lieu of an inflectional H, a root-initial long penult in an H verb realizes H as a falling tone. A root-initial H syllable before the penult has level H.

(4)	kʊ́[hí̱iza]	'to hunt'
	kʊ́[zá̱ázama]	'to taste'
	kʊ́[sá̱ángaara]	'to be happy'

Penult level long H contrasts with fall as a consequence of melodic H being added to the stem, compare with ake[só̱ó̱ma] 'he is still reading', ndáá[dé̱é̱ka] 'I cooked (remote)'.

The final relatively general tone rule is Meeussen's rule (Goldsmith 1984), which deletes H after H. In Logoori, this takes place between an object prefix (OP) and a root H. The following examples show that the OP has H, and when added to an H root, the root H is missing.

(5)	a.	kʊ[sya]	'to grind'	kʊ́-vʊ̱́[sya]	'to grind it$_{14}$'
		ko[sooma]	'to read'	kó-ké̱[sooma]	'to read it$_{7}$'
		kʊ[variza]	'to count'	kʊ́-vá̱[variza]	'to count them$_{2}$'
	b.	kʊ́[ryá̱]	'to eat'	kʊ́-gí̱[rya̱]	'to eat it$_{9}$'
		kʊ́[vé̱ga]	'to shave'	kʊ́-vá̱[ve̱ga]	'to shave them$_{2}$'[5]
		kʊ́[ɲá̱gʊra]	'to catch'	kʊ́-kʊ̱́[ɲa̱gʊra]	'to catch us'

Meeussen's rule only applies to a root H after an OP. Crucial evidence for this comes from constructions with multiple OPs.

(6) kʊ́-gí̱-vá̱[variza] 'to count it$_9$ for them$_2$'
kʊ́-gí̱-vá̱[ɲa̱gʊlla] 'to catch it$_9$ for them$_2$'

While /kʊ-gí̱-vá̱[variza]/ and /kʊ-kʊ̱́[ɲá̱gʊra]/ have parallel underlying representations—H on an OP followed by one H—the surface forms kʊ́-kʊ̱́[ɲa̱gʊra] versus kʊ́-gí̱-vá̱[variza] are rather different, with the rightmost underlying H being deleted in the single-OP structure but not in the double OP structure. If Meeussen's rule applied indiscriminately to any H after H, we would expect *kʊ́-gí̱-va̱[variza] and *kʊ́-gí̱-va̱[ɲa̱gʊlla]. Only a root-initial H deletes, and when two object prefixes are concatenated, their Hs fuse into one, thus kʊ́-gí̱-vá̱[variza] and not *kʊ́-gí̱-ꜝvá̱[variza].

The interaction between Meeussen's rule and leftward spreading at the phrasal level reveals a covert phonological effect of the deleted root tone: in H roots, leftward spread stops at the second stem syllable.

(7) a. kʊ́-vʊ̱́ꜝ[syá] gárá̱ha 'to grind it$_{14}$ slowly'
kó-ké̱ꜝ[sóómá] gárá̱ha 'to read it$_7$ slowly'
kʊ́-gí̱[rya̱] gárá̱ha 'to eat it$_9$ slowly'
kʊ́-vá̱[ve̱gá] gárá̱ha 'to shave them$_2$ slowly'

The form kʊ́-vá̱[ve̱gá] gárá̱ha has the underlying form /kʊ-vá̱[vé̱ga] gará̱ha/, and the surface form involves the combined effect of Meeussen's rule and leftward spread. One analysis of the failure of leftward spread to apply to the stem-initial syllable is that leftward spread precedes Meeussen's rule, and the underlying H limits the extent of leftward spread, but is later deleted. An alternative is that Meeussen's rule changes H to L, and on the premise that leftward spreading targets toneless syllables (not L syllables), leftward spread could not apply to the output of Meeussen's rule.

These patterns, identified in Goldsmith (1987) as the simple stem tone pattern, are found in many tenses, where just general phonological rules—syllable internal spread, fall-creation, leftward spread, Meeussen's rule—are responsible for the surface tone of the verb. The surface characteristics of the basic pattern are as follows:

(8) Toneless verbs with no OP are entirely toneless
H verbs have H on the first root syllable: if that syllable is long, it has level H unless it is also phrase-penult, in which case it has a falling tone.
H in a following word spreads leftward to an underlying H.
Root-initial H deletes after the H of an OP; this leaves a toneless gap between H tones, when an H root is followed by a complement with H.

A second tense with this pattern is the remote future.[6]

(9)	a.	va-ra-ka[syɪ]	'they will grind'
		n-da-ka[rore]	'I will see'
		va-ra-ka[rɪɪndɪ]	'they will watch'
		va-ra-ka[homoore]	'they will anoint'
	b.	va-rá-ká[ryí̲]	'they will eat'
		va-rá-ká[ká̲re]	'they will cut'
		va-rá-ká[ré̲ete]	'they will bring'
		va-rá-ká[ná̲gɪllane]	'they will catch for e.o'
	c.	a-rá-ká-kʊ̲́[varizɪrɪ]	'he will count for us'
		va-rá-ká-kʊ̲́[ra̲sɪrɪ]	'they will throw for us'
	d.	va-rá-ká[gwí] gárá̲ha	'they will fall slowly'
		va-rá-ká[ryí̲] ꜜgárá̲ha	'they will eat slowly'
		a-rá-ká-kʊ̲́ꜜ[várízírí] gáráha	'he will count for us slowly'
		va-rá-ká-kʊ̲́[ra̲sírí] gárá̲ha	'they will throw for us slowly'

The recent past likewise exhibits this pattern.

(10)	a.	nd-aa-ka[sya]	'I ground'
		w-aa-ka[rora]	'you saw'
		nd-aa-ka[homoora]	'I anointed'
	b.	y-aa-ká[ryá̲]	'he ate'
		kw-aa-ká[rá̲sa]	'we threw'
		w-aa-ká[ré̲eta]	'you brought'
	c.	nd-aa-ká-vá̲[variza]	'I counted them$_2$'
		nd-aa-ká-gí̲[ra̲sa]	'I threw it$_9$'
	d.	v-aa-ká[várízá] gárá̲ha	'they counted slowly'
		kw-aa-ká[dé̲éꜜká] gárá̲ha	'we cooked slowly'
		kw-aa-ká-vá̲ꜜ[várízá] gárá̲ha	'I counted them$_2$ slowly'
		nd-aa-ká-gí̲[ra̲sá] gárá̲ha	'I threw it$_9$ slowly'

The completive-focused variants of the recent and intermediate perfectives[7] behave the same way. The recent perfective is seen in (11).

(11)	a.	koo[ng'oodi]	'we have written'
		kʊʊ[rɪmi]	'we have plowed'
		koo[hoomori]	'we have anointed'
	b.	kʊ́ʊ́[ká̱ri]	'we have chopped'
		kʊʊ[ká̱raanji]	'we have fried'
	c.	koo-ké̱[rori]	'we have seen it$_7$'
		koo-ké̱[de̱echi]	'we have cooked it$_7$'
	d.	kʊ́ʊ́[túúmí] gárá̱ha	'we have pulled slowly'
		koo[vé̱ꜜjí] gárá̱ha	'we have shaved slowly'

The intermediate perfective completive-focused form is given in (12).

(12)	a.	nd-á̱a[shɪɪ]	'I ground'
		nd-á̱a[rori]	'I saw'
		nd-á̱a[ng'oodi]	'I wrote'
		nd-á̱a[ganagani]	'I thought'
	b.	nd-á̱a[nwɪ̱́ɪ]	'I drank'
		nd-á̱a[ká̱ri]	'I cut'
		nd-á̱a[ká̱raanji]	'I fried'
		nd-á̱a[tʊ̱́ʊ́ngamiɲi]	'I inverted'
	c.	nd-á̱a-kɪ̱́[gʊrizi]	'I sold it$_7$'
		nd-á̱a-kɪ̱́[ka̱raanji]	'I fried it$_7$'
	d	nd-áa[gánágání gárá̱ha]	'I thought slowly'
		nd-áa[vó̱ꜜdóng'ání] gárá̱ha	'I went around slowly'

Other tenses manifesting the basic pattern are the hodiernal future (13a), immediate past (13b), and the remote future with -ri-ka- (13c).

(13)	a.	a-ra[variza]	'he will count'
		a-rá[dé̱eka]	'he will cook'
		a-rá-vá̱[rora]	'he will see them'
		a-rá-kó̱[ve̱ga]	'he will shave us'
		a-rá-kɪ̱́ꜜ[háándííká] gárá̱ha	'he will write it$_7$ slowly'
		a-rá-gɪ̱́[za̱azámá] gárá̱ha	'he will taste it$_9$'
	b.	v-aa-ko[veenzegera]	'they have belched'
		kw-aa-kʊ́[vʊ̱́gʊra]	'we have received'
		kw-aa-kʊ́-vá̱[rora]	'we have seen them$_2$'
		kw-aa-kʊ́-kɪ̱́[vʊ̱gʊra]	'we have received it$_7$'
		kw-aa-kó[rímá] gárá̱ha	'we have cultivated quickly'
		nd-aa-kó[vé̱ꜜgá] gárá̱ha	'I have shaved quickly'

c. a-ri-ka[haandiikɪ] 'he will write'
a-rí-ká[dé̳eke] 'he will cook'
a-rí-ká[háándííkí] gáráha 'he will write quickly'
a-rí-ká[dé̳éꜜké] gáráha 'he will cook quickly'

Thus in a wide range of tenses, no special modifications are made to the stem.

4.3. Melodic Pattern 2

Other tenses evince different patterns. The analytic goal of abstracting a tone melody as an exponent of tense-marking is to identify the constant tonal content of these tenses, just as we seek to identify the constant content of segmental morphemes such as /-kɪ-/, which may be realized as [kɪ, ke, gɪ, ge, j, ch]. The representational content of these patterns is generally just an H (occasionally two Hs). Despite representational impoverishment, there are many patterns.

4.3.1. Main Variant

An example of the M2 pattern is found in the consecutive tense "(X happened) and then V." If the root is lexically toneless, the melodic H (double-underlined except when assignment of that H is blocked) appears on the second stem mora (unless the stem has only one mora, in which case it appears on that mora).

(14) maní váꜜ[gwá̳] 'they fell'
maní váꜜ[rírá̳] 'they cried'
maní váꜜ[móró̳ma] 'they spoke'
maní váꜜ[vúrú̳ganyirana] 'they stirred for e.o'
maní váꜜ[kúú̳ta] 'they scraped'
maní váꜜ[téé̳vaana] 'they asked'
maní vá[ꜜrákú̳úra] 'they released'

A noteworthy feature of this pattern is that long penults with H spread the H to the second mora of the syllable and do not have a falling tone.

In lexically H verbs there is loss of the lexical H and the inflectional H appears on the final vowel, which then spreads leftward.

(15)	maní vá[rya̱]	'they ate'
	maní vá[ve̱ga]	'they shaved'
	maní vá[de̱eká̱]	'they cooked'
	maní vá[vi̱táná̱]	'they passed e.o'
	maní vá[vo̱hóóllá̱]	'they tied'
	maní vá[za̱azámá̱]	'they tasted'
	maní vá[gɪ̱rʊ́ʊ́ngányá̱]	'they turned'

If the final vowel is moraically adjacent to the root-initial H—in mono- and dimoraic stems—no additional H appears within the stem. The lexical tone of the verb is deleted, whether or not the inflectional H is manifested on the surface. However, that lexical H still has an effect on leftward spreading of H from the final vowel—observe that the inflectional H spreads up to but not including the syllable containing the lexical H.[8]

We can identify three main features of this pattern that are familiar from other Bantu languages. First is the fact that H is added—this is the archetypical property of inflectional tone. The location of that H varies between the final vowel and the second stem mora, governed by whether the root has H or not. This is similar to the complex stem tone pattern identified by Goldsmith for Kihunde, and variants of the pattern are found throughout Bantu.

What is not typical is the pattern found in the presence of an OP. The melodic H is preserved in toneless roots in H (16a), but seems to disappear if the root is H in (16b).

(16)	a.	maní vá̱-kɪ̱[syá̱]	'they ground it$_7$'
		maní vá̱-ko̱[rórá̱]	'they saw us'
		maní vá̱-kʊ̱[várí̱za]	'they counted us'
		maní vá̱-ke̱[sóó̱ma]	'they read it$_7$'
		maní vá̱-kʊ̱[símʊ̱́gʊkiza]	'they revived us'
		maní vá̱-kɪ̱-kʊ̱[gúlí̱zɪra]	'they they sold it$_7$ to us'
	b.	maní vá̱-kɪ̱[ryá̱]	'they ate it$_7$'
		maní vá̱-va̱[vé̱ga]	'they shaved them$_2$'
		maní vá̱-ke̱[dé̱éka]	'they cooked it$_7$'
		maní vá̱-kɪ̱[ká̱raanga]	'they fried it$_7$'
		maní vá̱-kɪ̱[zá̱ázama]	'they tasted it$_7$'
		maníí m̱-ba̱-ke̱[dé̱ékera]	'I cooked it$_7$ for them'
		maní vá̱-kɪ̱-kʊ̱[rá̱sɪra]	'they threw it$_7$ for us'

Although H verbs superficially appear to revert to the basic pattern, there are important differences between the pattern in (16b) and the non-melodic pattern. First, the H of OPs deletes and the root H is preserved, but with the basic pattern in (5b), the H of the OP is retained at the expense of the root H. Second, we see from maní vá̱-ke̱[dé̱éka] that a long penult has a level H and not a fall, which contrasts with the fall found with the basic pattern (kó[dé̱eka] 'to cook').

The tonal content of this pattern is straightforward: H. The mapping of that H within the stem is not as straightforward. The choice of association locus, between final and second stem vowels, can be rationalized as reflecting avoidance of multiple adjacent Hs—final H is selected when Vowel 2 (V2) association would lead to a sequence of Hs on adjacent vowels. A seemingly minor complication is that addition of the melodic H causes deletion of preceding Hs—those of the root and the object prefix. Across-the-board deletion of H at the hands of an inflectional H is found in Interlacustrine languages such as Kerewe and Haya. The main puzzle pertaining to the location of this melodic H is that the root H prevails over both the H of the OP and the melodic H, when all three Hs are present, but when just two of those tones are present, it is the root H that deletes. Or, the locus of melodic H mapping switches to the root-initial syllable, just in case the stem already contains three Hs. A further complication in the derivation of the M2 pattern involves the effect of a following word, but proper consideration of that pattern requires enumerating the tenses that select the M2 pattern.

A second tense following the M2 pattern is the indefinite future. Toneless verbs have H on the second stem mora, which spreads to the left (17a); H verbs with fewer than 3 moras are surface toneless (17b), but longer verbs have H from the final vowel to the second syllable (17c). With a toneless root, an OP creates no complication, and the H of OPs deletes (17d), but when the root is H, the melodic tone shifts its locus wholesale to the root-initial syllable. In all contexts, a long penult with H is realized with a level H rather than a falling tone.

(17)	a.	va-ri[syá̱]	'they will grind'
		va-ri[séká̱]	'they will laugh'
		va-ri[róó̱nda]	'they will follow'
		va-ri[hómó̱óra]	'they will anoint'
	b.	va-ri[rya̱]	'they will eat'
		va-ri[ve̱ga]	'they will shave'
	c.	va-ri[de̱eká̱]	'they will cook'
		va-ri[tu̱ng'ámíɲá̱]	'they will invert'

d. a-ri-kɪ̲[syá̲] 'he will grind it$_7$'
a-ri-ke̲[rórá̲] 'he will see it$_7$'
a-ri-ke̲[sóó̲ma] 'he will read it$_7$'
va-ri-kɪ̲-kʊ̲[vʊ́rʊ̲́ganyɪra] 'they will stir it$_7$ for us'
e. va-ri-kɪ̲[ryá̲] 'they will eat it$_7$'
n-di-va̲[vé̲ga] 'I will shave them$_2$'
a-ri-ke̲[ré̲éta] 'he will bring it$_7$'
va-ri-ke̲-ko̲[dé̲ékera] 'they will cook it$_7$ for us'

The persistive tense likewise follows the M2 tone pattern (gloss 'they are still Ving').

(18) a. va-kɪ[syá̲] '. . . grind'
va-ke[góná̲] '. . . sleep'
va-ke[róó̲nda] '. . . follow'
va-kɪ[rákʊ̲́ʊra] '. . . release'
b. va-kɪ[rya̲] '. . . eat'
va-ke[vega̲] '. . . shave'
c. va-ke[de̲eká̲] '. . . cook'
va-ke[ko̲rórá̲] '. . . cough'
va-kɪ[za̲azámá̲] '. . . taste'
d. va-gɪ-kɪ̲[syá̲] '. . . grind it$_7$'
va-kɪ-va̲[rórá̲] '. . . see them$_2$'
va-kɪ-va̲[hómó̲óra] '. . . anoint them$_2$'
va-kɪ̲-kʊ̲[gʊ́lɪ̲́zɪra] '. . . sell it for us'
e. va-kɪ-kɪ̲[ryá̲] '. . . eat it$_7$'
va-kɪ-va̲[vé̲ga] '. . . shave them$_2$'
va-ke-ke̲[dé̲éka] '. . . cook it$_7$'
va-kɪ-kɪ̲[ká̲raanga] '. . . fry it$_7$'

The phrasal behavior of the M2 pattern points to an additional aspect of inflectional tone melodies, indicating that there are at least two surface variants of the M2 pattern. In the remote future and persistive, we observe in (20) that the melodic H found in citation forms is lacking (gloss (a) 'they will V quickly', and (b) 'they are Ving quickly').

(19) a. va-ri[rya̲] vwaangʊ '. . . eat'
va-ri[ve̲ga] vwaangʊ '. . . shave'
va-ri[ve̲gana] vwaangʊ '. . . shave e.o'
va-ri[rɪma] vwaangʊ '. . . cultivate'

va-ri[vʊrʊganya] vwaangʊ '. . . stir'
va-ri[homoora] vwaangʊ '. . . anoint'
b. va-ke[vega] vwaangʊ '. . . shave'
va-ke[karaanga] vwaangʊ '. . . fry'
va-kɪ[vʊrʊganya] vwaangʊ '. . . stir'
va-ke[homoora] vwaangʊ '. . . anoint'

Although the melodic H is missing, one of its effects is still present: it still triggers deletion of H in lexically H verbs (va-ke[karaanga] vwaangʊ). The lexical H can be indirectly detected by the fact that leftward spreading does not extend past the deleted H (gloss (a) 'they will V slowly', and (b) 'they are Ving slowly').

(20) a. va-ri[rya] gáráha '. . . eat'
va-ri[vegá] gáráha '. . . shave'
va-ri[vegáná] gáráha '. . . shave e.o'
va-ri[gʊ́rá] gáráha '. . . buy'
va-ri[vʊ́rʊ́gányá] gáráha '. . . stir'
va-ri[hómóórá] gáráha '. . . anoint'
b. va-ke[vegá] gáráha '. . . shave'
va-ke[vegáná] gáráha '. . . shave e.o'
va-kɪ[rímá] gáráha '. . . cultivate'
va-kɪ[vʊ́rʊ́gányá] gáráha '. . . stir'
va-ke[hómóórá] gáráha '. . . anoint'

In these examples, the phrasal behavior of verbs with the M2 pattern could be predicted by deriving the citation form of the verb, then deleting the melodic H. This view of the derivation of the phrase-medial form potentially runs into problems explaining how far H spreads to the left. Data such as vake[vegáná] gáráha show that spreading does not target a syllable with an underlying H, even when the H is deleted by a melodic tone or, as we have seen, by the H of a preceding OP. Yet the vowels that would otherwise receive the melodic H can be targeted by leftward spreading. In other words, we find evidence that phrase-medially the melodic H is present so it triggers deletion of lexical Hs, but there is no evidence that the H is associated to specific vowels.

Not all tenses selecting the M2 pattern delete that H phrase-medially. The consecutive tense is one tense where the melodic H is retained (gloss 'then they V slowly').

(21) maní vá[vega] vwaangʊ '. . . shaved'
maní vá[vegáná] vwaangʊ '. . . shaved e.o'
maní vá[ꜝsyá] vwaangʊ '. . . ground'
maní vá[ꜝváríza] vwaangʊ '. . . counted'

When the following complement has an H tone, leftward spreading stops at the end of the verb (gloss 'then they V quickly').

(22) maní vá[rya] gáráha '. . . ate'
maní vá[deeká] ꜝgáráha '. . . cooked'
maní vá[vegáná] ꜝgáráha '. . . shaved e.o'
maní vá[ꜝsyá] ꜝgáráha '. . . ground'
maní vá[ꜝróónda] gáráha '. . . followed'
maní vá[ꜝváríza] gáráha '. . . counted'
maní vá[ꜝháándiika] gáráha '. . . wrote'

Since the melodic H is retained in this tense, it is not surprising that spreading is blocked in longer H verbs, given that the melodic tone occupies the final vowel. What is surprising is blockage in dimoraic H verbs, where the melodic H is never realized, and in toneless verbs, where the melodic H is associated toward the beginning of the stem, not the end. In other words, the surface realization of the melodic tone itself cannot be held responsible for the blockage of spreading, rather, it is the very presence of the melodic tone that blocks spreading.

4.3.2. Perfective Variants (1)

The M2 pattern has variants that seem to challenge the integrity of M2 as "a pattern" rather than a family of patterns. These variants can largely be accommodated by minor elaborations to the mapping principles, in particular the statement of when the melodic H is lost in H roots. Previous examples of the M2 pattern have selected the final inflectional affix /-a/, which is a general default suffix employed in verbs. Some tenses such as the nonfocused hesternal perfective have a different final affix, the perfective suffix, which can be represented as /-i/.[9] For the most part, the tone pattern of the hesternal perfective is the same as that found in other M2-selecting tenses.[10]

(23) a. nd-aa[séchí] 'I laughed'
nd-aa[kúúti] 'I scraped'

	nd-aa[búrúchi]	'I flew'
	kw-aa[háándiichi]	'we wrote'
b.	nd-aa[deechí]	'I cooked'
	nd-aa[hakízí]	'I scorched'
	nd-aa[vohóólé]	'I untied'
	v-aa[deekéráníráánjí]	'they cooked continuously for e.o'
c.	kw-aa-kɪ[sáví]	'we borrowed it$_7$'
	y-aa-ko[róóndi]	'he followed us'
	kw-aa-va[vúrúganyɪrɪɪ]	'we stirred for them$_2$'
d.	nd-aa-vi[rúmi]	'I bit them$_8$'
	nd-aa-ke[dééchi]	'I ate it$_7$'
	y-aa-kɪ[túng'amiɲi]	'he turned it over$_7$'

Stems that have a final long vowel in the perfective realize the H as a phonetic fall, but there is no contrast between level H and fall in prepausal position, and from a phonological perspective nd-aa[ɲagúʊ] 'I ran' is as good a transcription as nd-aa[ɲagúú]. What is special about the tone of the hesternal perfective is that short H stems such as /ry-, vit-/ have final H.

(24)	nd-aa[ríí]	'I ate'
	nd-aa[vití]	'I passed'

Compare ndaavití with arivita 'he will pass', where the melodic H is deleted in the latter case. This complication can be accommodated into the analysis very simply by restricting deletion of melodic H—the rule does not apply if the tone is realized on the perfective suffix -i.

4.3.3. Perfect Variants (2) and Negative Subjunctive

The recent perfective and negative subjunctive evince another subpattern of M2, the systematic deletion of melodic H in lexically H stems. Beginning with the recent perfective, with toneless verbs in (25a), the observed pattern is the expected H on the second stem mora; in (25b), an OP has no effect on toneless verbs, as expected; and in (25c), an OP on an H verb results in wholesale migration of Hs to the root-initial vowel, as is also typical of M2-inflected verbs.

(25)	a.	va[séchí]	'they laughed'
		ko[ng'óódi]	'we wrote'
		ke[ng'éréng'ani]	'it is shiny'

b.	a-ko[rórí̱]	'he saw us'
	va-ke[ng'óó̱di]	'we wrote it$_7$'
c.	va-ke[dé̱échi]	'they cooked it$_7$'
	kʊ-kɪ[vú̱gʊri]	'we received it$_7$'

The exceptionality of this tense resides in the fact that regardless of the length of the stem, lexically H verbs with no OP have no H at all.

(26)	ko[ve̱ji]	'we shaved'
	ko[de̱echi]	'we cooked'
	kʊ[su̱gumi]	'we pushed'
	ko[vo̱hoolle]	'we untied'

We expect *kove̱jí̱, *kʊsu̱gúmí̱, the latter given the general realization of the M2 pattern in H verbs and the former given that the melodic H is not deleted in short perfective stems as we observed in section 4.3.2. Yet we find that the melodic H is phonetically missing in all H verbs. Indirect evidence for the melodic H is that the root H is deleted. Confirming evidence for the presence of the melodic H is that leftward spreading is blocked—as is typical of verbs with a melodic.

(27)	kʊ[háá̱ndiichi] gáráha	'we wrote slowly'
	ko[de̱echi] gáráha	'we cooked slowly'
	ko[ve̱ji] gáráha	'we shaved slowly'

This same pattern is found in the negative subjunctive: H on the first two stem moras in toneless verbs (28a) including after an OP (28c), total loss of H in H verbs (28b), and switch of H to stem-initial position in H verbs with OP (28d) (gloss 'you should not V').

(28)	a.	ʊ-ta[shá̱] ꜜdáave	'. . . grind'
		ʊ-ta[gúrá̱] ꜜdáave	'. . . buy'
		ʊ-ta[véé̱zegera] dáave	'. . . belch'
	b.	ʊ-ta[nwa̱] dáave	'. . . drink'
		ʊ-ta[ve̱ga] dáave	'. . . shave'
		ʊ-ta[vo̱ora] dáave	'. . . tell'
	c.	ʊ-ta-kɪ̱[shá̱] ꜜdáave	'. . . grind it$_7$'
		ʊ-ta-gɪ̱[gúrá̱] ꜜdáave	'. . . buy it$_9$'
		ʊ-ta-kɪ̱[gáná̱gana] dáave	'. . . think of it$_7$'
		ʊ-ta-gɪ̱[nwá̱] ꜜdáave	'. . . drink it$_9$'
		ʊ-ta-va̱[kóó̱ɲa] dáave	'. . . help them$_2$'

ʊ-ta-gɪ[kaáraanga] dáave '. . . fry it$_9$'
ʊ-ta-va[vɔ́don'ana] dáave '. . . go around them$_2$'

The resolution of this complication resides in a special deletion of melodic H, deleting the melodic H in just these tenses, and only in underlyingly H verbs (cf. va[séchí] 'they laughed' where the melodic H ends up on the final vowel). The problem this analysis creates—which will remain unresolved here—is that deletion of the lexical H would seem to logically preclude that same tone being a conditioning factor for deletion of the melodic H.

4.3.4. Progressive and Persistive Continuous Variants

A final variant of the M2 pattern arises in the persistive and present continuous, which have the final suffix -aa. Because of this suffix, stems are always longer than two moras and there is no deletion of melodic tone in shorter H verbs. In lieu of an OP, the pattern of the progressive conforms to the general pattern of other tenses selecting this melody. Indeed, even with an OP in a toneless verb in (29c), the data conform to the general pattern of M2 in other tenses.

(29)	a.	va[kɪnáá]	'they're playing'
		va[deekáá]	'they're cooking'
		va[karáángáá]	'they're frying'
		va[deekéránáá]	'they're cooking for e.o'
		va[fʊnyíírízáníráá]	'they're smelling for e.o'
	b.	va[gónáá]	'they're sleeping'
		va[sáámbaa]	'they're roasting'
		va[bʊ́rʊ́kaa]	'they're flying'
		va[hómóóraa]	'they're anointing'
		va[zíízagɪllaa]	'they're continuing'
	c.	n-ga[syéézaa]	'I'm grinding it$_6$'
		m-ba[dúyáá]	'I'm hitting them$_2$'
		n-ge[sóómaa]	'I'm reading it$_7$'
		vaa-m[bálízɪranaa]	'they are counting me'
		a-ko[séémbellaa]	'he's cultivating for me'
		n-gɪ[vʊ́rʊ́ganyaa]	'I'm stirring it$_7$'

A variant of the persistive also selects -aa (contributing the meaning 'expected to continue for some time').

(30)	a.	va-ke[gónáá]	'they are still sleeping'
		va-kɪ[vágáraa]	'they are still spreading'
		va-ke[hómóóraa]	'they are still anointing'
	b.	n-gɪ[vináá]	'I am still dancing'
		n-ge[deekáá]	'I am still cooking'
		va-ke[vohóólláá]	'I am still untying'
	c.	va-kɪ-kʊ[vágállaa]	'they are still spreading for us'
		va-ke-ko[hómóóraa]	'they are still anointing us'

A more substantial difference arises in H verbs with an OP. The root-initial vowel has a surface H, which is separated from the melodic H by a downstep.[11] We will refer to this pattern as the "double H pattern."

(31)	va-kɪ[nwɛ́ɛ́ꜜzáá]	'they are drinking it$_7$'
	va-kʊ[rʊ́ꜜmáá]	'they're biting us'
	a-va[kɔ́ɔ́ꜜnyáá]	'he is helping them$_2$'
	a-kɪ[fʊ́ꜜnyíírízáá]	'he's smelling it$_7$'
	va-kɪ[tʊ́ꜜng'ámínyáá]	'they are inverting it$_7$'

Previously under the broader M2 pattern, we have seen that H roots with an OP undergo a radical shift in pattern, whereby H appears just on the root-initial syllable. These aa-affixing tenses are immune to that radical change, and their pattern is closer to what one would expect just given the melodic H at the end of the verb. That is, just given underlying Hs and the primary loci of tone mapping, without the complications of melodic realignment with three Hs, we would expect *va-kɪ́[tʊ́ng'aminyaá], which is close to va-kɪ[tʊ́ꜜng'ámínyáá], save for the fact that the melodic H has failed to cause general deletion of preceding H, and H has shifted from the OP to the root-initial vowel. It is not clear in this context what is the precise exceptional mechanism and what is the default case. One could posit a special shift of H from the OP in these tenses and attempt to let the double H pattern emerge automatically, or one could block the wholesale shift of H tones to root-initial position and strive to make the double H pattern be the result of failing to consolidate those tones. As we will see in section 4.4, a version of the double H pattern is found in other tenses, where the complication is not limited to OPs. It turns out that there are multiple tense-determined double H patterns.

In summary, we have enjoyed considerable success in pursuing the strategy of reducing tonal variation to underlying representational differences (lexical tone of roots, selection of a melodic H) and relatively general rules (mapping melodic H to particular positions; deleting the melodic H immediately after root H). Nevertheless, accommodating the full range of these patterns requires recourse to tense-specific rules that systematically delete a final melodic H in some tenses or that provide other special rearrangements of the underlying tones in subcontexts of particular tenses.

4.4. Melodic Pattern 3

In another tense, a subset of those using the subjunctive form (suffix -e/-ɪ), a rather different tone pattern prevails. One hallmark of this pattern is that H and toneless verbs are treated alike—H verbs lose their H. H is assigned to the second mora after the initial syllable (a generalization noticed in Ebarb 2014). When σ_2 is light, the melodic H is on σ_3, otherwise it is on σ_2. Within a long syllable, the realization of H depends on the position of that syllable, per section 4.2.

The data in (32) show the pattern of H (32a) and toneless (32b) roots with a light second syllable (gloss 'they will V').

(32)	a.	na va[ryɪ̳́]	'. . . eat'
		na va[rá̱sé̳]	'. . . throw'
		na va[dé̱éké̳]	'. . . cook'
		na va[zá̱ázámé̳]	'. . . taste'
		na va[tʊ̱́ng'ámɪ̳́ɲɪ]	'. . . invert'
		na va[kó̱rórá̳ange]	'. . . cough continuously'
		na va[vé̱gánɪ̳́rane]	'. . . shave for e.o'
		na va[zá̱ázámá̳ange]	'. . . taste continuously'
	b.	na va[gwɪ̳́]	'. . . fall'
		na va[séké̳]	'. . . laugh'
		na va[róóndé̳]	'. . . follow'
		na va[várízɪ̳́]	'. . . count'
		na va[sʊ́ng'ʊ́sá̳nɪrane]	'. . . shake for e.o'
		na va[véénzégé̳re]	'. . . belch'

If the second vowel is long, that syllable defines the rightmost extent of the melodic H. If it is the penult, the tone is falling tone (33a), otherwise, it is level H.

(33)	a.	na va[ká̱ráa̳nge]	'. . . fry'
		na va[rákʊ́ʊ̳rɪ]	'. . . release'
		na va[sáángáa̳re]	'. . . be happy'

b. na va[ká̱ráá̱ngɪrane] '. . . fry for e.o'
na va[fʊ̱́ɲíɪ̱́rizɪ] '. . . smell'
na va[sʊ̱́gáá̱ɲanɪrane] '. . . mix for e.o'
na va[ká̱ráá̱ngaange] '. . . fry continuously'
na va[ká̱ráá̱nganɪrane] '. . . fry for e.o'
na va[rákʊ́ʊ̱́rane] '. . . release e.o'

Like the basic pattern and unlike the M2 pattern, the M3 melody undergoes the penult fall rule.

The M3 pattern has a different realization when an OP is present. From a comparative perspective, this is expected—see Marlo (2013) and Meeussen (2014) for an overview of the tone of subjunctive plus OP. The examples in (34) show that the tone pattern is virtually the same as for the M2 pattern—H verbs have their H on the root-initial vowel and toneless verbs have H on V2—the only difference being the fall in the penult.

(34) a. na va-kɪ̱[syɪ̱́] '. . . grind it$_7$'
na va-kɪ̱[gʊ́rɪ̱́] '. . . buy it$_7$'
na va-ko̱[róo̱nde] '. . . follow us'
na va-kɪ̱-kʊ̱[gʊ́rɪ̱́zɪrɪ] '. . . sell it$_7$ for us'
na va-ko̱[séé̱mbelle] '. . . cultivate for us'
na va-ko̱[rórá̱ange] '. . . see us continuously'
na va-kʊ̱[rákʊ̱́ʊ́llanɪrɪ] '. . . release us for e.o'
b. na va-kɪ̱[ryɪ̱́] '. . . eat it$_7$'
na va-ko̱[vé̱ge] '. . . shave us'
na va-ke̱[dé̱eke] '. . . cook it$_7$'
na va-kʊ̱[vɪ̱́nɪrɪ] '. . . dance for us'
na va-kʊ̱[ká̱raangɪrɪ] '. . . fry for us'
na va-gɪ̱-kʊ̱[ká̱raangɪrɪ] '. . . fry it$_9$ for us'
na va-kʊ̱[kʊ̱́ʊ́tɪrɪ] '. . . scrape for you'

At the phrasal level, there is no deletion of the melodic H, and leftward spreading is blocked.

(35) na va[vé̱gé̱] ꜜgáráha '. . . shave slowly'
na va[gɪ̱́rʊ́ʊ̱́nganye] gáráha '. . . turn slowly'
na va[véénzégé̱re] gáráha '. . . belch slowly'

In other words, the M3 pattern is like the M2 pattern in blocking leftward spreading and having an added H, but unlike the M2 pattern in neutralizing the H/toneless distinction, in the location of the melodic

H, and in whether a long penult has level H rather than a falling tone. M3 has a different cluster of defining behavioral properties: the surface pattern does not just reduce to an underlying representational distinction (adding a floating H or not).

4.5. Melodic Pattern 4

Another pattern is found in the remote past and habitual aspect. As in the M3 pattern, the distinction between H and toneless roots is neutralized (as long as no OP is present): an H appears on the first syllable of roots that are longer than one mora, and long penultimas do not have falling tones (unlike M3).

(36)	a.	nd-áá[sya̲]	'I ground'
		nd-áá[rɪ̲́ra]	'I cried'
		nd-áá[sá̲ámba]	'I roasted'
		nd-áá[vá̲riza]	'I counted'
		nd-áá[vʊ̲́rʊganya]	'I stirred'
	b.	nd-áá[rya̲]	'I ate'
		nd-áá[rʊ̲́ma]	'I bit'
		nd-áá[dé̲éka]	'I cooked'
		nd-áá[ká̲raanga]	'I fried'
		v-áá[vɪ̲́nɪrana]	'they danced for e.o'

Like other tenses selecting melodic Hs, leftward spreading fails to apply to a verb with the M4 pattern, even when the stem is a toneless monosyllable and the melodic H is not realized.

(37)	v-áá[gwa̲] gárá̲ha	'they fell slowly'
	v-áá[vʊ̲́rʊganya] gáráha	'they stirred slowly'
	v-áá[vé̲gana] gárá̲ha	'they shaved e.o slowly'
	v-áá[dé̲éka] gárá̲ha	'they cooked slowly'

Blockage of leftward spreading again points to the generalization that the rule is blocked by melodic Hs, regardless of where they end up, or even whether they are realized (but recall from section 4.3.1 that the melodic H is deleted phrase-medially in some tenses and leftward spread is then not blocked).

As we are coming to expect, a different tone pattern is found when an OP is present. The lexical H of the root is lost after the object prefix

(38a) and there is no sign of the melodic H, but with toneless roots (38b), a melodic H appears on the second stem mora.

(38)	a.	nd-áá-kí̱[rya̱]	'I ate it$_7$'
		nd-áá-vá̱[ve̱ga]	'I shaved them$_2$'
		nd-áá-ké̱[de̱eka]	'I cooked it$_7$'
		nd-áá-vá̱[ka̱raangɪra]	'I fried for them$_2$'
	b.	v-áá-kí̱[sya]	'they ground it$_7$'
		nd-áá-kó̱[ꜜrórá̱]	'I saw you'
		nd-áá-vá̱[ꜜríí̱nda]	'I waited for them$_2$'
		nd-áá-vá̱[ꜜkúú̱tɪra]	'I scraped for them$_2$'
		v-áá-kʊ̱́[ꜜvárí̱zɪra]	'they counted for us'

No H appears in a consonant-vowel (CV) stem, as in váá-kí̱[sya]. This contrast with the pattern of second-mora tone assignment found with CV stems after an object prefix, for example, a-ri-kɪ̱[syá̱] 'he will grind it$_7$', na va-kɪ̱[syí̱] 'they will grind it$_7$'. The reason for this different treatment of CV toneless stems lies in the fact that with this melodic pattern, the OP has an H, whereas the OP usually does not bear an H when there is a melodic tone. In other words, a preceding H has a blocking effect on mapping of the melodic tone.

The habitual follows this tone pattern, though owing to the presence of the suffix -aa, the significance of the level H on the penult (máá ꜜkó[déékaa] 'we usually cook') cannot be assessed.

(39)	a.	máá ꜜkú[gʊ̱́raa]	'we usually buy'
		máá ꜜkú[gʊ̱́rizaa]	'we usually sell'
		máá ꜜkú[há̱ándiikaa]	'we usually write'
	b.	máá ꜜkó[vé̱gaa]	'we usually shave'
		máá ꜜkó[dé̱ékaa]	'we usually cook'
		máá ꜜkú[ká̱raangaa]	'we usually fry'
		máá ꜜvá[tʊ̱́ʊ́ngamiɲaa]	'they usually invert'

4.6. Melody 5: Imperatives

A fifth tone pattern is found in bare imperatives, that is, those having no prefixes. That pattern is almost the same as the M2 tone pattern. H verbs have a final H that spreads to the left, the root H is deleted, and short stems also delete the melodic H.[12]

(40)	[rya̱]	'eat!'
	[ve̱ga̱]	'shave!'
	[ro̱otá̱]	'dream!'
	[za̱azámá̱]	'taste!'
	[fʊ̱nyíírízá̱]	'smell!'
	[gɪ̱rʊ́ʊ́ngányá̱]	'turn!'
	[tʊ̱ng'ámíɲánínání̱]	'invert for e.o!'

Toneless verbs, on the other hand, have no H at all.

(41)	[sya]	'grind!'
	[gona]	'sleep!'
	[sooma]	'read!'
	[seembera]	'cultivate!'
	[vʊrʊganya]	'stir!'

When followed by another word, the melodic H of H verbs is deleted, just as we found is possible (but tense-specific) with the M2 pattern, and if the following word has H, H spreads up to—excluding—the root-initial syllable. H spreads to the beginning of a toneless verb.

(42)	a.	gʊ́rá gárá̱ha	'buy slowly!'
		gávʊ́rá gárá̱ha	'divide slowly!'
	b.	ve̱ga vwaangʊ	'shave quickly!'
		ka̱raanga vwaangʊ	'fry quickly!'
		ve̱gá gárá̱ha	'shave slowly!'
		ka̱ráángá gárá̱ha	'fry slowly!'

The derivation of the imperative pattern thus reduces to the M2 pattern, except that across-the-board loss of the melodic H in toneless stems is unique to the imperative.

4.7. Melody 6: Double H

Finally, some tenses select a representationally distinct melody with two Hs. We encountered a limited version of a double H pattern in section 4.3.4, in the continuous tense of H verbs with an OP. This section investigates tenses where a similar pattern is found more broadly. The similarity in these tenses is partial, and there are significant difference in where the first tone of this pattern is mapped.

4.7.1. Imperative with OP

When an imperative has an object prefix, the segmental form of the verb switches to that of the subjunctive with the final suffix /-e/, but lacking a subject prefix. Lexical tone is obliterated so H and toneless verbs behave alike: there is H on the final vowel, and another H on the second stem syllable if there are at least three syllables in the stem.

(43)	a.	ga[syí̱]	'grind it$_6$'
		ji[gʊré̱]	'buy them$_4$'
		ko[roondé̱]	'follow us'
		ji[varíꜝzí̱]	'count them$_4$'
		kɪ[haandíꜝíkí̱]	'write it$_7$'
		kʊ[haandííꜝkírí̱]	'write for us'
		va[vʊrʊ́ꜝgányírí̱]	'stir$_{pl}$ for them$_2$'
	b.	ga[nwé̱]	'drink it$_6$'
		va[rʊ̱mí̱]	'bite them$_2$'
		ke[de̱eké̱]	'cook it$_7$'
		ko[ve̱géꜝré̱]	'shave for us'
		kɪ[ka̱ráꜝángé̱]	'fry it$_7$'
		vi[tʊ̱míꜝránírí̱]	'send$_{pl}$ them$_8$ for e.o'
		ga[ka̱ráꜝángírání̱]	'fry$_{pl}$ them$_6$ for e.o'
		kɪ[za̱azáꜝmírání̱]	'taste$_{pl}$ it$_7$ for e.o'

4.7.2. Relative Tenses

While verbs in relative clauses in Logoori are generally the same as verbs in main clauses, in some cases they have a special pattern. The subject relative of the recent perfective is an example (see section 4.3.3 for the pattern in main clauses). The examples in (44) show that this tense selects a double H pattern (gloss 'the people who V').

(44)	a.	avááándʊ va[shíꜝí̱]	'. . . ground'
		avááándʊ va[gʊ́ꜝrí̱]	'. . . bought'
		avááándʊ va[róóꜝtí̱]	'. . . dreamed'
		avááándʊ va[gʊ́ꜝrízí̱]	'. . . sold'
		avááándʊ va[hííꜝríítí̱]	'. . . snored'
		avááándʊ va[nwí̱ꜝí̱]	'. . . drank'
	b.	avááándʊ va[rá̱ꜝsí̱]	'. . . threw'
		avááándʊ va[dé̱éꜝchí̱]	'. . . cooked'

	aváándʊ va[vʊ̱́ꜜrʊ́gányɪ̱́]	'. . . stirred'
	aváándʊ va[vɔ̱́ꜜdɔ́ng'ánɪ̱́]	'. . . went around'
c.	aváándʊ va-kɪ̱́ꜜ[háándííchí]	'. . . wrote it$_7$'
	aváándʊ va-kʊ̱́ꜜ[ká̱ráángíríí]	'. . . fried for us'

The same pattern is found in the continuous subject relative (gloss 'the people who are V').

(45)	a.	aváándʊ va[vá̱ꜜgárá̱á̱]	'. . . spreading'
		aváándʊ va[há̱áꜜndííká̱á̱]	'. . . writing'
	b.	aváándʊ va[hɪ̱́ɪ́ꜜmá̱á̱]	'. . . hunting'
		aváándʊ va[ká̱ꜜráángá̱á̱]	'. . . frying'
	c.	aváándʊ va-kɪ̱́ꜜ[há̱ándííká̱á̱]	'. . . writing it$_7$'
		aváándʊ va-kɪ̱́ꜜ[ká̱ráángá̱á̱]	'. . . frying it$_7$'

A significant difference between the double H pattern of relative verbs and that of the imperative with OP in (43) centers around the assignment of the first H. The initial H appears on the OP if there is one, and on the root-initial vowel otherwise. A morphophonological constituent "macrostem," which begins with the OP if there is one and otherwise with the root-initial syllable, is generally recognized in Bantu (Hyman and Ngunga 1994). Thus we can say that the first H appears at the beginning of the macrostem. In the OP imperative, on the other hand, the initial H is on the second stem vowel.

4.8. Conclusion

We have seen that the concept of abstracting tone patterns from segmental content is utterly essential to an analysis of verb inflection in Logoori. However, these patterns have evaded analysis in purely representational terms—it is not enough to say that a certain tense adds an H, or two Hs, one must say what happens when these tones are added. Not only must one specify a particular target of initial association, a fact that has been well known throughout the history of autosegmental analysis of Bantu tone, one must say what that melodic tone does to other tones.

Notes

Versions of this chapter have been presented at numerous venues over the past decade. I would like to thank numerous colleagues for their insightful comments as this project has progressed, especially Michael Marlo, who started the Logoori project with me in 2004. I owe a prominent debt of gratitude to my Logoori consultants, especially Rose Kamwesa and Editon Mulera, whose dialect is represented here. Research for this chapter was supported in part by National Science Foundation Grant BCS-1355750. The name of the language is [llógoori], and it is known variously as Llogooli, Llogori, Logoori, Luragoli, Maragoli, among others.

1. Leung's data generally agrees with ours, but there are a number of empirical divergences.
2. Although Logoori has only two surface tonal distinctions, H and non-H, there is evidence that surface non-H realizes both toneless and specified L. Specified L only plays a role in blocking leftward spreading of H and is usually predictable based on underlying H tone, which is deleted/lowered.
3. Lexically H-toned vowels are indicated in this chapter by single underlining, and the initial association position of melodic H, which signals a particular tense, is indicated via double-underlining. Stems themselves are enclosed in brackets. Thus in nava[zá̲ázá̳mé] 'they will taste', the stem is zaazame, based on the root zaazam, which has an underlying H tone on the first vowel and an inflectional melodic H on the penult. When there are both melodic and lexical Hs on the same tone-bearing unit, the lexical tone is the one that is marked.
4. Whenever two Hs are concatenated, either one of the Hs deletes, or they are separated by a downstep.
5. Subscripted numerals indicate the noun class of the pronominal referent.
6. These and other examples of finite verbs exemplify the systematic blocking of leftward spread by the subject prefix. There is independent evidence that subject prefixes have underlying H, including the fact that H appears on the phrase preceding the verb.
7. The neutral variants are discussed in sections 4.3.2 and 4.3.3.
8. By analogy to maní vá[vi̲táná̳] one expects *maní vá[de̲éká̳], but there are no rising tones in the language.
9. The suffix is overtly [-i] in most contexts; it also appears as a long vowel after a vowel-final stem and causes the deletion of final /r/ in certain contests.
10. There is speaker variation in this respect: some speakers assign the M2 lexically H pattern to both H and toneless roots. This variant is not discussed here.
11. Notice in analogous forms of the hesternal perfective in (23d), such as ndaa-vi̲[rʊ̲́mi], that only a single H appears, as is the general case with M2—this exception is limited to continuous verb forms.
12. When the subject of the imperative is plural, the final suffix is -i rather than -a.

References

Cheng, C-C., and Charles Kisseberth. 1979. Ikorovere Makua tonology (part 1). *Studies in the Linguistic Sciences* 9, no. 1: 31–64.

Clements, G. N. 1984. Principles of tone assignment in Kikuyu. In Clements and Goldsmith 1984a, 281–339.

Clements, G. N., and John Goldsmith, eds. 1984a. *Autosegmental Studies in Bantu Tone*. Dordrecht: Foris Publications.

———. 1984b. Autosegmental studies in Bantu tone: Introduction. In Clements and Goldsmith 1984a, 1–17.

Ebarb, Kristopher. 2014. Tone and variation in Idakho and other Luhya varieties. PhD dissertation, Indiana University.

Ebarb, Kristopher, Christopher Green, and Michael R. Marlo. 2014. Luyia tone melodies. *Africana Linguistica* 20:121–143.

Goldsmith, John. 1976. Autosegmental phonology. PhD dissertation, Massachusetts Institute of Technology. Bloomington: Indiana University Linguistics Club. http://people.cs.uchicago.edu/~jagoldsm/Papers/dissertation.pdf. Published by Garland Press, New York [1979].

———. 1984. Meeussen's rule. In *Language Sound Structure*, ed. Mark Aronoff and Richard T. Oehrle, 245–259. Cambridge, MA: MIT Press.

———. 1987. Stem tone patterns of the lacustrine Bantu languages. In *Current Approaches to African Linguistics*, vol. 4, ed. David Odden, 175–185. Dordrecht: Foris Publications.

———. 1991. Tone and accent in Llogori. *Afrikanistische Arbeitspapiere* 25:7–30.

Hyman, Larry, and Armindo Ngunga. 1994. On the non-universality of tonal association conventions: Evidence from Ciyao. *Phonology* 11:25–68.

Leung, Elizabeth. 1986. A phonological study of the Llogoori language of Kenya. MA thesis, Cornell University.

———. 1991. *The Tonal Phonology of Llogoori: A Study of Llogoori Verbs*. Working Papers of the Cornell Phonetics Laboratory 6. Ithaca, NY: CLC Publications.

Marlo, Michael R. 2013. Verb tone in Bantu languages: Micro-typological patterns and research methods. *Africana Linguistica* 19:137–234.

Meeussen, A. E. 2014. Tones of the subjunctive and the imperative in Bantu. *Africana Linguistica* 20:15–28.

Odden, David. 1984. Stem tone assignment in Shona. In Clements and Goldsmith 1984a, 255–280.

———. 2014. Melodic tones in Karanga Shona. *Africana Linguistica* 20:331–348.

Odden, David, and Lee Bickmore. 2014. Melodic tone in Bantu: Overview. *Africana Linguistica* 20:3–13.

C. Extensions of the Theory

FIVE

Autosegments Are Not Just Features

D. ROBERT LADD

5.1. Introduction

Because a great deal of my career has been devoted to the study of intonation, I have often had occasion to wonder about the relation between the simultaneous and the sequential in language. Syllables follow syllables and words follow words: there is something essentially one-dimensional about speaking. But speaking also involves the precise coordination of several semi-independent physical systems, and some of what is conveyed by an utterance (such as question contours and emphatic accents) is conveyed not sequentially, but in parallel with other parts of the message. Modeling utterances as strings of elements is therefore fundamentally inadequate in some way that we still struggle to make sense of.

In 2006 I obtained financial support for a leave of absence that was to allow me time to explore the relation between the simultaneous and the sequential and write a book about it. My hope was that I could find a connection between low-level phenomena such as the coordination of multiple articulators in speech and higher-level ones such as the coordination between parallel streams of information in intonation and text. I did eventually produce a short monograph (Ladd 2014) in which I brought together various reflections on these issues, but I never really felt that I had achieved the aim of figuring out in some new way how these apparently contradictory aspects of language structure coexist and complement each other.

For one thing, in the course of writing the book I found that I spent a lot of time thinking about purely phonological issues. Perhaps this is because sound structure provides the most obvious example of the difficulty of idealizing utterances as strings. Many beginning linguistics courses work primarily with a segment-based description of phonetics—IPA transcription, phonemes and allophones, and so on—yet at the same time often encourage students to think about the way the articulators (vocal folds, velum, tongue tip, etc.) are in continuous motion. The incompatibility between these two ways of thinking about phonetic reality—what Laver (1994) called the "linear" and the "parametric"—is seldom confronted, certainly not in Linguistics 101.

The closest the field has come to dealing with this contradiction is the massive literature on phonological features. Feature theory is fundamentally an attempt at formalizing the relation between the simultaneous and the sequential, and features inevitably became a focus of my work on the monograph. As a result, I found myself repeatedly coming back to ideas that John Goldsmith had articulated in his PhD thesis some forty years earlier (Goldsmith 1976). I also came to realize that his ideas had largely been cast aside by subsequent developments, and the first half-chapter of my monograph ended up as an attempt to show why moving away from Goldsmith's early insights was a step in the wrong direction.

I can think of few more convincing ways to celebrate a scholar's achievements than to make the case that they were right and that what came after them was wrong, so I have decided that the most appropriate contribution I can make to this volume is simply to reprint what I said in that half-chapter. Except for a few minor emendations for continuity or consistency of style and for keeping references up-to-date, I have changed nothing. The evaluation implicit in the discussion speaks for itself.

5.2. Features: Particles or Attributes?

I begin by examining the role of features in classical generative phonology, as set forth by Chomsky and Halle in *The Sound Pattern of English* (1968; henceforth *SPE*). The Chomsky-Halle model is based on the system of phonological and phonetic representation that was developed by Jakobson, Fant, and Halle (1952; henceforth JFH). The model's crucial characteristic, for our present interests, is that it sharply distinguishes between the sequential and the simultaneous—or, more accurately, between the ordered and the unordered. The stream of speech is idealized as an ordered string of phonemes or segments, each of which is a bundle of concurrent unordered features. In JFH we read: "A speech message carries information in two dimensions. On the one hand, distinctive features are superposed upon each other, i.e., act concurrently (lumped into phonemes), and, on the other, they succeed each other in a time series" (p. 3). In *SPE* we read: "The phonetic representation consists of a sequence of 'phonetic segments,' each of which is nothing other than a set of 'phonetic feature specifications' . . . [A] phonetic representation is a 'phonetic matrix' in which the columns correspond to segments and the rows to features and in which each entry states the extent to which a given segment possesses the corresponding feature" (p. 164). There are minor differences between the JFH version and the *SPE* version, but both versions share the assumption that there is a fundamental distinction between segments, which are ordered with respect to one another, and features, which "act concurrently."

The JFH/*SPE* idealization is very clear about the existence of segments and seems very clear about the relation between segments and features. In this respect it simply does not make any provisions for the kinds of phenomena that concerned people such as J. R. Firth or Zellig Harris in the 1940s and 1950s—"prosodies" (Firth 1948), "long components" (Harris 1944), and the like. (In fact, Postal [1968: 93–94] explicitly argued against Harris's notion of long components, though on somewhat different grounds.) At the same time, though, the idealization is compatible with two quite different understandings of the features themselves. As we shall see, these two different conceptions of the feature suggest very different approaches once we start to deal with "prosodic" questions.

Consider the distinctive feature representation of the word *pin* shown in table 5.1. The horizontal dimension shows the temporally ordered sequence of phonological segments, while the vertical dimension specifies, for each segment, the values of the various phonological features that define it. Such two-dimensional matrices are presented in JFH (pp. 44–45) and are discussed (and sometimes illustrated; e.g., Harms 1968: 14; Schane 1973: 41–42) in early textbook presentations of generative phonology. Yet different textbook presentations treat the significance of such representations in rather different terms. Some contain

Table 5.1 Jakobsonian feature representation of English *pin* given by Harms (1968: 14)

	/p	ɪ	n/
consonantal	+	–	+
vocalic	–	+	–
nasal	–	0	+
continuant	–	0	0
grave	+	–	–
diffuse	+	+	0
tense	0	–	0
voice	–	0	0

passages implying that features are "things" and segments merely composite or even epiphenomenal—at most, convenient abbreviations for bundles of features:

The fundamental unit of generative phonology is the distinctive feature. . . . The phoneme—specifically, the systematic phoneme—clearly has a secondary status, but, for matters of presentation, it is frequently convenient to refer to phonemes as the underlying segments used to designate or "spell" morphemes. (Harms 1968: 1)

Although the phonological rules in Chapter 1 are all written in terms of segments, such notation is actually only an abbreviation. . . . [S]ymbols such as *p, t, k, a, i, u* are used as convenient shortcuts for the feature compositions which combine to produce these segments. (Hyman 1975: 24–25)

Others go out of their way to emphasize the primacy of segments and separately note that segments can be given a systematic description in terms of features. Schane, for example, says this in his first chapter ("The Segment"):

Although a speech signal may be physically *continuous*, we seem to perceive it as a sequence of *discrete* entities. That utterances can be represented as a sequence of discrete units is one of the basic theoretical assumptions of phonology. Because of this assumption we are able to talk about individual segments and sequences of segments. (Schane 1973: 3)

It is not until his third chapter ("Distinctive Features") that he shows how "it is advantageous to view segments as composed of sets of properties rather than as indivisible entities" (Schane 1973: 25). In the same way, Kenstowicz and Kisseberth (1979) take a page and a half to summarize the "prima facie evidence for the discrete segment hypothesis," citing such things as the invention and successful spread of alphabetic writing, the existence of segment-based speech errors such as spoonerisms, and "phonological operations" such as metathesis. Only then do they go on to say that "in addition to analyzing an utterance into a string of segments, generative phonologists have assumed that each segment is represented as a matrix of phonetic features which describe the articulatory and acoustic properties of the segment" (Kenstowicz and Kisseberth 1979: 238–239).

The difference between these two interpretations of segments betrays a crucial tension in the feature concept as it has developed since the 1930s. In *Principles* ([1939] 1958), Trubetzkoy began with segments—*Lautgebilde* or 'phones'—and his theory of distinctive oppositions was intended to describe the ways in which the segments of a given language enter into complex relationships with other segments. Trubetzkoyan oppositions are characterized in phonetic terms that describe various *Eigenschaften* (properties or attributes) of segments. These feature-based descriptions of segments are based primarily on the dimensions of IPA classification. Among other things, this means that Trubetzkoyan oppositions can be of different types (privative, equipollent, or continuous), depending on the phonetic nature of the classifying dimension. In certain cases (notably privative oppositions such as voicing or nasalization) the phonetic property on which an opposition is based can be described as the presence or absence of a specific *Merkmal* (mark or feature), but in other cases (such as the continuous oppositions of vowel height) the phonetic property refers to the position of a given segment type along some abstract dimension. The segment remains primary.

As is well known, Jakobson's subsequent work on feature theory treats all oppositions as binary—in Trubetzkoyan terms, as privative—and consequently assumes that they are based on the presence or absence of some *Merkmal*. *Merkmal* is now the standard German term for the technical linguistic sense of feature. *Eigenschaft* and *Merkmal* can both easily be translated by the English word *feature*, but they differ in concreteness: an *Eigenschaft* is an abstract characteristic (like English *feature* in collocations such as *the unusual feature of this theory* or *the best feature of her presentation*), whereas *Merkmal* often applies to actual physical objects (like English *feature* in expressions such as *features of the landscape* or *delicate facial features*). In the case of phonetic segments, *Merkmal* can be used for actual phonetic events or states such as velic opening or voicing. A similar difference exists in French between *caractéristique* (which is the term used for *Eigenschaft* in the French translation of *Principles*) and *trait* (which is now the standard French term for feature in linguistics). Although the distinction seems subtle, the shift from *Eigenschaft* to *Merkmal* and the accompanying reinterpretation of oppositions as privative represents a substantial reorientation of Trubetzkoy's original notion of the feature. In what follows I will use the English terms *attribute* and *particle* to convey the sense of the two terms.

The attribute/particle ambiguity remained largely hidden in the theoretical context of *SPE*. There was no explicit discussion of the issue, and, so far as I am aware, no sense that (say) Hyman's (1975) textbook was propounding a different view from Kenstowicz and Kisseberth's (1979). This was largely because the theory continued to assume the existence of segments and to work with a completely sequential segmented idealization of the phonological structure of utterances. But that began to change in the 1970s with the advent of autosegmental phonology, the first attempt within the JFH/*SPE* tradition to deal with broadly "prosodic" phenomena such as tone. As soon as this work raised questions about the nature (or the very existence) of segments, the unresolved questions about the nature of features quickly surfaced.

5.3. The Rise and Fall of the Autosegment

To set autosegmental phonology in context, I need to summarize first how "prosody" was accommodated in the JFH/*SPE* idealization. The JFH theory assumes that there are two types of features, which are referred to as "inherent" and "prosodic" features. Inherent features are the ones we normally think of when we think of features—things such as [voice] and [continuant] and [coronal]—which correspond to acoustic properties that can be identified in the signal at the idealized point in time corresponding to a given segmental phoneme. Prosodic features, as the name suggests, include features of stress, tone, and duration. Unlike inherent features, these are said to require reference to at least two different points in a time series, such as a difference between a stressed and an unstressed vowel, or between a low-pitched point in time and a high-pitched one. (See Ladd 2014, chapter 3 for further discussion.) However, both kinds of features share the same abstract relation to the phoneme: "The latter [i.e., prosodic features] are superposed upon the former [i.e., inherent features] and are lumped together with them into phonemes" (JFH, p. 13). That is, for JFH, the bundle of features corresponding to a given phoneme includes prosodic properties as well as inherently segmental ones. Chomsky and Halle simply assumed this view in *SPE*, treating stress features as features of vowels along with [high] and [back] and [tense] and so on (*SPE*, chapter 3). Naturally, Chomsky and Halle did not deal with lexical tone, because *SPE* is about English, and they said nothing about intonation, as they acknowledged (p. ix). But it is clear (e.g., pp. 68, 329) that their conception of prosodic features is essentially that of JFH, and in this way, the JFH view became the standard classical generative view.

In the wake of *SPE*'s publication in 1968, phonologists began testing the *SPE* idealizations against a variety of language data. It was quickly pointed out that many African tonal systems involve phenomena that are conspicuously incompatible with *SPE*'s theoretical framework. In particular, the association of two tones to one syllable or one tone to two syllables, which is common in West Africa, is at odds with the *SPE* idea that tones are features of vowels, bundled with inherent features such as [high] and [back]. The most influential statements of this problem were a paper by Williams (1976 [first circulated 1971]) and PhD theses by Leben (1973) and Goldsmith (1976); Goldsmith gave the name "autosegmental phonology" to the line of theoretical work that dealt with this and related phenomena. Both Leben and Goldsmith worked toward a way of defining tones as segments that are comparable in most respects to consonants and vowels but do not fit into an ordered string. Both were attempting to escape from the strictures of the idealization in which phonological elements have to be either totally ordered feature bundles or unordered features within a bundle.[1]

The main representational device used by autosegmental phonology to go beyond *SPE* was the idea of distinct *tiers* of phonological elements. In the case of tone, the linearly arranged consonants and vowels might constitute one tier, while the string of tones would constitute another, and the two tiers could then be linked together in well-specified ways in the overall representation of a word or phrase. The theory takes its name from the term *autosegment*, which was proposed by Goldsmith to refer to the elements on tiers separate from the main tier of segments. With this idea, early autosegmental phonology seems to have been on the verge of extending *SPE*'s theory of phonological representations in a genuinely new direction, allowing for the possibility of phonological elements that are *neither features nor segments*. Goldsmith stated this goal very clearly in his thesis: "Our object, ultimately, will be to produce a notion of 'suprasegmentals' which makes specific predictions about the behavior of these elements. We shall try to show real differences between features *per se* and supra- (or auto-) segmentals. . . . Features by themselves do not spread; they merely identify a segment for what it is" (1976: 12).

Goldsmith explicitly endorsed something like the understanding of phonological representations expressed in Schane's (1973) or Kenstowicz and Kisseberth's (1979) textbooks, quoted earlier in this section. He took it as "axiomatic that the phonological system of a language is composed of a small number of *atomic* segments; each segment is *defined by* several feature specifications, but these segments act, in general, like discrete, atomic units" (Goldsmith 1976: 158; emphasis added). Segments, in other words, are not merely convenient abbreviations, but are rather the atoms of phonology; features are the attributes that define the place of any segment in the overall sound system. The autosegment was intended to be an entity whose manifestation in the phonetics seemed to favor treating it as a feature—an attribute of some segment—but whose function in the phonology suggested that it was some sort of segment in its own right.

But the particle view of the feature was in the ascendant. Autosegmental research rapidly became increasingly focused on the problem of the temporal coordination of features, implicitly abandoning the anchor of the segmental string. This came about because other investigators immediately seized on the idea of association between autosegments as a way of representing both nonlocal dependencies in phonology (notably vowel harmony) and local sandhi effects (notably assimilation). The idea of applying autosegmental representations to vowel harmony appears to have been suggested by Clements at the same time as Goldsmith was developing his ideas on tonal phonology (e.g., Clements 1980 [first circulated 1976]), and is briefly discussed by Goldsmith in his thesis (1976: 150–154). However, Clements's proposals were part of a more general program of research into what he called the "geometry" of phonological features (Clements 1985), which quickly led (e.g., Hayes 1986) to the rapid acceptance of "feature spreading" as the mainstream generative account of such things as the place assimilation in *ten past* [ˌtɛmˈpast], as shown in (1). The place features associated only with the labial stop at the beginning of *past* in (1a) may spread so that they are linked to both the labial stop and the preceding nasal in (1b) and (1c); the features associated with the nasal at the end of *ten* in (1a) may either remain linked to it (1b) or may be completely delinked (1c).

(1)

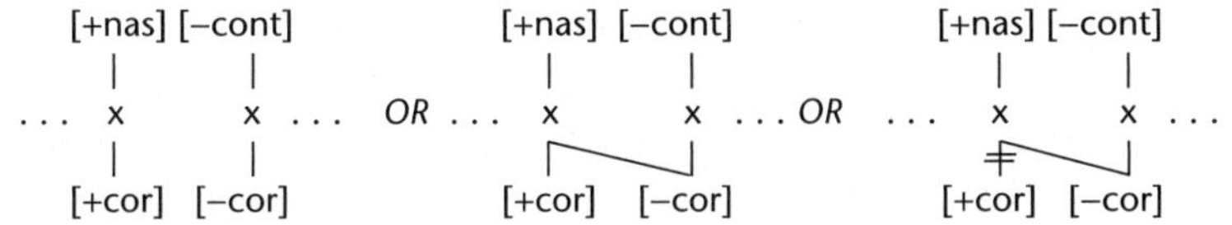

(a) unassimilated (b) partial assimilation (c) full assimilation

The basic idea of feature spreading had been around since the early 1970s (Daniloff and Hammarberg 1973; see also Fowler 1980), but the feature-based treatment of assimilation, like feature geometry more generally, struck many researchers as an obvious extension of the basic autosegmental idea. It clearly connected autosegmental theorizing to the ideas behind Harris's (1944) "long components" in phonology. It built on the increasing recognition of the physical continuousness of speech, which came about as instrumental phonetic data, especially acoustic data, rapidly became easier to collect and analyze in the 1980s. And it was broadly in harmony with a number of other fairly distinct post-*SPE* theoretical approaches such as "particle phonology" (Schane 1984), "government phonology" (Harris 1990; Kaye, Lowenstamm, and Vergnaud 1990), and "dependency phonology" (Anderson and Ewen 1987; van der Hulst 1989), all of which endeavored to understand phonology in terms of primitives that are in some sense smaller than segments. But it directly contradicts Goldsmith's explicit statements (1976: 13) that there may be a distinction "between a rule of feature-assimilation . . . and true spreading of a suprasegmental element," and that it is "a feature's behavior with respect to phonological rules that gives it away as suprasegmental, not any phonetic facts."

More importantly, treating assimilation as feature spreading removes any motivation for positing autosegments as a special phonological construct in the first place! If any feature can be multiply associated, then the multiple association of tones to syllables in West African languages is unremarkable. The relation between tones and syllables becomes just another aspect of the more general problem of the temporal coordination of features. The theoretical conundrum confronted by Leben (1973) and Goldsmith (1976) evaporates, and "autosegment" becomes equivalent to "feature." This consequence was recognized by Duanmu (1990: 13), who pointed out that "with the development of feature geometry . . . the idea of 'autosegment' has lost much content."[2] Instead, theorists began to take for granted that the structural behavior covered by the term is something that applies to all phonological features. This assumption is sufficiently uncontroversial that Kornai, in discussing the mathematical foundations of linguistics, explicitly treated the terms "autosegment" and "feature" as equivalent (Kornai 2008: 233). Similarly, Kenstowicz, in summary course notes, stated that "the study of tone in African [languages] raised serious conceptual problems for the representation of the phoneme as a bundle of distinctive features" and that "the solution to the problem (autosegmental representations) became a model for all other features" (Kenstowicz 2010).

5.4. Further Implications of Feature Spreading

If there were now broad agreement that feature spreading is the most appropriate treatment of assimilation (and if there were, by implication, agreement on the particle interpretation of features), the foregoing discussion would be of historical interest only. In fact, however, phenomena such as assimilation lie at the heart of a good deal of current debate about the relation between phonological abstractions and phonetic detail.

The central question is whether feature spreading is in principle an appropriate model of assimilation. Feature spreading notation can represent a small and discrete number of patterns of multiple association (e.g., partial and full assimilation; cf. Clements 1985), but it provides no ready way of expressing a continuous range of degrees of assimilation. It now appears that many phenomena of assimilation, deletion, and neutralization actually involve such continuous ranges of phonetic detail (e.g., Nolan 1992; Zsiga 1997). This means that some of the central phenomena for which feature geometry representations were developed might be more accurately and appropriately described by a quantitative physical model in which speech gestures can overlap to a greater or lesser extent. This is not to suggest that gestural overlap is the only basis for assimilation. Some studies seem to show that some cases of assimilation are phonologized and that in such cases gestural overlap is probably irrelevant to the phonetic detail (e.g., Ellis and Hardcastle 2002; Ladd and Scobbie 2003; Kochetov and Pouplier 2008). Others suggest that some cases of assimilation may involve complex patterns of modification of phonetic realization in specific segments; for example, Hallé and Adda-Decker (2010) found that voicing assimilation in French obstruent sequences may categorically affect the voicing of the affected segment while leaving various other phonetic details such as closure duration unchanged (cf. also Warner et al. [2004] on durational effects in final devoicing in Dutch). In short, gestural overlap may represent only one of a number of possibilities found in assimilation. The more general point here, however, is that the phonetic detail of assimilation appears too complex to be described in terms of a small inventory of particle-like features that are categorically either linked or not linked to segmental positions.

This raises the more fundamental question of whether symbolic representations such as feature geometry diagrams are ever suited to describing continuous physical phenomena such as speech. An early statement of this issue is Martin Joos's attempt to explain linguistics to telephone engineers (Joos 1950: 701): "Physicists describe speech with continuous mathematics, such as Fourier analysis or the autocorrelation function. Linguists describe language instead, using a discontinuous or discrete mathematics called 'linguistics.'" Essentially the same terms are used in a similar context half a century later by Kornai (1994: 22): "In the current academic division of labor, the cognitive aspects of speech are studied under the heading of *phonology*, while the physical aspects, including the biological mechanisms employed in speech perception and production, are studied under the heading of *phonetics*. The formal apparatus of these two fields reflects their primary concerns: phonologists tend to employ graphs, automata, rewrite rules, and other tools of discrete mathematics, while phoneticians prefer Fourier analysis, differential equations, and other tools of continuous mathematics." Both Joos and Kornai seemed to accept that discrete and continuous descriptions will both be required in a full account of how language is manifested in speech; the problem, of course, is deciding which phenomena need which kind of treatment. (For some discussion, see, e.g., Pierrehumbert 1990; Pierrehumbert, Beckman, and Ladd 2000; Smolensky, Goldrick, and Mathis 2014.) In this light, we might see the problem with modeling assimilation as feature spreading as being a matter of applying the wrong sort of model. Some of the puzzles and paradoxes of "precedence" that have taxed autosegmental theorists (e.g., Sagey 1988; Raimy 2000) probably arise at least in part from trying to use nonquantitative symbolic abstractions to describe details of physical phenomena (though see Kornai [1993] for a formal approach to this issue).

Perhaps the most serious problem with any particle interpretation of the feature is that it drastically changes the status of the segment without addressing the issue explicitly. The phenomena that motivate the segment idealization did not suddenly evaporate between the mid-1970s and the mid-1980s. The evidence summarized by Kenstowicz and Kisseberth (1979) and taken for granted by Goldsmith (1976) still needs to be accounted for in any overall theory of phonological structure. As long as features are seen as attributes of segments—as in Trubetzkoy's original conception—the segment idealization is unaffected. When features become multiply linked particles that are taken to be the atoms of phonological representations, though, conspicuous theoretical contradictions arise, and these remain unaddressed. Within autosegmental phonology, the need to allow for some sort of sequential segmentation led to notions such as the "root tier" (McCarthy 1981; Clements 1985) or the "CV tier" (Clements and Keyser 1983). This in turn allowed many theoretical phonologists to continue to focus on essentially segmental issues such as underspecification (e.g., Archangeli 1988, Hyman 1988). It also meant that feature geometry could be seen as being less about the phonetic independence of features and more about their hierarchical organization. For example, Vago (1988: 347) described feature geometry as "a model of *segment structure* in which features are hierarchically organized" (emphasis added), which at best glosses over the fact that feature geometry also makes it very difficult to say exactly what segments are. This contradiction within the field became even more pronounced with the development of optimality theory (Prince and Smolensky 2004 [first circulated 1993]). Optimality theory's entire architecture is based on segments, and many optimality theory analyses are still eminently compatible with the idea that features are attributes rather than particles.

So here we are back in the first week of Linguistics 101, with two apparently irreconcilable ways of thinking about phonology and phonetics. In the long run, we cannot continue to develop two central theoretical abstractions—the segment and the feature—in incompatible and contradictory directions. I believe that the field missed an opportunity when it began to identify autosegments with features; something like Goldsmith's original idea can and should be rehabilitated. We can see this by taking a fresh look at the nature of tone.

5.5. The Autosegment Redux: Temporal Sequence versus Abstract Order

Tone remains the most obvious challenge to any understanding of how the sequential and the simultaneous coexist in phonology, and it will be useful to step outside Western ways of thinking by considering the traditional Chinese approach to describing it. In the JFH/*SPE* view, segments are linearly ordered, and features are unordered; since tone is manifestly not linearly ordered, it is treated as a feature. The Chinese tradition, though, treats tone as comparable to elements that are roughly comparable to segments. In the traditional Chinese analysis of syllables, syllables consist of an "initial" (=onset), a "final" (=rime), and a tone (e.g., Chao and Yang 1962; Chen 2000). Initials are usually single segments in Western terms. The Chinese tradition lacks anything exactly like the phoneme concept, and finals sometimes consist—by standard Western phonological conventions—of two or even three phonemes, such as /aŋ/ or /uei/. But it is clear that finals are not at all like JFH features, and that on the whole initials and finals are more like segments than like features.[3] It therefore seems accurate to say that the Chinese tradition treats tones as being on a par with elements that are comparable to segments.

However, by saying that initial, final, and tone are the "segments" of which syllables are composed, the Chinese tradition implies something noteworthy about the way segments can be arranged. The segments of the Chinese tradition enter into a richer set of structural configurations than the phoneme-sized segments of the JFH/*SPE* view; formally speaking, the Chinese tradition is based on a partial ordering rather than a total ordering. Within each syllable, some pairs of segments are ordered (initials precede finals) while others are not (tones neither precede nor follow initials or finals). The JFH/*SPE* view assumes a strict and total linear ordering of all the segments; the Chinese tradition does not. Importantly, we are dealing here with formal notions of "ordered" and "unordered," not with actual simultaneity or with sequences of events in real time. This ordering can be treated as a formal relation of precedence, as it is, for instance, in the series of natural integers. Among other things, this means that we do not equate lack of defined precedence (which is an abstract, formal notion) with simultaneity or co-occurrence in real time.

The JFH view and the Chinese view do share one key premise, which is that tones do not enter into precedence relations with vowels. However, in the Chinese view this is very specifically a fact about tones and about the internal structure of syllables; it does not follow from anything else. In effect, it is just a fact about the way tones work—by their nature they neither precede nor follow finals, which makes them different from initials and finals. In the JFH/*SPE* view, by contrast, the fact that tones do not enter into precedence relations with consonants and vowels entails that tone is a feature rather than a phoneme. That is, the JFH/*SPE* view starts from the common-sense understanding that, phonetically, tones occur simultaneously with vowel and/or consonant features, and then fits this into a formal model in the only way it can. Given the following set of premises:

1. Segments are formally bundles of features
2. Strict precedence relations are defined for all segments
3. No precedence relations are defined for features (i.e., features are formally unordered)
4. Tones do not enter into precedence relations with vowels and consonants

it is a *logical necessity* for the JFH/*SPE* model that tones must be treated as features rather than as segments. In the traditional Chinese view, by contrast, the treatment of tone is based on the way things are in Chinese: some segments are ordered, while others are not. Unordered segments do not become something else merely by virtue of being unordered.

This is the theoretical understanding that Goldsmith was attempting to establish with the notion of the autosegment. If we accept the traditional Chinese view that tones are like segments rather than like features, and if we consequently try to formalize the intuition behind the original notion of the autosegment, then we can treat the simultaneity of pitch and the nonsynchronization of phonetic correlates of features as separate issues. The essence of autosegments is not that they overlap with other segments in real time but that they are abstractly unordered *while still having some of the phonological characteristics of ordered segments.* The multiple associations of tones to syllables and syllables to tones is a manifestation of partial ordering: tones differ from vowel and consonant phonemes in that their precedence relations to consonants and vowels are undefined. Nonsynchronization of the phonetic correlates of features, by contrast, is a matter of physical activity. Tones are not normal segments, but neither are they features on a par with phonetic attributes such as labiality. Goldsmith was correct to insist in his early work that the question of whether a given phonetic property is to be regarded as an autosegment or a feature cannot simply be reduced to matters of phonetic detail. The way to overcome the limitations of an ordered linear representation of phonology is not simply to exchange it for a parametric one, but to allow a greater range of ordering relations into what is still essentially a segmented string.

Several things follow if we acknowledge that the autosegment is not simply equivalent to the feature. For one thing, it suggests that autosegmental behavior is a specific phenomenon, not just a subtype of feature spreading. If we go back to the original intuitions that motivated Leben and Goldsmith and avoid following the theoretical logic that led to feature geometry, we can pose research questions that have the potential to make the difference clear. For example, it seems useful to distinguish vowel harmony, in the languages that have it, from ordinary assimilation; the former is grammatical in a way that the latter need not be. (Nevins [2010] toyed with this conclusion in chapter 6 of his book on vowel harmony.) In the same way, there is a sense in which nasality is autosegmental in many Amazonian languages but not in European languages (for a good summary, see Aikhenvald 2012: sec. 3.5.1). Further research can help make clear what this intuitively attractive distinction means: it is possible that more accurate phonetic description will show that autosegmental behavior is qualitatively distinct from the assimilation that results from articulatory phenomena such as gestural overlap.

However, it is important not to think of unordered segments solely in terms of the spreading or simultaneous manifestation of phonetic features. For example, the concept seems likely to apply to the "feature-shuffling" described by Henderson (1985) for various languages of Southeast Asia (see also Matisoff 1994). Henderson noted that, in both historical change and synchronic variation, certain phonetic properties seem to remain constant at the level of the syllable, while (from a strictly IPA-segmental viewpoint) the individual consonants and vowels vary considerably. For example, she cited the Bwe Karen word for 'snake' as varying between [ɰu2] and [wi2], and explained:

> The canonical form of syllables (and most morphemes) in Bwe is CV. In this word the C is further specified as a back glide and the vowel as high. Granted that, one can see that the [features of] the syllable as a whole include "rounding" or "labiality," and "spreading." (Henderson 1985: 5)

In connection with a similar example, she said:

> I prefer . . . to think of the feature "roundness" as dealt out to the syllable, rather than to specific segments. The difference between the two forms is then seen to be one of temporal distribution or phasing. (Henderson 1985: 6)

I observed a case like this in the early lexical development of one of my children. His earliest form for 'shoes' was something like [ɯɸ], but as his vocabulary reached the fifty-word mark almost all of his words were reshaped to fit a CV template with no fricatives. When this happened, 'shoes' became something like [p^wi] and remained stable in this form for three or four months. The change from [ɯɸ] to [p^wi] is difficult to explain in a purely string-based phonological description, but makes sense if we see it in terms of the realization of unordered phonological elements: the labiality of the rounded vowel (and of the [ʃ] of the adult form) are manifested in the onset consonant, and the vowel height (and perhaps the coronality of the adult [z]) are manifested as [i].

The notion of unordered segments has recently been independently proposed by Julian Bradfield (2014) as a solution to a quite different phonological problem, namely the analysis of clicks in the Khoisan languages. In many of these languages, click sounds are generally accompanied by other phonetic substance, such as prevoicing, concomitant nasalization, and prominent postrelease aspiration. Until the publication of Traill's detailed work on !Xóõ (Traill 1985), it was usual to treat the combinations of click and accompaniment as unit phonemes that were analyzed as bundles of features. However, because of the fact that in Khoisan languages any click can generally combine with any accompaniment, these languages were often said to have eighty or a hundred consonant phonemes. Traill floated the alternative idea of treating the combinations as clusters of two separate phonemes. Analyzing the accompaniments as features of unit phonemes makes the phonological representation conform to JFH/*SPE* assumptions, but it requires a slew of otherwise unmotivated features and understates the phonological independence of the click and the accompaniment—in addition to making the phoneme inventory of these languages look unusually large. The cluster analysis reduces the inventory of phonemes considerably, accounts for various phonological regularities, and generally makes the overall phonological system look more normal. However, it raises issues of the relation between phonetic realization and phonological representation, because the accompaniments, far from being clearly sequential, often overlap in time with the click (see, e.g., Miller et al. 2009).

Once again, the problem is with theoretical assumptions. If we assume that every phonological unit must be either a segment or a feature, and if we assume the segments must be sequentially ordered, we have no choice but to treat the temporally overlapping accompaniments as features. In doing so, we are forced to ignore evidence about the phonological independence of accompaniments and clicks. Instead, what Bradfield (2014) proposed is to treat accompaniments as segments, but to leave the ordering relation between the accompaniment and the click undefined: borrowing a concept from computer science, he referred to the relation between the two as one of *concurrency*. Allowing for the rather different phonetic contexts, it appears that Bradfield's concurrent segments and my unordered segments are the same thing, and that both correspond to Goldsmith's (1976) original notion of autosegment. Since the ostensible theoretical issue between sequence and feature analyses of clicks is unrelated to feature spreading and is concerned instead with the phonological representation of complex articulatory events, it is significant that the idea of concurrent or unordered segments seems to apply to both. Khoisan clicks may therefore also provide us with another source of insight into what it means to be an autosegment.

5.6. Prospect

In closing, I want to emphasize that my concern with the fate of the autosegment since 1976 is not just an exercise in intellectual history. Much modern phonological theorizing deals almost exclusively with the form of phonological grammars and takes the representations manipulated by those grammars for granted. I think this is a mistake: representations matter.

The dichotomy between "theories of rules" and "theories of representations" in phonology was the unifying theme of Stephen Anderson's (1985) brilliant history of twentieth-century phonology. As Anderson noted, some of the most influential works of twentieth-century phonology (such as the derivational approach to morphophonemics in classical generative phonology) dealt primarily with "rules"—the grammar governing phonological phenomena, however it is conceived. Others (such as the Prague School notion of distinctive features) focused on "representations," which might be best characterized as abstractions away from actual phonetic activity, abstractions that reveal the implicit categories that give rise to phonological phenomena in the first place. So far, so good—but Anderson's presentation of the rules/representations dichotomy suggests that the balance between the two is primarily a matter of theory-internal coherence.

This point of view is deeply rooted in phonological thinking. Consider, for example, Paul Kiparsky's (1968) influential article "How Abstract Is Phonology?" Kiparsky asked whether the systematic phonemic representations of Chomsky and Halle (1968) are too "abstract"—abstract in the very specific sense of being remote from observable phonetic forms. Yet most of the considerations he brought to bear on this question dealt with the form of the phonological grammar that relates the abstract representations to the phonetic observations. For example, he proposed that phonological theory might prohibit rules of absolute neutralization, which allow systematic phonemic representations to be more abstract. In effect, his paper is a discussion of how to constrain the rules in order to limit the abstractness of the representations: the abstractness of representations is treated as little more than the consequence of theoretical decisions about the grammar, not something to be considered in its own right.

What I am suggesting here is that defining the elements of our representations is fundamental to any adequate account of phonology and is largely an independent enterprise from formulating phonological grammars. Specifically with regard to the autosegment, I have tried to show that by equating autosegment with feature, we have forgone important insights about the potential diversity of phonological objects and the ways they can be arranged. Sooner or later it will be necessary to recover those ideas.

Notes

1. The possibility of hierarchical relations among the features that characterize a segment is mentioned in several sources (e.g., Postal 1968: 61; *SPE*, p. 300), but this idea was not really developed until the emergence of the notion of feature geometry in the 1980s, discussed in this section.
2. Duanmu's observation is borne out by searching Google Scholar for the term "autosegment"; the vast majority of the citations are for articles published before about 1990. A Google n-gram charting the frequency of occurrence of the term in Google's text database shows a rapid rise from 1976 (when Goldsmith's thesis appeared) to a peak in 1985 (when Clements's feature geometry article appeared), then a rapid decline until the early 1990s followed by a continued slow decline ever since. Of the small number of citations since 1990, most deal with floating tones and similar phenomena, which would have been covered by Goldsmith's original definition of autosegment. This in itself suggests that there continues to be a need for such a theoretical construct.
3. One reason for treating initials and finals as comparable to segments is that it is straightforward to analyze them further in terms of features: the inventory of initials in particular shows extensive symmetries of the sort that feature analyses are intended to describe, and these symmetries play a role in the Chinese tradition. For example, they form the basis for the standard order of the *Zhùyīn fúhào* or 'bopomofo' characters used for writing words phonetically in Taiwan: similar sounds are grouped together (e.g., the labial initials *bo po mo fo*) and the same order is used within related groups (e.g., the rich set of sibilant initials is ordered into alveopalatal, retroflex, and alveolar groups and within each group the sounds are ordered by manner in the same way, namely unaspirated affricate, aspirated affricate, fricative).

References

Aikhenvald, Alexandra Y. 2012. *Languages of the Amazon*. Oxford: Oxford University Press.

Anderson, John, and Colin Ewen. 1987. *Principles of Dependency Phonology*. Cambridge: Cambridge University Press.

Anderson, Stephen R. 1985. *Phonology in the Twentieth Century: Theories of Rules and Theories of Representations*. Chicago: University of Chicago Press.

Archangeli, Diana. 1988. Aspects of underspecification theory. *Phonology* 5:183–207.

Bradfield, Julian. 2014. Clicks, concurrency, and Khoisan. *Phonology* 31:1–49.

Chao, Yuen-Ren, and Lien-Shang Yang. 1962. *Concise Dictionary of Spoken Chinese*. Cambridge, MA: Harvard University Press.

Chen, Matthew. 2000. *Tone Sandhi: Patterns across Chinese Dialects*. Cambridge: Cambridge University Press.

Chomsky, Noam, and Morris Halle. 1968. *The Sound Pattern of English*. New York: Harper and Row.

Clements, G. N. 1980. *Vowel Harmony in Nonlinear Generative Phonology: An Autosegmental Model*. Bloomington: Indiana University Linguistics Club.

———. 1985. The geometry of phonological features. *Phonology Yearbook* 2:225–252.

Clements, G. N., and S. J. Keyser. 1983. *CV Phonology*. Cambridge, MA: MIT Press.

Daniloff, Raymond, and R. Hammarberg. 1973. On defining coarticulation. *Journal of Phonetics* 1:239–248.

Duanmu, San. 1990. A formal study of syllable, tone, stress and domain in Chinese languages. PhD dissertation, Massachusetts Institute of Technology.

Ellis, Lucy, and William J. Hardcastle. 2002. Categorical and gradient properties of assimilation in alveolar to velar sequences: Evidence from EPG and EMA data. *Journal of Phonetics* 30:373–396.

Firth, J. R. 1948. Sounds and prosodies. *Transactions of the Philological Society* 47:127–152. Reprinted in. *Prosodic Analysis*, ed. F. R. Palmer, 1–26. Oxford: Oxford University Press, 1970; and *Phonological Theory: Evolution and Current Practice*, ed. V. B. Makkai, 252–263. New York: Holt, Rinehart, and Winston, 1972.

Fowler, Carol A. 1980. Coarticulation and theories of extrinsic timing. *Journal of Phonetics* 8:113–133.

Goldsmith, John. 1976. Autosegmental phonology. PhD dissertation, Massachusetts Institute of Technology. Bloomington: Indiana University Linguistics Club. http://people.cs.uchicago.edu/~jagoldsm/Papers/dissertation.pdf. Published by Garland Press, New York [1979]. (Page references in the text refer to the Indiana University Linguistics Club version.)

Hallé, Pierre, and Martine Adda-Decker. 2010. Voice assimilation in French obstruents: Categorical or gradient? In *Tones and Features: Phonetic and*

Phonological Perspectives, ed. John Goldsmith, Elizabeth Hume, and Leo Wetzels, 149–175. Berlin: De Gruyter Mouton.

Harms, Robert T. 1968. *Introduction to Phonological Theory*. Englewood Cliffs, NJ: Prentice-Hall.

Harris, John. 1990. Segmental complexity and phonological government. *Phonology* 7:255–300.

Harris, Zellig S. 1944. Simultaneous components in phonology. *Language* 20:181–205. Reprinted in *Readings in Linguistics I*, ed. M. Joos, 124–138. Chicago: University of Chicago Press, 1966; and *Phonological Theory: Evolution and Current Practice*, ed. V. B. Makkai, 115–133. New York: Holt, Rinehart, and Winston, 1972.

Hayes, Bruce. 1986. Assimilation as spreading in Toba Batak. *Linguistic Inquiry* 17:467–499.

Henderson, Eugénie. 1985. Feature shuffling in Southeast Asian languages. In *Southeast Asian Linguistic Studies Presented to André-G. Haudricourt*, ed. Suriya Ratanakul, Suwilai Premsrirat, and David D. Thomas, 1–22. Bangkok: Mahidol University. Available online from Southeast Asian Linguistics Archives. http://sealang.net/sala/archives/pdf4/henderson1985feature.pdf.

Hyman, Larry M. 1975. *Phonology: Theory and Analysis*. New York: Holt, Rinehart, and Winston.

———. 1988. Underspecification and vowel height transfer in Esimbi. *Phonology* 5:255–273.

Jakobson, Roman, C. Gunnar M. Fant, and Morris Halle. 1952. *Preliminaries to Speech Analysis: The Distinctive Features and Their Correlates*. Cambridge, MA: MIT Press.

Joos, Martin. 1950. Description of language design. *Journal of the Acoustical Society of America* 22:701–708.

Kaye, Jonathan, Jean Lowenstamm, and Jean-Roger Vergnaud. 1990. Constituent structure and government in phonology. *Phonology* 7:193–231.

Kenstowicz. Michael. 2010. *24.901 Language and Its Structure I: Phonology, Fall 2010*. Cambridge, MA: Massachusetts Institute of Technology: MIT OpenCourseWare. http://ocw.mit.edu.

Kenstowicz, Michael, and Charles Kisseberth. 1979. *Generative Phonology*. Orlando, FL: Academic Press.

Kiparsky, Paul. 1968. *How Abstract Is Phonology?* Bloomington: Indiana University Linguistics Club.

Kochetov, Andrei, and Marianne Pouplier. 2008. Phonetic variability and grammatical knowledge: An articulatory study of Korean place assimilation. *Phonology* 25:399–431.

Kornai, András. 1993. The generative power of feature geometry. *Annals of Mathematics and Artificial Intelligence* 8:37–46.

———. 1994. Relating phonetic and phonological categories. In *Language Computations*, vol. 17, ed. Eric Sven Ristad, 21–36. Philadelphia: American Mathematical Society.

———. 2008. *Mathematical Linguistics*. Berlin: Springer.

Ladd, D. Robert. 2014. *Simultaneous Structure in Phonology*. Oxford: Oxford University Press.

Ladd, D. Robert, and James M. Scobbie. 2003. External sandhi as gestural overlap? Counter-evidence from Sardinian. In *Phonetic Interpretation: Papers in Laboratory Phonology 6*, ed. John Local, Richard Ogden, and Rosalind Temple, 164–182. Cambridge: Cambridge University Press.

Laver, John. 1994. *Principles of Phonetics*. Cambridge: Cambridge University Press.

Leben, William. 1973. Suprasegmental phonology. PhD dissertation, Massachusetts Institute of Technology. Published by Garland Press, New York [1980].

McCarthy, John. 1981. A prosodic theory of nonconcatenative morphology. *Linguistic Inquiry* 12:373–418.

Matisoff, James. 1994. Tone, intonation, and sound symbolism in Lahu: Loading the syllable canon. In *Sound Symbolism*, ed. Leanne Hinton, Johanna Nichols, and John Ohala, 115–129. Cambridge: Cambridge University Press.

Miller, Amanda L., Johanna Brugman, Bonny Sands, Levi Namaseb, Mats Exter, and Chris Collins. 2009. Differences in airstream and posterior place of articulation among N|uu clicks. *Journal of the International Phonetic Association* 39:129–161.

Nevins, Andrew. 2010. *Locality in Vowel Harmony*. Cambridge, MA: MIT Press.

Nolan, Francis. 1992. The descriptive role of segments: Evidence from assimilation. In *Papers in Laboratory Phonology II: Gesture, Segment, Prosody*, ed. Gerard Docherty and D. Robert Ladd, 261–280. Cambridge: Cambridge University Press.

Pierrehumbert, Janet. 1990. Phonological and phonetic representation. *Journal of Phonetics* 18:375–394.

Pierrehumbert, Janet, Mary E. Beckman, and D. Robert Ladd. 2000. Conceptual foundations of phonology as a laboratory science. In *Phonological Knowledge: Conceptual and Empirical Issues*, ed. N. Burton-Roberts, P. Carr, and G. J. Docherty, 273–303. Oxford: Oxford University Press. Reprinted in *Oxford Handbook of Laboratory Phonology*, ed. A. Cohn, C. Fougeron, and M. K. Huffman, 17–39. Oxford: Oxford University Press, 2012.

Postal, Paul M. 1968. *Aspects of Phonological Theory*. New York: Harper and Row.

Prince, Alan, and Paul Smolensky. 2004. *Optimality Theory: Constraint Interaction in Generative Grammar*. Oxford: Blackwell.

Raimy, Eric. 2000. Remarks on backcopying. *Linguistic Inquiry* 31:541–552.

Sagey, Elizabeth. 1988. On the ill-formedness of crossing association lines. *Linguistic Inquiry* 19:109–118.

Schane, Sanford A. 1973. *Generative Phonology*. Englewood Cliffs, NJ: Prentice-Hall.

———. 1984. The fundamentals of particle phonology. *Phonology Yearbook* 1:129–155.

Smolensky, Paul, Matthew Goldrick, and Donald Mathis. 2014. Optimization and quantization in gradient symbol systems: A framework for integrating the continuous and the discrete in cognition. *Cognitive Science* 38:1102–1138.

Traill, Anthony 1985. *Phonetic and Phonological Studies of !Xóõ Bushman*. Hamburg: Buske.

Trubetzkoy, Nikolai Sergeevich. [1939] 1958. *Grundzüge der Phonologie*. Göttingen: Vandenhoeck and Ruprecht. Reprinted as *Principles of Phonology*, trans. C. Baltaxe. Berkeley: University of California Press, 1969.

Vago, Robert M. 1988. Underspecification in the height harmony system of Pasiego. *Phonology* 5:343–362.

van der Hulst, Harry. 1989. Atoms of segmental structure: Components, gestures and dependency. *Phonology* 6:253–284.

Warner, Natasha, Allard Jongman, Joan Sereno, and Rachèl Kemps. 2004. Incomplete neutralization and other sub-phonemic durational differences in production and perception: Evidence from Dutch. *Journal of Phonetics* 32:251–276.

Williams, Edwin. 1976. Underlying tone in Margi and Igbo. *Linguistic Inquiry* 7:463–484.

Zsiga, Elizabeth C. 1997. Features, gestures, and Igbo vowels: An approach to the phonology-phonetics interface. *Language* 73:227–274.

SIX

The Importance of Autosegmental Representations for Sign Language Phonology

DIANE BRENTARI

6.1. Introduction

In the ideal scenario, evidence from data motivates theory, and, subsequently, the theory makes testable predictions, leading to evidence that supports or challenges the original theory. There is no doubt, however, that our perception of new data is colored by the theoretical lens through which we view it. Two central aspects of Goldsmith's work have fundamentally changed the lens through which we see phonological data, especially data from sign languages, which is the focus here. This chapter addresses two arenas where sign language phonology was inspired by topics that Goldsmith put on the map, either single-handedly or with others. First, the autosegmental tier allowed the field to expand phonological representations in ways that were more simultaneous and multidimensional in nature than ever before. This leap expanded the general conception of phonology to better accommodate sign language phonology, allowing signed and spoken language phonology to find some common ground within the field. Second, because the autosegmental tier was autonomous from segments and intimately linked to the field of prosodic analysis starting with the syllable, it paved the way for advances in the formalisms that express prosodic generalizations. The syllable was largely ignored in Chomsky and Halle's (1968) *The Sound Patterns of English* (*SPE*) phonology (but see Hooper 1972), and autosegmental phonology was largely responsible for resuscitating it.

Since phonological theory should aim to describe the abstract organization of the meaningless units of language, it is implicit that it should adequately describe the facts and make predictions about the organization of both signed and spoken phonological systems. Discussions between phonologists working on both types of languages allow for the possibility to consider aspects of phonology that might be universal, rather than dependent on the modality of transmission. Autosegmental phonology created two paths for such interchanges with the construct of autosegmental tier and subsequent work on the syllable. The autosegmental tier provided a means to capture, for the first time, the sign language "parameters" of handshape, movement, location, and orientation, rendering them more comprehensible to phonologists working on spoken languages. Since the autosegmental tier is an explanatory tool for both sign and spoken languages, it adds to its permanence within the field. This is described in section 6.2. In addition, developments regarding the syllable that grew out of autosegmental phonology allowed for syllable weight and sonority to be assessed simultaneously or sequentially within the syllable, which are essential when analyzing sign language data. The discussion of these issues in section 6.3 suggests that the sonority sequencing principle (SSP) is modality specific (i.e., relevant only to spoken languages), while the general concept of sonority applies to both signed and spoken languages in assigning and determining syllable weight.

6.2. Multidimensionality in Representation

Often, when Goldsmith talked about his own conceptualization of autosegmental phonology he produced a co-speech gesture showing a three-dimensional dynamic space rotating on an axis similar to one of Alexander Calder's mobiles. This gesture communicates in an optimal way what Goldsmith was seeking to reveal about phonological representation in a multidimensional space.[1] Multidimensional images of phonological features, such as those in figure 6.1 from Clements (1985) and Clements and Hume (1995), clearly made visible that the notion of

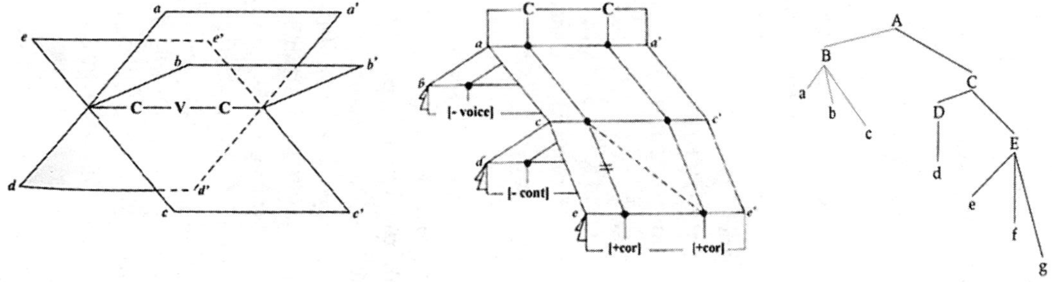

6.1 Multidimensional representations of features. (From Clements 1985; Clements and Hume 1995.)

phonemes as beads on a string was insufficient to capture a wide range phonological phenomena (Goldsmith 1976, 1985, 1990, 1992; Clements and Goldsmith 1984).[2] Such representations were an essential step in allowing sign language phonologists to conceptualize the sublexical elements of those languages, as will be described in section 6.2.1.

Without explicitly saying so, autosegmental phonology (Goldsmith 1976) and feature geometry (Clements 1985; Sagey 1986; Clements and Hume 1995) are sometimes invoked as if they were a single theory. Part of this has to do with the dual nature of association lines. Association lines serve two purposes: first, to encode patterns of temporal alignment and coordination among elements in phonological representations; and second, to group elements into constituents that function as single units in phonological rules. Because they are used in both feature trees and autosegmental phonological rules, their distinct theoretical roles in these two theories can be confused. Features produced by a single articulator—that is, the glottis—can be grouped together using an articulatory-based account of feature geometry, but they can have different autosegmental roles. For instance, the features of both tone and voicing are produced by the vocal folds, so features of tone ([high], [low]) and voicing ([spread glottis], [constricted glottis]) could be placed together physiologically; however, since tone is autosegmental in some languages, it will be assigned to an autosegmental tier, but [spread glottis] and [constricted glottis] will not. As we will see handshape and place of articulation (POA) behave in a similar fashion in sign languages.

In Goldsmith (1976), the criteria for establishing autosegmental tiers are phonological and not anatomical or physiological; they include stability, many-to-one association, morphological identity, and long-distance effects. One might think that autosegments are simply a way of representing nonlocal dependencies of all kinds—those that are based on physiology and those that are not, but autosegmental tiers have more flexibility and perform more organizational work in a phonological representation than features do. Goldsmith (1976: 13; cf. Ladd, chapter 5 of this volume) argued for a distinction "between a rule of feature-assimilation . . . and true spreading of a suprasegmental [autosegmental] element," and that it is "a feature's behavior with respect to phonological rules that gives it away as suprasegmental, not any phonetic facts." While analyses of the mechanics of articulation and phonetic spreading have a place in phonological theory, the goal should be to arrive at the underlying principles that govern these sensorimotor activities.

6.2.1. Multidimensionality in Spoken Languages: A Brief Sketch

The prototypical cases of autosegmental spreading are not simply cases of assimilation due to the mechanics of the articulators, but rather are factors about their organization according to specific phonological and morphological domains. Tone is the most obvious case. As Goldsmith and Mpiranya (2011) stated, "one particular characteristic of tone that keeps it distinct from other aspects of phonology is tone's tendency to shift its point of realization among a word's syllables based on a global metrical structure which is erected on the entire word." In this volume, Hyman (chapter 3) and Odden (chapter 4) provide excellent examples of this. Nasal harmony (Piggott 1989), vowel harmony (van der Hulst and van de Weijer 1995; Henderson 1985), and more recently clicks in the Khoisan languages (Bradfield 2014) have also shown characteristics of autosegmental spreading rather than generic feature spreading. The articulatory mechanics of feature spreading can be used to describe how the articulatory gestures are coordinated as a gestural score in spoken and sign languages (Browman and Goldstein 1989; Tyrone et al. 2010), but they do not account for other important aspects of these operations; for example, why feature spreading *stops* or is *blocked* when there is no opposing gesture present. For example, the tongue tip can move quite quickly and quite easily, and the velum moves more slowly, and these facts affect assimilation phenomena, to be sure, but to explain other facts of assimilation, such as those of the blocking of voice assimilation in Rendaku phenomena in Japanese via Lyman's law (Itô and Mester 1995), the nature of feature specifications (underlying versus redundant) as well as phonological and prosodic constituents are needed, including the autosegmental tier and the phonological word, among others (see also Piggott 2000; Goldsmith and Mpiranya 2011).

In addition, as Ladd (2014; see chapter 5 of this volume) pointed out, an autosegmental tier combines characteristics of both segments and features. The autosegment was intended to be an entity whose manifestation in the phonetics favor treating it as a feature—an attribute of some segment—but whose function in the phonology suggests that it is a segment in its own right. Treating autosegmental assimilation and feature spreading as the same phenomenon removes any motivation for positing autosegments as an innovative phonological unit with its own criteria. Ladd pointed out that the utility (the genius) of autosegments is that they have this dual character as unordered units with respect to the segment (*Merkmale)* and as properties (*Eigenschaften*) that are ordered at some level of the representation. These are characteristics of features that can be traced to Trubetzkoy (1939).

In sections 6.2.2 and 6.3.2 I will outline ways that sign language data have validated these two roles of features as unordered (*Merkmale*) and ordered (*Eigeneschaften*) units within the word. I claim that sign languages have a greater capacity than spoken languages do for having independent articulators active at one time. As such, in sign languages there are more possibilities for unordered phonological units, and it may be the case that they depend on autosegmental tiers even more heavily than spoken languages do, validating the constructs of autosegmental phonology as Goldsmith intended.

6.2.2. Multidimensionality in Sign Languages

Sign language phonology has developed very rapidly since its inception in 1960, but in general, theoretical developments proposed for spoken languages do not get tested on sign language data immediately. I will illustrate the development of the field using the American Sign Language (ASL) sign INFORM (figure 6.2) as an example and will consider three of the five parameters of a sign—handshape, place of articulation (POA, or location), and movement. The remaining two parameters of orientation and nonmanual behaviors will not be discussed. *Handshape* concerns the particular fingers that are used and the way the joints of the wrist and hand are configured. In the sign INFORM, all of the fingers are bent at the knuckle joint and the fingertips make contact with the forehead. *POA* is where the sign is articulated on the body or in front of the signer; INFORM starts at the forehead and ends in the neutral space in front of the signer. *Movement* is the dynamic part of the sign characterized by a particular direction or shape of movement as the hands from one place to another. INFORM is articulated with a direction of movement away from the signer's forehead and an opening gesture of the hand.

The earliest model of sign language phonology proposed by Stokoe (1960; sometimes called the cheremic model) emphasized the unordered, simultaneous nature of the three parameters. He treated handshape, movement, and POA as phonemes in the structuralist sense of the term (Bloomfield 1933). Like spoken language models in the 1950s, Stokoe (1960) focused on providing evidence for features using phonemic contrast, as was practiced in a phonemic account (Bloomfield 1933), but Stokoe was unsure about how to label the bundles of features that made up the three sign language parameters, because phonemes in spoken languages occur one after the other, while sign language par-

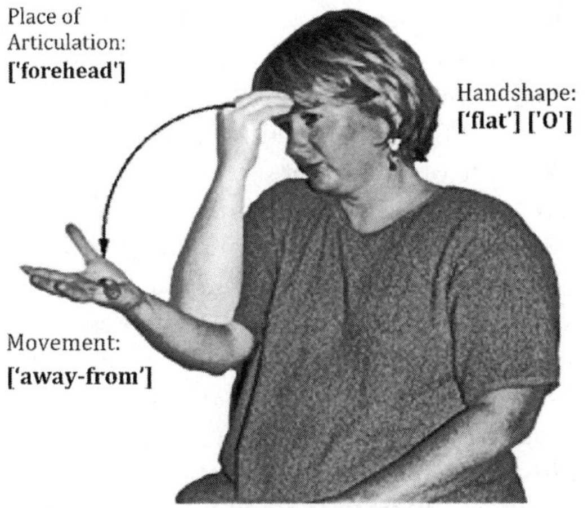

6.2 The ASL sign INFORM with its phonological description for handshape, place of articulation, and movement. (From Brentari 2016.)

ameters are articulated at the same time. He initially suggested a completely new vocabulary for sign language units (i.e., cheremes), but this was ultimately considered to be counterproductive to the enterprise of promoting dialogue between phonologists working on signed and spoken languages.

Stokoe obtained his PhD in 1941, and during the 1940s and 1950s, the interest in sign languages came primarily from the discipline of anthropology, since Plains Indian Sign Language was of interest to several students of Franz Boas (see Kroeber 1958; Voegelin 1958; West 1960; a review of this work in the field of anthropology appears in Davis 2010). A point of contact between the formal advances made in spoken language phonology using a pre-generative framework (Jakobson, Fant, and Halle 1952; Jakobson and Halle 1956) and those in sign language phonology did not occur at this crucial juncture. Moreover, phonologists responsible for pointing out the weaknesses in *SPE* for a wide range of phenomena—including tone, metrical structure, and prosodic structure—were not aware that *SPE* also did a poor job of accounting for sign language facts. By the time Stokoe's work became widely known at the beginning of the 1970s, spoken language phonology was deeply immersed in *SPE* phonology, and one of the most common questions in the early years of working with Stokoe's model was whether the sign language parameters were features or segments; in other words, How did they fit into a *SPE* framework?

In 20-20 hindsight we can see that the parameters of handshape, movement, and POA are autosegmental tiers, but the evidence for them was not proposed until almost sixteen years after Stokoe's initial 1960 publication (Sandler 1986). Additional work in the Stokoe tradition did a great deal to elaborate on the set of features responsible for contrast in ASL, but not on their hierarchical organization (Frishberg 1975; Klima and Bellugi 1979; Lane, Boyes Braem, and Bellugi 1976; Friedman 1977; Battison 1978; Mandel 1981; Poizner 1983).

Four subsequent models of phonological representation will be discussed in more detail (figure 6.3): the hold-movement model, the hand tier model, the dependency model, and the prosodic model. The hold-movement model (figure 6.3a) was largely inspired by *SPE* (Liddell 1984; Liddell and Johnson 1989). This work advanced the field of sign language phonology, and these authors proposed for the first time an organization of the phonological features of a sign. It was based on and biased toward a sequential representation of ordered segments. The hold-movement model answered the question "how did they fit into a *SPE* framework?" by proposing temporally ordered segments, within which in all features in each segment were bundled together. Holds (i.e., static elements) were compared to consonants, and movements (i.e., dynamic elements) were compared to vowels.

Within each segment, the features were implicitly organized by parameter, similar to the way the place, manner, and voicing features were implicitly placed together in an *SPE* feature matrix for a speech segment. Regarding the sign INFORM in figure 6.2 this meant that there was a shift from the simultaneous, unordered treatment of units in the cheremic model to sequential treatment of units in the hold-movement model: the temporal change as the hand moves from the hold at the forehead to hold in the space in front of the signer, and the movement in between (H-M-H)—three segments in total. By the time the hold-movement model became widely accepted within the sign language community in the 1980s, however, spoken language phonologists had moved on and were working out the details of autosegmental phonology and feature geometry in the ways described in section 6.1. There was still a substantial difference between how signed and spoken language phonology was represented.

The hold-movement model captured some important facts about assimilation and moved the field forward; however, the features associated within each segment in the hold-movement model contained a substantial amount of redundant information when compared to their spoken language counterparts—consonants (Cs) and vowels (Vs). The

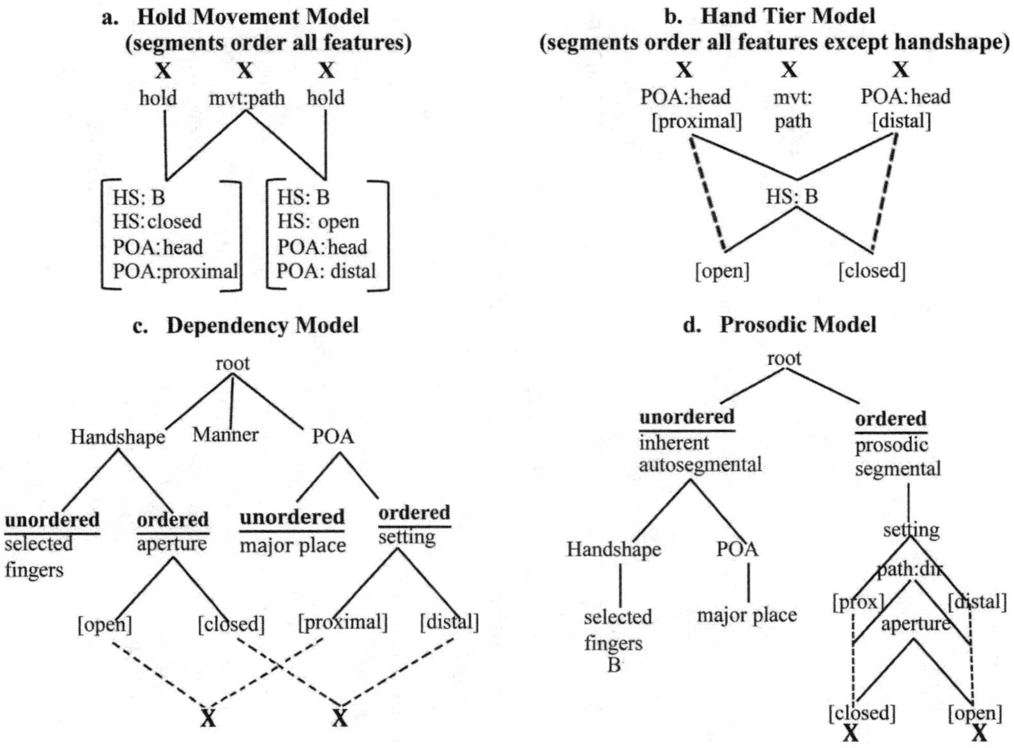

6.3 Four sign language models of phonological representation: (*a*) the hold-movement model, (*b*) the hand tier model, (*c*) the dependency model, and (*d*) the prosodic model.

hand tier model (Sandler 1986, 1989; Sandler and Lillo-Martin 2006) (figure 6.3b) would be the first to address some of the shortcomings of the hold-movement model by representing handshape as an autosegmental tier, thus partially reanimating Stokoe's original insights about the simultaneous nature of sign structure. Evidence for handshape as an autosegment is provided by the *handshape sequence constraint* (Sandler 1986), which formalized the generalization, first observed by Mandel (1981), that a sign only has only one set of *selected fingers*. Selected fingers are the features that typically denote which fingers can have contact with the body in a sign (note that all of the fingers contact the forehead at the start of the sign). In a sign, such as INFORM (figure 6.2), there is a change in the handshape from closed to open ; however, all four of the fingers plus the thumb are selected throughout the sign. The [closed] to [open] movement of the fingers is expressed by *aperture* features. A change in aperture such as this > is permitted in a monomorphemic sign,[3] while a change in selected fingers such as this * > or * > is not permitted in a monomorphemic sign. The relevant domain for the handshape sequencing constraint has been proposed to be the morpheme (Sandler 1986) or the phonological word (Brentari 1998), since historical change progresses in this direction. As compounds containing stems with two different sets of selected fingers become more integrated into the phonology as single words, one of the handshapes assimilates to the other—for example, RED^SLICE has become RED ^SLICE (tomato). Crucially, the domain of selected finger spreading is confined to the word; the phonetic facts have nothing to do with this.

The handshape parameter thus has a dual role with regard to selected fingers features, which are autosegmental and *unordered* within the word, and aperture features, which are segmental and *ordered*, just as the laryngeal features have a dual role in tone languages: tone (autosegmental, unordered) and voice (segmental, ordered). The sign language parameter of location (POA) also has this dual role in phonology. POA consists of *major POA*—four areas of the body where a sign is produced: the torso, head, arm, or nondominant hand. These features are autosegmental and unordered (like selected fingers) and appear only once per monomorphemic sign. Within a monomorphemic sign, however, *setting* features such as [top], [bottom], [ipsilateral], or [contralateral] are allowed to change in an ordered fashion, and are thus segmental and ordered (like aperture).

The dependency model (van der Hulst 1993; van der Kooij 2002; van der Kooij and van der Hulst 2005) (figure 6.3c) and the prosodic model (Brentari 1998) (figure 6.3d) unite both the sequential (ordered) and simultaneous (unordered) nature of signs in their respective representations even further than the hand tier model does. In both the dependency and prosodic models, the X-slots (timing slots) are demoted from the "root node" status they have in spoken languages; they are derived from features in the underlying form that generates them (van der Hulst 2000; Brentari 2002). Unlike segmental structure in spoken languages, which can be contrastive—in singleton versus geminate consonants or long versus short vowels—length is not contrastive in the sign languages that have been documented thus far. Although these two models differ in important details,[4] both ascribe autosegmental status to features of selected fingers and to major POA because they meet the phonological criteria established by Goldsmith (1976).

One important difference between the dependency and prosodic models is the principle guiding the organization of features. For INFORM, the two respective models' representations would look like those in figures 6.3c and 6.3d. In the dependency model, physiology is the major guide in organizing features; both selected fingers (autosegmental, unordered) and aperture (segmental, ordered) are dominated by the same class node in the tree, despite their different phonological roles, because they are handshape features. Major POA and setting features are united for this reason as well. In contrast, in the prosodic model, the phonological behavior is the primary guide in organizing features. All unordered, autosegmental features are located together in the tree in the inherent features branch (i.e., selected fingers, major POA), and inherent features do not generate segments. Ordered features that generate, such as aperture and setting features are found in a different place in the structure, called the prosodic features because ultimately these features also generate syllable nuclei.

Presenting more specific arguments for one or the other of these models is beyond the scope of this chapter, but there are three points to take away from the discussion thus far. First, autosegmental phonology is absolutely essential to signed and spoken language phonology. The domain of selected fingers and major POA are determined by phonological constituency, and not by phonetic facts. The impact of the notion of the autosegmental tier and its properties helped to initiate a great deal of work demonstrating that sign language phonology did not require theoretical tools that were different from those of spoken languages. Second, as Ladd (chapter 5 of this volume) points out, whether a property is ordered or unordered with respect to segments is a crucial distinction for phonology regardless of whether it concerns a spoken or signed language. Finally, since middle of the 1990s it has no longer been in doubt (at least to phonologists) that sign languages have important data to contribute to the discussion of the abstract categories that constitute phonology. In order to describe the full range of extant phonological systems, theories must strive to handle both types of data. Work by Hale and Reiss (2008) has gone so far as to propose "substance-free" phonology. Although we are still a very long way from achieving that goal, the organization of sign language phonology confirms and validates the need for autosegmental tiers.

6.3. Sonority and Syllable Weight

The study of the syllable was a natural development of autosegmental phonology. The connections between prosodies and autosegmental tiers have been well documented (Firth 1948; see also Coleman, chapter 1 of this volume; Leben, chapter 2 of this volume). Three of the primary motivators of this development were that (i) tone-bearing units were syllabic rather than segmental units (Goldsmith 1976), (ii) the syllable more elegantly accounted for a wide variety of phenomena than the segment in *SPE* (Hooper 1972), and (iii) segmental identity itself was often determined by the role the feature bundle played in the syllable (e.g., vowel~glide alternations; Dell and Elmedlaoui 1985; Levin 1985; Itô 1986). Goldsmith and Larson (1990) also contributed the insight that there are two different levels of sonority—inherent sonority based on a segment's underlying form and derived sonority (see also Wiltshire, chapter 8 of this volume), which also considers the segment's context. Spoken languages employ a sonority hierarchy, such as the one in (1), and we will see that a sonority hierarchy is employed in sign languages as well.

(1) Sonority hierarchy in spoken languages (Dell and Elmedlaoui 1985)
low V > high V > glide > liquid > nasal > voiced fricative > voiceless fricative > voice stop > voiceless stop

In addition to assigning syllable peaks, sonority can also important in both signed and spoken languages for assigning syllable weight (Gordon 2006, Gordon et al., 2008). Moraic (or weight) units are employed to assign syllable weight—one mora results a light syllable, while two or more morae results in a heavy syllable—and heavy syllables are more likely to be stressed in many languages (Trubetzkoy 1939; Hayes 1989). In the following sections, two lines of research about the syllable that have been pursued for spoken languages will be discussed as they pertain to sign languages—(i) the correlation of energy with sonority and (ii) the contribution of simultaneous elements in the syllable to weight—both of which Goldsmith's early work on the syllable inspired (Goldsmith 1992).

6.3.1. Sonority and Syllable Weight in Spoken Languages: A Brief Sketch

Sonority and syllable weight are related in important ways, which led Gordon (2006) and Gordon et al. (2008) to propose that, particularly in languages that treat CVC syllables as light, both sonority and syllable weight are determined by the amount of energy used to produce the form. In Gordon et al. (2008), the perceptual energy in rimes calculated using Cricket, a custom-made software designed to map an acoustic signal to one that more accurately reflects the perception of that signal by the human auditory system, showed a number of important results. In particular, a rime that ends in a sonorant or voiced coda has greater energy than one closed by an obstruent or a voiceless coda, respectively, particularly in languages that treat CVC as light. The correlation of energy expenditure is important for associating high energy generally with sonority peaks, and with higher syllable weight as well, in both signed and spoken languages.

6.3.1.1. Energy and Sonority in Spoken Languages: The SSP

Evidence for the importance of sonority in spoken language phonology also comes from the SSP, which captures the fact that syllable onsets typically increase in sonority from one segment to the next and codas typically decrease in sonority from one segment to the next. The SSP has been shown to be important for determining syllable well-formedness both theoretically (Clements 1990) and experimentally (Berent 2013). Unless there is an L-specific pattern allowing violations—for example, Polish (Rubach and Booij 1990)—even languages that do not allow consonant clusters, such as Korean, show evidence of the SSP. Berent (2013) argued that the SSP is a core property of phonology because Korean speakers are more likely perceive a sequence such as *bnif* as one syllable and *nbif* as two syllables (see figure 6.4); that is, falling sonority in the onset (a violation of the SSP) will facilitate the perception of a schwa and hence a second syllable. The data for Korean speakers are shown in figure 6.4, reprinted from from Berent's figure 8.6 (2013). Similar results exist for English, but might be explained by language experience (i.e., onset

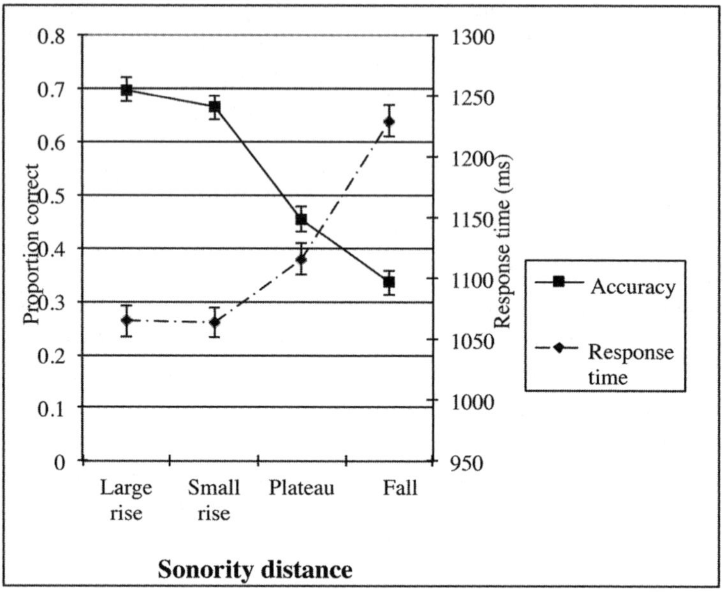

6.4 Accuracy and response time of Korean speakers when listening to words with a large rise in sonority, a small rise, no rise, a plateau, and a fall. Note that accuracy falls and response time rises as sonority moves from a rising to falling cline. (Reprinted with permission from Berent 2013, fig. 8.6.)

clusters exist in English and statistically English speakers hear more *bnif* than *nbif* forms); however, a statistical interpretation cannot be the explanation for the results in Korean because speakers have no experience with onset clusters. In section 6.3.1.2, we will see that speakers, without exposure to a sign language, naturally associate movements to syllable peaks, just as signers do.

6.3.1.2. Energy and Syllable Weight in Spoken Languages

Energy expenditure is also relevant for syllable weight. Syllable weight is correlated with the amount of energy expended, particularly if we examine tone languages that treat high tone as moraic. Gordon (2006) argued that syllable weight in such languages is not associated exclusively with length, but also with tonal properties that co-occur simultaneously with the vowel. In several tone languages—Crow (Kaschube 1967), Ijo (Williamson 1989), Kongo (Reh 1983), Iraqw (Mous 2007), and Llogoori (Goldsmith 1992)—a vowel plus high tone is treated as heavy. Vowels uttered with high tones have more energy than those with a low tone do. In these languages, syllables that would otherwise be treated as light, and not stress-attracting, are allowed to be stressed if they occur with a high tone. Discussions on this topic with Goldsmith about Llogoori in the late 1980s led to an analysis of simultaneous syllable weight in ASL (Brentari 1990, 1998) that predates Gordon's work on spoken languages.

6.3.2. Sonority and Syllable Weight in Sign Languages

Movements are the most visually salient part of a sign, just as vowels are the most acoustically salient part of a spoken word. Movement also plays a central organizing role at the phonological level in infants acquiring ASL from their deaf parents, and at the same as the stage of development as syllabic babbling in infants acquiring a spoken language (Pettito and Marentette 1991). Movement is used to count syllables in sign languages. The criteria for counting syllables in sign languages are outlined in (2).

(2) Syllable Counting Criteria (Brentari 1998):

a. The number of syllables in a sequence of signs equals the number of sequential movements in that string.

b. When several shorter (e.g., secondary) movements co-occur with a single (e.g., path) movement of longer duration, the longer movement is the one to which the syllable refers.

c. When two or more movements occur at exactly the same time, it counts as one syllable, e.g., ASL INFORM is one syllable containing an aperture change and a path movement.

These syllable counting criteria incorporate both issues relevant in this section. First, considering the three parameters of handshape, movement, and location syllables are counted according to the number of movements—the ordered elements aperture and setting—and not the unordered autosegmental tiers—selected fingers and major POA. Second, if two types of movements co-occur (e.g., a smaller one embedded in a single larger one), the energy is calculated across both, such that two simultaneous movements have higher energy than one. In other words, syllable count and syllable weight are based on sequential and simultaneous information.

6.3.2.1. Sonority Is Associated with Movements

The association of vowels with movements was originally proposed by Liddel (1984) because, functionally speaking, movements behave like vowels insofar as they are the medium of the signal. Without vowels, the speech signal would be of very low intensity, just as without movements, the sign signal would be low intensity (Brentari 2002). The idea that movement conveys the notion of sonority has been shown experimentally as well (Berent, Dupuis, and Brentari 2013) for both signers and nonsigners. The design of these studies was very similar to the ones reported earlier for Korean. Korean speakers were asked to judge the number of syllables, and they employed the sonority hierarchy instinctively even though their language has no CC clusters. Signers and nonsigners were asked to determine whether movements or handshapes are the default syllable nucleus. Novel signs were constructed with one or two different handshapes and with one or two different movements as shown in figure 6.5.

Analogous English examples of the ASL stimuli are given in each cell. (These were not part of the experiment and are intended to be illustrative examples of the analogous syllabic and morphological structure in a familiar spoken language.) Each experiment consisted of two tasks. In one task participants were asked to judge the number of parts *without* meaning (i.e., syllables) and in another to judge the number of parts *with* meaning (i.e., morphemes). Judgments of parts without meaning were taken to be syllabic units, and judgments of parts with meaning were interpreted as morphemes. Those in the top right and bottom left cells in figure 6.5 (outlined with bold lines) with incongruent meaningless and meaningful parts were the most informative (i.e., syllables or morphemes), because these items clearly would show differences in the participants responses if they are making different associations for handshape and movement.

The results of the four experiments are shown in figure 6.6. With just a few training examples prior to the experiment and no feedback, ASL signers readily associated movement with meaningless units (syllables) and handshape with meaningful ones (morphemes); this is evident from the interaction seen in (figure 6.6a). Nonsigners did not perform like the signers when given the same training without instruction (figure 6.6b); they seem to associate movement with both meaningless parts (syllables) and meaningful parts (morphemes). In prior work (Brentari 2006; Brentari et al. 2011) it has been shown that nonsigners tend to ignore handshape in judging the number of words in a string and to focus heavily

6.5 ASL examples containing (i) one handshape and one movement (a form such as English *can*), (ii) one handshape and two movements (a form such as English *candy*); (iii) two handshapes and one movement (a form such as English *cans*); and (iv) two handshapes and two movements (a form such as English *candies*). The incongruent stimulus items are *darkly outlined in black*. (From Berent et al. 2013.)

on movement, so this result was not surprising. Two additional experiments with nonsigners were conducted to see whether they could be taught to pay attention to both dimensions independently (handshape and movement). One of these new studies provided nonsigners "natural" feedback after the training items; it was called "natural" because it corresponded with the judgments of the signers. Participants were instructed to associate movement with meaningless units (syllables) and handshape with meaningful ones (morphemes). With natural feedback, nonsigners were able to learn the task and reliably associate movement with meaningless units (syllables) and handshape with meaningful ones (morphemes) (figure 6.6c). A final experiment with nonsigners included "unnatural" feedback after the training items; it was called "unnatural" because it did not correspond with the judgments of the signers. Here participants were instructed to associate handshape with meaningless units (syllables) and movement with meaningful ones (morphemes). When provided unnatural feedback, they were not able to learn the rule (figure 6.6d). They were able to associate movement with meaningful units as instructed (note the blue line), but they did not learn to associate handshapes with meaningless units.

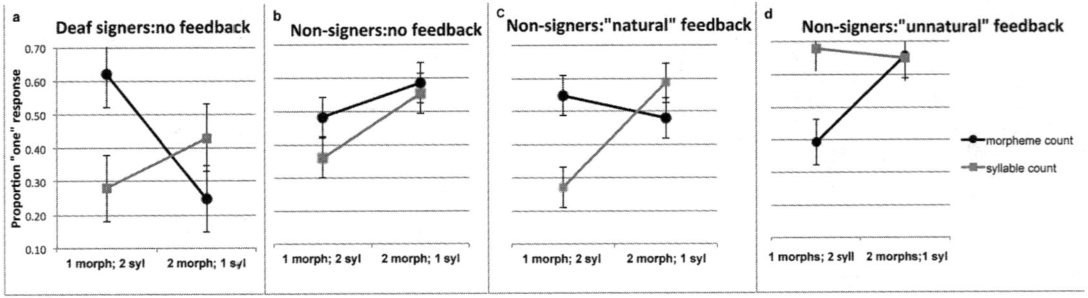

6.6 Responses of "one part" for novel ASL signs containing one handshape, two movements (*left* in each frame) and two handshapes, one movement (*right* in each frame) for (*a*) deaf ASL signers, (*b*) nonsigners without training, (*c*) nonsigners with "natural" training (training aligned with the signers responses), and (*d*) nonsigners with "unnatural" training (training not aligned with the signers responses). (From Berent et al. 2013.)

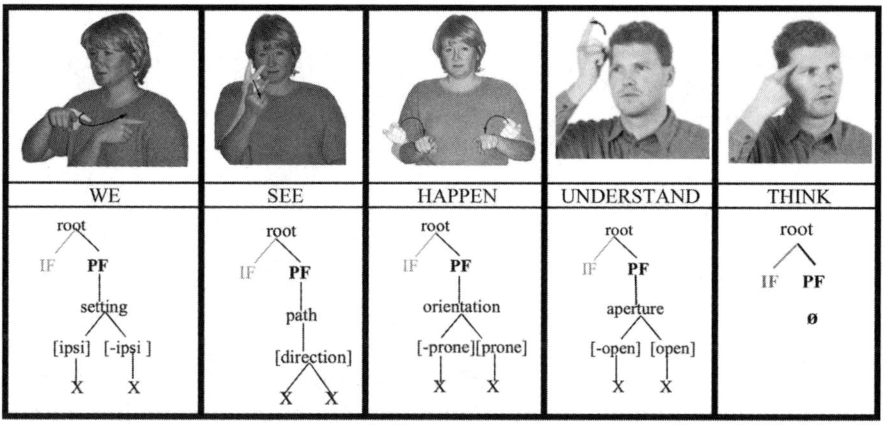

6.7 Sonority hierarchy in sign languages: path movements (those of the shoulder and elbow) are higher in sonority than local movements (those of the wrist and hand), which are more sonorant than no movement at all.

These results show that even without the relevant language experience (Korean speakers who have not heard CC clusters for spoken languages, and nonsigners who have never experienced sign languages), sonority is readily applied to the perceptually salient, high-energy elements of form and syllable nuclei are inferred correctly. This work also shows that despite the differences between articulators in signed and spoken language, comparative work such as this can ultimately lead to a better understanding of the universality of some of the principles of language organization, such as sonority.

Sonority hierarchies have been proposed for sign languages and many have several features in common which will be described will be described in this section (Corina 1990; Perlmutter 1992; Brentari 1993; Sandler 1993; van der Hulst 1993) (see figure 6.7). Assuming that movements made with larger articulators are produced with more energy, we see that the amount of energy correlates with proposed sonority hierarchies in sign languages: path movements produced by the elbow or shoulder are higher in sonority than are local movements, produce by the forearm, wrist, or hand. Lack of any movement (stasis) is lowest on the hierarchy, but there are no well-formed signs without a movement.

A sonority hierarchy is needed in sign languages to account for at least two phenomena. First, the sonority hierarchy is needed to explain why some ASL compounds are produced as disyllabic words and others as monosyllabic words. In ASL compounds if the first stem of the compound

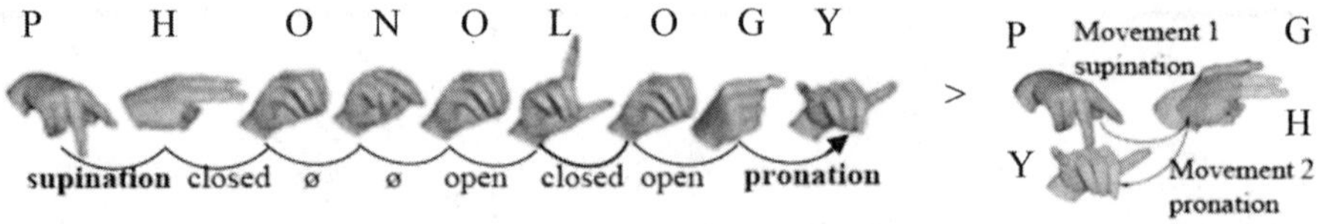

6.8 The fingerspelled form for P-H-O-N-O-L-O-G-Y (*left*) and its reduced form, which includes only the two wrist movements.

has a path movement (relatively high on the sonority hierarchy), the movement is retained and the resulting compound is disyllabic. If, instead, the first stem of the compound has a trilled movement (relatively low on the sonority hierarchy), the movement is deleted and the resulting compound is monosyllabic. This can be seen in the difference between BLACK^NAME (*bad reputation*) versus SPEAK^NAME (*mention*). As a stem, BLACK is articulated with a path movement, which is retained in the compound, and the resulting compound is disyllabic. As a stem, SPEAK is articulated with a trilled movement, which is not retained in the compound, and the resulting compound is monosyllabic. Another phenomenon in ASL that requires a sonority hierarchy is the nativization of fingerspelled sequences (e.g., #P-H-O-N-O-L-O-G-Y becomes [P-H]σ [G-Y]σ, with the other handshapes deleted) (figure 6.8). In such forms, the syllable nuclei are constructed on the transitional movements between handshapes. While these transitions typically involve only finger or hand movements, a few transitional movements between letters involve the wrist and forearm. These are preferred as syllable peaks over movements of the fingers, precisely because elbow and wrist movements are larger than finger or hand movements (see figure 6.8).

Despite the fact that a sonority hierarchy is needed, there is no evidence for the SSP at work in sign languages. In the hold-movement model of sign language phonology, movements have conceptually been associated with vowels, and holds could be considered syllable margins. Perlmutter (1992) presented a proposal that used positions instead of holds, and he also observed that complex onsets or codas clusters do not exist in ASL. Due to the lack of complex clusters, coupled with the fact that syllable margins in the majority of monomorphemic cases are largely redundant (most material in the "onset" and "coda" would be the same), Meier (2002) argued that sign languages do not employ the SSP. This is because, unlike spoken languages that have one major oscillator (i.e., the mandible), sign languages have many (i.e., body, arms, hand, head). This demotes the SSP in sign languages; however, sonority is one of the truly universal organizing principles of phonology.

6.3.2.2. Syllable Weight and Movement

The possibility of combining simultaneous properties for syllable weight in spoken languages was not widely known until Gordon (2006), which was the first large typological study of these phenomena. It is clear now, however, that the salience of a syllable nucleus can be determined sequentially or simultaneously in spoken languages. With regard to syllable weight with sonority in sign languages, there is a heavy/light sensitivity that is important for the application of reduplication and demonstrates that sign syllables are also sensitive to simultaneous layering of movement components as syllable weight. This distinction can be traced to expenditure of energy if we assume that one movement element requires less expenditure of movement than two. To be concrete, a group of ASL verbs containing one movement element are permitted to undergo reduplication, resulting in derived nominal forms (e.g., the path movement in ASL SIT can be repeated to derive the nominal form CHAIR; Supalla and Newport 1978); in contrast, signs consisting of two or more movements, such as ASL INFORM, which contains both a path and aperture movement, cannot be reduplicated to obtain a derived nominal form (*INFORMATION via reduplication). This suggests that forms allowing reduplication have one simultaneous movement component and are light syllables, while those that disallow reduplication have two or more simultaneous movement components and can be therefore considered heavy. This distinction has been argued for in Finnish Sign Language as well (Jantunen and Takkinen 2010). Light syllables readily allow reduplication, while heavy syllables do not.

Returning to the dependency model (figure 6.3c) and the prosodic model (figure 6.3d) of sign language phonology, in the dependency model the root node is a single "segment" structure linked to handshape and POA (NB, segment is not equal to timing units in this model). Within that model, movement is given a minor role as a manner feature, since van der Hulst (1993) argued that movement could be derived from transitions between handshape and POA features, at least for signs that are monomorphemic. In contrast, the prosodic model ascribes a central role in sign language phonology to movements, which not only unites all features that have ordered elements, as described in section 6.2.2, but also provides a coherent backbone on which to build syllable nuclei, to calculate sonority and syllable weight, and to provide the foundation for higher-order prosodic structure.

The ASL sonority hierarchy is built into the representation of the prosodic model (figure 6.3d), with components of movements that create a setting change or a particular direction of movement (path movements) located higher in the representation than those with a change produced at the wrist or hand (local movements) because path movements are in general larger, more visually salient, and require more energy than those of the wrist and fingers. Further, each additional movement component is argued to be a weight unit, a mora. The relationship of the syllable, sonority, and syllable weight is organized in a transparent way in this model. This model was inspired by Goldsmith's version of the autosegmental phonology and of the syllable.

Carstairs-McCarthy (2001) asked whether the syllable, as a unit of phonological description, is modality-neutral (with fundamentally the same sense in descriptions of signed and spoken languages), or whether the syllables of signed and spoken languages are really different phenomena. He asserted that it was legitimate to appeal to aspects of spoken syllables that are undoubtedly modality-dependent, such as their physiological underpinnings, perhaps in the number and type of oscillators available in the vocal apparatus versus the sign apparatus. Such differences are reflected in the presence versus absence in spoken and signed languages, respectively, of the SSP. By examining more basic notions, however, such as energy and perceptual salience, we see that the notion of sonority is truly universal.

6.4. Conclusion

It is rare in the history of science that we can speak of a paradigm shift, but I believe that autosegmental phonology constituted exactly that with respect to phonological representation. The constructs introduced (autosegmental tiers) or reintroduced (the syllable) by autosegmental theory have changed the way that phonology is practiced today, so much so that these ideas are often taken for granted. From the point of view of sign language phonology, autosegmental phonology made it possible to see cross-modal similarities and differences and to make predictions about structure that were not possible previously, changing theories of phonological representation (spoken and signed) ever since.

Notes

1. Goldsmith's recent, ten-dimensional visualizations displaying eigenvector analyses of the lexical and morphological structure of English and

French are also evidence of his longstanding interest in the multidimensional space within which a grammar operates (Goldsmith 2014; Lee and Goldsmith 2017).

2. Both the "rolladeck" structure of features as in (1a) and the hierarchical feature geometry as in (1b) are often represented as if they were flat in an attempt to make printing and viewing a bit easier on the page, but, as we know, printable simplicity is completely irrelevant to simplicity of phonological representations in the mind.
3. In the case of an aperture change, specific order is respected ( not *).
4. For ease of exposition I have simplified many details of both models. For example, in both models the handshape node is part of a larger structure known as the articulator, and orientation has been omitted.

References

Battison, Robbin. 1978. *Lexical Borrowing in American Sign Language.* Silver Spring, MD: Linstok Press. Reprint, Burtonsville, MD: Sign Media, 2002.

Berent, Iris. 2013. *The Phonological Mind.* Cambridge: Cambridge University Press.

Berent, Iris, Amanda Dupuis, and Diane Brentari. 2013. Amodal aspects of linguistic design: Evidence from sign language. *PLoS One* 8, no. 4: 1–17.

Bloomfield, Leonard. 1933. *Language.* New York: Henry Holt.

Bradfield, Julian. 2014. Clicks, concurrency, and Khoisan. *Phonology* 31:1–49.

Brentari, Diane. 1990. Licensing in ASL handshape change. In *Sign Language Research: Theoretical Issues*, ed. Ceil Lucas, 57–68. Washington, DC: Gallaudet University Press.

———. 1993. Establishing a sonority hierarchy in American Sign Language: The use of simultaneous structure in phonology. *Phonology* 10:281–306.

———. 1998. *A Prosodic Model of Sign Language Phonology.* Cambridge, MA: MIT Press.

———. 2002. Modality differences in sign language phonology and morphophonemics. In *Modality in Language and Linguistic Theory*, ed. Richard Meier, David Quinto, and Kearsy Cormier, 35–64. Cambridge: Cambridge University Press.

———. 2006. Effects of language modality on word segmentation: An experimental study of phonological factors in a sign language. In *Laboratory Phonology 8*, ed. Louis Goldstein, Doug Whalen, and Catherine Best, 155–164. Berlin: Mouton de Gruyter.

Brentari, Diane, Carolina González, Amanda Seidl, and Ronnie Wilbur. 2011. Sensitivity to visual prosodic cues in signers and nonsigners. *Language and Speech* 54, no. 1: 49–72.

Browman, Catherine, and Louis Goldstein. 1989. Articulatory gestures as phonological units. *Phonology* 6:201–251.

Carstairs-McCarthy, Andrew. 2001. ASL "syllables" and language evolution: A response to Uriagereka. *Language* 77:343–349.

Chomsky, Noam, and Morris Halle. 1968. *The Sound Pattern of English*. New York: Harper and Row.

Clements, G. Nick. 1985. The geometry of phonological features. *Phonology Yearbook* 2:225–252.

———. 1990. The role of the sonority cycle in core syllabification. In *Papers in Laboratory Phonology I: Between the Grammar and Physics of Speech*, ed. John Kingston and Mary Beckman, 282–333. Cambridge: Cambridge University Press.

Clements, G. Nick, and John Goldsmith. 1984. *Autosegmental Studies in Bantu Tone*. Dordrecht: Foris Publications.

Clements, G. Nick, and Elizabeth Hume. 1995. Internal organization of speech sounds. In *The Handbook of Phonological Theory*, ed. John Goldsmith, 245–306. Oxford: Blackwell.

Corina, David. 1990. Reassessing the role of sonority in syllable structure: Evidence from a visual-gestural language. In *Proceedings from the 26th Annual Meeting of the Chicago Linguistic Society*, vol. 2: *Parasession on the Syllable on the Syllable in Phonetics and Phonology*, 33–44. Chicago: Chicago Linguistic Society.

Davis, Jeffrey E. 2010. *Hand Talk: Sign Language among American Indian Nations*. Cambridge: Cambridge University Press.

Dell, François, and Mohammed Elmedlaoui. 1985. Syllabic consonants and syllabification in Imdlawn Tashlhiyt Berber. *Journal of African Languages and Linguistics* 7:105–130.

Firth, J. R. 1948. Sounds and prosodies. *Transactions of the Philological Society* 47:127–152.

Friedman, Lynn. 1977. Formational properties of American Sign Language. In *On the Other Hand: New Perspectives in American Sign Language*, ed. Lynn Friedman, 13–56. New York: Academic Press.

Frishberg, Nancy. 1975. Arbitrariness and iconicity. *Language* 51:696–719.

Goldsmith, John. 1976. Autosegmental phonology. PhD dissertation, Massachusetts Institute of Technology. Bloomington: Indiana University Linguistics Club. http://people.cs.uchicago.edu/~jagoldsm/Papers/dissertation.pdf. Published by Garland Press, New York [1979].

———. 1985. Vowel harmony in Khalkha Mongolian, Yaka, Hungarian and Finnish. *Phonology Yearbook* 2:253–75.

———. 1990. *Autosegmental and Metrical Phonology*. Oxford: Basil Blackwell.

———. 1992. Tone and accent in Llogoori. In *The Joy of Syntax*, ed. D. Brentari, G. Larson, and L. McLeod, 73–94. Philadelphia: John Benjamins.

———. 2014. Language and the mind: Encounters in the mind fields. Nora and Edward Ryerson Lecture. Filmed April 23, 2014. University of Chicago video, 1:06:50. Posted June 17, 2014. https://www.youtube.com/watch?v=CdgPpM9aC9k.

Goldsmith, John, and Gary Larson. 1990. Local modeling and syllabification. In *Papers from the 26th Annual Regional Meeting of the Chicago Linguistic Society*, vol. 2, ed. K. M. Ziolkowski, K. Deaton, and M. Noske, 129–142. Chicago: Chicago Linguistic Society.

Goldsmith, John, and Fidéle Mpiranya. 2011. Rhythm, quantity and tone in the Kinyarwanda verb. In *Tones and Features: Phonetic and Phonological Perspectives*, ed. L. Wetzels, E. Hume, and J. Goldsmith, 25–49. Berlin: Mouton de Gruyter.

Gordon, Matthew. 2006. *Syllable Weight: Phonetics, Phonology, Typology*. New York/Oxon: Routledge.

Gordon, Matthew, Carmen Jany, Carlos Nash, and Nobutaka Takara. 2008. Vowel and consonant sonority and coda weight: A cross-linguistic study. *Proceedings of the West Coast Conference on Formal Linguistics* 26:208–216.

Hale, Mark, and Charles Reiss. 2008. *The Phonological Enterprise*. Oxford: Oxford University Press.

Hayes, Bruce. 1989. Compensatory lengthening in moraic phonology. *Linguistic Inquiry* 20:253–306.

Henderson, Eugénie. 1985. Feature shuffling in Southeast Asian languages. In *Southeast Asian Linguistic Studies Presented to André-G. Haudricourt*, ed. S. Ratanakul, S. Premsirat, and D. Thomas, 1–22. Bankok: Mahidol University Press. Available online from Southeast Asian Linguistics Archives, http://sealang.net/sala/archives/pdf4/henderson1985feature.pdf.

Hooper, Joan B. 1972. The syllable in phonological theory. *Language* 48:525–540.

Itô, Junko. 1986. Syllable theory in prosodic phonology. PhD dissertation, University of Massachusetts. Published by Garland Press, New York [1989].

Itô, Junko, and Armin Mester. 1995. Japanese phonology. In *The Handbook of Phonological Theory*, ed. John Goldsmith, 817–838. Oxford: Blackwell.

Jantunen, Tommi, and Takkinen Ritva. 2010. Syllable structure in sign language phonology. In *Sign Languages*, ed. Diane Brentari, 312–331. Cambridge: Cambridge University Press.

Jakobson, Roman, and Morris Halle. 1956. *Fundamentals of Language*. The Hague: Mouton.

Jakobson, Roman, Gunnar Fant, and Morris Halle. 1952 *Preliminaries to Speech Analysis: The Distinctive Features and Their Correlates*. Cambridge, MA: MIT Press.

Kaschube, Dorothea. 1967. *Structural Elements of Crow*. Boulder: University of Colorado Press.

Klima, Edward, and Ursula Bellugi. 1979. *The Signs of Language*. Cambridge, MA: Harvard University Press.

Kroeber, Albert. 1958. Sign language inquiry. *International Journal of American Linguistics* 24:1–19.

Ladd, Robert. 2014. *Simultaneous Structure in Phonology.* Cambridge: Cambridge University Press.

Lane, Harlan, Penny Boyes Braem, and Ursula Bellugi. 1976. Preliminaries to distinctive feature analysis of handshapes in American Sign Language. *Cognitive Psychology* 8:263–289.

Lee, Jackson, and John Goldsmith. 2017. Linguistica: Unsupervised learning of linguistic structure. Paper presented at the North American Chapter of the Association for Computational Linguistics.

Levin, Juliette. 1985. A metrical theory of syllabicity. PhD dissertation, Massachusetts Institute of Technology.

Liddell, Scott. 1984. THINK and BELIEVE: Sequentiality in American Sign Language. *Language* 60:372–392.

Liddell, Scott, and Robert Johnson. 1989. American Sign Language: The phonological base. *Sign Language Studies* 64:197–277.

Mandel, Mark A. 1981. Phonotactics and morphophonology in American Sign Language. PhD dissertation, University of California, Berkeley.

Meier, Richard. 2002. Why different, why the same? Explaining effects and non-effects of modality on linguistic structure in sign and speech. In *Modality in Language and Linguistic Theory*, ed. R. Meier, D. Quinto, and K Cormier, 35–64. New York: Cambridge University Press.

Mous, Maarten. 2007. *A Sketch of Iraqw Grammar.* Leiden: Leiden University Centre of Linguistics.

Perlmutter, David. 1992. Sonority and syllable structure in American Sign Language. *Linguistic Inquiry* 23:407–442.

Pettito, Laura A., and Paula Marantette. 1991. Babbling in the manual mode: Evidence for the ontogeny of language. *Science* 251:1493–1496.

Piggott, Glyne. 1989. A parametric approach to nasal harmony. In *Features, Segmental Structure and Harmony Processes*, ed. H. van der Hulst and N. Smith, 132–167. Dordrecht: Foris Publications.

———. 2000. Against feature alignment. *Journal of Linguistics* 36:85–129.

Poizner, Howard. 1983. Perception of movement in American Sign Language: Effects of linguistic structure and linguistic experience. *Perception and Psychophysics* 33:215–231.

Reh, Mechthild. 1983. Krongo: A VSO language with postpositions. *Journal of African Languages and Linguistics* 5:45–55.

Rubach, Jerzy, and Geert Booij. 1990. Syllable assignment in Polish. *Phonology* 7:121–158.

Sagey, Elizabeth. 1986. The representation of features and relations in non-linear phonology. PhD dissertation, Massachusetts Institute of Technology.

Sandler, Wendy. 1986. The spreading hand autosegment of American Sign Language. *Sign Language Studies* 50:1–28.

———. 1989. *Phonological Representation of the Sign.* Dordrecht: Foris Publications.

———. 1993. A sonority cycle in American Sign Language. *Phonology* 10:243–279.

Sandler, Wendy, and Diane Lillo-Martin. 2006. *Sign Language and Linguistic Universals*. Cambridge: Cambridge University Press.

Stokoe, William. 1960. *Sign Language Structure: An Outline of the Visual Communication Systems of the American Deaf*. Studies in Linguistics, Occasional Papers 8. Buffalo, NY: University of Buffalo, Department of Anthropology and Linguistics. (Available from Linstok Press, Silver Spring, MD.)

Supalla, Ted, and Elissa Newport. 1978. How many seats in a chair? The derivation of nouns and verbs in ASL. In *Understanding Language through Sign Language Research*, ed. P. Siple, 91–132. New York: Academic Press.

Trubetzkoy, Nicholai. 1939. *Grundzüge der Phonologie*. Göttingen: Vandenhoeck and Ruprecht. English translation, *Principles of Phonology*. Berkeley: University of California Press, 1969.

Tyrone, Martha E., Hosung Nam, Elliot Saltzman, Gaurav Mathur, and Louis Goldstein. 2010. Prosody and movement in American Sign Language: A task-dynamics approach. In *Conference Proceedings of Prosody 2010*, Chicago. N.p.

van der Hulst, Harry. 1993. Units in the analysis of signs. *Phonology* 10:209–241.

———. 2000. Modularity and modality in phonology. In *Phonological Knowledge: Its Nature*, ed. N. Burton-Roberts, P. Carr, and G. Docherty, 207–244. Oxford: Oxford University Press.

van der Hulst, Harry, and van der Weijer, Jeroen. 1995. Vowel harmony. In *The Handbook of Phonological Theory*, ed. J. Goldsmith, 495–534. New York: Blackwell.

van der Kooij, Els. 2002. Phonological categories in Sign Language of the Netherlands: The role of phonetic implementation and iconicity. PhD dissertation, Leiden University.

van der Kooij, Els, and Harry van der Hulst. 2005. On the internal and external organization of sign segments: Some modality specific property of sign segments in NGT. In *The Internal Organization of Phonological Segments*, ed. M. van Oostendorp and J. van de Weijer, 153–180. Studies in Generative Grammar 77. Berlin: Mouton de Gruyter.

Voegelin, Carl. 1958. Sign language analysis: On one level or two? *International Journal of American Linguistics* 24:71–77.

West, La Mont, Jr. 1960. The Sign Language, an analysis. 2 vols. PhD dissertation, Indiana University.

Williamson, Kay. 1989. Tone and accent in Ịjọ. In *Pitch Accent Systems*, ed. Harry van der Hulst and Norval Smith, 253–278. Dordrecht: Foris Publications.

SEVEN

Abstract Underlying Representations in Prosodic Structure

BERT VAUX AND BRIDGET D. SAMUELS

7.1. Introduction

The centuries-old tension between rationalism and empiricism manifests itself in a number of areas in phonology. This debate has perhaps become most obvious over the past quarter century with the emergence of surface-oriented, parallelist models of phonology built on a connectionist conception of cognition (Goldsmith and Larson 1990, 1993; Goldsmith 1992, 1993, 1994; Prince and Smolensky 1993 [2002]; Pater 2009) as well as exemplar-based, statistically oriented approaches (Bybee 2001). Many of these models of phonology blur the line between phonology and phonetics (e.g., Flemming 2002; Hayes, Kirchner, and Steriade 2004), and in doing so depart from the more abstract views of phonological representations advocated by Saussure (1916), Sapir (1933), Jakobson (1949), and Chomsky and Halle (1968), among others. In the present work, we follow Goldsmith (2011) in investigating whether such a move is empirically or conceptually warranted in the domain of prosodic representation in particular. The answer has significant implications for several areas of phonological theory, as well as for the architecture of grammar more broadly.

Here we take on the question of whether phonological representations include predictable abstract prosodic structure. We find this question to be particularly interesting because it cross-cuts the empiricist versus rationalist debate: even some proponents of highly abstract, derivational models of phonology forgo lexically stored representations of prosodic structure (e.g., Chomsky and Halle 1968; Samuels 2011; see Goldsmith 2011 for a historical overview of this line of thinking).[1] The debate over whether to store prosodic structure in the lexicon is also couched in a larger discussion regarding the degree to which underspecification of other phonological features is allowed in lexical entries (Goldsmith and Noske 2006). There is compelling evidence for at least some degree of underspecification in certain situations, which we review in section 7.2. However, the situation with respect to the underspecification of prosodic structure is less clear; in section 7.3, we lay out arguments for and against storing syllabification in the lexicon. Finally, in section 7.4, we illustrate the consequences of this debate for moraification and stress in Abkhaz and the problem of lexical prosody in Optimality Theory (OT). We ultimately conclude that the weight of the evidence supports the existence of abstract underlying phonological representations, and that in the domain of prosodic structure, languages appear to employ a surprising degree of redundancy.

7.2. Underspecification of Phonological Features

From a certain perspective (see, e.g., Bromberger and Halle 1989), it seems desirable for phonology—like other modules of grammar—to strike a balance between two conflicting sets of demands: (i) the need to reduce long-term memory burden and (ii) the need to provide a full set of instructions to its interfaces (in this case, the sensory-motor system). Steriade formalizes these demands as in (1):

(1) a. Lexical Minimality: underlying representations must reduce to some minimum the phonological information used to distinguish lexical items.
b. Full Specification: the output of the phonological component must contain fully (or at least maximally) specified feature matrices. (Steriade 1995: 114)

In order to satisfy Lexical Minimality and Full Specification simultaneously, all predictable information must be left out of the lexicon, to be supplied instead by rules or other means in the phonological component. This is indeed the tack that has been taken by proponents of various underspecification theories over the past half-century. For example, Halle (1959) employed feature-filling "segment structure rules" (later known as "redundancy rules") interleaved with feature-changing rules. On the basis of work by Lightner (1963) and Stanley (1967), this position was revised, and Chomsky and Halle (1968) in *The Sound Pattern of English* (*SPE*) moved the feature-filling redundancy rules into the lexicon. This move was a response to the position held by Stanley in particular: if unvalued features are allowed into the phonology, then the binary ± feature-value system effectively becomes ternary, +/–/Ø. At the time, this was seen as an abuse of the notation, though more recently Inkelas (1995) and others argued that Stanley's objections to ternarity were unwarranted.

Because ordering all redundancy rules before other phonological rules eliminates the possibility of using underspecified representations to do any work in phonology, it also eliminates any empirical advantages to adopting underspecification. Lexical Minimality is its only motivation. However, there is empirical evidence that Stanley's (1967) position cannot be maintained. Consider, for example, the arguments put forth by Archangeli and Pulleyblank (1994) based on the Kalenjin languages, which have a process of [ATR] harmony. In this system, some affixes freely alternate between [+ATR] and [–ATR], but a handful of opaque affixes invariably surface as [–ATR] and block [+ATR] from spreading across them. One such morpheme is the negative affix, *-ma-*. Thus, when the [+ATR] root *ke:r* is prefixed with *-ma-* as in (2b), *-ma-* and the prefix to the left of it surface as [–ATR].[2] Archangeli and Pulleyblank attributed the different behavior of vowels with respect to [±ATR] alternation to differences in their underlying representation. They hypothesized that invariant roots and affixes carry their [ATR] specifications throughout the derivation, but the vowels that alternate remain unvalued for [ATR] until the harmony rule (for them, a rule of autosegmental spreading) fills in those values. Specifically in the case of (2b), *-ma-* is underlyingly specified [–ATR] and prevents the root's [+ATR] value from spreading across to *kA-*. Crucially, both values of [ATR] must be present in the lexicon: [+ATR] must spread and [–ATR] must be present to block it. The correct pattern is derived only by maintaining a three-way +/–/Ø distinction at the time the harmony rule applies.

(2) Kalenjin ATR harmony

Underlying form	Surface form	Gloss
kI-A-ke:r-In	[kiạge:rin]	'I saw you-SG'
kA-ma-A-ke:r-Ak	[kamaạge:rạk]	'I didn't see you-PL'

This analysis is reminiscent of the Prague School view of how to analyze such alternations; the Ø-valued segment is similar to the notion of "archiphoneme" employed by Jakobson (1929) and Trubetzkoy (1939). Inkelas (1995), Reiss (2008), and Samuels (2009) argue, on the basis of such cases, that underspecification occurs for a given feature where there is evidence of alternating forms that contrast with nonalternating ones, and the alternation is predictable.

Several approaches admitting this much or more underspecification have emerged in the phonological literature, spanning a considerable range of variation: for instance, among theories that hold that unmarked feature values are underspecified, there are some that take markedness to be universal, while others take it to be language-specific or contextually determined. "Radical" underspecification theories only permit one value of a given feature in the lexicon, whereas "contrastive" underspecification is based on the notion that only "feature values predictable on the basis of universal co-occurrence conditions or on the basis of positional neutralization statements can be omitted from underlying representations" (Steriade 1995: 142).

We have discussed our views on underspecification in the segmental domain elsewhere, arguing for the archiphonemic view, in which features that undergo predictable phonological alternations are underspecified (see, e.g., Samuels 2009, 2011). We now take up a related yet independent question, whether predictable prosodic structure such as syllables and moras should also be underspecified in underlying representations.

7.3. Prosodic Structure in the Lexicon

The question of how to divide labor between lexical storage and online derivation arises frequently in phonology and morphology. Three general types of evidence can bear on the question of whether a particular prosodic structure is stored: (i) whether it can be unpredictable/contrastive, (ii) whether there is evidence for processes that occur prior to the introduction of the structure in question, and (iii) psycholinguistic evidence. However, these arguments may be asymmetric: while the existence of unpredictable or contrastive syllabification would argue in favor of lexical storage of syllabic structure, storage and derivation are not necessarily mutually exclusive. We must avoid what Langacker (1987) called the "rule/list fallacy" and acknowledge that language may employ redundant systems: some forms within a given language may be stored with prosodic structure, while other forms may be prosodified by rule. For this reason, we focus here solely on cases in which prosodic structure is predictable, yet there is still evidence that the structure may be stored. Such cases in some sense represent a departure from Bloomfield's (1933: 274) conception of the lexicon as "an appendix of the grammar, a list of basic irregularities."

Given this perspective, we find a number of arguments in the literature inconclusive. For example, Blevins gives three arguments against underlying syllabification:

(3) Arguments against syllable structure in underlying representations
   a. Minimal pairs distinguished by syllabification alone are rare, and are nonexistent in many languages.
   b. Segments in many languages exhibit syllabicity alternations which can be viewed as the simple result of derived syllabification.
   c. Individual morphemes often fail to conform to the possible [surface] syllable types of a given language. (Blevins 1995: 221)

Several counter examples have been adduced against the claim that syllabification is always predictable (3a): see Bloomfield (1933) on English, Kenstowicz and Kisseberth (1979: 261–264) on Barra Gaelic, and Elfner (2006) on Blackfoot. We set this issue aside here, as we are concerned with whether prosodic structure may be stored in cases of predictable syllabification or moraification as well.

Blevins (1995) further claims that evidence of derived syllabification, such as alternations like opin[iə]n ~ opin[jə]n, argue against lexical syllabification (3b). First, it is important to note that not all languages have the potential for resyllabification; languages permitting only consonant-vowel (CV) or CVC syllables, for example, do not. Even in languages where resyllabification could occur, Ramoo (2014) provides a number of converging lines of evidence that storage plus resyllabification accords better with psycholinguistic evidence than syllabifying online and provides additional computational benefits. Evidence from priming studies remains inconclusive: some find syllable priming effects, whereas others find segmental priming effects instead (Schiller 1998, 2000; Brand, Rey, and Peerman 2003; Cholin, Neils, and Levelt 2004). Overall, however, the picture is consistent with the view that syllable structure is stored in the lexicon; see Ramoo (2014: sec. 1.5.4.3) for an overview.

Ramoo's study of resyllabification rates in English, Hindi, and Italian suggests that the computational burden of resyllabification is quite low (Ramoo 2014, sec. 2.3). In the Hindi and Italian corpora that Ramoo studied, the average resyllabification rates were 0.25 and 1 percent, respectively. English has a much higher rate of resyllabification (33 percent on average), but this difference is due almost entirely to high-frequency vowel-initial functional items (*a, an, and, in, it, of, on*). These items are only infrequently resyllabified—for example, *and it* becomes [æn.dɪt] only 7 percent of the time—but drive the overall rate higher because they occur quite frequently in the corpus as a whole. Even the English resyllabification rate of 33 percent still represents significant computational savings over a model in which 100 percent of syllabification is computed online.

Storing syllable structure may also allow the lexicon to be organized according to the principles of content-addressable storage rather than serial order. The small set of permissible syllable types in a given language (e.g., V, CV, CVC) can be used to define the storage space, eliminating the need to maintain addresses and storage for the huge number of phonotactically illicit sequences that do not conform to these syllabic templates. This could improve the efficiency of lexical storage and retrieval, as well as phonological acquisition. This view is compatible with the Lexicon with Syllable Structure model of speech production (Romani et al. 2011), which links syllable structural nodes to phonemes on the phonological level of representation and converts these phonemes to articulatory units on a different level. Such a model can account for connected speech phenomena by permitting online resyllabification, unlike Dell's (1986, 1988) model, which specifies segments with syllabic (allophonic) information at the lexical level and does not permit resyllabification.

The status of Blevins's third objection to underlying syllable structure, namely that morphemes can be stored in phonotactically illicit shapes (3c), is also unclear. We return to this issue in section 7.4 in our discussion of Abkhaz, which provides several such examples. We concur that roots (e.g., *rhythm* /rɪðm/, *meter* /mitr/) and affixes (e.g., plural *-z*, past tense *-d*) may be lexically stored in forms that cannot be exhaustively syllabified. Szigetvári (2011) points out that such forms are not problematic if syllabification in the lexicon can be partial. Monosyllabic bound morphemes like *-d* could be stored unsyllabified, and forms such as /hɪmn/ (*hymn*) could be allowed to contain an unsyllabified /n/ in the lexical entry.[3] Maintaining the OT principle of Lexicon Optimization (LO) (4) precludes this alternative, however.

(4) Lexicon Optimization

Suppose that several inputs $I_1, I_2, \ldots, I_n$ when parsed by a grammar G lead to corresponding outputs $O_1, O_2, \ldots, O_n$ all of which are realized as the same

> phonetic form Φ—these inputs are all *phonetically equivalent* with respect to G. Now one of these outputs must be the most harmonic, by virtue of incurring the least significant violation marks: suppose this optimal one is labelled O*k*. Then the learner should choose, as the underlying form for Φ, the input I*k*. (Prince and Smolensky 2004: 225–226)

As Prince and Smolensky (2004: 226) put it, "Lexicon Optimization entails that the constraints on surface syllable structure will be echoed in the lexicon as well." We will return to this issue in section 7.4.2.

Further evidence for underlying syllabification has been claimed to come from tip-of-the-tongue (TOT) states, misremembered words, and malapropisms. Brown and McNeill (1966) and many subsequent studies, catalogued by Brown (2012), noted that the number of syllables is often remembered in a TOT state (60 percent of the time in Brown and McNeill's [1966] study and 80 percent of the time in Koriat and Lieblich's [1974] study); in fact, this is the most common type of structure to be remembered about a target word (Lovelace 1987). It was already noted by Fromkin (1971) that this suggests syllabification is stored in the lexicon. However, as Koriat and Lieblich (1974) and Brown (1991) have pointed out, successful guesses of syllable number may in part be attributed to general (or even extralinguistic) knowledge about the word; for example, animal names are more likely to be two syllables than four, while medical terms are more likely to be four syllables than two. In short, evidence from the TOT state remains inconclusive. In the absence of strong evidence from the literature presented in this section, we now ask whether attested phonological phenomena that depend on moraification or syllabification can shed some light on this matter.

7.4. Case Studies

In this section we focus on two case studies, with the goal of showing in more detail the theoretical consequences of assuming storage or underspecification of predictable prosodic structure. Section 7.4.1 develops an explicit account of the core systems of moraification and stress assignment in Abkhaz, on the basis of which we argue that predictable moraic structure may be stored in lexical representations. Section 7.4.2 examines consequences of this assumption for optimality-theoretic learning algorithms and suggests that they are able to account for neither syllabified nor unsyllabified underlying representations without abandoning central tenets of the model.

7.4.1. Abkhaz Moraification and Parasitic Unpredictability

One element of prosodic structure, the mora,[4] differs from the syllable in being uncontroversially *un*predictable (and hence necessarily encoded in some form lexically) in certain situations, namely ones involving contrastive vowel or consonant length (e.g., Hayes 1989: 256–257; Elfner 2007). Proponents of Moraic Theory assume however that *predictable* moraic structure is *not* stored in lexical entries, but instead is inserted by rules or constraints (e.g., Hayes 1989: 258).

In a language where all closed syllables count as heavy, for example, a hypothetical form such as /apta/ would according to Hayes (1989) be stored in the lexicon with the form in (5a). The /p/, which is predictably moraic by virtue of closing a syllable, is then assigned a mora by a rule of Weight by Position (5d).

(5) Assignment of predictable prosodic structure in Moraic Theory (Hayes 1989: 259)

a. underlying form

b. σ assignment

c. adjunction: prevocalic consonants

d. adjunction: Weight by Position

With the exception of (some) short vowels, then, Moraic Theory maintains that predictable prosodic structure is not stored in lexical entries.

The stress system in the Northwest Caucasian language Abkhaz may pose a problem for this assumption. We argue here that in Abkhaz an unpredictable property (lexical accent) is best analyzed in Moraic Theory as being hosted in the lexicon by moras. This becomes a problem when these moras are predictable from the phonological contexts in which their host segments occur and hence by the principle of underspecifying predictable prosodic structure should not be stored in the lexicon.

The core stress system in Abkhaz is governed by Dybo's Rule, which can be formulated as in (6):

(6) Dybo's Rule

Assign word stress to (i) the leftmost underlyingly accented element (ii) not followed by another accented element; otherwise (iii) stress falls on the final element.[6] (Dybo 1973, 1977; Dybo, Nikolayev, and Starostin 1978; cf. Hewitt 1979, 1989; Spruit 1986: 38; Kathman 1992, 1994, 1996; Trigo 1992)

We illustrate the workings of Dybo's Rule with the forms in (7) and (8).[7] In the notation employed here, an underscore (e.g., x̲) represents a lexically accented element and an acute accent (e.g., x́) represents an element that is stressed in the surface form.

(7) Nominal root: /madza/ 'secret' (Spruit 1986: 42)

a. [á̲-madza] 'DEF-secret'

b. [madzá-k'] 'secret-INDEF'

(8) Verbal roots (Spruit 1986: 46)

	unaccented root			*accented root*	
a.	á̲-p^{h}a-ɾa̲	'jump'	d.	a̲-p^{h}a̲-ɾá̲	'pleat'
b.	á̲-fa-ɾa̲	'eat'	e.	a̲-ja̲-ɾá̲	'lie down'
c.	á̲-t^{h}a-ɾa̲	'give'	f.	a̲-ts^{h}a̲-ɾá̲	'go'

We can see the workings of condition (i) of Dybo's Rule in (7a) and (8a)–(8c). In (7a), the lexically accented definite prefix /a̲-/ is followed by the unaccented root /madza/; by dint of (6i) the /a̲-/, being the leftmost underlyingly accented element, receives the surface stress. The forms in (4) are verbal infinitives, which are constructed from the root by prefixing the accented definite morpheme /a̲-/ and suffixing the accented infinitive ending /-ɾa̲/. In the forms in (8a)–(8c) the verbal roots are underlyingly unaccented; the lexical accents of the prefix and suffix are therefore nonadjacent, and condition (i) of Dybo's Rule therefore holds again, assigning stress to the leftmost of these accents.

The forms in (8d)–(8f) involve lexically accented roots, as a result of which these infinitives each contain a sequence of three consecutive accented elements. This configuration triggers condition (ii) of Dybo's

Rule, assigning surface stress to the rightmost accented element. The interaction of conditions (i) and (ii) can be seen in (9):

(9) /x̲ x̲ x x̲/ strings

a. verbal: [a̲-tʰá̲-la-ɾa̲] 'go into' (DEF-into-go-INF) (Spruit 1986: 47)

b. nominal: [a̲-dzá̲ɾa-p'a̲] 'go into' (DEF-waist-slender) (Spruit 1986: 42)

In (9a) we have a string of two lexically accented elements (/a̲-tʰa̲-/), followed by an unaccented one (/-la-/), followed by another lexical accent (/-ɾa̲/). Here if (i) alone determined the outcome we would expect *[átʰalara], but condition (ii) prevents the /a̲-/ prefix from being stressed since it is immediately followed by another accented element, /-tʰa̲-/. The leftmost accented element not followed by an accented element is this same /-tʰa̲-/, so it is assigned the surface stress.

Condition (iii) of Dybo's Rule is at work in (7b), a form assembled from the unaccented root /madza/ 'secret' and the unaccented indefinite suffix /-k'/. Since this form contains no lexical accents the elsewhere condition in (6iii) kicks in, and surface stress is assigned to the final element.

So far we have used Spruit's term "element" to refer to the entities that can host lexical accents. Spruit considers each Abkhaz word to consist for stress-placement purposes of a string of elements drawn from the set {C(ɨ), Ca, a, aa}, with a and aa occurring only in morpheme-initial position and C representing any consonant (Spruit 1986: 37). Each of these four elements can host a lexical accent, in which case Spruit refers to it as dominant (D); elements not bearing a lexical accent are recessive (R). The element C(ɨ) normally surfaces as [Cɨ] when assigned a surface stress, and [C] when unstressed (though unstressed D C(ɨ)'s can surface as [Cɨ] under certain conditions). In Spruit's system, a form such as [madzá-k'] 'secret- INDEF' in (7b) would contain three elements: the Ca element /ma/, which is R, the Ca element /dza/, which is also R, and the C(ɨ) element /k'/, also R.

7.4.1.1. Moraic Analysis of the Abkhaz Facts

Kathman (1992: 211) suggests that the Abkhaz system may not be as idiosyncratic as it might appear from Spruit's description, if we think of the accent-bearing unit in Abkhaz as the cross-linguistically familiar mora instead of the Abkhaz-specific "element," and if we recast the language-specific heuristic in (6) in terms of a more familiar stress formalism designed for use with all human languages. Starting with the idea that the Abkhaz stress system manipulates moras rather than elements, let us suppose for the moment that Abkhaz assigns moras in the manner depicted in (10) and (11).[8]

(10) Metaprinciples of Abkhaz prosodification (provisional)

a. Unpredictable moraic structure is stored in the lexicon: long vowels are stored with two moras (Hayes 1989: 256, figure 3), and geminate consonants are stored with a single mora (Hayes 1989: 257, figure 6).

b. Predictable moraic structure is not stored in the lexicon.

(11) Algorithm for assignment of moraic structure to Abkhaz forms[9]

a. *σ Assignment* (cf. (5b) and Hayes 1989: 259, figure 11): Project a mora from each vowel, and project a syllable from each such mora.

b. *Adjunction of prevocalic consonants*: Attach to each new syllable as many immediately preceding unsyllabified adjacent consonants as are allowed in syllable-initial position (cf. Hayes's (1989: 259, figure 11) adjunction of prevocalic consonants (5c)).

c. *Weight by Position*: Project a mora for each unprosodified consonant that is immediately preceded by a vowel. Attach this mora to the syllable that dominates the left-adjacent mora (cf. Hayes 1989: 258, figure 10).

d. Attach to a left-adjacent mora as many unsyllabified adjacent consonants as are phonotactically allowed.[10]

We provide in (12) sample derivations produced by the system in (10) and (11) for /a-pʰʃa/ 'wind (n)', /d-a-m-ba-j/ 'didn't it see him?', /a-tʰa-χː-ɾa/ 'to run into', and /a-χʲʃˀtsʰba/ 'sparrowhawk'.

(12) Derivations of Abkhaz moraic structures

a. UR[11] by (10) /a-pʰʃa/ 'wind (n)'

(11a) 

(11b) 

(11c) N/A

(11d) N/A

b. UR by (10) /d-a-m-ba-j/ 'didn't it see him?' (Spruit 1986: 64)

(11a) 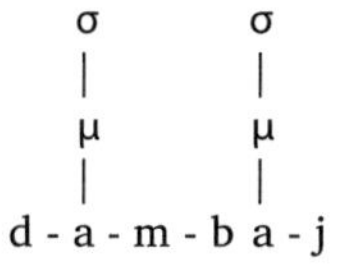

(11b) 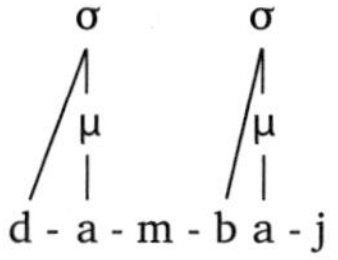

(11c) 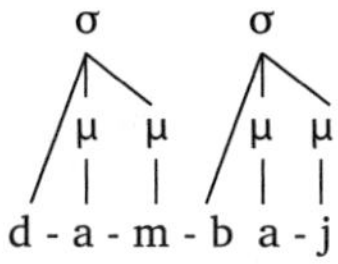

(11d) N/A

c. UR by (10) /a-tʰa-χ:-ɾa/ 'to run into' (Spruit 1986: 48)

(11a) 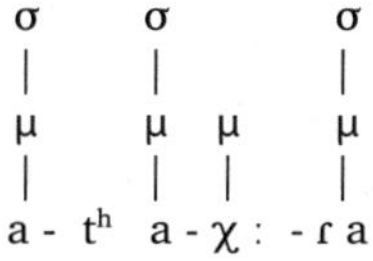

(11b) 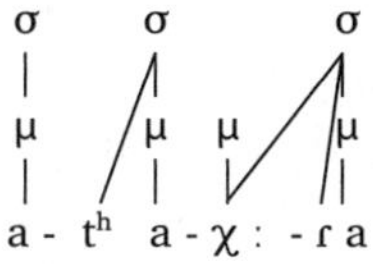

(11c) 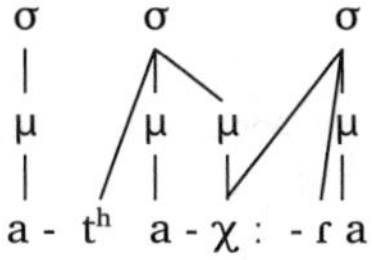

(11d) N/A

d. UR by (10) /a-χʲʃʲtsʰba/ 'sparrowhawk' (Spruit 1986: 44)

(11a) 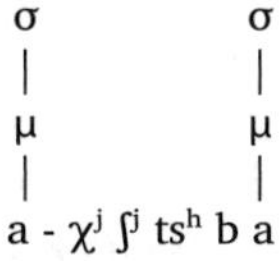

(11b)

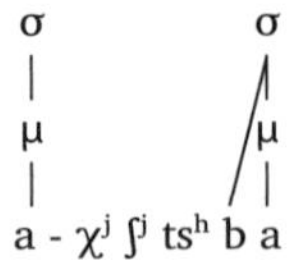

(11c)

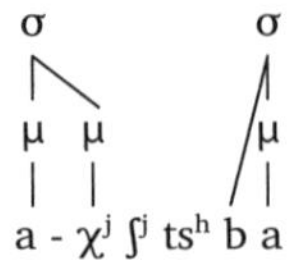

(11d)

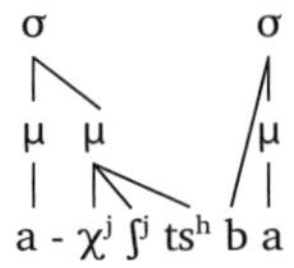

Moving on to the stress computation system, we can model the core Abkhaz facts in terms of Halle and Idsardi's (1995) formalism in the manner outlined in (13).[12]

(13) Algorithm for assignment of stress in Abkhaz

i. Project all moras onto Line 0 of the metrical grid.
ii. For each lexically accented mora, project a right bracket) to the right of the Line 0 element associated with the mora.
iii. Line 0 edge marking: LLL
iv. Clash Deletion:) → Ø / _ *) [iterative, L→R]
v. Project the rightmost element of each Line 0 foot to Line 1.
vi. Project the leftmost element of each Line 1 foot to Line 2.

In the formalism in (13), the conflicting directionality identified by Dybo ([6i] versus [6iii]) results from left (L) versus right (R) headedness on Lines 0 and 1, respectively, in (13v) and (13vi), and the iterativity and directionality via (13iv) (cf. Howard 1972).

We illustrate in (14) how the algorithm in (13) assigns metrical structure to madzá-k' 'secret-INDEF' (7b), á-pʰa-ra 'jump' (8a), and a-pʰa-rá 'pleat' (8d).

(14) Sample derivations

a.	(13i)	Line 0	* * *	* * *	* * *
			a-pʰa-rá	á-pʰa-ra	madzá-k'
b.	(13ii)	Line 0	*) *) *)	*) * *)	* * *
			a-pʰa-rá	á-pʰa-ra	madzá-k'

c.	(13iii)	Line 0	(*) *) *)	(*) * *)	(* * *
			a̲-p^ha̲-ɾá̲	á̲-p^ha-ɾa̲	madzá-k′
d.	(13iv)	Line 0	(* * *)	(*) * *)	(* * *
			a̲-p^ha̲-ɾá̲	á̲-p^ha-ɾa̲	madzá-k′
e.	(13v)	Line 1	*	* *	*
		Line 0	(* * *)	(*) * *)	(* * *
			a̲-p^ha̲-ɾá̲	á̲-p^ha-ɾa̲	madzá-k′
f.	(13vi)	Line 2	*	*	*
		Line 1	*	* *	*
		Line 0	(* * *)	(*) * *)	(* * *
			a̲-p^ha̲-ɾá̲	á̲-p^ha-ɾa̲	madzá-k′

When viewed in this way, the workings of the Abkhaz stress system are strikingly similar to those of Sanskrit and Proto-Indo-European (Kiparsky and Halle 1977; Halle 1997), save that these lack the Abkhaz rule of Clash Deletion (13iv) and do not project consonants onto the stress grid.

Now that we have set out an explicit system for the computation of Abkhaz accentuation, let us justify some of its less obvious components. First of all, why do we say that lexical accents are hosted by moras rather than simply by vowels? The reason is that (moraic) consonants also appear to be able to host lexical accents, as with the morpheme /-χː-/ in a̲-t^ha̲-χː-ɾá̲ 'to run into' (Spruit 1986: 48; Kaslandzia 2005: 662). If only vowels were able to bear lexical accents and the /-χː-/ was therefore underlyingly unaccented, we would expect *a̲-t^há̲-χː-ɾa̲, with the unaccented χː blocking Clash Deletion by intervening between the lexical accents on t^ha and ɾa, incorrectly leading to stress surfacing on the second syllable.

One might then object that consonants simply do not participate in the Abkhaz stress system; this move would straightforwardly account for the behavior of a̲-t^ha̲-χ̲ː̲-ɾá̲, which in the revised analysis would be a̲-(t^h)a̲-(χː-ɾ)á̲, with parentheses enclosing segments not projected onto the stress grid. Since in this scheme neither the t^h nor the χ would be visible for purposes of stress computation, we would have a string of three consecutive accented elements, which according to (6) should correctly produce final stress.

The problem for this analysis is that moraic consonants are contrastive with respect to lexical accent: they may either bear a lexical accent or not, whereas the invisible-consonant theory allows for only one of these two options. Consider [dámbaj] 'didn't it see him?' in (8b), which has the underlying structure /d-a̲-m-ba̲-Ø-j/ 3.SG.HUMAN.ABS-3.SG.NONHUMAN.OBLIQUE-NEG-see-AOR-WHQ.NONHUMAN. If only vowels were visible to stress computation, that is, (d-)a̲(-m-b)a̲(-Ø-j), Line 0 of the stress plane would contain only the lexically accented elements -a̲- and -a̲-, which would incorrectly generate *[dambáj]. Crucially the negative morpheme /-m-/ must project to Line 0 (by virtue of being moraic) but be lexically unaccented; this combination of assumptions leads to the first -a̲- being the leftmost lexically accented element not followed immediately by another lexical accent, and it is therefore assigned the surface word stress. By similar reasoning, the morpheme /-ɥ-/ 'two' in á̲-ɥ-lá̲-k' 'the two dogs' must project onto Line 0 (by virtue of being moraic) but be lexically unaccented. The contrast between a̲-tʰa̲-χ̲ː-rá̲ on the one hand and d-á̲-m-ba̲-Ø-j on the other suggests that moraic consonants can be either lexically accented (as with -χ̲ː-) or not (as with -m-).

The next question is why we single out moraic consonants, rather than having all consonants be able to bear lexical accents. Non-weight-bearing consonants normally do not participate in stress systems in human languages (see Gordon 2005 for a review of possible cases). Abkhaz conforms to this expectation; while there is ample evidence for moraic consonants participating in stress computations, there is no evidence for nonmoraic consonants being accentable. It therefore makes sense from both Abkhaz-internal and cross-linguistic perspectives to assume that only moraic elements can bear lexical accents in Abkhaz, and only moras can project elements onto the stress grid.

7.4.1.2. Problems with the Moraic Analysis

These assumptions, while well-grounded both internally and externally, pose at least two problems. First, there is the problem that all consonants except immediately prevocalic ones count for the purposes of stress computation in Spruit's (1986) and Kathman's (1992) systems: they are moraic in Kathman's system, or are "elements" in Spruit's system. The word [apʰstʰá] 'DEF-ravine', for example, has the prosodic structures in (15a) and (15b) for Spruit and Kathman, respectively:

(15) Prosodic structure of consonant sequences

a. Spruit (1986: 43)

D		D	D	D
a	-	pʰ	s	tʰ a

b. Kathman (1992: 211) (Line 1 asterisks are equivalent to Ds in Spruit's model and lexical accents in our model)

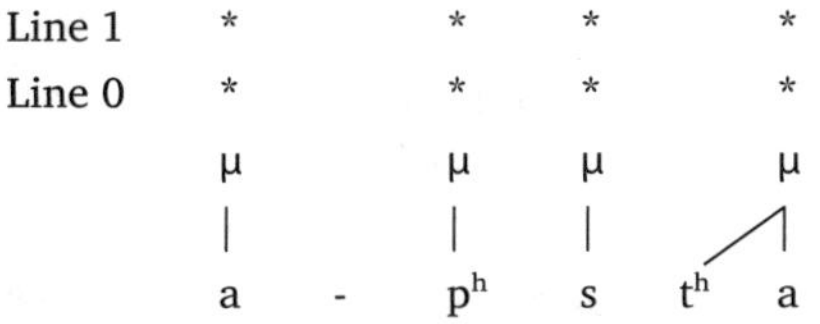

The problem here is twofold. First, a mora is assigned to every non-prevocalic consonant, allowing in principle for unbounded numbers of moras per syllable; [pʰstʰák'] 'ravine-INDEF' for example would have four moras in a single syllable. An unconstrained system of this sort would lose the ability to capture the generalization that languages never contrast more than two (or at most three) phonological weights. Second, by projecting all non-prevocalic consonants onto the stress grid we would be forced to stipulate that all consonants immediately following a lexically accented consonant must themselves bear a lexical accent. In [apʰstʰá] 'DEF-ravine', for example, both the /pʰ/ and the /s/ have to be specified as lexically accented, otherwise they would separate the lexical accent of the definite prefix /á̲-/ from that of the final /-á̲/ of the root, incorrectly predicting that the form should surface as *[ápʰstʰa].

Having all non-prevocalic consonants be moraic and capable of hosting a lexical accent predicts moreover that one should find contrasts between for example /a̲-p̲ʰstʰa̲/ and /a̲-pʰstʰa̲/, with the non-prevocalic consonants in the former bearing lexical accents and those in the latter not doing so. We would expect these configurations to surface as [apʰstʰá] and [ápʰstʰa], respectively. Minimal pairs of surface forms such as this do exist; in this particular case, [apʰstʰá] means 'the ravine' and [ápʰstʰa] means 'the lead (metal)'. Similarly [apʰʃdzá] means 'weasel', whereas [ápʰʃdza] means 'beautiful' (Kaslandzia 2005: 573), and so on.

All forms of the 'lead'/'beautiful' type appear to involve an entirely unaccented root rather than unaccented moraic consonants, however. Take, for example, [ápʰstʰa] 'the lead', which could in principle come from /a̲-pʰstʰa̲/, /a̲-pʰs̲tʰa̲/, or /a̲-pʰstʰa/. The fact that the indefinite form alternates between [pʰstʰák'] and [pʰstʰak'ɨ́] reveals that the correct underlying form of the root is unaccented /pʰstʰa/. If the root were /pʰstʰa̲/ or /pʰs̲tʰa̲/, with a root-final lexically accented vowel, we would expect combination with the unaccented indefinite suffix /-k'/ to produce only [pʰstʰák'], with no [pʰstʰak'ɨ́] option; compare the behavior of lexically accented CV̲-final roots such as /la̲-k'/ 'dog-INDEF' → [lák'], which has no option to be pronounced *[lak'ɨ́]. With lexically unaccented

CV-final roots such as /la-k'/ 'eye-INDEF' → [lák'] ~ [lak'ɨ́], on the other hand, a special condition of Abkhaz stress kicks in when an unaccented root combines with unaccented /-k'/, namely that one can assign surface stress either to the first of the two unaccented elements (yielding [lák'], [pʰstʰák']), or to the second, which triggers epenthesis: [lak'ɨ́], [pʰstʰak'ɨ́] (Spruit 1986: 39). Assuming an idiosyncratic condition of this sort on the behavior of strings containing no lexical accents is formally simpler than, and hence (ceteris paribus) preferable to, an alternative account that stipulates that *both* unaccented strings *and* strings of non-prevocalic consonants (of which one or more are unaccented) followed by an accented vowel can trigger stress shift and epenthesis.

The result of our discussion of consonant clusters thus far is that sequences of non-prevocalic consonants (i.e., ones that would typically share a single mora in Moraic Theory) never bear more than a single lexical accent. This is what we expect if the hosts of lexical accents are moras, but not if (following Spruit 1986 and Kathman 1992) the hosts are vowels and *all* non-prevocalic consonants.

Consider for example a-χʲʃʲtsʰbá 'sparrowhawk'. In Spruit's (1986) system this has the structure D-DDDD in (16a); in our system, which draws on Hayes-style Moraic Theory, it has the simpler structure in (16b).

(16) Underlying structure of 'sparrowhawk'

a. Spruit (1986: 44)	a-	χʲ	ʃʲ	tsʰ	ba		
	D	D	D	D	D		
b. Moraic analysis	a-	χʲ	ʃʲ	tsʰ	b	a	
	|	\	|	/	\	|	
	μ[13]		μ			μ	

Spruit's (1986) structure in (16a) contains five lexically accented elements: the definite prefix a-, the χʷ, the ʃʷ, the tsʰ, and ba. This is necessary in order to obtain surface stress on the final -a of the root, given that we know the definite prefix bears a lexical accent; if the intervening consonants were not specified as D/ lexically accented, the stress would be expected to surface on the prefix. The number of lexical accents here seems excessive: we need the string of non-prevocalic consonants to include at least one accent, as otherwise stress would surface on the prefix, but the other two accents do no work in the language other than to generate the desired surface form.

The moraic representation in (16b), on the other hand, reduces the number of idiosyncratic elements to the minimum required, three. It moreover has the advantage of conforming to what is commonly assumed about moraic structures and stress systems cross-linguistically and correctly predicts the absence of lexical accent contrasts in strings of non-prevocalic consonants.

We have now resolved the overmoraification problem in Spruit's (1986) and Kathman's (1992) models by recasting the Abkhaz system in the more conventional moraic framework of Hayes (1989). This leaves the second problem with the moraic analysis of Abkhaz stress alluded to earlier, which is that many of the moraic hosts for lexical accents are predictable in Abkhaz, and therefore by (10a) are not expected to be stored in the lexicon. The form a̱-p^{h}a̱-ɾá̱ 'pleat' in (8d), for example, requires lexical accents on each of its three moras in order for the correct stress [ap^{h}aɾá] to surface, but each of these three moras is entirely predictable by the algorithm in (11), and therefore by (10a), these moras should not be stored in the lexical entries for the three morphemes in question.

This is the crux of our discussion of Abkhaz in this section: put in general terms, it is difficult to reconcile the general philosophical tenet that the lexicon is a repository for unpredictable information with the proposal that idiosyncratic lexical diacritics such as accents can be parasitic on moras in the lexicon. And it is not just accents that raise this problem: one finds a similar situation with tones in Makhuwa, a Bantu language of northern Mozambique (Samuel Andersson, pers. comm.).

In Makhuwa moraic structure is predictable, with vowels and coda consonants each bearing a mora. (The language allows only simple codas, so the issue of mora assignment to strings of non-prevocalic consonants that we saw in Abkhaz does not arise in Makhuwa.) The language is tonal, and all moraic elements (both vocalic and consonantal) are able to host tones, as exemplified in (17).

(17) Makhuwa tones

a. Moraic C with high tone: 'plant with spikes'

UR /nańtata/ 'plant with spikes'

SR[14] [nàńtátà] (with high tone doubling onto the following mora)

b. Moraic C with low tone: '3-problem'

UR /n-láʈu/

SR [ǹláʈù]

c. Both high and low tones on moraic Cs: 'Christians'

UR /ma-ḵ́ristáo/

SR [màḵ́.rís̀.tá(.)ò] (with expected failure of high tone doubling onto a word-final vowel)

The forms in (17a)–(17c) demonstrate that moraic consonants can surface with either a high or a low tone, and that one cannot predict from context which of these will surface in a given word. These tonal specifications therefore must be stored with the relevant consonants in the corresponding lexical entries. The problem that arises at this point is that the moras that arguably license the tones (bearing in mind that nonmoraic consonants cannot host lexical tones) are entirely predictable from the surface phonological sequence, and therefore are not expected to be stored in lexical entries.

The Makhuwa case closely parallels the Abkhaz one with respect to the hosting of unpredictable elements by predictable moras, the primary difference being that the parasitic elements are accents in Abkhaz and tones in Makhuwa. Interestingly, Dybo, Nikolaev, and Starostin (1978) have observed that in the Tapanta dialect of Abaza, which despite its name is a mutually intelligible variety of Abkhaz (Chirikba 1996), what in our framework are lexically accented moras surface with high tone and unaccented moras with low tone, making the Abkhaz and Makhuwa cases appear even more similar.

How can one reconcile the theory that only unpredictable information is stored in lexical entries with the proposal that idiosyncratic lexical accents and tones can be parasitic on predictable moraic structure? One possibility is to maintain that predictable moraic structure is derived by rule rather than stored and state that lexical accents in Abkhaz and tones in Makhuwa are simply associated with vowels or consonants in the lexicon, with no stipulation that these hosts be moraic. This move would miss the insight that only weight-bearing ones can bear lexical accents and tones in the respective languages and would incorrectly predict that nonmoraic consonants should also be able to serve as hosts.

Another possibility would be to observe that in Hayes's (1989) system, vowels actually bear moras underlyingly (p. 259) and therefore should be able to host lexical accents and tones. This analysis encounters at least two difficulties: it seems unnecessarily asymmetrical in representing short vowels in the same way as long rather than short consonants (i.e., as lexically attached to a single mora), and it incorrectly predicts that short vowels but not short consonants should be able to host lexical accents and tones.

A third possibility, in the spirit of Evolutionary Phonology (Blevins 2004), is that the restriction of lexical accents and tones to moraic segments should receive a grammar-external account. In this analysis, accents are free in principle to occur on any consonant or vowel, but for perceptual and/or historical reasons, accents never end up being postulated on nonmoraic consonants by learners. In this scheme, the existence of extragrammatical explanations for the absence of lexical accents on nonmoraic consonants obviates the need to encode this restriction in the synchronic grammar, and therefore there is no need to store predictable moraic structure in lexical entries. At least two possible problems for this approach to moraic structure come to mind: first, it is not entirely clear what the relevant perceptual and/or historical restrictions on the hosts of lexical accents might be; second, we arguably still require synchronic mechanisms to assign moraic structure, lexical accents, and so on to novel forms that are not presented to the learner complete with such information, or which contain information that violates the putative extragrammatical restrictions (compare the point made by Scheer [2012] in the next paragraph).

For these reasons, we prefer a fourth alternative to make sense of the apparent storage of predictable moraic structure. In this scheme, morphemes are assigned moraic and/or syllabic structure when they are first acquired by the learner; the processes that assign this structure function as redundancy rules over lexical entries, but these processes are also able to apply in the course of derivations (LeSourd 1993). Scheer makes a similar proposal within a Government Phonology framework:

> It may seem at first sight that [it] is not true [that there is no syllabification algorithm accounting for the predictability of most syllabic structure in] Government Phonology, where lexical entries are fully syllabified and hence no syllabification algorithm builds syllable structure during phonological computation. . . . The presence of syllable structure in the lexicon does not mean that syllable structure is not a projection of melodic primes. For one thing, it must somehow get into the lexicon, and hence children must transform a linear phonetic signal into a syllabified lexical entry. The same is true for adults when they lexicalise new lexical material (loans, acronyms etc.). Hence just like in other theories there is a syllabification algorithm in Government Phonology—which however is active upon lexicalisation, rather than during regular phonological computation. (Scheer 2012: 105)

In this analysis, then, the predictability of moraic/syllabic structure is a product of the prosodification algorithm employed when morphemes are first introduced into the lexicon. This allows us to account for both the predictability of prosodic structure (via the aforementioned prosodification algorithm) and the existence of predictable prosodic structure in lexical entries (by waiving requirement [10b]); this is in keeping with our conclusions regarding (3b) and Langacker's (1987) list fallacy in section 7.2. An alternative analysis without stored moras would seem to require that lexical accents can only be stored on segments that will end up being moraic, which is unsatisfying at best and runs the risk of involving derivational look-ahead.

In sum, we have argued in this section that (i) idiosyncratic accents and tones need to be stored in the lexicon; (ii) these accents and tones are only hosted by moraic[15] segments; (iii) whether a segment is weight-bearing or not is entirely predictable from the segmental context in these languages; therefore (iv) predictable prosodic structure (in this case moras or rimes) must be stored in lexical entries in Abkhaz and Makhuwa. We account for the predictability of prosodic structure by assuming the existence of a prosodification algorithm that assigns syllabic and/or moraic structure to morphemes at the point of their introduction into the lexicon.

7.4.2. Lexical Prosody in Optimality Theory

Up to this point we have considered arguments for (under)specification of predictable prosodic structure within an essentially rule-based framework. One might reasonably object that these arguments do not hold within an optimality-theoretic framework, which is powerful enough to derive the phenomena in question regardless of whether one assumes underspecification or Full Specification in lexical entries. This then raises the question of what (if anything) OT has to say about storage of predictable prosodic structure.

7.4.2.1. Storage of Predictable Prosodic Structure

OT inherits from classic rule-based phonology (Halle 1959, 1962; Chomsky and Halle 1968; et seq.) the idea that surface syllable structure is predictable and therefore not stored in lexical entries. As McCarthy (2003) put it (and recall [3]), "no language is known to contrast tautomorphemic pa.ta with pat.a or pa.kla with pak.la. . . . This observation is usually taken to mean that syllabification is absent from underlying representations (e.g., Blevins 1995: 221; Clements 1986: 318; Hayes 1989: 260)." A typical example of this assumption in OT is Kenstowicz's (1994) article "Syllabification in Chukchee," the purpose of which is to demonstrate how an OT constraint system can derive fully syllabified Chukchee surface forms, complete with epenthetic vowels, from unsyllabified underlying forms.

McCarthy (2003) continues on to point out, though, that it is "more in keeping with OT's thesis of Richness of the Base (ROTB; Prince and

Smolensky 1993) to assume that underlying representations may be syllabified or not and in diverse ways—freely but pointlessly, since no constraints of UG [Universal Grammar—BV and BS] lobby for the conservation of underlying syllabification." His reason for stipulating this invisibility of prosodic structure to faithfulness constraints, which we term "prosodic invisibility," is that "a necessary condition for ensuring that syllabification is never contrastive is that syllabification is faithfulness-free, so an unsyllabified input like /maba/ or a syllabified input like /mab.a/ will be associated by GEN with all of the following fully faithful and fully syllabified candidates: *m.a.b.a, ma.b.a, m.a.ba, m.aba, m.ab.a, ma.ba, mab.a, maba*. Many of these candidates are sure losers for markedness reasons, such as the absurd monosyllable *maba*. But they are still fully faithful in the sense that they incur no faithfulness violations" (McCarthy 2002: 51).

For McCarthy, then, ROTB allows underlying representations to be "syllabified or not and in diverse ways" (McCarthy 2003: 55). But does classic OT (Kager 1999) actually generate this range of syllabification options? The answer depends on the sort of acquisition algorithm one assumes. It is fairly standard in classic OT to employ some version of LO (Prince and Smolensky 1993: 191), according to which the UR selected for a given surface form will be the one whose relationship to the SR best satisfies the ranking of faithfulness constraints in the language. With morphemes that have only one surface realization, the logic of LO dictates that their underlying form will in fact be *segmentally* identical to this surface realization. With *prosodic* structure, though, the picture is less clear. Does LO produce prosodified URs (cf. Gouskova 2007), or do prosodic invisibility and/or *Spec ("underlying material must be absent," Prince and Smolensky 2002: 213) produce conventional unsyllabified URs? In what follows we will suggest that without the addition of problematic restrictions to the model, classic OT predicts neither Full Specification nor full underspecification of prosodic structure, but rather a profusion of tied candidate URs.

7.4.2.2. UR Acquisition with LO and Prosodic Invisibility

In order to determine what UR prosody is constructed for a given SR, one would expect that it would first be necessary to determine the extent to which prosodic structure is present in the surface forms to which the learner is exposed.[16] Scheer (2012), as we saw earlier, assumes that children receive only a "linear phonetic signal," devoid of syllabic structure. Other phoneticians and phonologists appear to share the belief that information about syllables and their constituents is not encoded in the phonetic signal (see Ladefoged 1982 and Ohala and Kawasaki 1984 for discussion). For example, Tesar and Smolensky (2000) assume that the learner does not have access to the full prosodic structure of surface forms in the primary linguistic data, but only to elements easily inferable from the acoustic signal, such as the location of stresses. Tauberer (2008) assumes in a similar vein that learners have access only to the number of syllables in the utterance, each syllable's weight, and which syllables have primary and secondary stress.

For the present purposes we will assume by contrast that surface forms do encode syllabic structure and that learners are sensitive to this information. If this were not the case, it would be difficult to explain how children learn systems that contrast [VC.RV][17] and [V.CRV] parses of /VCRV/ strings, such as German (Rubach 1990) or Proto-Romance (Steriade 1988). Maddieson (1984) provides additional phonetic evidence from closed syllable vowel shortening, along with a review of other phonetic cues to syllable structure that have been proposed in the literature.

Let us assume then that learners are exposed to fully syllabified surface forms. If learners hear an SR [.ka.pa.], what UR will they postulate if learning is guided by an optimality-theoretic algorithm? In (18) we provide a tableau demonstrating the expected outcome if we assume that UR construction is guided by LO.

(18) LO tableau for [.ka.pa.][18]

[.ka.pa.]	ONSET	NOCODA	FAITH constraints
a. /<kapa>/			
b. /.ka.pa./			
c. /.kap.a./			
d. /.kapa./			
e. /.k.apa./, /.k.a.p.a./, . . .			

The process of LO essentially reverses the normal course of OT input-output evaluations: the input in the upper-left-hand corner of the tableau is now the observed SR, and the candidate outputs of the evaluation in the remainder of the leftmost column are the forms being considered for selection as the UR to be stored in the lexicon. In this mirror-image evaluation, the markedness constraints are irrelevant: they are violated equally by each candidate input–output pair, as each pair has the same SR, and markedness constraints refer only to SRs, not URs. We have illustrated this with the markedness constraints ONSET and NOCODA in (18): it can be seen for example that none of the candidate URs for the SR [ka.pa] violate ONSET—no matter how many times they would violate this constraint if they were URs—because this constraint refers only to the SR [ka.pa], which is the same for each candidate UR and does not contain any ONSET violations.

None of the candidate URs in (18) will violate any of the faithfulness constraints in the language either. By virtue of McCarthy's tenet of prosodic invisibility, "no constraints of UG lobby for the conservation of underlying syllabification" (McCarthy 2003: 55). The differences in syllabification in the UR candidates in (18) are therefore irrelevant; all that matters to the constraints in the universal constraint set CON is the syllable structure of the SR [ka.pa], which is legislated by markedness rather than faithfulness constraints. Candidate URs that differ in components *other* than syllabification, such as individual distinctive features, may well trigger violations of individual faithfulness constraints, but all such UR candidates will lose out to the candidates in (18), which are identical to the SR in all respects except syllable structure.

Since by the tenet of prosodic invisibility, syllabification differences between the UR and SR are ignored, all candidate URs that are fully faithful to the SR in everything except for syllable structure will tie for selection as the UR to be inserted into the lexicon as the underlying form of the observed data point [ka.pa]. The number of UR candidates that will tie in this way is potentially quite large, as GEN currently places no limits on the number of relevant candidates that can be generated from [ka.pa]. Under present assumptions about GEN, the list of candidate URs that differ from the observed SR [ka.pa] only with respect to syllabification will include at least the forms in (19):

(19) A selection of candidates that tie for selection as the UR for [ka.pa]

a. .ka.pa.	b. .kap.a.
c. .kapa.	d. .k.apa.
e. .k.a.p.a.	f. .ka.p.a.
g. .k.ap.a.	h. .k.a.pa.
i. <kapa>	j. <k>.a.pa.
k. <ka>.pa.	l. <kap>.a.
m. <k>.a.<p>.a.	etc. etc.

It should be clear from (18) and (19) that the addition of prosodic invisibility to a conventional optimality-theoretic learning algorithm (such as the one proposed by Tesar and Smolensky 2000) poses a nontrivial indeterminacy problem, with unreasonably large numbers of candidates tying as the optimal UR for each observed SR. Is it viable to store such a large number of URs for each SR, or are further mechanisms required to weed out all but a single UR?

McCarthy (2003) rightly observed that this issue does not matter for *SRs*—all of the tied URs will generate SRs that are licit in the language. In (18), for example, each of the candidates that ties for selection as the UR will produce the licit surface form [ka.pa]. The problem lies not on the surface of the language, but beneath it: how can learning, which in OT involves comparison of UR–SR mappings, proceed (efficiently or at all) in cases where each SR has an indeterminately large number of URs?

7.4.2.3. Solution: *Spec?

A possible solution to the indeterminacy problem might involve the classic OT constraint *Spec, which dictates that "underlying material must be absent" (Prince and Smolensky 2002: 213). Adding *Spec to the evaluation in (18) would yield something like the tableau in (20).

(20) Evaluation of [.ka.pa.] with *Spec

[ka.pa]	Onset	NoCoda	*Spec
☞/k a p a/			****
			*****!***
			*****!****

Here UR candidates incur a violation of *Spec for each representational element they contain; abstracting away from the featural content of segments, the unsyllabified UR /<kapa>/ would therefore violate *Spec four times, once for each of its segments; the syllabified UR /.ka.pa./ would contain these four violations plus (at least) an additional four violations, one for each mora and one for each syllable; the syllabified UR /.kapa./ would contain these eight violations plus (at least) an additional violation for the mora attached to the p; and so on. When legislated by *Spec in this way, the universal evaluation mechanism EVAL is able to select a unique, unsyllabified winning UR.

Like the *Spec scheme just described, Krämer's (2012) "Lexicon Optimization 2.0" also uniquely selects the unsyllabified candidate as the winning UR. Krämer's model does this by allowing markedness constraints to legislate URs and not just SRs; this move enables candidates (14b)–(14e) to be ruled out by virtue of containing violations of markedness constraints such as Onset and NoCoda.

7.4.2.3.1. PROBLEMS WITH THE *SPEC AND LEXICON OPTIMIZATION 2.0 ANALYSES Though *Spec and Lexicon Optimization 2.0 make it possible for a classic OT evaluation to produce a single unsyllabified winner, that is, the UR that is assumed in traditional Chomskyan phonology, doing so undermines the spirit of classic OT. Both *Spec and Krämer's UR markedness constraints resemble morpheme structure constraints in placing constraints on the structure of underlying representations (albeit universal in the former case and language-specific in the latter)—a concept that is explicitly antithetical to the core OT notion of ROTB, according to which GEN contains *no* constraints on URs.[19]

A further potential problem with the introduction of morpheme structure constraints into OT is that doing so leads to selection of an unsyllabified UR, which runs afoul of the evidence that we have considered in this chapter for storage of predictable prosodic information such as mora and syllable structure in URs. Selecting a unique, *syllabified* UR of the sort suggested by the TOT evidence or the Abkhaz and Makhuwa facts remains a significant unsolved challenge for any combination of existing OT principles and mechanisms, despite what one might expect from superficial consideration of LO in the manner of Gouskova (2007). If one wants to derive unique syllabified underlying representations in OT, it appears necessary to abandon prosodic invisibility and introduce faithfulness constraints that legislate syllabic structure. This move comes at a cost, though: it loses Hayes's (1989) generalization that syllabification is not intramorphemically contrastive in any human language.

7.5. Conclusions

In this chapter we considered the question of whether underspecification of predictable abstract prosodic structure is permitted in lexical entries. We reviewed evidence for underspecification of segmental material in section 7.2 and turned to prosodic structure in section 7.3 with an overview of psycholinguistic and other arguments that have been made both for and against lexical storage of predictable syllable and mora structures. We argued in section 7.4 that the available empirical evidence appears most consistent with a theory in which morphemes are assigned moraic and syllabic structure in the lexicon, even if this structure is predictable from the surface representation of the form. We have suggested that currently popular optimality-theoretic learning algorithms equipped with ROTB, LO, and prosodic invisibility encounter nontrivial problems with the assignment (or not) of predictable underlying prosody: generating unique *un*prosodified underlying representations requires abandoning ROTB and adopting morpheme structure constraints; generating unique prosodified underlying representations requires introducing syllabic faithfulness constraints and thereby abandons Hayes's (1989) generalization about the predictability of syllable structure.

Notes

I have John Goldsmith to thank for my shift from Indo-European philology to phonological theory, after being inspired by his Introduction to Phonology course at the University of Chicago as a sophomore in 1987–1988. I still remember clearly the day during the fall quarter when the professor for that term was late, and after fifteen minutes or so a lanky graduate student rose from the back row and began an impromptu lecture on structuralist phonology. I could not understand why this grad student would randomly step in, but I was impressed by his clear, level-headed style and his ability to make structuralism comprehensible and to connect it to current theoretical debates. By the end of the class it became clear from the lecturer's command of the material that youthful appearances can be deceiving, and this was actually our professor for the second quarter, John Goldsmith. [BV]

1. Authors who deny the storage of predictable prosody in URs include Anderson (1992); Béland, Caplan, and Nespoulos (1990: 130); Bloomfield (1933); Bromberger and Halle (1989); Chomsky and Halle (1968: 12); Gringon (1984); Hall (1992); Halle and Marantz (1993); Harris (1983); Kenstowicz (1994); Noske (1992); Steriade (1982); and Zhang (2006). Proponents of including predictable prosody in URs include Anderson (1982: 549); Benua (1997); Borowsky (1983: 95); Burzio (1996, 2000); Cairns and Feinstein (1982); Calabrese (2005: 150); Caramazza, Laudanna, and Romani (1988); Dell (1986); Giegerich (1985); Goldinger (1997); Golston and van der Hulst (1999); Hagstrom (1997); Hogg and McCully (1987); Inkelas (1990); Iosad (2013); Kaye (1995); Kaye and Lowenstamm (1984); Kaye, Lowenstamm, and Vergnaud (1985); Kenstowicz (1997: 335); Kintsch (1974); Laeufer (1985); Leben and Robinson (1977); LeSourd (1993); Pisoni (1997); Romani

et al. (2011); Rudes (1976); Scheer (2004, 2012); Selkirk (1980: 596, 1982: 356ff); Stemberger (1985); and Vennemann (1974).

2. Following convention, vowels that are observed to alternate in their values for [ATR] are capitalized. The vowel transcribed as [ạ] is the [+ATR] counterpart of [a].
3. Szigetvári (2011) contends that Level 1 (nonanalytical) affixes such as *-al* are not stored in the lexicon independently; thus, *hymn* [hɪm] and *hymnal* [hɪmnəl] derive from two different lexical entries, /hɪm/ and /hɪmnəl/, respectively. This analysis eliminates the need for a phonotactically illicit lexical entry /hɪmn/. We set this issue aside here, but see Samuels (2015) for some related discussion.
4. Some of the themes addressed here are also discussed in Brentari and Bosch (1990), which captures aspects of John Goldsmith's thinking about the mora at the time.
5. It is not clear to us why Hayes assumes that short vowels have moras underlyingly, given that their surface moraic representation is predictable. He proposes (1989: 256, following Guerssel 1986) that moraless vowels are glides, and one might therefore say that the underlying mora is necessary to distinguish short vowels from glides, but this step is not necessary for the vowel /a/ in (1), which has no glide counterpart. On p. 257, Hayes relies on vowels having moras to drive his syllabification algorithm, which targets moraic elements to build syllables from. This move seems unnecessary; it is possible to assign the desired syllabic structures without assuming that vowels are underlying moraic, as we do in (7).
6. Spruit (1986) discusses several classes of exception to generalization (6iii) that we will not consider here as they are not germane to the point of this chapter.
7. We transcribe using the International Phonetic Alphabet, on the basis of the pronunciation of Zihni Şener, a speaker of the Cwyzhy dialect.
8. Our system requires assuming that Abkhaz possesses a /ɨ/ phoneme that undergoes deletion when unstressed in certain contexts. (Spruit [1986] proposes, in contrast, that all or most tokens of Abkhaz [ɨ] result from either epenthesis or assigning stress to a consonant.) We adopt the inverse of Spruit's position because doing so allows for a significantly simpler moraification algorithm and accounts for the existence of unstressed schwas that result neither from phonotactically driven epenthesis nor from stressed consonants, as in the Cwyzhy Abkhaz form /a-tsʰɨgʷɨ/ [atsʰɨgʷɨ́] 'cat-DEF', or Abzhuy /a̲-k'ɨ̲lɨχ:a/ [ak'ɨ́lɨχ:a] 'lattice-DEF' (Kaslandzia 2005: 369; compare /a̲-k'ɨ̲lχ:a/ [ak'ɨ́lχ:a] 'full of holes-DEF', which demonstrates that [lχ] is a possible coda cluster in Abzhuy).
9. We leave aside the treatment of unsyllabifiable consonants via epenthesis, as this is not directly relevant to our point in this chapter.
10. This stage of moraification is not discussed by Hayes (1989), but it is required for languages that allow (the moraic equivalent of) branching codas.

11. UR=underlying representation.
12. We believe that the range of facts considered here works equally well in comparable serial, rule-based stress assignment systems such as that of Prince (1983), which Kathman employs in his discussion of the Abkhaz facts.
13. Following Spruit's (1986) notation, we use an underscore to represent the fact that an element (in our case a mora) is lexically accented.
14. SR=surface representation.
15. Or rime segments in onset-rime theories that eschew moras.
16. We shall see later in this section that the syllable structure of the surface form does not necessarily have any bearing on the syllable structure of its corresponding underlying form, under standard assumptions about prosodic invisibility.
17. V=vowel, C=consonant, R=liquid.
18. Angled brackets enclose unsyllabified material; periods enclose syllabified material.
19. For further learnability arguments against Richness of the Base, see Rasin and Katzir (2015).

References

Anderson, Stephen. 1982. The analysis of French shwa: Or, how to get something for nothing. *Language* 58, no. 3: 534–573.

———. 1992. *A-morphous Morphology*. Cambridge: Cambridge University Press.

Archangeli, Diana, and Douglas Pulleyblank. 1994. *Grounded Phonology*. Cambridge, MA: MIT Press.

Béland, Renée, David Caplan, and Jean-Luc Nespoulos. 1990. The role of abstract phonological representations in word production: Evidence from phonemic paraphasias. *Journal of Neurolinguistics* 5, nos. 2–3: 125–164.

Benua, Laura. 1997. Transderivational identity: Phonological relations between words. PhD dissertation, University of Massachusetts, Amherst.

Blevins, Juliette. 1995. The syllable in phonological theory. In *The Handbook of Phonological Theory*, ed. John A. Goldsmith, 206–244. Oxford: Blackwell.

———. 2004. *Evolutionary Phonology: The Emergence of Sound Patterns*. Cambridge: Cambridge University Press.

Bloomfield, Leonard. 1933. *Language*. New York: Holt.

Borowsky, Toni. 1983. Geminate consonants in Luganda. In *Current Approaches to African Linguistics*, vol. 2, ed. Jonathan Kaye, 81–97. Dordrecht: Foris Publications.

Brand, Muriele, Arnaud Rey, and Ronald Peerman. 2003. Where is the syllable priming effect in visual word recognition? *Journal of Memory and Language* 48:435–443.

Brentari, Diane, and Anna Bosch. 1990. Mora: Autosegment or syllable constituent? In *Proceedings from the 26th Annual Meeting of the Chicago Linguistic Society*, vol. 2: *Parasession on the Syllable in Phonetics and Phonology*, ed. Michael Ziolkowski, Manuela Noske, and Karen Deaton, 1–15. Chicago: Chicago Linguistic Society.

Bromberger, Sylvain, and Morris Halle. 1989. Why phonology is different. In *The Chomskyan Turn*, ed. Asa Kasher, 56–77. Oxford: Blackwell.

Brown, Alan S. 1991. A review of the tip-of-the-tongue experience. *Psychological Bulletin* 109:204–223.

———. 2012. *The Tip of the Tongue State*. New York: Psychology Press.

Brown, Roger, and David McNeill. 1966. The "tip of the tongue" phenomenon. *Journal of Verbal Learning and Verbal Behavior* 5:325–337.

Burzio, Luigi. 1996. Surface constraints versus underlying representations. In *Current Trends in Phonology: Models and Methods,* vol. 1, ed. Jacques Durand and Bernard Laks, 97–112. Manchester: European Studies Research Institute, University of Salford.

———. 2000. Segmental contrast meets output-to-output faithfulness. *Linguistic Review* 17, nos. 2–4: 367–384.

Bybee, Joan. 2001. *Phonology and Language Use*. Cambridge: Cambridge University Press.

Cairns, Charles, and M. Feinstein. 1982. Markedness and the theory of syllable structure. *Linguistic Inquiry* 13:193–226.

Calabrese, Andrea. 2005. *Markedness and Economy in a Derivational Model of Phonology*. Berlin: Walter de Gruyter.

Caramazza, Alfonso, A. Laudanna, and Christina Romani. 1988. Lexical access and inflectional morphology. *Cognition* 28:297–332.

Chirikba, Viacheslav. 1996. *A Dictionary of Common Abkhaz*. Leiden: N.p.

Cholin, Joana, Niels O. Schiller, and Willem J. M. Levelt. 2004. The preparation of syllables in speech production. *Journal of Memory and Language* 50:47–61.

Chomsky, Noam, and Morris Halle. 1968. *The Sound Pattern of English*. New York: Harper and Row.

Clements, G. N. 1986. Compensatory lengthening and consonant gemination in Luganda. In *Studies in Compensatory Lengthening*, ed. Leo Wetzels and Engin Sezer, 37–77. Dordrecht: Foris Publications.

Dell, Gary S. 1986. A spreading-activation theory of retrieval in sentence production. *Psychological Review* 93:283–321.

———. 1988. The retrieval of phonological forms in production: Tests of predictions from a connectionist model. *Journal of Memory and Language* 27:124–142.

Dybo, Vladimir. 1973. Balto-slavjanskaja akcentnaja sistema s tipologicheskoj tochki zrenija i problema rekonstrukcii indoevropejskogo akcenta. In *Kuznecovskie chtenija 1973: Istorija slavjanskix jazykov i pis'mennosti*, 8–10. Moscow: Akademija Nauk SSSR, Institut slavjanovedenija i balkanistiki.

———. 1977. Zapadnokavkazskaja akcentnaja sistema i problema eë proisxozhdenija. In *Konferencia "Nostraticheskie jazyki i nostraticheskoe jazykoznanie" (Tezisy dokladov)*, ed. Vjacheslav Ivanov, 41–45. Moscow: Akademija Nauk SSSR, Institut slavjanovedenija i balkanistiki.

Dybo, Vladimir, S. Nikolayev, and Sergey Starostin. 1978. A tonological hypothesis on the origin of paradigmatic accent systems. In *Estonian Papers in Phonetics: Papers of the Symposium (Tallinn, November 1978). Studies on Accent, Quantity, Stress, Tone*, ed. Arvo Eek, 16–20. Tallinn: Academy of Sciences of the Estonian SSR, Institute of Language and Literature. http://www.inslav.ru/images/stories/people/dybo/dybo_nikolaev_starostin1978.pdf.

Elfner, Emily. 2006. Contrastive syllabification in Blackfoot. In *Proceedings of WCCFL 25*, ed. Donald Baumer, David Montero, and Michael Scanlon, 141–149. Somerville, MA: Cascadilla Proceedings Project.

———. 2007. Moraic faithfulness: Evidence from Blackfoot and English. Paper presented at the 15th Manchester Phonology Meeting, University of Manchester, UK, May 26, 2007

Flemming, Edward. 2002. *Auditory Representations in Phonology*. New York: Routledge.

Fromkin, Victoria A. 1971. The non-anomalous nature of anomalous utterances. *Language* 47:27–52.

Giegerich, Heinz. 1985. *Metrical Phonology and Phonological Structure: German and English*. Cambridge: Cambridge University Press.

Goldinger, S. D. 1997. Words and voices: Perception and production in an episodic lexicon. In *Talker Variability in Speech Processing*, ed. Keith Johnson and John W. Mullennix, 33–65. San Diego: Academic Press.

Goldsmith, John A. 1992. Local modeling in phonology. In *Connectionism: Theory and Practice*, ed. Steven Davis, 229–246. Oxford: Oxford University Press.

———. 1993. Harmonic phonology. In *The Last Phonological Rule*, 21–60. Chicago: University of Chicago Press.

———. 1994. Grammar within a neural net. In *The Reality of Linguistic Rules*, ed. Pamela Downing, Sue Lima, and Gregory Iverson, 95–113. Philadelphia: John Benjamins.

———. 2011. The syllable. In *The Handbook of Phonological Theory*, 2nd ed., ed. J. Goldsmith, J. Riggle, and A. C. L. Yu, 164–196. Oxford: Wiley-Blackwell.

Goldsmith, John A., and Gary Larson. 1990. Local modeling and syllabification. In *Papers from the 26th Annual Regional Meeting of the Chicago Linguistic Society, Part 2*, ed. K. M. Ziolkowski, K. Deaton, and M. Noske, 129–142. Chicago: Chicago Linguistic Society.

———. 1993. Using networks in a harmonic phonology. In *Papers from the 28th Annual Meeting of the Chicago Linguistic Society*, vol. 2, ed. Costas Canakis, Grace Chan, and Jeannette Denton, 94–125. Chicago: Chicago Linguistic Society.

Goldsmith, John A., and Manuela Noske. 2006. Autosegmental phonology and underspecification theory. In *History of the Language Sciences*, ed. S. Auroux, K. Koerner, H.-J. Niederehe, and K. Versteegh, 2280–2291. Berlin/New York: Walter de Gruyter.

Golston, Chris, and Harry van der Hulst. 1999. Stricture is structure. In *The Derivational Residue in Phonological Optimality Theory*, ed. Ben Hermans and Marc van Oostendorp, 153–173. Amsterdam: John Benjamins.

Gordon, Matthew. 2005. A perceptually-driven account of onset-sensitive stress. *Natural Language and Linguistic Theory* 23:595–653.

Gouskova, Maria. 2007. Prosodic faithfulness and contrastive syllabification. Unpublished manuscript, New York University. https://goo.gl/dR4uxj.

Grignon, Anne-Marie. 1984. Phonologie lexicale tri-dimensionelle du japonais. PhD dissertation, Université de Montréal.

Guerssel, Mohamed. 1986. Glides in Berber and Syllabicity. *Linguistic Inquiry* 17:1–12.

Hagstrom, Paul. 1997. Contextual metrical invisibility. In *PF: Papers at the Interface*, ed. Benjamin Bruening, Yoonjung Kang, and Martha McGinnis, 113–181. Cambridge, MA: Department of Linguistics and Philosophy, Massachusetts Institute of Technology.

Hall, Tracy Alan. 1992. *Syllable Structure and Syllable-Related Processes in German*. Tübingen: Niemeyer.

Halle, Morris. 1959. *The Sound Pattern of Russian*. The Hague: Mouton.

Halle, Morris. 1962. Phonology in generative grammar. *Word* 18, nos. 1–3: 54–72.

———. 1997. On stress and accent in Indo-European. *Language* 73:275–313.

Halle, Morris, and William J. Idsardi. 1995. General properties of stress and metrical structure. In *A Handbook of Phonological Theory*, ed. John Goldsmith, 403–443. Oxford: Blackwell.

Halle, Morris, and Alec Marantz.1993. Distributed morphology and the pieces of inflection. In *Distributed Morphology and the Pieces of Inflection. The View from Building 20: Essays in Honor of Sylvain Bromberger*, ed. Kenneth Hale and Samuel Jay Keyser, 111–176. Cambridge, MA: MIT Press.

Harris, James. 1983. *Syllable Structure and Stress in Spanish: A Nonlinear Analysis*. Cambridge, MA: MIT Press.

Hayes, Bruce. 1989. Compensatory lengthening in moraic phonology. *Linguistic Inquiry* 20:253–306.

Hayes, Bruce, Robert Kirchner, and Donca Steriade. 2004. *Phonetically Based Phonology*. Cambridge: Cambridge University Press.

Hewitt, B. George, ed. 1979. *Abkhaz*. Amsterdam: North-Holland.

———. 1989. *The North West Caucasian Languages*. The Indigenous Languages of the Caucasus, vol. 2. Delmar, NY: Caravan Books.

Hogg, Richard, and C. B. McCully. 1987. *Metrical Phonology: A Coursebook*. Cambridge: Cambridge University Press.

Howard, Irwin. 1972. A directional theory of rule application in phonology. PhD dissertation, Massachusetts Institute of Technology.

Inkelas, Sharon. 1990. *Prosodic Constituency in the Lexicon.* New York: Garland.

———. 1995. The consequences of optimization for underspecification. In *Proceedings of NELS 25*, ed. Jill Beckman, 287–302. Amherst, MA: GLSA (Graduate Linguistic Student Association), Department of Linguistics, University of Massachusetts.

Iosad, Pavel. 2013. Glottal stop insertion in Scottish Gaelic and contrastive syllabification. Paper presented at Teangeolaíocht na Gaeilge/Cànanachas na Gàidhlig [The Linguistics of the Gaelic Languages 15], Dublin, Ireland, April 19 and 20. http://www.research.ed.ac.uk/portal/files/9665525/tnag15.handout.pdf.

Jakobson, Roman. 1929. *Remarques sur l'évolution phonologique du russe comparée à celle des autres langues slaves.* Prague: Travaux du Cercle Linguistique de Prague.

———. 1949. On the identification of phonemic entities. *Travaux du Cercle Linguistique de Copenhague* 5:205–213.

Kager, René. 1999. *Optimality Theory.* Cambridge: Cambridge University Press.

Kaslandzia, Vladimir. 2005. *Abkhazko-Russkij Slovar'.* Sukhumi, Republic of Abkhazia: OLMA Press.

Kathman, David. 1992. Stress and accent in Abkhaz. In *ESCOL '91: Proceedings of the Eighth Eastern States Conference on Linguistics*, ed. Germán Westphal, Benjamin Ao, and Hee-Rahk Chae, 210–221. Columbus: The Ohio State University Department of Linguistics.

———. 1994. Floating grids and the independence of metrical structure. In *CLS 29: Papers from the 29th Regional Meeting of the Chicago Linguistic Society*, ed. Katherine Beals et al., 239–250. Chicago: Chicago Linguistic Society.

———. 1996. Abkhaz stress and morphological templates. In *NSL 8: Linguistic Studies in the Non-Slavic Languages of the Commonwealth of Independent States and the Baltic Republics*, ed. Howard Aronson, 221–238. Chicago: Chicago Linguistic Society.

Kaye, Jonathan. 1995. Derivations and interfaces. In *Frontiers of Phonology*, ed. Jacques Durand and Francis Katamba, 289–332. London: Longman.

Kaye, Jonathan, and Jean Lowenstamm. 1984. In *De la syllabicité*, ed. François Dell, Daniel Hirst, and Jean-Roger Vergnaud, 123–159. Paris: Hermann.

Kaye, Jonathan, Jean Lowenstamm, and Jean-Roger Vergnaud. 1985. The internal structure of phonological elements: A theory of charm and government. *Phonology Yearbook* 2:305–328.

Kenstowicz, Michael. 1994. Syllabification in Chukchee: A constraints-based analysis. *Proceedings of the Formal Linguistics Society of the Midwest* 4:160–181.

———. 1997. Uniform exponence: Extension and exemplification. In *Selected Papers from the Hopkins Optimality Workshop 1997*, ed. Viola Miglio and Bruce Morén, special issue, *University of Maryland Working Papers in Linguistics* 5:139–154.

Kenstowicz, Michael, and Charles Kisseberth. 1979. *Generative Phonology: Description and Theory*. San Diego: Academic Press.

Kintsch, Walter. 1974. *The Representation of Meaning in Memory*. Hillsdale, NJ: Lawrence Erlbaum.

Kiparsky, Paul, and Morris Halle. 1977. Towards a reconstruction of the Indo-European Accent. In *Studies in Stress and Accent: Southern California Occasional Papers in Linguistics*, vol. 4, ed. Larry Hyman, 209–238. Los Angeles: Department of Linguistics, University of Southern California.

Koriat, Asher, and Israel Lieblich. 1974. What does a person in a TOT state know that a person in a don't know state doesn't know. *Memory and Cognition* 2:647–655.

Krämer, Martin. 2012. *Underlying Representations*. Cambridge: Cambridge University Press.

Ladefoged, Peter. 1982. *A Course in Phonetics*. 2nd ed. New York: Harcourt Brace Jovanovich.

Laeufer, Christiane. 1985. Some language-specific and universal aspects of syllable structure and syllabification: Evidence from French and German. PhD dissertation, Cornell University.

Langacker, Ronald W. 1987. *Foundations of Cognitive Grammar*. Vol. 1. Stanford, CA: Stanford University Press.

Leben, William, and O. Robinson. 1977. Upside-down phonology. *Language* 53:1–20.

LeSourd, Philip. 1993. *Accent and Syllable Structure in Passamaquoddy*. New York: Routledge.

Lightner, Theodore. 1963. A note on the formulation of phonological rules. *Quarterly Progress Report, MIT Research Laboratory of Electronics* 68:187–189.

Lovelace, Eugene A. 1987. Attributes that come to mind in the TOT state. *Bulletin of the Psychonomic Society* 25:370–372.

Maddieson, Ian. 1984. Phonetic cues to syllabification. *UCLA Working Papers in Phonetics* 59:85–101.

McCarthy. 2002. Comparative markedness [long version]. In *Papers in Optimality Theory II*, ed. Angela C. Carpenter, Andries W. Coetzee, and Paul de Lacy, 171–246. University of Massachusetts Occasional Papers in Linguistics 26. Amherst, MA: GLSA (Graduate Linguistic Student Association), Department of Linguistics, University of Massachusetts.

———. 2003. Sympathy, cumulativity, and the Duke-of-York gambit. In *The Syllable in Optimality Theory*, ed. Caroline Féry and Ruben van de Vijvereds, 23–76. Cambridge: Cambridge University Press.

Noske, Roland. 1992. Syllabification and syllable changing rules in French. In *The Structure of Phonological Representations*, vol. 2, ed. Harry van der Hulst and Norval Smith, 257–310. Dordrecht: Foris Publications.

Ohala, John, and H. Kawasaki. 1984. Prosodic phonology and phonetics. *Phonology Yearbook* 1:113–127.

Pater, Joe. 2009. Weighted constraints in generative linguistics. *Cognitive Science* 33:999–1035.

Pisoni, D. 1997. Some thoughts on "normalization" in speech perception. In *Talker Variability in Speech Processing*, ed. Keith Johnson and John W. Mullennix, 9–32. San Diego: Academic Press.

Prince, Alan. 1983. Relating to the grid. *Linguistic Inquiry* 14:19–100.

Prince, Alan, and Paul Smolensky. 2004. *Optimality Theory: Constraint Interaction in Generative Grammar.* Malden, MA: Blackwell.

Ramoo, Dinesh Kumar. 2014. Syllable structure in the mental lexicon: Neuropsychological and computational evidence. PhD dissertation, University of Birmingham.

Rasin, Ezer, and Roni Katzir. 2015. A learnability argument for constraints on underlying representations. In *NELS 45: Proceedings of the Forty-Fifth Annual Meeting of the North East Linguistic Society*, vol. 2, ed. Thuy Bui and Deniz Özyıldız, 267–274. Amherst, MA: Graduate Linguistics Student Association.

Reiss, Charles. 2008. The OCP and NOBANANA. In *Rules, Constraints, and Phonological Phenomena*, ed. Bert Vaux and Andrew Ira Nevins, 252–301. Oxford: Oxford University Press.

Romani, Cristina, Claudia Galluzzi, Ivana Bureca, and Aandrew Olson. 2011. Effects of syllable structure in aphasic errors: Implications for a new model of speech production. *Cognitive Psychology* 62:151–192.

Rubach, Jerzy. 1990. Final devoicing and cyclic syllabification in German. *Linguistic Inquiry* 21:79–94.

Rudes, B. 1976. Lexical representation and variable rules in natural generative phonology. *Glossa* 10:111–150.

Samuels, Bridget. 2009. The structure of phonological theory. PhD dissertation, Harvard University.

———. 2011. *Phonological Architecture: A Biolinguistic Perspective*. Oxford: Oxford University Press.

———. 2015. Stem vs. word-level effects: can a structural analysis succeed? In *NELS 45: Proceedings of the 45th Annual Meeting of the North East Linguistic Society*, vol. 3, ed. Thuy Bui and Deniz Özyildiz, 29–38. N.p.: CreateSpace Independent Publishing Platform.

Sapir, Edward. 1933. La réalité psychologique des phonèmes. *Journal de Psychologie Normale et Pathologique* 30:247–265.

Saussure, Ferdinand de. 1916. *Cours de linguistique générale*. Ed. C. Bally and A. Sechehaye, with the collaboration of A. Riedlinger. Lausanne/Paris: Payot.

Scheer, Tobias. 2004. *A Lateral Theory of Phonology*. Berlin: Mouton de Gruyter.

———. 2012. *Direct Interface and One-Channel Translation*. Berlin: Mouton de Gruyter.

Schiller, Niels O. 1998. The effect of visually masked syllable primes on the naming latencies of words and pictures. *Journal of Memory and Language* 39:484–507.

———. 2000. Single word production in English: The role of subsyllabic units during phonological encoding. *Journal of Experimental Psychology: Learning, Memory and Cognition* 26:512–528.

Selkirk, Elisabeth. 1980. The role of prosodic categories in English word stress. *Linguistic Inquiry* 11, no. 3: 563–605.

———. 1982. The syllable. In *The Structure of Phonological Representations, Part 2*, ed. Harry van der Hulst and Norval Smith, 337–385. Dordrecht: Foris Publications.

Spruit, Arie. 1986. Abkhaz studies. PhD dissertation, Leiden University.

Stanley, Richard. 1967. Redundancy rules in phonology. *Language* 43:393–436.

Stemberger, Joseph. 1985. CV phonology and French consonants: A concrete approach. *Journal of Linguistics* 21, no. 2: 453–457.

Steriade, Donca. 1982. Greek prosodies and the nature of syllabification. PhD dissertation, Massachusetts Institute of Technology.

———. 1988. Gemination and the Proto-Romance syllable shift. In *Advances in Romance Linguistics*, ed. David Birdsong and Jean-Pierre Montreuil, 371–409. Dordrecht: Foris Publications.

———. 1995. Underspecification and markedness. In *The Handbook of Phonological Theory*, ed. John A. Goldsmith, 114–174. Oxford: Blackwell.

Szigetvári, Péter. 2011. Syllable. In *Continuum Companion to Phonology*, ed. Bert Botma, Nancy C. Kula, and Kuniya Nasukaw, 64–94. London: Continuum.

Tauberer, Joshua. 2008. Learning in the face of infidelity: Evaluating the Robust Interpretive Parsing/Constraint Demotion Model of Optimality Theory Language Acquisition. PhD dissertation, University of Pennsylvania.

Tesar, Bruce, and Paul Smolensky. 2000. *Learnability in Optimality Theory*. Cambridge, MA: MIT Press.

Trigo, Loren. 1992. Abkhaz stress shift. In *Caucasian Perspectives*, ed. B. George Hewitt, 191–235. Unterschleissheim/München: Lincom Europa.

Trubetzkoy, Nikolai S. 1939. *Grundzüge der Phonologie*. Prague: Jednota Československých Matematiků a Fysiků.

Vennemann, Theo. 1974. Words and syllables in natural generative grammar. In *Papers from the Parasession on Natural Phonology*, ed. A. Bruck, R. A. Fox, and M. W. La Galy, 346–374. Chicago: Chicago Linguistic Society.

Zhang, Jisheng. 2006. The phonology of Shaoxing Chinese. PhD dissertation, Leiden University.

EIGHT

Sonority Waves in Syllabification

CAROLINE WILTSHIRE

8.1. Introduction

The current emphasis on constraints in phonology has deep historical roots in the development of syllable phonotactics, with sonority playing a salient role from the beginning. Goldsmith (2011) pointed to the use of sonority in syllabification dating back to ancient languages, including Pānini, studied by pregenerativists,such as Whitney (1874) and Jesperson (1904) among others. Pike and Pike (1947) borrowed the formalism of syntactic structure to introduce the syllable as a hierarchical structure dominating subconstituents, and many modern accounts of sonority focus on its role within syllable constituents such as onset or coda (e.g., Steriade 1982; Selkirk 1984; Gouskova 2001). However, sonority fits uneasily into the standard formalism of generative theory in two main ways: (i) it is not a binary contrast that can be represented in a [±feature] contrast, but rather a gradient/scalar one with multiple values (Hankamer and Aissen 1974) and (ii) what matters often is relative sonority, or the sonority of one segment relative to its neighbors (Goldsmith and Larson 1990).

In opposition to the hierarchical approach to stating sonority constraints within syllable constituents, Goldsmith (2011) also discussed a more "wave-like" understanding of sonority, in which speech consists of rises and falls of sonority, with the peaks defining the number of syllables and the trough marking the beginning of a syllable. This understanding emphasizes the use of both gradience in sonority values and contextual factors in determining sonority, both of which can be lacking in hierarchical approaches. As with wave and particle theories in physics (Pike 1959), Goldsmith suggested that both approaches add to our understanding of sonority and its function in the syllable.

In this chapter, I will review examples of several of the major applications of sonority in phonological description and analysis, where we find it useful for (i) motivating alternations within languages, (ii) motivating alternations in languages in contact, and (iii) determining order of acquisition (in first [L1] and second [L2] language acquisition). I provide examples from my own work that required reference to sonority in (i) alternations within L1s (Spanish, Malayalam), (ii) adaptations of words borrowed from L2s, in order to meet L1 syllable phonotactics (Indonesian), and (iii) acquisition of L2's syllables and consonant clusters (Indian Englishes). Where they differ, I compare the use of hierarchical syllable structure versus sonority waves as explanations for the generalizations and alternations, confirming the importance of the latter. While accounts that restrict sonority based on syllable constituency can be developed to provide a formal account for (most of) the examples, the sonority-wave approach provides not only an account, but also a motivation.

8.2. Background

The Sound Pattern of English (Chomsky and Halle 1968) was noted for its avoidance of syllable-related phenomena and its insistence that segments are characterized in terms of distinctive features with binary values. There have been several approaches to dealing with the issue of sonority as gradient, rather than an all or nothing feature like [±voice] or [±coronal]. One approach in keeping with the use of binary distinctive features is that of Clements, who proposed combining the plus values of a set of four major class features—sonorant, approximant, vocoid, syllabic (1990: 294)—to give a relative sonority ranking:

(1) Sonority class rankings in Clements (1990: 294)

Obstruents	< Nasals	< Liquids	< Vowels
1	2	3	4

Exactly the opposite of this approach is to use an n-ary sonority feature (Vennemann 1972; Hankamer and Aissen 1974; Hooper 1976; Selkirk 1984), in some cases dispensing with the major class features entirely (Hankamer and Aissen 1974: 142; Selkirk 1984: 110). Segments or segment classes each are indexed with a numerical value to represent sonority levels and ranked by their sonority index into a hierarchy as in (2).

(2) Sonority index in Selkirk (1984: 112)

p, t, k	b, d, g	f, θ	v, z, ð	s	m, n	l	r	i, u	e, o	a
.5	1	2	3	4	5	6	7	8	9	10

In Optimality Theory (OT), a set of constraints relate segments to syllable positions, with a fixed ranking ensuring that a segment of higher sonority is preferred as a peak and one of lower sonority is preferred as a margin (Prince and Smolensky 1993). Baertsch (2002) and Baertsch and Davis (2009) extended this approach further toward capturing sonority relationships by proposing a syllable internal segment that allows onsets to consist of two margin segments (M_1 followed by optional M_2) and considering the coda as M_2 as well, in order to capture sonority relationships within onsets and between onsets and codas, again using fixed rankings.

(3) Fixed ranking for fixed relative sonority (Prince and Smolensky 1993: 141)
*P/t>> . . . *P/l . . . >>*P/i>>*P/a
*M/a>>*M/i . . . >>*M/l . . . >>*M/t

(4) Split margin to handle sonority relationship within and between constituents (Baertsch 2002; Baertsch and Davis 2009: 303)
M_1/[+lo]>>M_1/[+hi]>>*M_1/r>>*M_1/l>>*M_1/Nasal>>*M_1/Obstruent
M_2/Obstruent>>M_2/Nasal>>*M_2/l>>*M_2/r>>*M_2/[+hi]>>*M_2/[+lo]

The treatment of classes of sounds as having a numerical sonority is compatible with the wave approach to sonority. For diagramming this approach, I will use a less detailed scale (5) than the index in (2), to map the rise and falls of sonority within words as in (6):

(5) Sonority hierarchy (à la Selkirk 1984; Steriade 1982)

Obstruent stops <	fricatives <	nasals <	liquids <	glides <	vowels
1	2	3	4	5	6

(6)
```
6      *        *      *            *   *   *
5     /\       /\     /\           /\  /\  /\
4    * \     /  \   /  \          /  \/  *  \
3   /   \   /    \ /    \        /    *      *
2  *     \/       \/      *     *             \
1         *        *                           *
   f  ɹ  ɪ  k  ə  t  ɪ  v      s o n ə ɹ æ n t
```

These waves can be constrained by a minimum value for the peak, a depth requirement for the trough, and an obligatory alternation between the two that requires sonority to fall between peaks and troughs, and rise between troughs and peaks, monotonically. A syllable is well-formed when it meets these requirements, and one syllable is more optimal than another if it has a higher peak, lower trough, greater rise in sonority between neighboring segments in the onsets, and lesser fall between neighboring segments in a coda.

The main distinction for hierarchical structures, as Goldsmith (2005/2016) described it, is that information "does not pass from one terminal element to another, but flows up and down a tree" so that the "link between two adjacent elements is expressible directly iff they are sisters" (2005/2009: slide 9). A more hierarchical approach to syllables is therefore based on constraints within subsyllabic constituents, especially onset and coda:

(7)
```
        σ
       / \
  Onset   Rhyme
           /   \
    Nucleus     Coda
```

With the nucleus as a peak of sonority, we generally appeal to three basic principles to deal with the effects of sonority in the context of neighboring segments: sonority sequencing within onsets/codas, sonority distance within onsets/codas, and contact between codas/onsets. Again drawing on a sonority scale as in (2) and (5), these constraints are stated as:

(8) Sonority sequencing generalization: consonant clusters in the onset must rise in sonority toward the nucleus, while clusters in the coda fall in sonority (Hooper 1976; Steriade 1982; Selkirk 1984)

(9) Minimal sonority distance (MSD) requirement: consonants in a cluster in onset or coda differ from each other in sonority to a degree determined language-specifically (Steriade 1982)

(10) Syllable contact: sonority falls across a syllable boundary; codas should be more sonorous than following onsets (e.g., Murray and Vennemann 1983)

It is also generally observed that cross-linguistically, less sonorous onset consonants and more sonorous coda consonants are preferred (Clements 1990; Carlisle 2001), and that there may be limits on the number of consonants in coda and or onset (Harris 1983; Itô 1986), although often these limits seem to result from the limits on sonority sequence and distance.

8.3. Case Studies

The following examples illustrate some of the uses of sonority as a factor in phonological analyses, comparing the insights of hierarchical syllable structure versus sonority waves. I begin with language-internal alternations (section 8.3.1), and then move to extensions involving languages in contact, as in borrowing and L2 acquisition (section 8.3.2–8.3.3).

8.3.1. Alternations within L1s

Two general types of processes are attributed to sonority and its roles in syllabification: (i) realization of phonemes differently in different syllable positions, including lenition and fortition, and (ii) insertion or deletion of segments in order to fit sonority/syllable requirements. I discuss one example of each.

First, an example of fortition from Argentinian Spanish, as discussed in Baker and Wiltshire (2003). High vocoids [i, j] in nucleus or coda position are realized as a fricative [ʒ] in onset, as shown in (11).

(11)	a. *bueyero*	'ox driver'	[bweˈ**ʒ**ero]	*buey*	'ox'	[bwe**j**]
	b. *yendo*	'going'	[ˈ**ʒ**en̪do]	*ir*	'to go'	[**i**r]

We attributed fortition to a constraint HONSET: be strong in onsets (2003: 37). The term *strong* is a reference to sonority: "a consonant strength hierarchy is basically an inverted sonority hierarchy" (Lavoie 2000: 213), so that fricatives are stronger than approximants or vowels; hence the constraint HONSET favors fortition as seen in the change from a vocoid (indeterminate between a vowel and an approximant) to a fricative in onsets. In Baker and Wiltshire (2003) we assumed a gradient HONSET, as not all varieties of Spanish strengthen onsets to the same extent.

The use of a constraint such as HONSET fits with the hierarchical view: consonants must be parsed in onsets to be evaluated by this constraint. Under a wave view of sonority peaks and troughs, Goldsmith argued that "we might expect to find a difference in the realization of consonants depending on where in the wave of sonority they appear. On this view, a consonant that appears in a context of *rising* sonority at the beginning of a syllable—that is, before the peak of the syllable—is in a qualitatively different environment compared to those that appear in the context of *falling* sonority, at the end of the syllable" (2011: 4).

In the sonority profile of a word without fortition, as in (12) on the right, the distinction between onset and peak may be minimal, while fortition in the onset on the left, exaggerates the depths of a trough preceding a peak, providing perhaps a better formed wave in terms of a relationship between two neighboring elements. In the constituent view, the increased strength of an "onset" is relatively unmotivated, a matter of fiat. Constraints like HONSET or fixed rankings like that in (3) can be motivated as functionally grounded, but that grounding is provided in terms of the sonority relationships between neighbors.

(12) Sonority profile with and without fortition

```
6       *       *   *              *   *       *
5      * \     / \ /             *   *   \   /
4     /   \   /   *             /          *
3    /     \ /                 /
2   /       \/                /
1  *        *                *
   [b we 'ʒ e   r o]        *[bwe 'ʝ e   r   o]
```

A second kind of alternation related to sonority is epenthesis, found cross-linguistically when a cluster of consonants exceeds language-specific limits. Malayalam provides an example of typical epenthesis, despite the fact that K. P. Mohanan (1982, 1986) and T. Mohanan (1989) attracted attention to Malayalam by arguments for an atypical syllabification. K. P. Mohanan (1982) analyzed Malayalam as lacking in codas, so that all consonant clusters had to be syllabified in onsets, while T. Mohanan (1989) argued that codas were allowed in initial lexical syllabification, but that different constraints hold at different lexical levels and postlexically.

Wiltshire (1992) proposed that there are only two levels of syllabification: one with codas and one without. Among the evidence presented in these arguments was data on the distribution of vowel epenthesis. As in many languages, epenthesis is motivated by input consonant clusters that cannot be syllabified within the constraints of the language. In Malayalam, schwa appears in word-final position after clusters such as liquid+stop (ɾp, lt), homorganic nasal+stop (mp, h̪d̪), and geminates (pp, tt, etc.).

(13)	[wijaɾppə]	'sweat'	[bʰraʂʈə]	'excommunication'
	[cempə]	'copper'	[pan̪t̪ə]	'ball'

These schwas generally can be understood to repair clusters that cannot fit into codas word-finally without violating sonority sequencing, and statements about possible clusters word-initially, medially, and finally are more complicated if we cannot refer to codas that are required to fall in sonority. In Malayalam, word-initial sequences rise in sonority (stop+glide, for example) and we never find the opposite (*glide+stop). Morpheme-final and word-final sequences (preceding the epenthetic schwa) include clusters that show a fall in sonority (mp) or level sonority (geminates). The same sequences and more are found word-medially; we find both falls in sonority and falls followed by rises; such clusters are not found word-initially:

(14)	[kalpana]	'king's order'	[wakt̪ram]	'fence'
	[swapnam]	'dream'	[can̪d̪ran]	'moon'

A coda-less analysis, treating all intervocalic consonant clusters as onsets, would violate sequencing by parsing a fall and rise together into the onset, and we could not explain why such sequences occur medially but not initially. An analysis with codas would describe them as containing up to two consonants, a continuant followed by a stop, while onsets likewise contain maximally two consonants, the second of which is a continuant. By this analysis, the words that end in an epenthetic schwa cannot be syllabified without it.

Arguments in favor of postlexical syllabifications entirely without codas are generally considered external to the phonology proper (e.g., evidence from language games, native speaker pauses, rhyme and the writing system, see especially K. P. Mohanan [1982, 1986]), but they may nonetheless refer to some characteristic that is accessible to native speakers. In order to refer to this, previous analyses provided for a distinct syllabification at some level. However, consider the sonority-wave representation for some words in Malayalam:

(15) Sonority representation for some Malayalam words

```
6    *         *          *         *         *     *
5  *  \       / \          * \      / \        /\    /
4      \    *    \        /    \   /   \      / \   /
3       \  /       *     /      \ *     *    /  *  /
2        \/             *        \/         /   \/
1        **                       *         *    *
    w a k t̪ ɾ a m     s w a p  n a m      p a n̪ t̪ ə
       'fence'        'dream'             'ball'
```

In the usual interpretation of a sonority wave, Goldsmith wrote, "Just as a peak of derived sonority corresponds to the nucleus of a syllable, so the local minimum (or trough) of sonority marks the boundary between syllables; in general, syllables are stretches from one trough of derived sonority up to, but not including, the next trough of sonority" (Goldsmith 1993: 53). The wave approach can provide a way for native speakers to create a new interpretation of a unit, one that runs from the segment immediately after one peak to the end of the next peak, which is independent from the syllable and its constituents.

From the hierarchical point of view, with sonority sequencing invoked to constrain onsets and codas, the epenthesis of Malayalam improves the underlying forms to make syllabifiable surface forms. From the wave point of view, we can create units from one peak to the next, providing for native speaker behavior. The fortition example is not so clearly motivated in a hierarchical approach, as the syllables may already have respectable onsets, but in a wave approach fortition can be seen to improve the shape of the sonority wave.

8.3.2. Loanword Adaptations

Words borrowed into a language are often adapted to conform to the sound structure of the language; in some cases, borrowed words present a language with challenges that its phonology has never encountered and thus provide evidence of hidden phonological tendencies. A large body of literature now addresses the factors involved in adapting loanwords (e.g., LaCharité and Paradis 2005; Peperkamp 2005; Kenstowicz

2006; de Jong and Cho 2012) including adaptations of borrowed words in order to meet L1 syllable phonotactics (e.g., Gouskova 2001; Kabak and Idsardi 2007; Batais and Wiltshire 2015).

I illustrate with examples from Indonesian, a language in which 34 percent of the vocabulary is borrowed (Tadmor 2009); approximately 12 percent of the vocabulary (or one-third of the borrowings) comes from Arabic and Dutch. Indonesian allows simple syllable structures with only a single consonant at the beginning or end of the syllable/word, and therefore has no strategy for dealing with consonant clusters word-initially or finally. Words from Arabic and Dutch can have such clusters, and as found in Batais (2013) and discussed in Batais and Wiltshire (2015), monosyllabic words with a cluster of consonants at the beginning or end have an epenthetic vowel added, when borrowed into Indonesian. This epenthesis resembles that of Malayalam (section 8.3.1), improving the syllabifiability of consonants by providing a nucleus. However, the location of the epenthetic vowel depends on the sonority pattern within the consonant cluster. A word-final sequence of consonants in Arabic can have rising, equal, or falling sonority; epenthesis adds the vowel between the two consonants if the sonority of the cluster rises (table 8.1, a–f) and after the cluster if its two consonants are equal or falling in sonority (table 8.1, g–j).

Two-consonant clusters in Dutch monosyllables have rising sonority, and have the epenthetic vowel added between the two consonants (table 8.2, a–c), while three-consonant clusters have an initial /s/ and the epenthetic vowel appears immediately after the /s/ (table 8.2, d and e):

While epenthesis in a single location into the two-consonant clusters (always between or after the two consonants word-finally) would provide a form that is syllabifiable in Indonesian, the location reflects an aspect

Table 8.1 Borrowings from Arabic in Indonesian

	Arabic	Indonesian	Gloss
a.	/sˤubħ/	[subuh]	'dawn prayer'
b.	/fikr/	[pikir]	'to think'
c.	/fahm/	[paham]	'to understand'
d.	/siħr/	[sihir]	'sorcery'
e.	/ʕasˤr/	[ʔasar]	'late afternoon prayer'
f.	/ʕumr/	[ʔumur]	'age'
g.	/waqt/	[waktu]	'time'
h.	/sabt/	[sabtu]	'Saturday'
i.	/θalʤ/	[salʤu]	'snow'
j.	/ʕilm/	[ʔilmu]	'science'

Table 8.2 Borrowings from Dutch in Indonesian

	Dutch	Indonesian	Gloss
a.	/krax/	[kərah]	'collar'
b.	/blus/	[bəlus]	'blouse, dress'
c.	/slɔt/	[səlot]	'door lock'
d.	/sxruf/	[səkrup]	'screw driver
e.	/strok/	[sətruk]	'invoice'

of sonority: a preference for sonority to fall across the intervocalic consonant cluster, known as syllable contact (10). Note that this preference is not necessarily expressed all the time; for example, within the three-consonant clusters such as /str/, the falling sonority cluster that remains after a single vowel is epenthesized [sətr] does not trigger another epenthesis (*[sətəruk]). However, the preference for a fall in sonority is a factor that can be used to choose between otherwise equally viable options such as [pikir] versus [pikri].

In Batais and Wiltshire (2015), we analyzed this using a constraint based on (10), referring to sonority contact and a preference for more sonorous codas adjacent to less sonorous onsets. Can a wave approach to sonority offer any insights?

(16) Sonority representations for syllable contact

```
6        *      *                    *       *
5       / \    / \                  /\      /
4      /   \  /   *                /  \    *
3     /     \ /                   /    \  /
2    /       \/                  /      \/
1    *        *                  *       *
     p   i   k  i  r     vs.    *p  i   k  r  i
```

Both would seem to be well-formed waves, with rises to each peak. Following Indonesian syllabification, which does not allow clusters in onsets or codas, the correct form [pi.kir] benefits from a lower sonority [k] in the onset rather than the higher sonority [r], which would form the onset of the second syllable of *[pik.ri]. Furthermore, interpreting the graphs into syllables defined from trough to trough, as was already mentioned, would lead to an incorrect syllabification for the *[pi.kri] case. In terms of sonority waves, the sonority contact preference could be seen as a way to provide for lower sonority onsets and syllabifications compatible with a trough as the beginning of the syllable.

8.3.3. L2 Acquisition

As with borrowing, L2 acquisition can provide a probe into the phonological system of languages. L1 acquisition has provided evidence of the importance of sonority (Barlow 2005; Gnanadesikan 2004; Pater and Barlow 2003). Gnanadesikan's (2014) L1 English learner shows a preference for less sonorous onsets and, when faced with a complex cluster, deletes the more sonorous consonants, a pattern that can result from the same HONSET constraint in section 8.3.1. L1 acquisition is understood to provide evidence for universal tendencies, and while L2 acquisition involves transfer as well, acquiring an L2 may present learners with structures not present in their L1 for which transfer may not be relevant. Instead, how they deal with those structures can reveal relatively hidden aspects of L1 or universal tendencies. The role of syllable structure during the L2 acquisition of consonant clusters in onsets or codas by speakers of L1s that lack those clusters reveals yet again the role of sonority in syllabification (e.g., Hancin-Bhatt and Bhatt 1997; Wiltshire 2005, 2014). One of the earliest papers applying OT to this observation was Hancin-Bhatt and Bhatt (1997), who used a combination of universal constraints on sonority and constraint rankings transferred from L1 to predict patterns of L2 learners in producing new clusters for the L2.

A large body of work on the pronunciation of consonant clusters in coda positions by L2 learners who lack codas or coda clusters has provided evidence that the acquisition follows a pattern based on sonority, as discussed in Wiltshire (2014). To illustrate, I draw on an example from Indian English, which is generally learned as an L2 by speakers of Indian L1s. In studies of speakers of different L1s (Gujarati, Hindi, Angami, Ao, and Mizo), I have found that L2 productions of final-consonant clusters also revealed the effects of sonority sequencing (Wiltshire 2005, 2017), but, in addition, suggested that L2 speakers of English treat final clusters ending in /s/ as special, just as L1 speakers do.

Of the five Indian languages, the three Tibeto-Burman ones are the simplest in syllable structure: Angami allows no coda consonants at all, while Ao and Mizo allow exactly one consonant in coda. The two Indo-Aryan languages, Hindi and Gujarati, both allow consonant clusters in codas, but only those obeying the sonority sequencing generalization by falling in sonority. The productions of consonant clusters of the target L2 English differs based on the L1 of the speaker, with speakers of languages that do not allow clusters (Angami, Ao, Mizo) deleting consonants more

Table 8.3 Percentages of word-final cluster reductions in Indian English, by L1 groups

Cluster type (tokens per L1)	Angami	Ao	Mizo	Gujarati	Hindi
Nasal-stop (30), %	6.7	3.3	13.3	6.7	0
Lateral-stop or lateral-nasal (25), %	12	16	28	12	4
Fricative-stop (20), %	35	15	45	10	5
Stop-s (30), %	0	0	6.7	6.7	0
Stop-stop (20), %	45	45	65	10	5
CC-s (35), %	51.4	42.8	57.1	34.3	14.3
CC-stop (10), %	30	30	70	20	0
Total tokens altered	42/170	38/170	62/170	25/170	8/170
% altered	24.7	20.6	36.5	14.7	4.7

Note: C = any consonant.

often than speakers of languages that do allow clusters (Gujarati, Hindi), as shown in table 8.3.

Not all types of clusters were treated equally. Nasal-stop clusters and lateral-stop clusters, which follow the sonority sequencing principle, and stop-fricative clusters, which do not, were produced more often by speakers of all L1s, while clusters of two stops, with flat sonority, and fricative-stop (surprisingly) were more often reduced by deletion or epenthesis. For example, Tibeto-Burman speakers generally had no systematic problems producing nasal+stop (*stamp*), and liquid+stop (*held*); all speakers more surprisingly produced stop+/s/ (*slabs*) as well. The more problematic clusters included /s/+stop (*ask*), stop+stop (*project*), and some three-consonant clusters (*lifts, asks, sculpt*). Overall, apart from sequences involving stops and fricatives, the clusters that are more frequently produced follow the sonority sequencing generalization (8), and the clusters that are reduced violate it or sonority distance (9).

Wiltshire (2017) analyzed the data in OT, using a constraint against complex consonant clusters in codas, plus constraints that directly translate the sonority-related principles from (8) and (9).

(17) Markedness constraints on coda consonant clusters:

*COMPLEXCODA:	No consonant clusters in coda.
SONSEQ:	Consonant clusters fall in sonority in the coda.
MSD:	Consonants in the coda differ in sonority by a minimum of two steps.

In an OT analysis of L2 acquisition, we begin by considering the results of L1 acquisition, which is assumed to be transferred when beginning

L2. In the L1 acquisition, we assume that markedness constraints outrank correspondence constraints initially (Gnanadesikan 2004) and then constraints are reranked based on exposure to the L1 data. In acquiring languages like Ao, Angami, and Mizo, with no coda clusters, the markedness constraints in (17) would remain ranked above correspondence constraints as learners encounter no data causing them to rerank. To acquire languages like Hindi and Gujarati, which do allow clusters, learners must demote at least *COMPLEXCODA in their L1 grammars. Such a ranking would leave coda clusters subject to constraints on sonority sequencing and distance, but not rule them out altogether.

(18) a. Markedness outranks Correspondence in Angami, Ao, and Mizo L1 grammars

*COMPLEXCODA, SONSEQ, MSD >> MAX(C), DEP(V)

b. Markedness and Correspondence interleaved in Gujarati and Hindi L1 grammars

SONSEQ, MSD >> MAX(C), DEP(V) >> *COMPLEXCODA

Transfer of these L1 rankings predict that Angami, Ao, and Mizo speakers will initially reduce consonant clusters of all kinds, while Hindi and Gujarati speakers will repair only the more marked clusters in their L2 English productions. Once Angami, Ao, and Mizo speakers begin to learn, they will lower *COMPLEXCODA first, as all coda clusters will violate that markedness constraint while only a subset will also violate the SONSEQ and MSD constraints. At that point, they should first produce the less marked clusters, those that satisfy SONSEQ and MSD, thus producing an emergence of the unmarked effect. While the SONSEQ and MSD constraints were obscured in the L1 grammars due to the effect of a constraint eliminating all clusters, once *COMPLEXCODA is lowered they can make their presence known. As in table 8.3, these speakers of L1s that lack complex codas deleted consonants from a greater number of target clusters, from 20.6 percent for Ao speakers up to 36.5 percent for Mizo speakers; Hindi and Gujarati speakers had much lower rates of deletion, at 4.7 percent and 14.7 percent, respectively. Furthermore, the clusters that were more marked for sonority sequencing, such as stop+stop, are also the clusters more often reduced, while the well-formed nasal+stop rarely is.

The predictions of sonority sequencing do not perfectly hold, however, as fricatives are considered higher in sonority than stops and should therefore precede them in codas; however, the speakers of Indian English, regardless of their L1, tended to produce stop+fricative clusters correctly more often than fricative+stop clusters.

(19) Markedness of two-consonant clusters by sonority sequencing and the MSD: (N = Nasal, S = Stop, L = Lateral, F = Fricative)

Least marked			Most marked
NS, LS	*FS*	*SF*	SS

Two-consonant cluster acquisition order by speakers of Indian English:

First/best			Last/worst
NS, LS	*SF*	*FS*	SS

The fricative in the stop+fricative cluster was generally /s/ or /z/, which leads to two types of explanations: either the sonority sequencing constraint does not count stop+/s/ as a markedness violation, or some other factor outweighs sonority. One such factor could be frequency, which is known to play a role in L1 acquisition (Zamuner, Gerken, and Hammond 2005); it is plausible that the frequency of stop+/s/ clusters in English provided learners with more opportunities to master it. However, applying the Gradual Learning Algorithm (Boersma and Hayes 2001) reveals that the special treatment of /s/ in clusters cannot result from frequency alone, supporting the claim that C+/s/ clusters should be treated as special in L2 as well as L1 phonology (Yildiz 2005).

So we are left with treating stop+/s/ in codas as not counting as a sonority sequencing violation. The finding for the L2 English speakers is similar to that of Kirk and Demuth (2005), who found two-year-old children acquiring English as an L1 were more accurate in nasal+/z/ and stop+/s/ clusters, before other clusters. Kirk and Demuth also rejected a frequency solution and attributed their finding to the ease of production for word-final fricatives, even in clusters, relative to other clusters. There are also a variety of representational approaches for making the claim that these sequences are structurally distinct from other clusters. For example, excess consonants word-finally have been treated as being outside of coda position and therefore not subject to the coda sonority sequencing constraints, particularly when they are often morphologically separate. Formalisms along those lines include the use of an appendix or extraprosodic position (e.g., Fudge 1969; Goldsmith 1990; Itô 1986) or treating consonants as the onset of an empty-headed syllable in government phonology (Kaye, Lowenstamm, and Vergnaud 1990).

Looking at the sonority waves in (20), examples such as *held* and *project* behave as expected, while *slabs* is unexpectedly good and *ask* is unexpectedly bad.

(20) Acquired (held, slabs) versus repaired (ask, project) final clusters

```
6          *            *            *               *        *
5         / \          / \            \              Λ        Λ
4        /   *        *   \            \           *  \     /  \
3       /     \      /     \            \          /   \   /    \
2      *       \    *       \ *          *        /     \/       \
1               *            *            *      *       *        * *
        h  e l d  s l a      bs        a s k   p r o j    e       c t
```

This simple representation of sonority sequencing provides no additional explanatory power, based as it is on simple relationships between neighboring segments. A more sophisticated model that allows neighbors to interact and influence each other's sonority value, as discussed next and in Larson (1992) would be required to explain the exceptional behavior of /s/.

8.4. Discussion and Conclusions

One main motivation for sonority hierarchies not yet discussed is the description of syllabification, and the classic case for the use of sonority in syllabification is Berber (Dell and Elmedlaoui 1985). As this is presumably familiar to the reader, I will sketch their analysis only enough to make a comparison between constituents and waves possible. According to Dell and Elmedlaoui, word syllabification precedes by searching left to right for the most sonorous unsyllabified element, setting that element up as a nucleus of a syllable, and taking the segment to its left as its onset. The algorithm begins by looking at elements of the highest sonority ([a]) and proceeding in order up the hierarchy to lower sonority elements ([i], [l], [n], etc.) until the entire word is syllabified or until there is no sequence of two unsyllabified elements in a row, in which case the stray segments are joined up into a syllable. The analysis is formalized using a scale of sonority with multiple levels, but otherwise follows a hierarchical approach; once a segment is taken as an onset to an adjacent nucleus, it cannot be syllabified in any other way. The analysis demonstrably works.

However, an alternative in terms of sonority waves has been developed by Goldsmith and Larson, together and individually (Goldsmith and Larson 1990; Larson 1992; Goldsmith 1993). Using a dynamic computational network that allows each segment to interact with its neighbors, Goldsmith and Larson create a derived sonority value for each segment in context that can explain syllabification in Berber, among other things (the model is discussed in greater detail in chapter 12 of this volume). Each segment enters the model with an inherent sonority, but segments affect the sonority of their neighbors on either side, raising or lowering their derived sonority until the model settles into equilibrium. The model sets variable α as a factor for the segment's influence on its left-hand neighbor and β, mutatis mutandis, to the right; if both values are set at 0, we have the simple sonority waves used in (6), (12), (15), (16), and (20). However, nonzero values allow the model to incorporate both gradience and context in a finer tuned and more interactive model of the calculation of sonority. While the input /tluat/ in Berber would show inherent values of sonority that look like a single peak/syllable, with negative (inhibitory) values for both α and β, the derived sonority creates the two peaks found in the analysis of Dell and Elmedlaoui (1985).

(21) Larson's (1992: 62) analysis of Berber in the dynamic computation model

Inherent: 0 5 7 8 0		Derived values:	−2.6	4.34	1.54	8.38	−.89
t l u a t	→		t	L	w	A	t

This model also offers insight into the treatment of /s/ in clusters with other consonants. Larson (1992: 67) provided data from English to a learning algorithm for the model, and the algorithm learned to give /s/ a low sonority, negative α, and positive β. This means segments to the left of /s/ have lowered sonority while segments to its right increase in sonority, resulting in sonority waves for coda /ts/ clusters that show a sonority fall.

Goldsmith stated that "syllabification is not simply an effect, of which the sounds are the cause" (2011: 28), and we have seen that here in examples ranging from the more traditional sources of data, language-internal alternations, to more novel types of data from language borrowing and acquisition. Syllabification and its relationship with sonority can affect the character of a segment in fortition, determine where epenthesis is required or best located, and explain which sequences are easier/harder to acquire. While the use of a simple model of sonority waves that incorporates gradience, peaks, and trough has enhanced our understanding of these processes, we may need the further sophistication of the dynamic computational model to capture further gradience and the influence of neighboring segments on the evaluation of sonority in sequence.

References

Baertsch, Karen. 2002. An optimality theoretic approach to syllable structure: The split margin hierarchy. PhD dissertation, Indiana University.

Baertsch, Karen, and Stuart Davis. 2009. Strength relations between consonants: A syllable-based OT approach. In *Strength Relations in Phonology*, ed. Kuniya Nasukawa and Philip Backley, 285–316. Berlin: Mouton de Gruyter.

Baker, Gary K., and Caroline Wiltshire. 2003. An OT treatment of palatal fortition in Argentinian Spanish. In *Romance Linguistics: Theory and Acquisition*, ed. Ana Teresa Pérez-Leroux and Yves Roberge, 33–48. Amsterdam: John Benjamins.

Barlow, Jessica. 2005. Sonority effects in the production of consonant clusters by Spanish-speaking children. In *6th Conference on the Acquisition of Spanish and Portuguese as First and Second Languages*, ed. D. Eddington, 1–14. Somerville, MA: Cascadilla Press.

Batais, Saleh. 2013. Consonantal and syllabic repairs of Arabic and Dutch loanwords in Indonesian: A phonological account. PhD dissertation, University of Florida.

Batais, Saleh, and Caroline Wiltshire. 2015. Word and syllable constraints in Indonesian adaptation: OT analysis. In *LSA Annual Meeting Extended Abstracts* 6:2.1–5. http://dx.doi.org/10.3765/exabs.v0i0.2998.

Boersma, Paul, and Bruce Hayes. 2001 Empirical tests of the graduate learning algorithm. *Linguistic Inquiry* 32:45–86.

Carlisle, Robert S. 2001. Syllable structure universals and second language acquisition. *International Journal of English Studies* 1:1–19.

Chomsky, Noam, and Morris Halle. 1968. *The Sound Pattern of English*. New York: Harper and Row.

Clements, G. N. 1990. The role of the sonority cycle in core syllabification. In *Papers in Laboratory Phonology*, vol. 1, ed. John Kingston and Mary E. Beckman, 283–333. Cambridge: Cambridge University Press.

De Jong, Kenneth, and M.-H. Cho. 2012. Loanword phonology and perceptual mapping: Comparing two corpora of Korean contact with English. *Language* 88, no. 2: 314–368.

Dell, François, and Mohamed Elmedlaoui. 1985. Syllabic consonants and syllabification in Imdlawn Tashlhiyt Berber. *Journal of African Languages and Linguistics* 7:105–130.

Fudge, E. 1969. Syllables. *Journal of Linguistics* 5:253–286.

Gnanadesikan, Amalia. 2004. Markedness and faithfulness constraints in child phonology. In *Constraints in Phonological Acquisition*, ed. René Kager, Joe Pater, and Wim Zonneveld, 73–108. Cambridge: Cambridge University Press.

Goldsmith, John A. 1990. *Autosegmental and Metrical Phonology*. Vol. 1. Cambridge: Blackwell.

———. 1993. Harmonic phonology. In *The Last Phonological Rule*, 21–60. Chicago: University of Chicago Press.

———. 2011. The syllable. In *The Handbook of Phonological Theory*, ed. John Goldsmith, Jason Riggle, and Alan Yu, 162–196. West Sussex, UK: Wiley-Blackwell.

———. 2005/2016. Dynamic computational networks. Presentation slides/notes. http://people.cs.uchicago.edu/~jagoldsm/slides/2016-dcn.pdf.

Goldsmith, John, and Gary Larson. 1990. Local modeling and syllabification. *Chicago Linguistic Society* 26, no. 2: 129–142.

Gouskova, Maria. 2001. Falling sonority onsets, loanwords, and syllable contact. *Chicago Linguistic Society* 37, no. 1: 175–185.

Hancin-Bhatt, Barbara, and Rakesh Bhatt. 1997. Optimal L2 syllables: Interactions of transfer and developmental effects. *Studies in Second Language Acquisition* 19:331–378.

Hankamer, Jorge, and Judith Aissen. 1974. The sonority hierarchy. In *Papers from the Parasession on Natural Phonology, April 18, 1974*, ed. Anthony Bruck, Robert A. Fox, and Michael W. LaGaly, 131–145. Chicago: Chicago Linguistic Society.

Harris, James W. 1983 *Spanish Syllable Structure and Stress: A Nonlinear Analysis*. Cambridge, MA: MIT Press.

Hooper, Joan. 1976. *An Introduction to Natural Generative Phonology*. New York: Academic Press.

Itô, Junko. 1986. Syllable theory in prosodic phonology. PhD dissertation, University of Massachusetts.

Jesperson, Otto. 1904. *Lehrbuch der Phonetik*. Leipzig: Teubner.

Kabak, Bariş, and William J. Idsardi. 2007. Perceptual distortions in the adaptation of English consonant clusters: Syllable structure or consonantal contact constraints? *Language and Speech* 50, no. 1: 23–52.

Kaye, Jonathan, Jean Lowenstamm, and Jean-Roger Vergnaud. 1990. Constituent structure and government in phonology. *Phonology* 7:193–231.

Kenstowicz, Michael. 2006. Salience and similarity in loanword adaptation: A case study from Fijian. *Language Sciences* 29:316–340.

Kirk, Cecilia, and Katherine Demuth. 2005 Asymmetries in the acquisition of word-initial and word-final consonant clusters. *Journal of Child Language* 32:709–734.

LaCharité, Darlene, and Carole Paradis. 2005. Category preservation and proximity versus phonetic approximation in loanword adaptation. *Linguistic Inquiry* 362:223–258.

Larson, Gary N. 1992. Dynamic computational networks and the representation of phonological information. PhD dissertation, University of Chicago.

Lavoie, Lisa M. 2000. Phonological patterns and phonetic manifestations of consonant weakening. PhD dissertation, Cornell University.

Mohanan, K. P. 1982. The theory of lexical phonology. PhD dissertation, Massachusetts Institute of Technology.

———. 1986. *The Theory of Lexical Phonology*. Dordrecht: D. Reidel.

Mohanan, T. 1989. Syllable structure in Malayalam. *Linguistic Inquiry* 20, no. 4: 589–625.

Murray, Robert, and Theo Vennemann. 1983. Sound change and syllable structure in Germanic phonology. *Language* 59:514–528.

Pater, Joe, and Jessica Barlow. 2003. Constraint conflict in cluster reduction. *Journal of Child Language* 30:487–526.

Peperkamp, Sharon. 2005. A psycholinguistic theory of loanword adaptations. *Berkeley Linguistics Society* 30:341–352.

Pike, Kenneth L. 1959. Language as particle, wave, and field. *Texas Quarterly* 2, no. 2: 37–54. Reprinted in *Kenneth L. Pike: Selected Writings*, ed. Ruth M. Brend. The Hague: Mouton, 1972.

Pike, Kenneth L., and Eunice V. Pike. 1947. Immediate constituents of Mazatec syllables. *International Journal of American Linguistics* 13:78–91.

Prince, Alan, and Paul Smolensky. 1993. *Optimality Theory: Constraint Interaction in Generative Grammar*. Report no. RuCCS-TR-2. New Brunswick, NJ: Rutgers University Center for Cognitive Science.

Selkirk, Elisabeth. 1984. On the major class features and syllable theory. In *Language Sound Structure*, ed. Mark Aronoff and Richard T. Oehrle, 106–136. Cambridge, MA: MIT Press.

Steriade, Donca. 1982. Greek prosodies and the nature of syllabification. PhD dissertation, Massachusetts Institute of Technology. Published by Garland Press, New York [1990].

Tadmor, Uri. 2009. Loanwords in Indonesian. In *Loanwords in the World's Languages: A Comparative Handbook*, ed. Martin Haspelmath and Uri Tadmor, 686–716. Berlin: Mouton de Gruyter.

Vennemann, Theo. 1972. On the theory of syllabic phonology. *Linguistische Berichte* 18:1–18.

Whitney, William Dwight. 1874. *Oriental and Linguistic Studies*. New York: Scribner, Armstrong.

Wiltshire, Caroline. 1992. Syllabification and rule application in harmonic phonology. PhD dissertation, University of Chicago.

———. 2005. The "Indian English" of Tibeto-Burman language speakers. *English World-Wide* 26, no. 3: 275–300.

———. 2014. New Englishes and the Emergence of the Unmarked. In *The Variability of Current World Englishes*, ed. Eugene Green and Charles Meyer, 13–40. Berlin: Mouton de Gruyter.

———. 2017. Emergence of the unmarked in Indian Englishes with different substrates. In *The Oxford Handbook of World Englishes*, ed. Markku Filppula, Juhani Klemola, and Devyani Sharma, 599–620. Oxford: Oxford Press.

Yildiz, Yasemin. 2005. The structure of initial /s/-clusters: Evidence from L1 and L2 acquisition. In *Developmental Paths in Phonological Acquisition*, ed. Marina Tzakosta, Claartje Levelt, and Jeroen van der Weijer. Special issue, *Leiden Papers in Linguistics* 2, no. 1: 163–187.

Zamuner, Tania, LouAnn Gerken, and Michael Hammond. 2005. The acquisition of phonology based on input: A closer look at the relation of cross-linguistic and child language data. *Lingua* 115:1403–1426.

NINE

Toward Progress in Theories of Language Sound Structure

MARK LIBERMAN

9.1. Introduction

The theme of this chapter is a crucial redundancy in the traditional organization of phonological theories. Serious consideration of this redundancy supports radical simplification of the theory. In technical terms, allophonic variation can be treated in two different ways: first, as a mapping from symbols to symbols, via phonological rules or constraints; or second, as a mapping from symbols to signals, via principles of phonetic realization. Careful examination of specific cases of allophonic variation generally supports (and never seems to refute) a mode of description of the second type, in which structured phonological representations are mapped onto classes of phonetic trajectories. We should therefore consider the null hypothesis: a theory that entirely eliminates the symbolic treatment of allophonic variation and makes postlexical representations subject to direct phonetic interpretation, without any intervening symbol manipulation, whether by rules or by constraints.

This leaves us with four well-motivated (indeed unavoidable) tools for dealing with sound-structure patterns:

1. Phonological inventory: the set of available phonological elements and structures.
2. Lexical entries: the phonological spelling of whatever entities are listed in the lexicon: roots, affixes, morphological templates, words, phrases.
3. Allomorphy: alternative lexical pronunciations, whether conditioned by morphological features and morphological or phonological context, or in (linguistically) free variation.
4. Phonetic interpretation: the mapping between symbols (from 1 to 3) and signals.

And we assume, following Liberman and Pierrehumbert (1984) and many others, that patterns of phonetic interpretation are variably conditioned by structured phonological representations, as well as by rhetorical, attitudinal, and physiological variables, in ways that can be specific to particular language varieties and even particular individual speakers.

Given those resources, the phenomena generally described under the heading of *allophonic variation* do not require the addition of a fifth tool, in the form of manipulation of symbolic phonological representations via rules or constraints. Occam's razor therefore suggests a null hypothesis that some may find surprising, since it is inconsistent with many aspects of the past century of phonological practice: phonological rules or constraints of the traditional symbol-manipulating sort do not exist.

This is not a novel idea. For example, Liberman and Pierrehumbert suggested that

> Our methods . . . combine the phonologist's traditional concern for relations among abstract representations with the phonetician's interest in accounting for the details of actual speech. Our experience with these hybrid methods suggests that the correct "division of labor" between abstract phonological descriptions and the process of phonetic interpretation is not easy to discover. This point, applied to the subject matter of segmental phonology, will lead us to raise some pointed questions . . . about the correct treatment of allophonic variation. A reasonable answer to these questions would force most "postlexical" phenomena (in the sense of Mohanan 1982 and Kiparsky 1982) to be treated as facts about the phonetic realization of phonological representations, rather than as modifications of phonological representations themselves. (1984: 166)

> In such a framework, the minimally required set of postlexical rules would combine lexical representations into a well-formed phrase-level phonological structure. One reasonable account of the division of labor between phonological representations and their phonetic implementation would limit postlexical rules to such a minimal set and assign all other postlexical regularities to phonetic implementation. (1984: 231)

A version of this null hypothesis can be framed in nearly all of the many alternative theories of phonology, though it is easier to carry through in some theories rather than in others. The hypothesis may turn out to be false, but somewhat surprisingly, there do not seem to be any strong theoretical or empirical arguments against it at present. And recent technological advances make it practical, for the first time, to mount careful empirical investigations of this null-hypothesis phonology as applied to a wide variety of relevant phenomena, as well as freeing us from the need to rely on arbitrary phonetic distinctions in order to make descriptive progress. Whatever the outcome, the search will enrich our understanding of language sound structure.

9.1.1. Symbols and Signals

When someone speaks, they assemble a structured sequence of words, which they somehow encode as a pattern of vocal gestures and sounds. When all goes well, a hearer reverses the process and perceives the same structured word sequence. The individual elements of this word sequence are drawn from a set of entities that are crisply differentiated one from another, and transmitted from speaker to hearer with remarkable fidelity. In contrast, the corresponding vocal gestures and sounds are essentially continuous trajectories in continuous articulatory and acoustic spaces. Linguists traditionally model this situation by representing words as *symbols* and vocal gestures and sounds as *signals*.

And as linguists for millennia have recognized, a second symbolic layer intervenes between words and sounds: *phonological representations*. These might be strings of phonemes as in traditional structuralist theories, or distinctive feature matrices as in Chomsky and Halle (1968), or linked autosegmental tiers as in Goldsmith (1976), or features arranged as moras, syllables, and feet. But in any phonological system, a simple structured combination of a small finite set of basic symbolic elements defines the claims that words make on articulations and sounds.

We should note in passing that the history of automatic speech recognition technology underlines the motivations for (cultural or biological) evolution of a phonological system. We want accurate transmission of messages composed of word sequences drawn from a vocabulary of tens of thousands of items. But the signals representing these messages also carry many other sorts of information: about the identity of the speaker, about the acoustic environment, about the style and rhetorical structure of the message, about speaking rate and vocal effort and the speaker's attitudes and emotions and so on. If words were arbitrary classes of vocal noises, learning a word would require hundreds or thousands of training examples from different speakers in different contexts, as was the case when automatic speech recognition "time warping" systems were based on stored word-level recordings. But when a word's pronunciation is encoded phonologically, every occurrence of every word helps us to learn the symbol-to-signal mapping of the phonological system and therefore helps us to learn to recognize all other words (in the same language) as well.

9.1.2. Some Other Relevant Concepts

There are many different theories about how to cash out these general ideas in formal or psychological detail. For the most part, these differences are orthogonal to the issue discussed here. Underlying all the alternatives is overwhelming evidence for the psychological reality and descriptive necessity of both lexical and phonological levels of representation as discrete, symbolic systems, and for the existence of variable, language-particular principles for the phonetic interpretation of phonological representations. However, we need to discuss a few additional concepts in order to clarify the proposal being made.

9.1.2.1. Morphological Structure

There can be lexical structure inside word forms (e.g., via inflection, derivation, and compounding) and also lexical entries that are phrasal in nature. These structures have consequences for pronunciation, through allomorphy and perhaps also through direct phonetic interpretation.

9.1.2.2. Phonological Structure

It is obvious that syllable structure, stress and foot structure, and phrasal structure play a role in speech patterns. For example, in most varieties of American English, the /t/ of 'at all' is pronounced as a voiced flap, whereas the /t/ of 'a tall' is pronounced as a voiceless aspirated stop. The relevant generalization is roughly that all nononset consonants are weakened, and in the case of intervocalic /t/, the closure is weakened to a ballistic tap and the laryngeal gesture is weakened to the point of disappearance. For phonetic interpretation to be an option in such cases, phonological structure must be available to be interpreted.

9.1.2.3. Allomorphy

It is clear that lexical entries can have multiple phonological forms. In some cases these forms are in more or less free variation, like /ɛ/ versus /i/ in the first syllable of *economics*. In other cases, the choice of form depends on phonological or morphological context, like the two versions of the English indefinite article *a* and *an*. And via lexicalization, what starts as a casual-speech reduction can become an alternative lexical form, as in the case of English 'going to' in the version conventionally spelled 'gonna'.

9.1.2.4. Exemplar Theory and Word-Specific Phonetics

Every theory has word-specific phonological representations (ignoring some radical and implausible proposals to do without phonology entirely). Some linguists (e.g., Bybee 2000; Hay 2000; Pierrehumbert 2001) have suggested that there might be lexically specific phonetic interpretation as well. If true, this would add yet another descriptive option to an already overcomplete set of alternatives, and the cited facts also lend themselves to accounts in terms of the well-established influence of frequency, register, dialect mixture, and so on, on lexical choice and phonetic interpretation. But to the extent that lexically specific phonetic interpretation exists, for example via lexical priming of gestural or acoustic variants, it further undermines the arguments for symbolic allophony.

9.1.2.5. Quasi-Regularity and Emergent Knowledge

There are several strands of recent work (e.g., Rumelhart and McClelland 1986; Pierrehumbert 2001; Liberman 2004a, 2004b; Seidenberg and Plaut 2014) that blur the distinction between table lookup and derivation by rule, noting that it is possible to devise systems in which the learning of specific examples gradually generalizes to treat novel inputs in terms of similar patterns. As applied to lexical representations, this can be seen as a new form of traditional ideas about analogy. Patterns that look like symbolic allophony and allomorphy can emerge from such approaches to lexical storage. More radically, such ideas might blur the symbol–signal distinction entirely, or at least offer a story about how symbolic representations might emerge out of learned trajectories in signal space, while simultaneously generating those trajectories. At present, however, these ideas seem too amorphous and protean to define a productive approach to everyday linguistic description.

9.1.3. A Little Disciplinary History

There was a time when linguists were forced by circumstances to explore language sound structure almost entirely in symbolic terms. The shared perception of words anchored one end of the problem, and the principles that underlie alphabetic writing provided a rich and reliable array of discrete categories for characterizing the relationship of words to sounds, which were generalized to extend symbolic representations deep into the domain of signals.

Although these phonetic symbols often have rather poor intersubjective stability (see, e.g., Shriberg and Lof 1991; Pitt et al. 2005; Oller and Ramsdell 2006), they are a convenient way to convey subjective impressions of contextual, dialectal, and historical patterns in language sound structure. And for more than a century, the manipulation of such symbols has been the standard method of describing such patterns. In the course of this process, linguists have evolved a number of ideas for generalizing representations beyond simple strings of symbols: phonological features, syllabic and prosodic structures, and the linked tiers of autosegments originally proposed by John Goldsmith (1976, 1990).

In contrast to symbol manipulation, quantitative measurements of speech signals, though clearly relevant, were once nearly impossible, and until recently were painfully difficult. And systematic models of such measurements, beyond ordinary statistical analysis, have been much less extensively explored. In recent years, technological innovation has changed this balance to some extent. Acoustic recording has become easy, and digital storage allows easy distribution of very large collections of sound recordings. Techniques borrowed from speech recognition give us convenient forced alignment of recorded audio to the words in transcripts, and increasingly reliable automatic classification and measurement of the pronunciation of those words. Database technology gives us instant access to arbitrary subsets of those annotated audio collections. We also have increasingly inexpensive and convenient articulatory measurement techniques such as ultrasound, electromagnetic articulography, and magnetic resonance imaging. And modern computer hardware and software makes it relatively easy to frame and test quantitative models relating linguistic symbols and signals.

This progress has a cost: linguistics faces an increasing embarrassment of theoretical and methodological riches. The new phonetic methodologies help us to discover many new patterns of sound in language. And for any set of such patterns, we can provide many descriptions and explanations that are conceptually very different, but describe almost exactly the same set of observations.

This was already an issue for purely symbolic accounts of linguistic sound structure, but a serious consideration of nonuniversal contextually constrained symbol-signal mapping releases a host of new descriptive options. In particular, these new methods make it practical to frame and test, on a large scale, theories that dispense with symbolic allophony.

9.2. Some Illustrative Examples

Across the world's languages, linguists have documented and analyzed thousands of cases of dozens of types of allophonic variation. Here we will take a brief look at just two well-documented phenomena. The point is not to prove that the proposed mode of analysis is correct, but simply to illustrate the sorts of patterns that arise, to sketch the way that linguists have treated them, and to suggest the alternative approaches that the proposed null-hypothesis phonology might take. If phonological theories without symbolic allophony should be treated as the null hypothesis, then we should accept the burden of proof to try to show that analyses based on such theories are inadequate.

9.2.1. Canadian Raising

Joos observed that in Ontario English, "the diphthongs /aj/ and /aw/ . . . each have two varieties. One, which I shall call the HIGH diphthong after its initial tongue-position, begins with a lower-mid vowel-sound; it is used before any fortis consonant with zero juncture: [hwɐɪt, nɐɪf; ʃʌʊt, hʌʊs]=*white, knife; shout, house*. The other, the LOW diphthong, is used in all other contexts: [haɪ, faɪnd, naɪvz; hɑʊ, fɑʊnd, hɑʊzɪz]=*high, find, knives; how, found, houses*" (1942: 141). Joos described this phenomenon both qualitatively, in terms of his impressions of relative tongue position, and symbolically, in terms of the difference between [ɐ, ʌ] and [a, ɑ]. He did not describe it quantitatively, because in 1942 the quantitative measurement of vowel sounds was in practice impossible.

Joos (1942: 142) suggested that the source of this difference was a "lesser movement of the tongue," associated with "the relative shortness of English vowels before fortis consonants," which has been modified in the case of those two vowels "from a difference essentially of length to a difference essentially of quality," conditional on a following "fortis consonant with zero juncture," that is, immediately following a voiceless consonant within the same word.

Joos argued that this is enough to lay the groundwork for the contrast to become a matter of phonemic opposition (that is, change in lexical entries) versus allophonic variation (that is, change by phonological rule):

> It is now possible for [ɐɪ, aɪ; ʌʊ, ɑʊ] to become four phonemes instead of two, while it would not have been possible if /aj, aw/ had continued to be split according to the same criterion as all other syllabics. This statement is here proposed as a criterion of the possibility of phonemicizing: A phoneme /x/ can be succeeded historically by two phonemes /x_1/ and /x_2/ only if there is a difference between the contrast [x_1] – [x_2] under the contextual opposition $C_1 \sim C_2$, and the contrast [y_1, z_1, . . .] [y_2, z_2, . . .] in other phonemes under the same C_1, C_2. Under this PRINCIPLE OF DIFFERENTIATION, when /k, g/ were split into Old English / č, ǰ / and /k, g/, there must have been a period when the articulatory contrast between [č, ǰ] before palatals and [k, g] elsewhere was different from the contrast between [p_1, b_1, t_1, . . .] before palatals and [p_2, b_2, t_2, . . .] elsewhere, but when [č, ǰ] and [k, g] were still allophones of /k, g/; for otherwise the palatalization-opposition would have affected all consonants equally, which is as much as to say that palatalization would have been a separate phoneme feature itself, or a classifier of part of the vowels: the history of palatalization in Russian is an example. (1942: 142)

And he suggested that "this possibility [is] beginning to become a reality," given the voicing of /t/ "between voiced sounds with the syllable-division within it" (Joos 1942: 143). He asserted that in his own speech, "it is not lenis [d]; it is a very short fortis," but "in the speech of a large part of my contemporaries in the General American area, however, it has become a lenis [d], so that *latter=ladder* and *diluted=deluded*, with no difference in the preceding vowels either" (143). And he further claimed that "such speakers divide into two groups according to their pronunciation of words like *typewriter*. Group A says [tɐɪpaɪdɚ], while Group B says [tɐɪpɐɪdɚ]" (143).

Joos also cited some lexical differentiation, noting that there are "about two dozen common words like bite, biting" where Group A "shifts /t/ to /d/ in the inflected forms while keeping the dipthong unchanged," whereas "in hundreds of common words like *bet, betting*, there is also a difference in the vowels . . . so that *betting=bedding* in all its phonemes" (1942: 143). He asserted that "this difference clearly establishes the phonemic splitting of the diphthongs" (143), and suggested that "from such a beginning, it need not be long before we hear high diphthongs before /b, g/ also, in contrast with low diphthongs, maybe in all homely words or on some such analogical basis" (143).

Without delving further into the interesting details of Joos's (1942) paper, we can already see the crucial outline of the story. There are lexical representations, printed between slashes and consisting of strings what Joos called "phonemes," and there are pronunciations, printed between square brackets and consisting of strings of symbols from a similar set that Joos called "allophones." Some phonetic changes are historically reanalyzed—here a length difference causes a "lesser movement of the tongue" (p. 142) and is therefore reanalyzed in some cases as a difference in vowel quality. And some of these allophonic changes may become "phonemicized" and thereby elevated to lexical status for some words. The interaction of allophonic patterns can create what has come to be called "opacity," as when the voicing of intervocalic /t/ in certain inflected forms obscures the environment for Canadian Raising.

Joos (1942) subscribed to some very restrictive ideas about the nature and relationship of phonemes and allophones. And there are some factual questions about his treatment as well—his belief in his own voiced "very short fortis" /t/ may well be an instance of the *phoneme restoration effect* (Warren 1970); and the existence of his Group B is controversial. The dozens of papers that have wrestled over the past seventy-five years with the issues that he raised have considered a much wider range of phonological theories and have brought in a wider range of less anecdotal data, including the variants of /ay/ raising that have developed, apparently independently, in many other varieties of North American English.

But one long-outmoded aspect of Joos's (1942) treatment has stayed stubbornly in place in this literature. Although Joos recognized the relevance of speech articulation and sound, through his mention of the "lesser movement of the tongue," his description remains entirely symbolic, expressed in terms of relationships among symbol strings. He had no real choice in this matter, since in 1942 there was no accessible method for quantifying vowel quality. This changed in 1946 with the declassification of the sound spectrograph and has changed further since that time with more and more accessible computer-based methods for measuring vowel formants or other proxies for vowel quality. And there have been a number of papers on /ay/ raising that take advantage of these methods and thereby shed additional light on the phenomenon (e.g., Thomas 2000; Moreton 2004; Moreton and Thomas 2007; Fruehwald 2007, 2013).

However, essentially all of the more recent treatments, whether or not they are based on phonetic measurements, continue to address the questions that Joos (1942) raised in essentially the same symbol-string terms that Joos used.

Thus Mielke, Armstrong, and Hume focused on ways to use the ranked constraints of optimality theory to show "that some cases of opacity that were previously considered problematic for a surface-oriented formal model of synchronic phonology can be reanalyzed in a manner that renders the phonological patterns transparent" (2003: 124), treating Canadian Raising as an alternation between the phonetic strings [ay] and [ʌy]. They noted, "While our analysis of Canadian Raising succeeds in transparently accounting for the observed data, we cannot help but speculate that a more satisfying explanation would directly incorporate the relationship between phonological voicing and preceding vowel length. . . . As Port (1996) observes, the tendency to view segments as discrete elements leads to the analysis of vowel raising and consonant voicing as separate contrasts, and this misses an important generalization about the interrelatedness of the phonetic realization of vowels and consonants in phonological contrast" (Mielke et al. 2003: 134). But this is no more than a modernized and expanded version of Joos's remark about a "lesser movement of the tongue."

Idsardi argued that "recent efforts by Mielke et al. (2003) to revive Joos's (1942) phonemic splitting analysis . . . and to deny the existence of allophonic opacity are incorrect" (2006: 119). He mentioned the "growing industry in the phonetic measurement of the raised dipthongs," but argued that "we need to resist the lure of the transcription systems," because "the importance of Canadian Raising for opacity comes from its interaction with the process that neutralizes the /t-d/ contrast (or the neutralization of the /s-z/ contrast between $house_{Noun}$ and $house_{Verb}$ by phonetic devoicing), not from the phonetic details of the raising process itself" (2006: 120). In other words, the relevant issues arise within an essentially discrete, symbolic system, and we can remain agnostic about the particular distinction's phonetic interpretation.

Pater offered yet another formal mechanism to account for "the distribution of the raised variant of the Canadian English diphthongs" (2014: 230). In his system, "the preflap raised diphthongs are licensed by a language-specific constraint . . . captured with a weighted constraint grammar"; and he "shows how correct weights can be found with a simple, widely used learning algorithm" (2014: 230). He noted, "As Idsardi (2006) points out, analyses of CANADIAN RAISING . . . are generally of two types: those that treat the low/raised diphthong distinction as phonemic (Joos 1942), and those that treat it as opaquely allophonic, with the surface vowel contrast derived from the underlying contrast between /t/ and /d/ that is itself neutralized to the flap" (2014: 230). Pater described his proposal as "a third type of analysis, intermediate between the phonemic and allophonic approaches, in which the distribution of these diphthongs is an instance of positionally restricted contrast" (2014: 230).

These intelligent and interesting analyses, along with many others that we could cite, share with Joos (1942) the property of seeing the problem in terms of the distribution of symbols on the phonological surface, in relation to their distribution in the basic lexical entries involved. And the interesting and significant research into the quantitative measures of vowel quality relevant to these phenomena does not fundamentally change this perspective.

Thus Moreton "found the /ai/ pattern of more peripheral F1 and F2 in the offglides /ɔi ei aʊ/ as well, showing that it is part of a general pattern of 'hyperarticulation before voiceless consonants'" (2004: 1). This claim about hyperarticulation essentially inverts Joos's "lesser movement of the tongue" idea, and Moreton's measurements also show that Joos got the phonetic transcription wrong, since "the diphthong nuclei were less affected than the offglides" (2004: 1). But this work echoes Joos (1942) in appealing to an articulatory and perceptual explanation of the forces leading to this sound change; and Moreton's careful production and perception experiments help to explain why similar changes have apparently developed independently in several different speech communities, without challenging the idea that these changes are symbolic.

Fruehwald (2013) tracked the /ay/ raising over several decades of sociolinguistic interviews from the Philadelphia Neighborhood Corpus and produced striking evidence to

> [challenge] the conventional wisdom that phonologization is a late-stage reanalysis of phonetic coarticulatory and perceptual effects. . . . Rather, it appears that phonologization occurs simultaneously with the onset of phonetic changes. (Fruehwald 2013: vi)

He observed that

> the factors which categorize contexts as undergoing or not undergoing a change are best defined on phonological, not phonetic, grounds. . . . Perhaps the most surprising result is that /ay/ raising has applied opaquely with respect to flapping from the

very outset of its phonetic change. Despite the demonstrable phonetic differences between surface /t/ and /d/, and their flapped forms, /ay/ raising has always applied according to the underlying voicing of the following segment. (Fruehwald 2013: 175)

And he argued for a modified version of the "Big Bang" theory of sound change proposed by Janda and Joseph (2003):

(6.4) The initial innovation in a conditioned sound change is phonological, thus abrupt.
(6.5) The phonetic correlates of this abrupt phonological innovation are not necessarily large. (Fruehwald 2013: 183)

So Fruehwald used sophisticated phonetic measurement and modeling to argue that the factors that characterize contexts for sound change are phonological, that is, in our terms "symbolic"—and so is "the initial innovation" (2013: 183).

As far as I can determine, none of the more than a hundred post-1942 treatments of this phenomenon gives serious consideration to the alternative account that would be forced by the null-hypothesis phonology under discussion here. In this alternative account, neither /ay/ raising nor the flapping and voicing of /t/ are symbolic changes, rewriting symbolically expressed phonological representations. Rather, both /t/ and /ay/ are unchanged on the phonological surface and are interpreted phonetically in diverse ways, depending on language variety and context, so as to reflect the observed patterns of pronunciation.

This account is consistent with overlaid processes of lexicalization, where some or all of the variation is moved up into the lexicon, by expanding the phonological inventory and/or modifying a suitable range of lexical entries. (And if we allow lexically specific phonetic implementation, lexicalization does not require a change in the phonological inventory, at least at first.) In fact, Fruehwald (2013) demonstrated that something of this kind has happened in Philadelphia, where some speakers have generalized the raised version of /ay/ vowel to a few words like *spider*.

Note that this account does away with all of the problems of opacity and "counter-feeding order." Contextually varied phonetic interpretation of /ay/ and of /t/, treated independently, still results in the observed patterns, since (in the simplest case) each phonetic-interpretation pattern operates on an unchanging phonological representation. And given the options of modifying the phonological inventory and the phonological spelling out of individual lexical entries, the more complex outcomes remain easy to model.

9.2.2. Spanish /s/ Lenition

The weakening of syllable-final /s/ in Spanish has been even more widely studied than English /ay/ raising, but the intellectual histories of linguistic approaches to these two phenomena have been quite different. As discussed in the previous section, /ay/ raising has (nearly?) always been analyzed in terms of symbolic allophony, even when the analysis is based on instrumental phonetic measurements. In contrast, some analyses of Spanish syllable-final /s/ lenition have viewed it as an aspect of phonetic realization, while others have treated it in terms of the rewriting of a symbol string.

Thus Navarro offered considerable impressionistic detail about the variable realization of /s/ in various environments in Puerto Rican Spanish, always treating the process as a matter of phonetic detail rather than phonological change. For example:

> Delante de p, t, c (k), la aspiración de la s reduce y atenúa su sonido: *respeto, pestaña, pescar*. En las palabras de esta clase con *es-* inicial en principio de grupo, no solo la s sino toda la silaba se apaga hasta un grado casi imperceptible. . . . Sería exagerado decir que vocablos como *abispa, cresta, casco,* se convierten en *abippa, cretta, cacco.* En realidad se percibe siempre cierto resto de la aspiración entre la vocal acentuada y la oclusion siguiente. (Navarro 1948: 71)

And Lloyd placed this approach in a broader historical perspective:

> The preponderance of open syllables in Spanish from earliest times, and the drive to make all syllables as open as possible, has had a continuous effect on syllable-final consonants. (Lloyd 1987: 347)

> Related, in part at least, to the preceding phenomenon is the weakening of syllable-final /-s / into an aspiration which may eventually become so weak that it disappears. (Lloyd 1987: 348)

On the other hand, much of the late twentieth-century literature treated this phenomenon in symbolic terms. Thus Beym (1963), describing Argentinian Spanish, discussed the geographic, social, and phonological conditioning of the symbolically represented allophones [s], [z], [h], [ɦ], [s], [x], and [Ø] (=0) as variants of phonemic /s/ in syllable-final position. Ma and Herasimchuk (1972) limited their account of Puerto Rican Spanish /s/ to the three allophones [s], [h], and [Ø]. Cedergren

(1973) described three "relevant variants" of syllable-final /s/ in Panamanian Spanish, with several symbolically represented "phonetic realizations" each:

Var.	*Phonetic Real.*
s	[s] [z] [sz]
h	[c] [h] [ɦ]
Ø	[] Ø

Poplack wrote that

Puerto Rican Spanish (s) is variably subject to two weakening processes, aspiration and deletion, so that a phrase such as *las cosas bonitas*, 'the pretty things' can also be realized [lah 'kosah bo'nitah] or [la 'kosa bo'nita]. (Poplack 1980: 55)

In some cases, these researchers assigned pronunciations to discrete classes in order to make the phenomena accessible to the then-popular computer programs for "variable rules" in sociolinguistics, which modeled the distribution of a binary variable using logistic regression. In other cases, the motivation is explicitly the problem of designing an intersubjectively valid coding scheme. For example, in a study of Cuban Spanish, Terrell wrote:

Certain methodological observations are in order. It was my intention to distinguish a variety of phonetic manifestations of /s/. However, it became quickly apparent that such a task, theoretically so simple, on a practical basis was impossible. It is imperative in any science to demand that others be able to replicate the results of any investigation. Replicability of the results would have been very difficult to achieve with a fine transcription. For this reason, the following system was selected.

s: all phones with some sibilance.
0: complete absence of a phone representing /s/.
h: normally aspirated, sometimes very weak, often voiced or nasalized and possibly assimilated resulting in a geminate consonant cluster.

It should be noted that this is essentially the same system used by others who have done quantitative studies of Spanish phonology. (Terrell 1979: 600)

In contrast, several more recent studies have used modern computer-based methods to solve Terrell's problem by applying appropriate regression models to the systematic measurement of spectral centroids, closure, voicing, and frication durations, and so on, treating these measurements with appropriate regression models. Thus Fox wrote:

Automated speech recognition methods were used to code three dependent variables for a corpus of over 50,000 tokens of syllable-final /s/: deletion or retention of /s/, duration of retained /s/, and the spectral center of gravity of retained /s/. Multiple regression was performed for each of the dependent variables, on all of the data combined and on several subsets of the data. (Fox 2006: iv)

Erker asserted that such approaches lead to greater insight:

Among the most compelling and often replicated findings to emerge from sociophonetic research is that correlations between linguistic form and social factors can be manifested not only at the level of the segment but also in fine-grained, subsegmental aspects of speech. That is, instrumental analysis has proven capable of uncovering systematic socio-phonetic variation within a single segmental category and also across more than one segmental category. (Erker 2010: 10)

And File-Muriel and Brown reinforced this conclusion:

Whereas previous studies of Spanish *s*-weakening have relied on impressionistic coding, the present study examines temporal and gradient acoustic details in the production of /s/ by eight females from Cali, Colombia, during sociolinguistic interviews. We propose a metric for quantifying *s*-realization by employing three scalar-dependent variables: *s*-duration, centroid, and voicelessness. The results of linear regressions indicate that the dependent variables are significantly conditioned by local speaking rate, word position, following and preceding phonological context, stress, and lexical frequency. This study sheds light on how each independent variable influences *s*-realization acoustically. For example, as local speaking rate increases, duration, centroid, and voicelessness decrease, which is indicative of lenition, and the same weakening tendency is observed when /s/ occurs in word-final position or is followed by a nonhigh vowel, whereas frequency contributes only to *s*-duration. We discuss the advantages of opting for instrumental measurements over symbolic representation. (File-Muriel and Brown 2011: 223)

As in the case of /ay/ raising, there is evidence for lexicalization. Thus Terrell wrote:

Informal experience and some direct work with the Spanish of illiterate and semi-illiterate Dominicans leads me to believe that many speakers in the Dominican Republic have speech with completely restructured lexicons, in which no word ends in /s/. (Terrell 1979: 610)

But Bullock, Toribios, and Amengual argued that "illiterate Dominicans are not 'lost-s speakers' who arbitrarily add coda-s" as a form of hypercorrection, because

> If such speakers did exist, we should not find that they are able to adjust their rates of s-realization according to different conversational styles. Their linguistic performance should demonstrate an accidental or random realization of coda-s, where each token produced would as likely be intrusive as lexical. But we already have available evidence that this is not the case. (Bullock et al. 2014: 23)

However, lexical identity does seem to be a relevant factor in determining rates of coda-s production in their data, suggesting that their speakers' lexical entries differ in the presence (or perhaps the strength) of s-less and s-ful variants.

To sum up, the literature on Spanish syllable-final /s/ lenition seems entirely consistent with the class of phonological theories suggested here, in which we rely entirely on the resources of the phonological inventory, the content of lexical entries including allomorphic variation, and contextually varied patterns of phonetic interpretation, without any use of symbolically defined allophony.

9.3. Conclusion

There are at least two good practical reasons that scholars over the centuries have described allophonic variation in terms of the manipulation of phonological symbols.

One source for this practice is the description of historical change, where we see systematic correspondences in phonological representations across time and space. Since allophonic variation is often a form of change in progress, it is natural to treat it in the same way as we treat the raw materials of historical-comparative reconstruction.

And a second source is descriptive convenience: extensions of the usual inventory of phonemes, features, and phonological structures are an obvious way to keep track of impressionistic data about instances of pronunciation.

But historical change, by definition, involves changes in lexical entries and phonological inventories. Our proposed class of null-hypothesis theories includes ways for patterns of phonetic interpretation to be reanalyzed as changes in lexical entries and phonological inventories, and so the needs of historical-comparative reconstruction are not prima facie a reason to add symbolic allophony to our toolkit.

And modern methods of phonetic research allow us to extract and model quantitative acoustic measurements from thousands of hours of speech. If the phonetic phenomena are quantal, in the sense of Stevens (1972, 1989), or otherwise fall into qualitatively different subsets, we can generate and apply appropriate (semi-)automatic classifiers. With increasing facility, we can select audio samples or generate artificial stimuli and run perception tests. So it may often remain convenient to use symbolic labels in discussing and thinking about allophonic variation, but we now have clear practical alternatives to the ontological commitment that this convenience too easily creates.

In sum, the symbolic treatment of allophony is a deeply ingrained habit that our field should not continue to accept without evidence. Discarding this habit will give us a fresh perspective on familiar phenomena, and even if we end up persuading ourselves to take it up again, the experience will be instructive.

Note

This essay is dedicated to John Goldsmith, from whom I learned the value of examining basic assumptions. Among the many people who have recently contributed to my thoughts on this topic, Larry Hyman and Neville Ryant deserve special acknowledgment. Errors and omissions are of course my responsibility.

References

Beym, Richard. 1963. Porteño /s/ and [h] [ɦ] [s] [x] [Ø] as variants. *Lingua* 12:119–204.

Bullock, Barbara, Almeida Toribio, and Mark Amengual. 2014. The status of *s* in Dominican Spanish. *Lingua* 143:20–35.

Bybee, Joan. 2000. The phonology of the lexicon: Evidence from lexical diffusion. In *Usage-Based Models of Language*, ed. Michael Barlow and Suzanne Kemmer, 65–85. Stanford, CA: Center for the Study of Language and Information.

Cedergren, Henrietta. 1973. The interplay of social and linguistic factors in Panama. PhD dissertation, Cornell University.

Chomsky, Noam, and Morris Halle. 1968. *The Sound Pattern of English*. New York: Harper and Row.

Erker, Daniel. 2010. A subsegmental approach to coda/s/weakening in Dominican Spanish. *International Journal of the Sociology of Language* 203:9–26.

File-Muriel, Richard, and Earl Brown. 2011. The gradient nature of s-lenition in Caleño Spanish. *Language Variation and Change* 23, no. 2: 223–243.

Fox, Michelle. 2006. Usage-based effects in Latin American Spanish syllable-final /s/ lenition. PhD dissertation, University of Pennsylvania.

Fruehwald, Josef. 2007. The spread of raising: Opacity, lexicalization and diffusion. Paper presented at New Ways of Analyzing Variation (NWAV) 36, November 11, 2007. http://repository.upenn.edu/cgi/viewcontent.cgi?article=1087&context=curej.

———. 2013. The phonological influence on phonetic change. PhD dissertation, University of Pennsylvania.

Goldsmith, John. 1976. Autosegmental phonology. PhD dissertation, Massachusetts Institute of Technology. Bloomington: Indiana University Linguistics Club. http://people.cs.uchicago.edu/~jagoldsm/Papers/dissertation.pdf. Published by Garland Press, New York [1979].

———. 1990. *Autosegmental and Metrical Phonology: A New Synthesis*. Oxford: Basil Blackwell.

Hay, Jen. 2000. Causes and consequences of word structure. PhD dissertation, Northwestern University.

Idsardi, William. 2006. Canadian raising, opacity, and rephonemicization. *Canadian Journal of Linguistics/La revue canadienne de linguistique* 51, no. 2: 119–126.

Janda, Richard, and Brian Joseph. 2003. Reconsidering the canons of sound-change: Towards a "Big Bang" theory. In *Historical Linguistics 2001: Selected Papers from the 15th International Conference on Historical Linguistics*, ed. Barry Blake and Kate Burridge, 205–219. Amsterdam: John Benjamins.

Joos, Martin. 1942. A phonological dilemma in Canadian English. *Language* 18, no. 2: 141–144.

Kiparsky, Paul 1982. Lexical phonology and morphology. In *Linguistics in the Morning Calm*, ed. I. S. Yang, 3–91. Seoul: Hanshin.

Liberman, Mark. 2004a. The curious case of quasiregularity. *Language Log*, January 15. http://itre.cis.upenn.edu/~myl/languagelog/archives/000344.html.

———. 2004b. The theology of phonology. *Language Log*, January 2. http://itre.cis.upenn.edu/~myl/languagelog/archives/000288.html.

Liberman, Mark, and Janet Pierrehumbert. 1984. Intonational invariance under changes in pitch range and length. In *Language Sound Structure*, ed. Mark Aronoff and Richard Oehrle, 157–233. Cambridge, MA: MIT Press.

Liberman, Mark, and Alan Prince. 1977. On stress and linguistic rhythm. *Linguistic Inquiry* 8, no. 2: 249–336.

Lloyd, Paul. 1987. *From Latin to Spanish*. Philadelphia: American Philosophical Society.

Ma, Roxana, and Elenor Herasimchuk. 1972. The linguistic dimensions of a bilingual neighborhood. In *Bilingualism in the Barrio*, ed. Joshua A. Fishman, Robert L. Cooper, and Roxana Ma Newman. Bloomington: Indiana University Press.

Mielke, Jeff, Mike Armstrong, and Elizabeth Hume. 2003. Looking through opacity. *Theoretical Linguistics* 29:123–139.

Mohanan, K. P. 1982. Lexical phonology. PhD dissertation, Massachusetts Institute of Technology. Bloomington: Indiana University Linguistics Club.

Moreton, Elliott. 2004. Realization of the English postvocalic [voice] contrast in F1 and F2. *Journal of Phonetics* 32, no. 1: 1–33.

Moreton, Elliott, and Erik R. Thomas. 2007. Origins of Canadian Raising in voiceless-coda effects: A case study in phonologization. *Laboratory Phonology* 9:37–64.

Navarro, Tomas. 1948. *El Espanol en Puerto Rico, Contribucion a la Geografia Linguistica Hispanoamerica.* Río Piedra: Editorial de la Universidad de Puerto Rico.

Oller, Kimbrough, and Heather Ramsdell. 2006. A weighted reliability measure for phonetic transcription. *Journal of Speech, Language, and Hearing Research* 49, no. 6: 1391–1411.

Pater, Joe. 2014. Canadian raising with language-specific weighted constraints. *Language* 90, no, 1: 230–240.

Pierrehumbert, Janet. 2001. Exemplar dynamics: Word frequency, lenition and contrast. In *Frequency Effects and the Emergence of Linguistic Structure*, ed. Joan L. Bybee and Paul J. Hopper, 137–158. Amsterdam: John Benjamins.

Pitt, Mark, Keith Johnson, Elizabeth Hume, Scott Kiesling, and William Raymond. 2005. The Buckeye corpus of conversational speech: Labeling conventions and a test of transcriber reliability. *Speech Communication* 45, no. 1: 89–95.

Poplack, Shana. 1980. The notion of the plural in Puerto Rican Spanish: Competing constraints on (s) deletion. In *Locating Language in Time and Space*, ed. William Labov, 55–67. New York: Academic Press.

Port, Robert. 1996. The discreteness of phonetic elements and formal linguistics: Response to A. Manaster-Ramer. *Journal of Phonetics* 24:491–511.

Rumelhart, David, and James McClelland. 1986. On learning the past tenses of English verbs. In *Parallel Distributed Processing: Explorations in the Microstructure of Cognition*, by David Rumelhart, James McClelland, and the PDP Research Group. Cambridge, MA: MIT Press.

Seidenberg, Mark, and David Plaut. 2014. Quasiregularity and its discontents: The legacy of the past tense debate. *Cognitive Science* 36, no. 6: 1190–1228.

Shriberg, Lawrence, and Gregory Lof. 1991. Reliability studies in broad and narrow phonetic transcription. *Clinical Linguistics and Phonetics* 5, no. 3: 225–279.

Stevens, Kenneth. 1972. The quantal nature of speech: Evidence from articulatory-acoustic data. In *Human Communication: A Unified View*, ed. Peter Denes and Edward David Jr., 51–66. New York: McGraw-Hill.

———. 1989. On the quantal nature of speech. *Journal of Phonetics* 17:3–45.

Terrell, Tracy. 1979. Final /s/ in Cuban Spanish. *Hispania* 62, no. 4: 599–612.

Thomas, Erik. 2000. Spectral differences in /ai/ offsets conditioned by voicing of the following consonant. *Journal of Phonetics* 28, no. 1: 1–25.

Warren, Richard. 1970. Perceptual restoration of missing speech sounds. *Science* 167, no. 3917: 392–393.

PART TWO

Computation and Unsupervised Learning

TEN

On the Discovery Procedure

JACKSON L. LEE

10.1. Introduction

On what linguistic theory is about, Chomsky (1957) discussed three views: the discovery procedure, the decision procedure, and the evaluation procedure. Chomsky rejected the discovery view for being "unreasonable" and argued for the evaluation view for being "practical." Among the subsequent works that make reference to this discussion is John Goldsmith's recent research on computational morphology, specifically the development of the unsupervised morphological learner Linguistica (Goldsmith 2001, 2006). Goldsmith contextualized his work in terms of a strongly empiricist approach to linguistics (Goldsmith 2015) and an explicit formulation of the evaluation device (Goldsmith 2011). Goldsmith stressed the connection of his work to the evaluation metric. This chapter argues, however, that Goldsmith's work actually also argues for what Chomsky believed to be too challenging and high order—namely, the discovery procedure. Goldsmith's emphasis on the use of unsupervised and machine learning approaches to inducing linguistic structure is precisely what the discovery procedure asks for, that is, explicit methods that take raw linguistic data as input and learn patterns analogous to what a linguistic description would look like. This chapter concludes by discussing the importance of the discovery procedure for doing linguistics, particularly in terms of reproducible, accessible, and extensible research.

10.2. Doing Linguistic Research Computationally

Put another way, this chapter is a brief reflection of what it means to come up with a linguistic analysis. This section discusses a strongly data-driven and empiricist perspective, leading to the discovery procedure and John Goldsmith's work on unsupervised learning of linguistic structure.

10.2.1. The Relationship between Data and Analysis

In linguistics, what does it mean to analyze some given data? This section reflects on this by discussing two seemingly incompatible positions as an answer to it and providing a view that reconciles the apparent paradox.

The first position for how a linguistic analysis comes into being is the more traditional approach. In theoretical linguistics, this actually goes largely unnoticed. Given data, the job of a linguist is to provide the best analysis that captures the full range of the available data. This is all too familiar to those who have undertaken graduate-level linguistic training in the field, in the sense that when you are given a linguistics problem set and asked to analyze the data, your job is to come back a week later with an analysis—the *best* analysis—in your write-up. Nobody would ask exactly what enables you to know the analysis and what has happened with you between the moment you receive the problem set and the moment you submit the analysis. What goes between the data and analysis—between input and output—is very much a black box.

The second position for doing linguistics can be regarded as "the algorithmic approach." Most importantly, what mediates between the data and analysis is an algorithm or procedure of some sort, entirely external to the human mind and, once established, free from any human biases. In this mode of doing linguistic analysis, the human analyst still has access to both data and analysis, but he or she restricts direct access and manipulation to only the algorithm that takes the data and outputs the analysis. If the analysis is suboptimal (as evaluated by the analyst with some criterion), then changes can be made only to the algorithm. At any given point, the algorithm can be externally and objectively examined, whereas the human brain in the first position cannot. Given its nature of absolute explicitness, the algorithmic approach to linguistics is usually practiced by the computationally oriented researchers who implement algorithms as computer programs.

Prima facie, these two approaches to linguistics appear incompatible, in the sense that the human linguist can directly manipulate an analysis without much attention to the precise steps taken in the traditional method, whereas in the algorithmic one, manipulation is disallowed in the analysis and focused on the steps that mediate between the input data and the analysis. It is important to recognize, however, that the algorithmic approach to linguistics depends on the insights of the human analyst who develops the algorithm. Such insights do stem from the human intuition. Also, whether an algorithm is deemed successful relies on some evaluation metric that is devised, necessarily, based on the human analyst's judgment as to what it means to be a good algorithm or analysis. Theoretical linguistics stemming from human insights, on the one hand, and computational linguistics built on rigorous implementation, on the other, complement each other. Neither of them are dispensable for the explicit modeling of the relationship between data and analysis.

10.2.2. Empiricism and Unsupervised Learning

The chapter takes a strongly empirical view of language and linguistic research. More specifically, the view is based on the position that the relationship between grammar and data is one that is partially overlapping:

(1) The partially overlapping nature of grammar and data

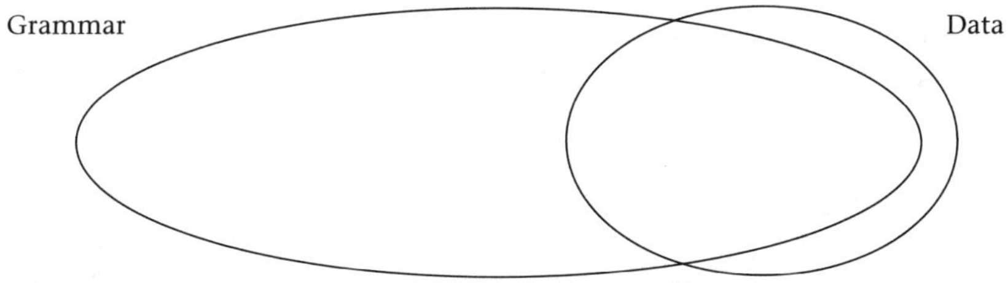

The term "data" refers to what is empirically observed in the real world, that is, what one actually hears and utters. "Grammar" refers to what an individual knows about a particular language. On the one hand, there is something that we have never heard or uttered but which we know is part of the language in question, that is, in the grammar but not in the data. On the other hand, there is a small portion of the observed data that can be considered the noise in the data, analogous to errors, slips of tongue, and the like—this is part of the observed data but not in one's grammar.

Arguably, mainstream linguistic research focuses on what is referred to as "grammar" here. Linguists are interested in characterizing what is *not* observed and yet considered part of grammar. This is reflected by the use of the introspection methodology leading to grammaticality judgments that advance theoretical arguments. A related and increasingly popular methodology is to conduct behavioral studies to obtain data from a much larger pool of subjects who are native speaker consultants for more fine-grained grammaticality judgments.

While one of the most intriguing aspects of language is our implicit knowledge of grammar, it is important to recognize that grammar, as a speaker's knowledge of a particular language, ultimately comes from data. A research program on how grammar results from data echoes the recent literature on learnability, especially regarding the observation that most mainstream theoretical linguistic work focuses on characterizing the grammar and ignores questions of how it comes into being (cf. Clark 2015). If we understand linguistic research as an enterprise about explicitly figuring out how grammar results from data, then the question is how to do so. Fortunately, a natural answer has long been available: unsupervised learning. By unsupervised learning, I refer to the ensemble of computational tools and concepts from computer science and statistics employed in learning patterns from unlabeled data. Particularly relevant in the study of language is the use of unsupervised learning techniques as a way to model first language acquisition (Clark and Lappin 2010), given that toddlers acquiring their first language have to induce a grammar based only on the unlabeled linguistic data from the ambient environment. Such linguistic data is unlabeled in the sense that it is unannotated at any levels of linguistic analysis.

10.2.3. Grammar Evaluation and Algorithms

Criss-crossing this chapter is the question of what it means for an analysis to be the best for some given linguistic data. Linguists seem to share the intuition—be it vague or not—for what makes an analysis good or bad, including such factors as how complex the formalism is and how much data the analysis can capture; see, for example, Halle (1962) on measuring grammar complexity in terms of counting symbols. Much as we have to be explicit about *what* it means for an analysis to be the best, it is no less important that we are explicit about *how* we advance an analysis. The "what" question is discussed in terms of the trade-off between grammar complexity and data compression, whereas the answer to the "how" question relies on the use of computationally implementable algorithms.

On the goal of linguistic theory, Chomsky (1957: 49–53) discussed several possibilities and argued for this particular one:

> Given a corpus and given two proposed grammars G_1 and G_2, the theory must tell us which is the better grammar of the language from which the corpus is drawn. In this case we might say that the theory provides an *evaluation procedure* for grammars. (Chomsky 1957: 51; emphasis in original)

This is graphically represented as follows:

(2) Chomsky (1957: 51) on the evaluation procedure of grammars:

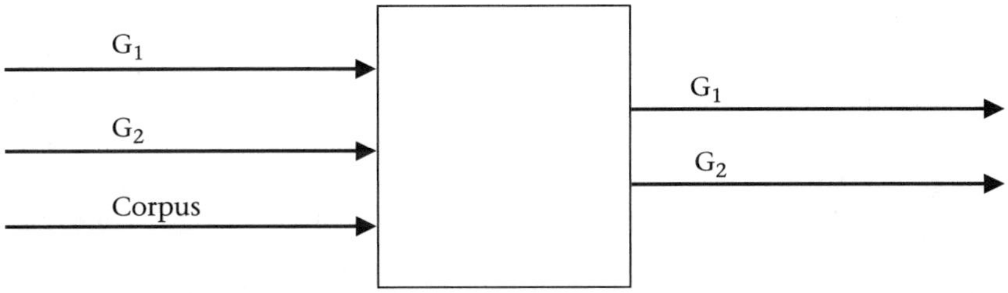

Among the subsequent works that make reference to Chomsky's (1957) evaluation procedure of grammars, a recent focal point is John Goldsmith's work on unsupervised learning of morphology. While this chapter does not do full justice to explaining Goldsmith's view on the "what" and "how" questions about the evaluation procedure, the rest of this section discusses its gist from a very brief, intuitive, and practical point of view. Goldsmith (2015) is an elaborate discussion of some of the ideas referred to in this chapter.

For any linguistic analysis, we would like a way of formalizing how complex it is. In the parlance of computer science, complexity can be formalized as description length in terms of bits: the longer the description length, the more complex the analysis is. There are two parts in the analysis: grammar complexity and data cost. For grammar complexity, consider a grammar that captures a good deal of some given data. The description length of the grammar is computed in terms of bits. We say that, for instance, a grammar encoded in 1,000 bits is more complex than one encoded in 800 bits. As for the second part of data cost, we ask how good the grammar is for fitting the given data, and for this we measure it by the number of bits needed to encode data using that particular grammar. This includes, for example, the exceptions that the grammar is unable to capture and therefore have to be encoded, also in bits, separately. The notion of the best analysis, then, is formalized as searching for the one with the smallest sum of the two measurements. This is the minimum description length (MDL) approach (Rissanen 1989). In other words, for grammar selection, an MDL analysis asserts that the best analysis is one that minimizes the sum of the grammar complexity and the data cost given the grammar (Goldsmith 2011). There are two major appealing aspects stemming from an MDL approach. First, MDL embodies Occam's razor. Minimizing grammar complexity is the computational analog to advancing the simplest analysis in theoretical linguistics. Second, MDL eschews overfitting. In traditional theoretical linguistics, an often unnoticed assumption is the emphasis placed on accounting for *all* the given data points at all costs, typical in linguistic training, and consequently the reduced concern over increasing grammar complexity. In other words, the insight from MDL is this: we do not want to fit the data too well at the cost of a highly complex grammar, and at the same time we also do not want a grammar that is too simple, one that fits the given data too poorly.

To execute the kind of complexity and description length computation described here requires precision at a level that the computer, as opposed to the human being, can practically handle. This necessarily means we need computer programs that can be considered realizations of explicit and precise algorithms representing ideas devised by the human analyst. More often than not, in theoretical linguistics, the focus is the analysis but not *how* that analysis comes into being. This claim is supported by the way that linguists are typically trained: given a linguistic data set, we are asked to come up with an analysis for a given question, but we are *never* asked to explicitly and meticulously pin down the steps through which the analysis is born. The procedure that leads to an analysis is as important as, if not more, the analysis itself (see also Goldsmith 2004). The important role of algorithms for linguistics is discussed further in section 10.3 in terms of what linguistics is about and in section 10.4 on methodological issues.

10.3. Toward the Discovery Procedure

Recall Chomsky's (1957) view in favor of the evaluation procedure. If there exists some evaluation metric and algorithmic approach appropriately defined with respect to a linguistic data analysis problem, then one might well say this should be the end of the chapter. No—this is far from it. The view that devising algorithms sits at the center of linguistic analytic work for executing the evaluation procedure as well as connecting data and analysis tightly together echoes squarely the *discovery procedure*:

> The strongest requirement that could be placed on the relation between a theory of linguistic structure and particular grammars is that the theory must provide a practical and mechanical method for actually constructing the grammar, given a corpus of utterances. Let us say that such a theory provides us with a *discovery procedure* for grammars. (Chomsky 1957: 50–51; emphasis in original)

The discovery procedure is illustrated as follows:

(3) Chomsky (1957: 51) on the discovery procedure of grammars:

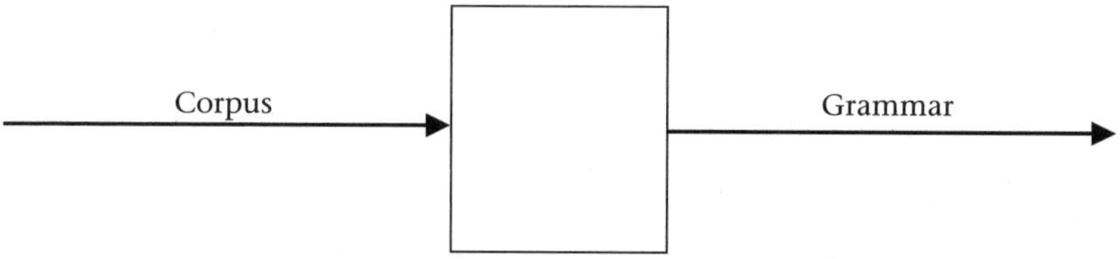

Chomsky rejected the discovery procedure, as it was deemed "unreasonable" (p. 52). Perhaps Chomsky's view is understandable given the circumstances in the 1950s with far fewer resources and technologies for data-intensive and computational research in linguistics. But from today's point of view, the research program envisioned by the discovery procedure is entirely feasible and reasonable. If we are able to even get close to what was once deemed unreasonable, there are no reasons why we should not devote research efforts to the deeper, more challenging aspects of linguistics.

If we take the discovery procedure to mean a procedure for finding the *best* grammar for some given data, then the discovery procedure, in this sense, encompasses the other procedures that Chomsky discussed: the decision procedure (one that decides whether a grammar accounts for some given data) and the evaluation procedure (one that decides which of the two given grammars is better for some given data, as discussed in section 10.2.3). More concretely, the procedure must be able to generate multiple grammars, decide which of them are compatible with the data, and evaluate the compatible ones for a winning grammar.

To illustrate doing linguistics in the style of discovery procedure, we briefly consider John Goldsmith's work on computational morphology (Goldsmith 2001, 2006) next.

10.3.1. An Example

For about two decades, John Goldsmith has been working on a project called Linguistica (Goldsmith 2001, 2006). On the surface, it is about unsupervised learning of natural language morphology. Underlyingly—and more importantly, especially in relation to this chapter—it is the platform where Goldsmith develops his empiricist approach to linguistic analysis, bridging generative grammar and machine learning. Goldsmith himself made it explicit that his work is closely connected to Chomsky's evaluation metric: "his [Chomsky's] notion of an evaluation metric for grammars was equivalent in its essential purpose to the description length of the morphology utilized in the present paper" (Goldsmith 2001: 190). In other words, Goldsmith's (2001) is an example of treating a linguistic problem (morphological learning in this case) with the evaluation procedure.

However, if one steps back and thinks about what Linguistica actually does, what it demonstrates is far beyond the evaluation procedure. In Chomsky's (1957) formulation of the evaluation procedure, it is agnostic about how the grammars in question come into being. In Goldsmith's (2001, 2006) Linguistica morphological analyzer, the input data is a raw text corpus. Linguistica generates morphological grammars for comparison and displays the results in its graphical user interface; among the results is the best grammar by the metric of description length. From the perspective of Chomky's (1957) discussion of what the goal of linguistic theory is, Goldsmith's (2001, 2006) Linguistica is an instantiation of the discovery procedure: Linguistica takes a raw corpus as input data and outputs the best grammar.

If we see John Goldsmith's work on unsupervised learning of morphology (Goldsmith 2001, 2006) as evidence that doing linguistics in the style of the discovery procedure is entirely feasible, then there is no reason why linguists should avoid engaging in this higher-order goal of linguistics, one that was once judged "unreasonable" by Chomsky (1957). Furthermore, there are important methodological benefits of setting the goal of linguistics as coming up with the discovery procedure. This chapter concludes with a few remarks in this regard.

10.4. Axioms

This chapter ends with a few remarks on the importance of doing linguistics as coming up with a discovery procedure in methodological terms.

10.4.1. Reproducible Research

Reproducible research, first articulated by Claerbout and Karrenbach (1992), refers to the idea that the publication of academic research is the ensemble of published papers together with all data sets and tools (experimental stimuli, computer code, etc.) that produce the reported results. Naturally, the notion of reproducible research is especially relevant for computationally oriented research, including the kind of linguistic research discussed in this chapter. From this perspective, the least that researchers should do is to properly maintain their computer code and data sets and make them available upon request.

Doing linguistics in pursuit of the discovery procedure naturally lends itself to reproducible research. The black box in theoretical linguistics (section 10.2.1) cannot be reproduced, as we do not (and probably should not be able to) possess the ability to examine one's brain for how thoughts evolve, whereas the algorithmic approach to linguistics is necessarily part of the discovery procedure and is amenable to the creation of computer code subject to external examination and free from human biases.

10.4.2. Accessible Research

Research should be accessible in multiple senses. This is significant for linguistics. For historical and institutional reasons, linguistics is usually housed in humanities and social sciences. Doing the particular kind of linguistics described in this chapter requires technical skills and background. Understanding linguistics in terms of the discovery procedure presents language, as linguists see it, as a machine learning problem to colleagues in such other fields as computer science and statistics, thereby facilitating scholarly pursuits.

Another component of accessible research for linguistics is data visualization. On the one hand, the focus of linguistic research in general has shifted from categoricity to gradience, thereby employing a wide range of experimental, quantitative, and computational methodologies. On the other, parallel with the current era of "big data," linguists are increasingly dealing with data sets whose sizes are ever-growing. This trend requires tools to explore patterns in large and complex data sets in a visually informative way. A recent and Linguistica-related example is the use of network visualization techniques on the clustering patterns of word distribution with only a raw corpus text as the input (Goldsmith 2014). The goal toward the discovery procedure encourages the use of large data sets and, in turn, innovation for how we understand linguistic data.

10.4.3. Extensible Research

Extensible research in linguistics refers to the idea that analyses should be amenable to extensions for both modularity and cross-linguistic coverage. If we study language in terms of various subfields, then our knowledge about language from all the fields has to all come together in some integrated way as a general model of language. If the goal of linguistics is to search for a general understanding of how language works, then research from any linguistic subfields must have ramifications for and contributions to other subfields. To make it possible for research to cross subfields given their compartmentalization, it is important for linguistic research to be modular with well-defined input and output points—explicitly linked by algorithms—so that different research can be connected.

The second aspect of extensible research is the familiar goal that general linguistic research be cross-linguistically relevant. Although many technical papers in linguistics are in-depth case studies of a very small number of languages, most of them attempt to convey the message that they have something to say about language in general according to the insights learned from their case studies. For noncomputational research, to see how claims based on a few languages bear on other languages usually requires the same huge amount of work in terms of time, labor, and mental energy as the original paper where the claims come from. To the extent that this is a form of extensible research, the search for the discovery procedure with computationally intensive work has the added advantage of being much more efficient to produce results—and reproduce—given suitably prepared data sets from other languages. As an example, Goldsmith (2001) showed how the Linguistica morphological analyzer uses the same algorithm and straightforwardly produces results for large data sets for languages ranging across English, French, Spanish, and Latin.

10.5. Conclusion

The discovery procedure as the goal of linguistic research is far from being untenable. As John Goldsmith's work on unsupervised learning of linguistic structure has demonstrated, the discovery procedure is the unavoidable—and much welcomed—result if one devises an evaluation metric couched within an algorithmic approach to linguistic analysis. We are now equipped with the prerequisites, both intellectual and technical, to put forward a research program for reproducible, accessible, and extensible work in linguistics.

References

Chomsky, Noam. 1957. *Syntactic Structures*. Berlin: Mouton.

Claerbout, Jon, and Martin Karrenbach. 1992. Electronic documents give reproducible research a new meaning. *SEG Technical Program Expanded Abstracts* 1992:601–604.

Clark, Alexander. 2015. Distributional learning of syntax. In *Empiricism and Language Learnability*, ed. Nick Chater, Alexander Clark, John A. Goldsmith, and Amy Perfors, 106–145. Oxford: Oxford University Press.

Clark, Alexander, and Shalom Lappin. 2010. Unsupervised learning and grammar induction. In *Handbook of Computational Linguistics and Natural Language Processing*, ed. Alexander Clark, Chris Fox, and Shalom Lappin, 197–220. Oxford: Wiley-Blackwell.

Goldsmith, John A. 2001. Unsupervised learning of the morphology of a natural language. *Computational Linguistics* 27:153–198.

———. 2004. From algorithms to generative grammar and back again. *Proceedings from the Annual Meeting of the Chicago Linguistic Society* 40, no. 2: 243–259.

———. 2006. An algorithm for the unsupervised learning of morphology. *Natural Language Engineering* 12:353–371.

———. 2011. The evaluation metric in generative grammar. Paper presented at the 50th anniversary celebration for the MIT Department of Linguistics, Cambridge, MA, December 9–11.

———. 2014. Language and the mind: Encounters in the mind fields. Nora and Edward Ryerson Lecture. Filmed April 23, 2014. University of Chicago video, 1:06:50. Posted June 17, 2014. https://www.youtube.com/watch?v=CdgPpM9aC9k.

———. 2015. Towards a new empiricism for linguistics. In *Empiricism and Language Learnability*, ed. Nick Chater, Alexander Clark, John Goldsmith, and Amy Perfors, 58–105. Oxford: Oxford University Press.

Halle, Morris. 1962. Phonology in generative grammar. *Word* 18:54–72.

Rissanen, Jorma. 1989. *Stochastic Complexity in Statistical Inquiry*. World Scientific Series in Computer Science 15. Singapore: World Scientific.

ELEVEN

Model Selection and Phonological Argumentation

JAMES KIRBY AND MORGAN SONDEREGGER

11.1. Introduction

A key theme that has run through much of John Goldsmith's work over the past twenty years is that of *model selection* as a guiding principle for linguistic analysis. Goldsmith's perspective on the issue of model selection is essentially information theoretic, suggesting that linguistic analysis is, at its core, a procedure in which the linguist chooses a model that maximizes the probability of the observed data while at the same time minimizing the overall description length of the grammar (Goldsmith 2001a, 2001b, 2011, 2015; Goldsmith and Riggle 2012). The objective function one might seek to optimize can vary, but the fundamental goal remains the same: for some set of data, we should seek to assess the goodness of fit between our model and the data, and select a model that minimizes our objective function.

As quantitative methods have become ever more prominent elements of the modern phonologist's toolbox, the theory and practice of model selection have become increasingly important—both in experimental work, where statistical methods have always been essential, as well as in theoretical work, where experimental results are more and more frequently being used as evidence for supporting or advancing a particular theoretical position. In daily practice, phonologists are frequently interested in assessing the importance (either in a technical or nontechnical sense) of a model parameter—does the underlying [voice] status of a German coda obstruent affect its surface realization, say, or does word frequency play a role in how likely trisyllabic shortening is to occur in English? Statistical results are then used to decide between different theories of the phenomenon: for example, is it necessary for phonological representations of English words to include information about word frequency, or can the effects of frequency be accounted for in other ways? In practice, this often ends up meaning: are there some factors that are found to be *significant* in a statistical model? As such, the issues of choosing between alternative statistical models and interpreting model parameters are becoming increasingly important for research on sound structure, and for linguistics as a whole.

Any model selection problem has two important aspects.[1] Given any pair of (nested) models in a set of candidate models, we want to assess (i) whether a particular term is justified ("is there an effect?"); and (ii) the value of the term (its *effect size*: "how big is the effect?")? Both issues play into linguistic argumentation; here we focus on the first of them, which currently plays a larger role in the practical application of statistical methods in linguistics. (We return briefly to the second in the conclusion.) We also focus on the case of a single term, in a model that may contain many terms. The issue is then: given the results of an experimental study, do we conclude based on a statistical model that there is an effect of X (which would support theory A) or not (which would support theory B)?

This choice is independent of whether there is, in reality, an effect of X or not. This means that there are two types of errors the researcher can make: falsely concluding there is an effect when none exists (*type I error*), or falsely concluding there is no effect when one in fact exists (*type II error*). The first is arguably more familiar and much more common in everyday statistical practice. If a term is found to be important (e.g., assessed via a p-value being below some cutoff, such as 0.05), in the sense of a type I error being unlikely, then we conclude there is a *significant* effect, which supports theory A. Although it is well known that a nonsignificant p-value does not support theory B, in many contexts researchers are understandably tempted to interpret the finding that a coefficient is not significantly different from 0, because ultimately the goal is to make a choice between two theories, with potentially important linguistic ramifications.[2] Null results *can* in fact be interpreted, but only by taking *power* (type II error) into account, in addition to significance. Power is less commonly covered than significance in introductory courses, and is trickier to think about, because it depends on considerations of sample size, effect size, and noise. Intuitively, a significant result is less likely to be found for an experiment with a smaller sample, where the effect is small, and/or where the variance is high, even where a true effect exists.

The purpose of this chapter is to provide a brief and accessible illustration of power analysis for a case study of phonological interest, motivated by two questions:

(Q1) What are we licensed to conclude on the basis of an individual study?
(Q2) What are we licensed to conclude from a body of studies?

11.2. Background

11.2.1. Incomplete Neutralization

As a case study, we consider the issue of so-called incomplete neutralization (IN) of word-final voicing in languages such as German, Catalan, or Dutch. An example from German is given in (1): in final position, the voicing contrast in stops is neutralized, leading to apparent homophony between *Rat* 'council' and *Rad* 'wheel'.

(1) a. *Rat* /ʁa:t/ > [ʁa:t] 'council', *Räte* [ʁɛ:tɐ] 'councils'
b. *Rad* /ʁa:d/ > [ʁa:t] 'wheel', *Räder* [ʁɛ:dɐ] 'wheels'

Word-final neutralization of this type has often been used as a textbook example of an exceptionless phonological rule. Beginning in the early 1980s, however, this picture was blurred by phonetic studies claiming to show a small but significant difference in the phonetic realizations of underlyingly voiced and voiceless obstruents, usually in terms of their effect on the durations of the burst, closure, and/or preceding vowel (e.g., Mitleb 1981; Fourakis and Iverson 1984; Port and O'Dell 1985; Jassem and Richter 1989; Port and Crawford 1989; Piroth and Janker 2004; Warner et al. 2004, 2006; Roettger et al. 2014). Much of the subsequent debate has been about methodological issues (see especially Winter and Roettger 2011; Kohler 2012), but what has primarily captured the interest of phonologists are the implications for phonological theory. For some, the existence of IN effects would have important theoretical ramifications, entailing either a major modification to the notion of contrast in order to accommodate these small but consistent differences (van Oostendorp 2008; Yu 2011; Braver 2013), or the incorporation of a large set of (possibly speaker-dependent) articulatory features into phonology (Port and Crawford 1989). This stands in opposition to the traditional position that phonological contrasts are amenable to discovery on the basis of native speaker and/or analyst intuitions (Manaster-Ramer 1996), and that the phonetic differences attributed to IN are the result of orthographic confounds, task effects, hyperarticulation, or other factors outside the purview of the phonology. Some have gone so far as to claim that the existence of IN would pose "a threat to phonological theory" (Port and Crawford 1989: 257) requiring that the field "rethink the whole process of collecting and evaluating claims of fact about the phonetics and phonology of the world's languages and dialects" (Manaster-Ramer 1996: 480), suggesting that the stakes for getting the model selection right are quite high.

Here, our focus is not on whether or not incomplete neutralization is real, or the theoretical implications in either case. Rather, we are interested in IN as a good example of an instance where the *absence of evidence* has been repeatedly interpreted by researchers as relevant for phonological argumentation. In the IN literature, we find studies that find statistically significant evidence for acoustically incomplete neutralization (Port and O'Dell 1985; Port and Crawford 1989; Roettger et al. 2014) alongside those that do not (Fourakis and Iverson 1984; Jassem and Richter 1989). What may we conclude from a single study that fails to find an effect? And, how should we interpret a body of results, some of which find an effect, and some of which do not?

11.2.2. Power

Interpreting a significant result requires consideration of one hypothetical scenario: if there were in reality no effect (the "true effect size" is 0), how likely would the result be? Interpreting the *lack* of a significant effect requires the researcher to consider a different hypothetical scenario: if there were a real effect of a given size, for a data set like this one, how likely would we be to detect it? This is statistical power, which is conceptually independent from significance. Power is the probability of committing a type II error (falsely concluding that there is no effect when in fact one exists); thus, we can describe an experimental design where there is a low probability of committing a type II error as having high power, and one with a high probability of committing a type II error as having low power. Although the concept of power is amply covered elsewhere (for a recent overview from a psycholinguistic standpoint, see Vasishth and Nicenboim 2016a), we give a motivating example here in the context of IN to provide some intuition.

Fourakis and Iverson (1984) examined production of German word-final stops for six repetitions of five voiced-voiceless pairs by four speakers and found that while the mean value of acoustic parameters for voiced and voiceless stops were in the expected direction (e.g., vowel duration preceding voiced stops was 3.8 milliseconds longer on average), this difference was not significant (assessed via *t*-tests). They concluded that "the traditional position that German devoicing constitutes phonologically irrecoverable merger is supported" (Fourakis and Iverson 1984: 149).[3] This conclusion, however, depends on how surprising it is to have *not* found a real effect if it exists—the power—which is quite low in this case (see section 11.4.1). Why is the conclusion not surprising, and what would change this? Intuitively, not detecting a 3.8 millisecond difference is less surprising than not detecting a 30 millisecond difference (as found in, e.g., English); not finding a significant result would be more surprising with twenty subjects instead of four; and finding the effect would be less surprising in natural versus in read speech. These three factors—the true effect size, sample size, and the amount of noise—all affect an experiment's power. (An additional factor, the data analysis method used, is discussed further in section 11.3.2.1.)

The dependence of power on these factors is often illustrated in the context of relatively simple examples, such as *t*-tests, and it is not necessarily obvious how power analysis should proceed in the more complex scenarios in which researchers now typically find themselves, such as nested model comparison between generalized linear mixed models with large numbers of interactions (but see Matuschek et al. 2015; Vasishth and Nicenboim 2016a, for related illustrations in the context of psycholinguistic studies). Our aim here is to provide an illustration of power analysis in a mixed-model setting, for a relatively simple case (one term of interest). In doing so, we illustrate how considerations of power interact with model selection strategies, and the impact this has on the interpretation of both single studies and bodies of studies.

11.3. Methods

We proceed via a simulation study, using a data set from a moderately powered study of IN in German where a significant effect was found. We use the results of this study to simulate data sets where two factors are varied—the sample size, and the true effect size—while holding all others constant; we also vary the criterion used to decide whether there *is* IN. This allows us to explore how power would be affected if the same experiment had been run, but with less data; if the true effect size were different; or if the data were analyzed differently.

11.3.1. Data Set

The case we consider is experiment 1 of Roettger et al. (2014), using the data set from this study.[4] Roettger et al. (2014) recorded sixteen native speakers of German producing singular forms of nonwords (e.g., [go:p]) in which the target consonant was in final position in response to auditory primes containing a voiced variant (e.g., [go:bə]). Each speaker produced one repetition of twenty-four critical items (a pair such as [go:bə]/[go:pə]). The statistical analysis, using a linear mixed-effects model, modeled duration of the vowel preceding the stop as a function of the stop's underlying voicing, as well as a number of control predictors. By-subject and by-item random intercepts and random slopes for voicing were included. The key result for our purposes is that speakers produced longer vowels before underlyingly voiced stops: the difference (corresponding to the voicing fixed-effect coefficient) was statistically significant in a likelihood-ratio test ($\chi^2(1)=13.76$, $p<0.0002$), and estimated to be 8.6 milliseconds (SE=2.03 milliseconds).

Since we do not know whether the incomplete neutralization effect is "real," by definition we also do not know its true size. However, since a number of studies of this effect have now been conducted, we have some basis for guessing what the true size of the effect might be. For German, published estimates have ranged from around 4 milliseconds (Port and Crawford 1989) to over 20 milliseconds (Mitleb 1981). For present purposes, these estimates will suffice to give us a range in which to explore the ramifications of effect size on power in a mixed-model setting.

11.3.2. Simulations

In our simulations, we varied three factors[5] to understand their effect on power: the sample size, the effect size, and the model selection criterion (table 11.1).[6] In terms of sample size, we altered the number of subjects, items, and repetitions, as these are the primary differences between studies of nominally the same phenomenon, both in the IN literature and in experimental work more generally. These parameters were varied in a range of values corresponding to previous work. Sweeping the effect size is important as well, because in a real-world study, we never know a priori the size of the effect we are looking for; we can only make an inference about likely effect size based on related work (see discussion in Vasishth

Table 11.1 Parameters swept in simulation study

Parameter	Range	Step
Number of subjects (n_s)	6–16	2
Number of items (n_i)	8–24	4
Number of repetition (n_r)	1–6	1
True effect size (β)	0–10	0.5
Model selection criterion	Likelihood ratio, AIC, BIC	

and Nicenboim 2016a). The effect size was swept from values corresponding to no effect (β=0) to a moderate IN effect (10 milliseconds). Finally, we considered power under three different model selection criteria (discussed in the next section) to show how different choices about data analysis might also affect a researcher's ability to detect an effect.

11.3.2.1. Simulation Procedure

For a given set of parameter values, a single simulation run was performed as follows.[7] A random subset of the original data set was taken corresponding to n_s subjects and n_i items; this data was concatenated n_r times, making a "resampled" data set. The fixed-effect coefficients of the original model were used to predict a vowel duration for each data point, excluding the effect of voicing. The random-effect parameters (variance components) of the original model were used to sample new intercept and slope offsets for each subset and item in the resampled data set. These, together with the desired true effect size (β), were used to adjust predicted vowel durations for each subject and item—including the effect of voicing. Finally, the estimated residual error was used to add observation-level noise to each prediction. The resulting data set can be thought of as one possible "smaller" version of the original data set, accounting for by-speaker and by-item variability, and with an adjusted effect size for voicing. Two statistical models were fitted to this new data set: the original statistical model (the *superset model*), and this model with the fixed effect of voicing removed (the *subset model*).

Given these two models, three model selection criteria were applied to decide whether the model with the voicing term was justified by the data:

1. *Likelihood-ratio test* (LR): Assess the significance (p) of the difference in log-likelihood between the two models, using a χ^2-test. Choose the superset model if $p < 0.05$, and the subset model otherwise.

2. *Akaike information criterion* (AIC): Assess the trade-off between the log-likelihood of the observed data under a proposed model (L), and the number of parameters in the model (Q), as $-2L+2Q$. Choose the model with the lower AIC.
3. *Bayesian information criterion* (BIC): Assess a similar trade-off, taking into account as well the number of observations in the data set N, as $-2L+\ln(N)Q$. Choose the model with the lower BIC.[8]

All three methods measure the trade-off between model complexity and fit to the data in some way. As N increases, BIC tends to favor simpler models than AIC, due to the $\ln(N)$ term imposing a higher penalty for each additional model parameter. In practice, BIC is expected to often be more conservative than AIC or LR: it will have lower type I error, but also lower power (higher type II error). Both LR and AIC are widely used in practice (in linguistic research in particular) as model selection criteria (AIC, for example, is often used in "stepwise" methods); we include BIC as well to help illustrate the effect of model selection criterion on power.

Thus, for each simulation run, we have three decisions on whether the voicing term is justified or not; concluding it is not would be a type II error (unless $\beta=0$). By performing n_{sim} runs and computing the fraction in which the subset model is chosen, we obtain an estimate of the power under each model selection strategy, for a given set of parameter settings. We performed simulations with $n_{sim}=500$. Although our results show the curves resulting from sweeping several parameters, note that a common cutoff for a "high power result," corresponding to the common 0.05 cutoff for a "significant" result, is 0.8 (i.e., at least an 80 percent chance of detecting the effect).

11.4. Results

Figure 11.1 shows the results of these simulations: how power (on the y-axis) varies as a function of the true effect size β (on the x-axis) for several different sample sizes and model selection criteria. Each curve in the figure thus represents a different study design—with different choices for the number of subjects, items, and repetitions—as well as a choice of model selection criterion and can be used to determine the power of the experiment as a function of the true effect size (which, in general, is not known to the analyst). The general pattern is quite clear: as the sample size and the true size of the effect increase, so too does power. The model selection criterion used also makes a difference; in general,

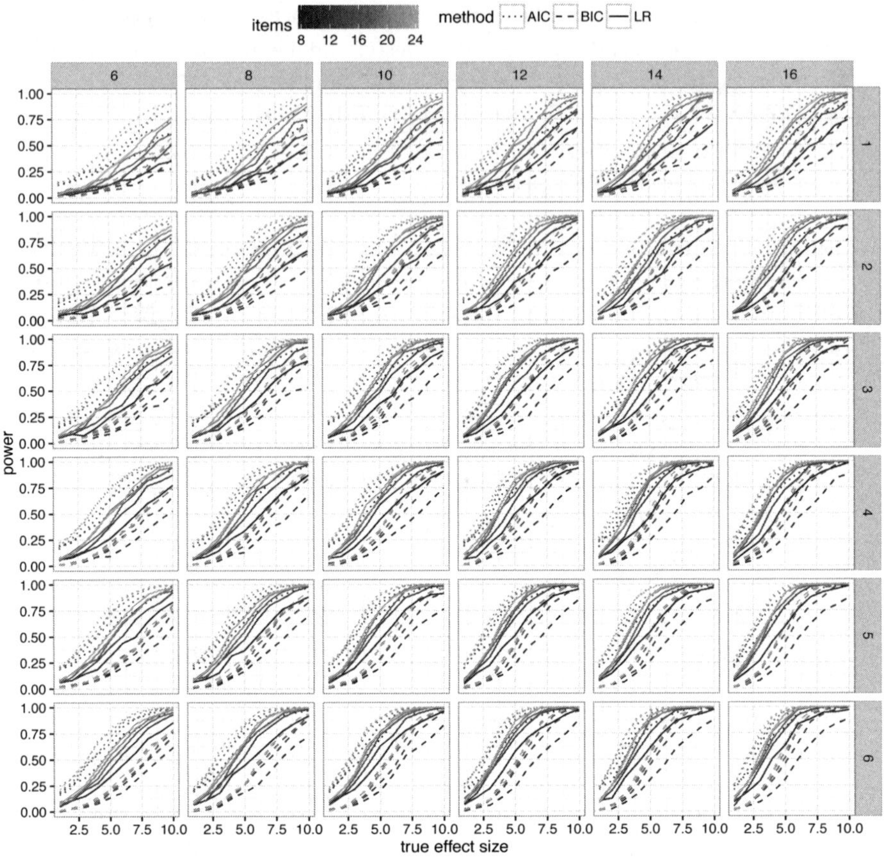

11.1 Power curves resulting from different sweeps simulated from the Roettger et al. (2014) data for three different model selection criteria. Columns show simulated number of subjects; rows show number of repetitions of each item per subject. *Darker-colored lines* are for runs with fewer items, *lighter-colored lines* for runs with more items.

using AIC will lead to greater power, followed by LR, and finally BIC. As discussed in section 11.3.2.1, this is expected based on the properties of these criteria: the AIC tends to favor predictive accuracy over model complexity, while the BIC more heavily penalizes model parameters, particularly as the number of observations increases. The greater power of AIC leads it to have the highest type I error (i.e., to wrongly conclude there is an effect when there is not), as can be seen by examining the power curves as the true effect size approaches 0.

Recall that we are interested in two main questions: (Q1) What are we licensed to conclude on the basis of an individual study? (Q2) What are we licensed to conclude from a body of studies? To gain some intuition for the patterns in this figure with respect to these two questions, we will consider three regimes (low-, medium-, and high-power) in detail, roughly corresponding to three studies from the existing IN literature. In each case, we pose the following question: suppose we reran the Roettger et al. (2014) study with a different sample size; what should we conclude in case of different outcomes (Q1)? We then consider some examples of how to interpret results from several studies together (Q2), assuming they are from different regimes. We then offer one possible interpretation of the German incomplete neutralization literature.

11.4.1. Low-Power Regime

To illustrate a low-power regime, we select the power curves from simulations with six subjects, eight items, and two repetitions per item (figure 11.2a). In this regime, power is always below 80 percent, regardless of model selection criteria or effect size (assuming that the effect is ≤ 10 milliseconds), and is below 50 percent for most values of β. The logic of interpretation is different in different cases (keeping in mind that, in an experimental setting, we do not know what the true size of the effect is; it could be 0). If we find a significant result (e.g., $p < 0.05$), we may conclude that observing an effect of this magnitude, or larger, is unlikely to have occurred if the true contribution of β is in fact 0. If we do not find a significant result, on the other hand, we should not be surprised, but we cannot interpret this lack of effect as evidence in favor of anything: a nonsignificant result would have been likely to occur whether there is in reality a true effect of ≤ 10 milliseconds (low power) or not (high *p*-value). In a low-powered study, then, a null result is not informative.

In terms of the IN literature, a possible analog is the "elicitation condition" study of Fourakis and Iverson (1984), with four subjects and six repetitions; *t*-tests are reported for subsets corresponding in our terms to one to two items, and none of these tests are significant.[9] Approximate power calculations for these *t*-tests can be carried out using the information in Fourakis and Iverson's table 2; even assuming a 10 millisecond true effect size (much larger than that reported), power is below 0.35 for all tests. Given what we might reasonably assume about the true size of the effect, the null result does not provide evidence to "falsify the claim

(a)

(b)

(c)

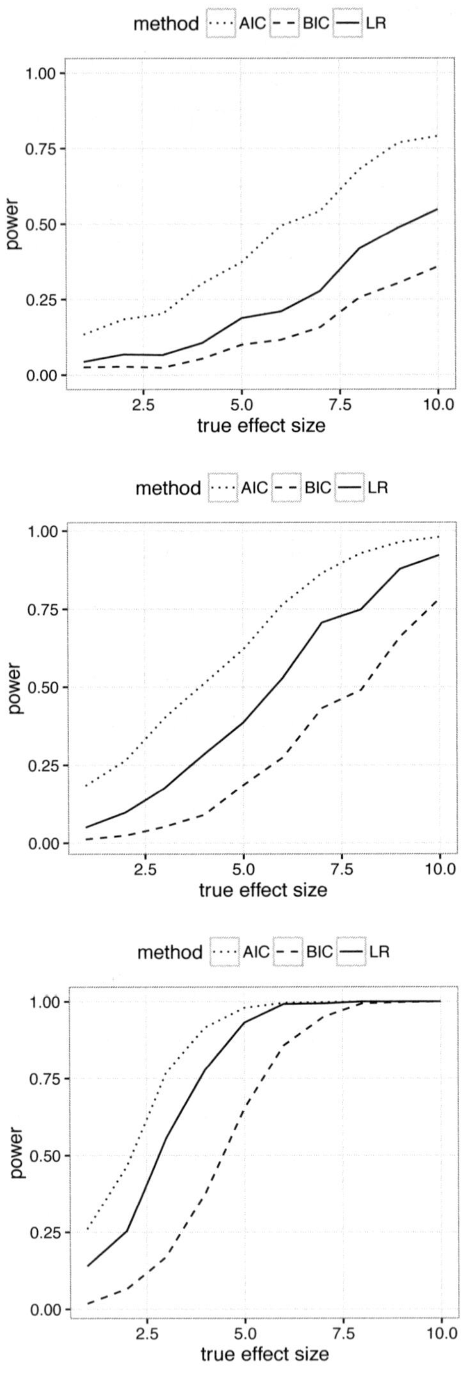

11.2 (*a*) Low-power regime (six subjects, eight items, two repetitions).
(*b*) Medium-power regime (eight subjects, twelve items, three repetitions).
(*c*) High-power regime (sixteen subjects, twenty-four items, six repetitions).

that final obstruent devoicing is not neutralizing in German," neither can it be claimed that "the traditional position that German devoicing constitutes phonologically irrecoverable merger is fully supported" (Fourakis and Iverson 1984: 149). When power is this low, a null result does not by itself contribute one way or the other to our understanding of the phenomenon under study.

11.4.2. Medium-Power Regime

The medium-power regime is illustrated by power curves for simulations with eight subjects and three repetitions each of twelve items (figure 11.2b). In this regime, power is above the 80 percent mark for a sufficiently large effect size using the less conservative model selection criteria (LR or AIC), but only for the upper range of effect size. Again, a significant result can be interpreted as meaningful (i.e., unlikely to happen by chance); but the interpretation of a null result is less straightforward. If we have reason to believe the true β is, say, 10 milliseconds or higher, we may reasonably expect to have detected it. Therefore, *not* finding a significant effect can be interpreted as evidence that *if* an incomplete neutralization effect exists, it is going to be smaller than 10 milliseconds. Note that this is *not* the same as saying we have evidence that there is no effect; rather, this is a statement about our ability to detect an effect *of a given size*.

In this regime, power is particularly sensitive to both the true effect size as well as the data analysis method. One practical consequence of this is that replications of the same experiment (or subsets of data from the same experiment) could well return a mix of significant and non-significant effects *even if there is a true effect*. Similarly, different results may obtain depending on the particulars of the data analysis method. A possible example from the literature is the study of Piroth and Janker (2004), who analyzed data from three repetitions of nine pairs uttered by six German speakers from different dialect areas. They found that the two Southern German speakers in their sample preserved acoustic differences in coda duration between underlyingly voiced-voiceless pairs, but that speakers from the other dialect regions did not. Given the power of the study, however, we should not necessarily be surprised that they failed to detect a (small) effect that may in fact be present. If the IN effect for the Southern German speakers is in reality larger than for speakers from other dialect areas, it will be easier to detect, all else being equal. So while we are licensed to conclude something about the Southern German speakers in this study, we have not really learned anything about other speakers, or about the ensemble of speakers as a whole.

11.4.3. High-Power Regime

Finally, we consider a design with sixteen speakers, twenty-four items, and six repetitions (i.e., the design of Roettger et al. 2014, but with six repetitions instead of just one). As seen in figure 11.2c, power is above the 80 percent mark for the majority of the range of possible effect sizes, at least for the AIC and LR model selection criteria. Once again, a significant result can be interpreted as evidence of an incomplete neutralization effect—if the true effect size were 0, such a result would be unlikely to occur (modulo of course the possibility of type I error). Unlike the low- and medium-power regimes, however, here a null result is also meaningful: if there *were* a true effect in this range of effect sizes, we would be surprised to not detect it, while if the true effect size were 0, we would not be surprised if we failed to find it. Therefore, in a high-powered design, we *are* licensed to interpret a null result as evidence for complete neutralization—at least in the sense of, if there is an effect, it has to be quite small.

In the IN literature, the studies of Warner et al. (2004, 2006) are illustrative in this regard. Warner et al. (2004) found that the Dutch word-final voicing contrast was incompletely neutralized, with vowels preceding voiced stops 3.5 milliseconds longer than those preceding voiceless stops. However, in their follow-on study (Warner et al. 2006), in which they carefully controlled for possible orthographic effects, they failed to find a significant effect. Because the 2006 study was sufficiently high-powered (as calculated by the authors, using the effect size from the 2004 study), Warner et al. are licensed to interpret their findings as indicating that "the current manipulation does not produce an incomplete neutralization effect, *at least not one comparable in size to the 3.5 msec differences found in the previous work*" (2006: 290; emphasis added). Because of the high power of the design, they are able to interpret the null result in a theoretically meaningful way.

11.5. Discussion

As the preceding examples illustrate, the conclusions that can be drawn on the basis of a null result, with respect to deciding between different theoretical stances, are heavily dependent on the power regime. This, in turn, is dependent on factors including the true effect size, the sample size, and the particulars of the data analysis method. This contrasts sharply with what may be inferred from a significant result, which (at least to a reasonably good first approximation) does not depend on sample size or model selection criteria.[10] This does not mean that only significant results are meaningful: if a high-powered study returns a null result, as in the case of Warner et al. (2006) (see section 11.4.3), it can be interpreted as evidence consistent with the null hypothesis, in the sense that it supports the selection of a simpler (less parameterized) statistical model.

Given what we have reviewed, what can we conclude from a collection of studies of (more or less) the same phenomenon, in which some studies find significant effects and others do not (or equivalently, select a model containing a term *T* versus reject a model containing *T* on the basis of some model selection criterion)? In such a scenario, do we have evidence for theory A, theory B, or truly conflicting evidence?

As the preceding discussion suggests, the answer depends on the power of the studies involved. If all of the studies concerned have high power, then those that find significant results provide us with evidence favoring/consistent with theory A, while those that find null results can be interpreted as favoring/consistent with theory B. In this scenario, the results are truly conflicting, because we have evidence that supports different, presumably incompatible theoretical positions. If, on the other hand, the high-powered studies find significant results, but the low-powered studies find null results, we only have evidence that supports theory A; the null results are not evidence for or against anything.

What consequences does this have for our interpretation of the German IN literature? The existence of a high-powered study on German IN similar to Warner et al. (2006)—which found a null effect, or a significant effect in the wrong direction—would indeed conflict with earlier findings. At least in the German case, however, the most highly powered study of which we are aware (Roettger et al. 2014) found a small but significant IN effect in the expected direction, in spite of numerous experimental controls. Previous low- to medium-powered studies have either similarly found small but significant effects in this direction or have returned null results. Thus, because null results are only informative in a high-power regime, it is not the case that there is conflicting evidence; rather, a reasonable interpretation of the existing literature is that there is, in fact, a small but real effect of IN in German, and the inconsistency between studies is due to lack of statistical power.

11.5.1. Further Issues

Our discussion has focused on interpreting the results of an experiment (or a set of experiments) with respect to whether or not an effect is 0, corresponding to a choice between two linguistic theories. There are of course further considerations that enter into the interpretation of experimental results, some of which might suggest that our concerns are unwarranted (at least for the IN case). Here, we discuss two of these: *prior belief* in one linguistic theory versus another, and (estimated) *effect size*.

First, is a null result informative if it agrees with (or fails to contradict) a more plausible theory? A researcher may have significant evidence (e.g., decades of agreement among experimentalists, or an assumption about phonological representation working well in daily practice) that leads them to think theory A (e.g., complete neutralization) is more plausible than theory B (e.g., IN). When an experiment then searches for evidence in favor of theory B, and finds a null result, it is tempting to conclude that this supports the researcher's strong prior belief in theory A. This is an implicitly Bayesian view of the scientific world: a researcher (or the field as a whole) has degrees of belief in different hypotheses, which are updated based on new information. This view makes intuitive sense, but is not consistent with the null hypothesis significance testing (NHST) statistical framework used almost exclusively in experimental studies in linguistics (including all studies of IN cited here). The NHST framework does not take prior beliefs into account, and a null result from an NHST statistical method cannot be interpreted as supporting the null, regardless of its plausibility. There are ways to explicitly combine prior beliefs with new evidence in performing statistical analysis, using Bayesian data analysis methods (e.g., Jaynes 2003; Gelman et al. 2014), the main alternative to NHST. Using these methods, a null result from a low-powered study tends to offer evidence both for and against a researcher's prior belief, since the observed outcome would be fairly likely under a number of different priors (Vasishth and Nicenboim 2016b). However, even within this framework, *a null result from a low-powered study is still uninformative*—as demonstrated in our simulation study.

Second, even if an effect can be demonstrated, it may not be of sufficient magnitude to warrant attention. For example, IN effects have often been suggested to arise from orthographic, hypercorrection, and/or task effects (e.g., Fourakis and Iverson 1984; Warner et al. 2006; Kharmalov 2014), and in any event to be too small to be of any communicative relevance (Kohler 2012). This gets at a broader issue in interpreting experimental results: the estimated *size* of an effect is just as important as whether it is significantly different from 0 or not, and these two things are independent. It is possible to have a tiny but significant effect (as in the Roettger et al. 2014 study) in a high-powered study, or a large but nonsignificant effect (in a low-powered study)—where "small" and "large" are always assessed relative to a particular domain (e.g., vowel duration differences between voiced and voiceless obstruents cross-linguistically). Thus, it is crucial to consider *both* the estimated size of effects and their significances when interpreting experimental data, as emphasized in modern approaches to data analysis across fields (e.g., Baayen 2008; Gelman and Hill 2007). An effect's estimated size (as for whether it is 0 or not) is subject to error, and it is important to take this into account in interpreting either a single experimental result or a body of studies. A thorough exposition is beyond the scope of this chapter (but see Vasishth and Nicenboim 2016a for a discussion in the context of linguistic data), but power turns out to again be crucial: for low-powered studies, estimated effect sizes are likely to have the wrong magnitude or sign, *even for a significant result*; for high-powered studies, estimated effect sizes are likely to be reliable, *even for null results*. Thus, effect sizes from a low-powered study should be trusted less than effect sizes from appropriately powered studies, which is important when interpreting experimental results in order to decide between competing theoretical models. In the IN literature, for example, a surprisingly large IN effect found in a low-powered study (such as the 20 milliseconds reported in Mitleb 1981) should be given little weight, while a near-0 (and not significant) effect found in a high-powered study (such as Warner et al. 2006, for Dutch) should be taken seriously.

11.6. Conclusion

Model selection is a powerful tool for linguistics and provides a rigorous basis for scientific understanding, but it must be approached with cautious respect. In this chapter, we have tried to demonstrate how a failure to take statistical power into account can potentially lead to unlicensed inference with respect to the theoretical issue(s) at stake. Similarly, we have tried to illustrate how choices about data analysis, such as model selection criteria, can impact statistical inference and subsequent reasoning based on it.

Notes

1. We set aside here the equally important aspect of deciding on an appropriate set of candidate models; for more on this issue, see Anderson (2008).
2. This issue is widespread both in linguistics and beyond; see, for example, Vasishth and Nicenboim (2016a) and Haller and Krauss (2002).
3. We are considering Fourakis and Iverson's "elicitation task." For a second experiment, they do find a significant IN effect, but they attribute it to the less communicatively natural setting and conclude that neutralization is complete in natural settings.
4. We thank Timo Roettger and Bodo Winter for sharing this data set with us.
5. We also explored varying the "noise"—the residual variance, and amount of variability among subjects and items—which also affects power, but we hold it constant in the simulations we report here in the interest of expositional clarity.
6. For discussion of how these factors effect type I error, see Barr et al. (2013), Matuschek et al. (2015), and Winter (2015).
7. Our methodology is a simplified version of the simulation-based power calculation method for mixed models described in chapter 20 of Gelman and Hill (2007). Our simulation script is available upon request.
8. Note that both the AIC and BIC are related to the notion of *minimum description length* (Rissanen 1978), a principle advocated by Goldsmith in much of his work (e.g., Goldsmith 2001b).
9. Although the words in this study were not organized into pairs, the corresponding power calculation is very similar. Note that we are considering only *t*-tests conducted across all speakers—which Fourakis and Iverson (1984) focused on—and not those conducted within individual speakers.
10. Note that this statement applies to the binary "is the effect 0?" question considered here, but not to the actual *estimate* of the effect size, which is affected by factors similar to those influencing power.

References

Anderson, David R. 2008. *Model Based Inference in the Life Sciences: A Primer on Evidence*. New York: Springer Verlag.

Baayen, R. H. 2008. *Analyzing Linguistic Data: A Practical Introduction to Statistics Using R*. Cambridge: Cambridge University Press.

Barr, Dale J., Roger Levy, Christoph Scheepers, and Harry J. Tily. 2013. Random effects structure for confirmatory hypothesis testing: Keep it maximal. *Journal of Memory and Language* 68:255–278.

Braver, Aaron, 2013. Degrees of incompleteness in neutralization: Paradigm uniformity in a phonetics with weighted constraints. PhD dissertation, Rutgers University School of Graduate Studies–New Brunswick.

Fourakis, Marios, and Gregory K. Iverson. 1984. On the "incomplete neutralization" of German final obstruents. *Phonetica* 41:128–143.

Gelman, Andrew, and Jennifer Hill. 2007. *Data Analysis Using Regression and Multi-Level/Hierarchical Models*. Cambridge: Cambridge University Press.

Gelman, Andrew, John B. Carlin, Hal S. Stern, and Donald B Rubin. 2014. *Bayesian Data Analysis*. 3rd ed. New York: Taylor and Francis.

Goldsmith, John. 2001a. Phonology as information minimization. *Phonological Studies* 5:21–46.

———. 2001b. Unsupervised learning of the morphology of a natural language. *Computational Linguistics* 27:153–198.

———. 2011. The evaluation metric in generative grammar. Paper presented at the 50th Anniversary Celebration for the MIT Department of Linguistics, Cambridge, MA, December 9, 2011.

———. 2015. Towards a new empiricism. In *Empiricism and Language Learnability*, ed. Nick Chater, Alexander Clark, John A. Goldsmith, and Amy Perfors, 58–105. Oxford: Oxford University Press.

Goldsmith, John A., and Jason Riggle. 2012. Information theoretic approaches to phonology: The case of Finnish vowel harmony. *Natural Language and Linguistic Theory* 30:859–896.

Haller, Heiko, and Stefan Krauss. 2002. Misinterpretations of significance: A problem students share with their teachers. *Methods of Psychological Research* 7:1–20.

Jassem, Wiktor, and Lutoslawa Richter. 1989. Neutralization of voicing in Polish obstruents. *Journal of Phonetics* 17:317–325.

Jaynes, Edwin T. 2003. *Probability Theory: The Logic of Science*. Cambridge: Cambridge University Press.

Kharmalov, Viktor. 2014. Incomplete neutralization of the voicing contrast in word-final obstruents in Russian: Phonological, lexical, and methodological influences. *Journal of Phonetics* 43:47–56.

Kohler, Klaus J. 2012. The phonetics-phonology issue in the analysis of word-final obstruent voicing. http://www.ipds.uni-kiel.de/kjk/pub_exx/kk2012_3/neutralization.pdf.

Manaster-Ramer, Alexis. 1996. A letter from an incompletely neutral phonologist. *Journal of Phonetics* 24:477–489.

Matuschek, Hannes, Reinhold Kliegl, Shravan Vasishth, Harald Baayen, and Douglas Bates. 2015. Balancing type I error and power in linear mixed models. *ArXiv e-prints*, arXiv:1511.01864. Submitted November 5, 2015. Last revision January 2, 2017. https://arxiv.org/abs/1511.01864. Published in *Journal of Memory and Language* 94:305–315 [2017].

Mitleb, Fares. 1981. Temporal correlates of "voicing" and its neutralization in German. *Research in Phonetics* 2:173–191.

Piroth, Hans Georg, and Peter M. Janker. 2004. Speaker-dependent differences in voicing and devoicing of German obstruents. *Journal of Phonetics* 32:81–109.

Port, Robert, and Penny Crawford. 1989. Pragmatic effects on neutralization rules. *Journal of Phonetics* 16:257–282.

Port, Robert F., and Michael O'Dell. 1985. Neutralization of syllable-final voicing in German. *Journal of Phonetics* 13:455–471.

Rissanen, Jorma. 1978. Modeling by shortest data description. *Automatica* 14:465–471.

Roettger, Timo B., Bodo Winter, Sven Grawunder, James Kirby, and Martine Grice. 2014. Assessing incomplete neutralization of final devoicing in German. *Journal of Phonetics* 43:11–25.

van Oostendorp, Marc. 2008. Incomplete devoicing in formal phonology. *Lingua* 118:1362–1374.

Vasishth, Shravan, and Bruno Nicenboim. 2016a. Statistical methods for linguistic research: Foundational ideas—part 1. *ArXiv e-prints*, arXiv:1601.01126. Submitted January 6, 2016. Last revised January 7, 2016. https://arxiv.org/abs/1601.01126?context=stat.AP. Published in *Language and Linguistics Compass* 10:349–369 [2016].

———. 2016b. Statistical methods for linguistic research: Foundational ideas—part 2. *ArXiv e-prints*, arXiv:1602.00245. Submitted January 31, 2016. https://arxiv.org/abs/1602.00245. Published in *Language and Linguistics Compass* 10:591–613 [2016].

Warner, Natasha, Erin Good, Allard Jongman, and Joan Sereno. 2006. Orthographic vs. morphological incomplete neutralization effects. *Journal of Phonetics* 34:285–293.

Warner, Natasha, Allard Jongman, Joan Sereno, and Rachèl Kemps. 2004. Incomplete neutralization and other sub-phonemic durational differences in production and perception: Evidence from Dutch. *Journal of Phonetics* 32:251–276.

Winter, Bodo. 2015. The other N: The role of repetitions and items in the design of phonetic experiments. In *Proceedings of the 18th International Congress of Phonetic Sciences*. Glasgow: University of Glasgow.

Winter, Bodo, and Timo Roettger. 2011. The nature of incomplete neutralization in German: Implications for laboratory phonology. *Grazer Linguistiche Studien* 76:55–74.

Yu, Alan C. L. 2011. Contrast reduction. In *The Handbook of Phonological Theory*, 2nd ed., ed. J. Goldsmith, J. Riggle, and A. C. L. Yu, 291–318. Oxford: Wiley-Blackwell.

TWELVE

The Dynamics of Prominence Profiles: From Local Computation to Global Patterns

KHALIL ISKAROUS AND LOUIS GOLDSTEIN

12.1. Introduction

All across language, from discourse and sentence structure to segment, syllable, and word structure, we see evidence of hierarchical computation. At each level, there are local computations affecting the combination of smaller units into larger units, resulting in some emergent global pattern. Syntacticians, have, for instance, been trying to identify universal local modes of combination that allow functional units to combine with lexical units to obtain sentences with emergent global patterns of displacement and dependency, due to the underlying local computations (Collins 1996; Borer 2013). At another end of language, phoneticians and phonologists have tried to understand local modes of combination of localized contrastive units into varied segmental types such as vowels and consonants, as well as asymmetrical syllables with their ends behaving differently from their beginnings, in other words, with a global pattern (Browman and Goldstein 1989; Saltzmann et al. 2006; Iskarous et al. 2013). Despite the enormous difference between the units involved, language seems to have a recurring motif:

local computation leading to global pattern—a type of computation that we usually call hierarchical computation.

A concrete example of a model for generating global structure out of local computational interaction was proposed by Goldsmith and Larson (1990) to account for syllabification of segments into syllables, through local interactions of segments, as opposed to structure-building rules that impose the global structure. Goldsmith (1994) extended this work to metrical phonology to show that this theory can allow global patterns of prominence profiles, such as rhythm, to emerge from local interactions between syllables, using dynamical systems theory. We believe that his dynamical model could serve as a prototype for more general theories of how local computation can lead to global patterns, a computational concept that seems to be needed across the various domains of language. The goal of this chapter is to deepen the analysis of the model, building on the work of Larson (1993), Prince (1993), and Goldsmith (1994, 2005/2016), with special emphasis on how local computation can actually generate global pattern for quantity-insensitive (QI) stress systems. We do so by introducing and using the powerful Green's function (GF) method, which derives from the fundamental theorem of calculus, and has been used for almost two centuries to analyze the working of many dynamical systems in physics, engineering, and computer science. One of the main questions we ask and attempt to answer is exactly what kind of dynamical system Goldsmith's model actually instantiates. There are two reasons we pursue this. First, we show that dynamical systems analysis is itself based on the idea of the generation of global patterns from local constraints/computations and argue that this is the reason it might be a useful tool of analysis in many linguistic domains. Second, by understanding the type of system involved, we can leverage established analytical tools to predict the typology of global patterns that the system will generate. Specifically, we will show, in tutorial style, how dynamical systems theory works and how the theory of GFs allows for the prediction of the global capability of a dynamical model. In section 12.2, we discuss the types of pattern found in stress systems, and then review how Goldsmith's dynamic computational network (DCN) generates the typology of observed patterns. In sections 12.3 and 12.4, we provide an introduction to dynamical systems of the boundary value type, then show how Goldsmith's model is of this type, and explain how tools of analysis can help us understand the linguistic properties that emerge from dynamical computation.

12.2. Dynamical Linear Model of Stress

Several generalizations have emerged within work on the prosody of stress languages regarding the prominence profiles of words (Trubetzkoy 1939; Hyman 1977; Hayes 1980; Halle and Vergnaud 1987; Kager 2007). The first, termed *culminativity*, is that content words in stress languages have at least one stress. That is, the prominence profile cannot be purely constant, but must be peaked, in other words, there must be a primary stress. There could be secondary or even tertiary weaker stresses, but there must be at least one primary stress. Another global feature of the prominence profile is that the primary peak is near the beginning or end of the word, a property termed *demarcativity*, because it could help segment the speech stream into words by marking edges. A third generalization is that languages are either rhythmic (*bounded*) allowing for more than one stress, on alternating syllables from the primary stress, or *unbounded* allowing for only a single stress in the word domain. A fourth property is *extrametricality*, where an initial or final syllable does not seem to count for the placement of stress. The last property is *quantity sensitivity*, where stress placement depends on properties such as the duration of vowels.

Typological work has shown how languages can be classified using these properties (Hayes 1980; Halle and Vergnaud 1982; Gordon 2002). The basic outline of such a classification system for QI languages, the focus of this chapter, provides eight basic categories, which can be seen in table 12.1. Some QI systems are more complex, but these will be seen as dynamical combinations of the basic ones. In each cell of table 12.1, we give an example of the prominence profile of an example word, with 0 meaning no stress, 1 primary stress, and 2 secondary stress. An example language is given for each system.[1]

The above-stated properties are global in that they involve the word as a whole and are not determinable by examining a single syllable. Globality is implicit in Liberman's (1975) original insight that became the basis of metrical theory: prominence is relative, not absolute, and is not a thing in itself, but an organizing structure (Beckman 1993). A very important question for any theory of stress systems is how these global properties arise. Several answers were given within early metrical phonology and later within optimality theory (Hayes 1980; Halle and Vergnaud 1987; Dresher and Kaye 1990; Prince and Smolensky 1993; Hayes 1995). In these frameworks, structure-building rules or constraints on metrical structure are proposed using a variety of theoretical devices. A

Table 12.1 Typology of QI stress systems

QI system basic types		Bounded		Unbounded	
		No extram.	Extram.	No extram.	Extram.
Demarc.	Word-initial	1 0 2 0 2 0 2 Maranungku	0 1 0 2 0 2 0 Paiute	1 0 0 0 0 0 0 Latvian	0 1 0 0 0 0 0 Lakota
	Word-final	2 0 2 0 2 0 1 Weri	0 2 0 2 0 1 0 Warao	0 0 0 0 0 1 French	0 0 0 0 0 1 0 Polish

Note: Demarc., demarcativity; Extram., extrametricality.

different type of theory was proposed by John Goldsmith (1994), who, showed that the global properties of prominence *emerge* from purely local interactive computations, rather than being imposed by rule or by constraints that favor or disfavor certain global profiles.

Goldsmith's (1994) dynamical model of metrical structure is based on iterative computation of prominence on each syllable based on the prominence of the syllables next to it. The model assumes a set of nodes, on each of which is defined a real numbered prominence. The basic equation of the model is the following (Goldsmith and Larson 1990):

$$a_i^{t+1} = P(i) + \alpha\, a_{i+1}^{t} + \beta\, a_{i-1}^{t} + N(i)$$

Here a is the prominence, α is a coefficient multiplying the prominence of the node/syllable to the right $(I+1)$, and β multiplies the node to the left $(i-1)$. $P(i)$ represents positional bias that is defined at the initial and final nodes, whereas $N(i)$ represents possible bias on the internal nodes, but is necessary only for quantity-sensitive systems, which we do not treat here. In this chapter, $P(i)$ will be specified by providing a bias for the initial syllable (I) and the final syllable (F). The computation is iterative, computing and recomputing each prominence. Goldsmith (1994) studied the convergence criteria of the model, that is for which α and β the model actually converges, that is, no longer varies. The basic criterion is that $|\alpha\,\beta| \leq \frac{1}{4}$. Figure 12.1 shows the well-known basic eight category typology of the QI systems. Each panel is labeled with one exemplar language, but Gordon (2002) provided many examples of each category. Larson (1993) provided arguments for alternative choices of each set of coefficients for each of the categories, and all of the systems discussed here were accounted for by Goldsmith (1994) and Larson (1993). The first two systems show initial and final primary stress, with secondary stress on alternating syllables. When the non-0 P coefficient

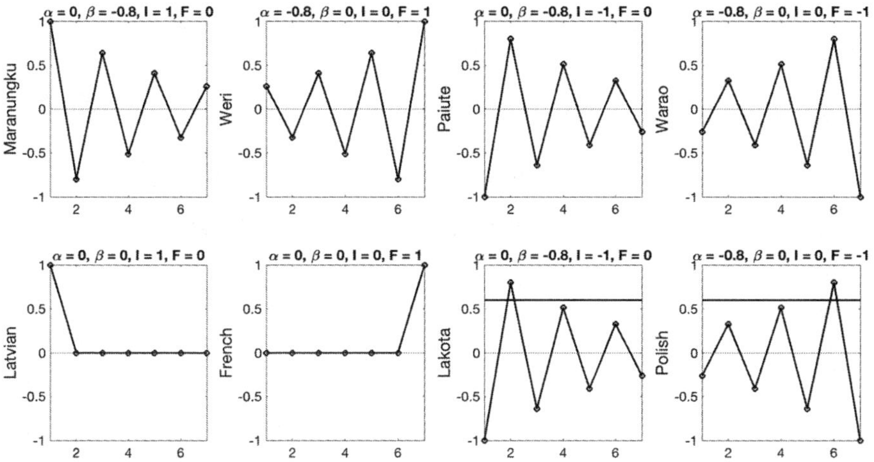

12.1 DCN-derived prominence patterns according to Goldsmith (1994) and Larson (1993).

(I or F) is switched from 1 to −1, we get systems just like the first two, except that they exhibit initial and final extrametricality, respectively. The unbounded systems of Latvian and French are modeled by the setting value only of the appropriate *P* coefficient (with α and β set to 0), whereas the unbounded systems with extrametricality are modeled as underlyingly rhythmic (non-0 α or β), with a threshold below which prominence is set to 0 (the threshold line is seen at prominence = 0.6 in the Lakota and Polish panels—by stipulation, only prominence above that level is interpreted as linguistically relevant in these languages). The difficulty of treating these systems could be linked to their typological rarity (Gordon 2002).

This computational system is also able to generate the patterns of more complex QI systems such as Garawa as in figure 12.2, where stress falls on the initial syllable and penult, and also systems such as Lenakel, where a minor modification of the coefficients yields the difference between stress in verbs and adjectives versus nouns.

When this system was first introduced, many concerns were raised regarding the possible predicted infinity of stress systems predicted since the two basic parameters α and β can vary continuously within the convergence region. This issue was addressed in Goldsmith (1994) and Prince (1993), who showed that there are qualitatively very few systems obtained through quantitative variation of the parameters. Furthermore, the few systems predicted correspond quite convincingly to attested ones.

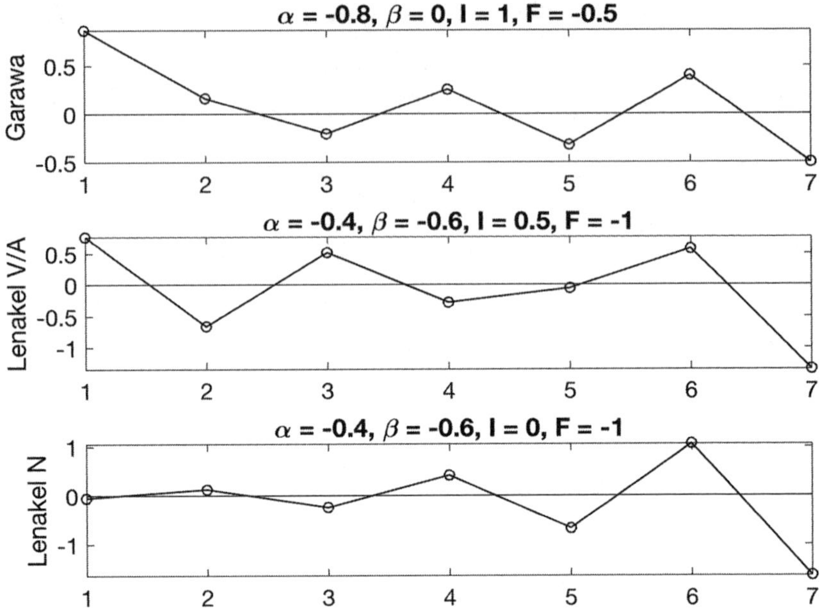

12.2 Complex stress patterns.

This was intended as a cursory introduction to the model as a whole, and the reader is referred to the works of Goldsmith, Larson, and Prince for the details. Our interest in this model is in the way it exemplifies a system in which local computation generates a global pattern, since we believe that this kind of computation is essential to understanding language at all of its levels. Part of clarifying how this model actually derives stress patterns is understanding its dynamical nature. In section 12.3, we provide a general introduction to a well-known physical dynamical system, the plucked string, whose fundamental equation, we believe, bares an important resemblance to the DCN model. Then, in section 12.4, we uncover the dynamical basis of the model's computation and argue for one possible simplification.

12.3. Dynamical Systems Analysis

The basic mathematical tool at the heart of the dynamical systems analysis of nature is the notion of a differential equation, originally proposed by Newton. He, along with the great mathematical physicists of the eighteenth and nineteenth centuries, developed the idea that the fundamental laws of physics, which describe how physical fields such as positions of particles, temperature, fluid density, and so on, depend on space and time, are fundamentally local in nature. These laws, stated as differential equations, describe how the physical field–dependent variable relates to the physical field at immediately neighboring nearby instants of time and points of space. What the mathematical physicists were interested in was the global behavior of a physical field–dependent variable, such as the entire trajectory of a particle, the flow of blood in an entire vein, or the temperature field of an entire bar of material. But Newton's insight, applied initially to the trajectories of particles due to applied forces, was that the laws of physics do *not* directly govern the global behavior of the field, rather they only specify the local relations between neighboring values of the physical field–dependent variable. Mathematical tools such as calculus can then be used to obtain the global behavior from the local description given by the physical laws. In the coming subsections we explore, in tutorial style but also in great detail, the idea of how global pattern arises from local relations in the specific area of mathematical physics, where it was first explored, and where it has mostly developed. The reason we go into this level of detail is that we believe, based on Goldsmith's original insight, that sonority in syllable structure and prominence in metrical structure are dependent field variables, and that the possible patterns of syllabification and metrical patterns we observe typologically are the result of local relations between sonorities in consecutive segments and prominence in consecutive syllables. And we hope to show that deep appreciation of how local computation leads to a global pattern in mathematical physics can be greatly rewarding for a linguist. To make this discussion more concrete, we will consider a mathematical physical–specific example: the behavior of a string, if it is plucked and held still. We will discuss how physicists were able to derive the global shape of such a string from local relations and forces by solving a differential (or difference) equation. The dynamical analysis of the string will be argued to be interesting in itself, since it has within it already a basic clash avoidance dynamic, but the equation will also to be an instance of a large family of dynamical systems, of which Goldmith's prominence dynamics belongs.

12.3.1. Poisson Equation

Imagine a string fastened at its ends; plucked up at a particular point, say one-third from its right end; and held steady (no vibration). Based

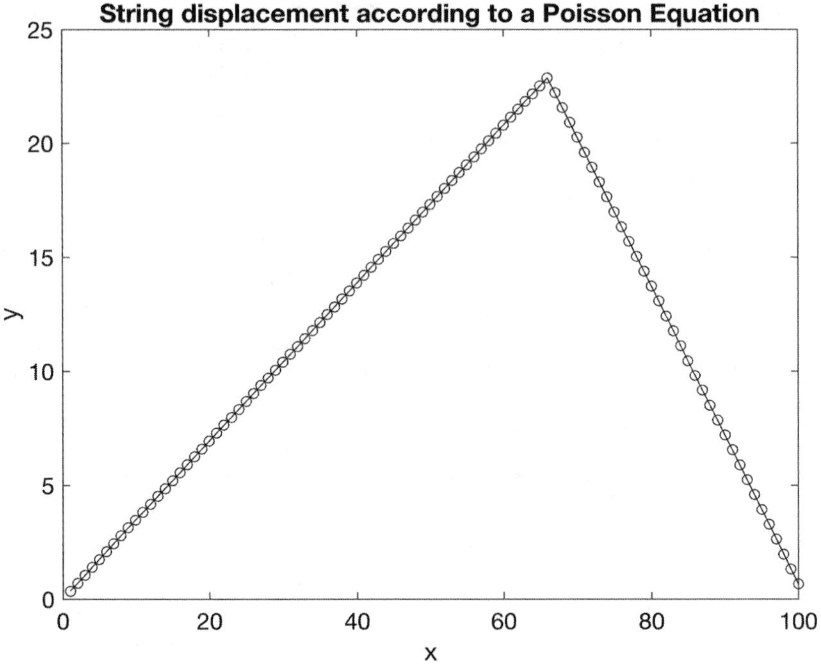

12.3 Solution of the Poisson differential equation due to a force one-third from the right.

on physical intuition, we know that the string will assume the shape in figure 12.3 if we assume that the string is perfectly elastic with negligible mass and that the extension of the string is small. The physical laws from which we can predict this shape mathematically are the laws of elasticity, from which can be deduced a single differential equation usually named the Poisson equation (Love 1906).

This equation is given in two versions, the differential one in (1a) and the discrete one in (1b), which are distinguished only by whether we take the spatial points of the string to be infinitesimally close to each other or whether we take them to be a finite distance (Δx) apart. We will only describe the discrete version (1b), since this is the one that will be most relevant for the discrete independent-variable differential equation proposed by Goldsmith and Larson (1990). The variable y refers to the vertical position of a point of the string, x refers to the horizontal position, f refers to the force applied to the string, and the position y at left and right ends equals 0.

$$\frac{d^2y}{dx^2} = -f \tag{1a}$$

$$-2\left(\frac{\frac{1}{2}(y_{x-\Delta x} + y_{x+\Delta x})}{\Delta x^2} - y_x\right) = f \tag{1b}$$

Equation (1b) can be conceptually understood in the following way. Consider the position y at any point x in the string, denoted by y_x in (1b). Now take the average of the positions y in surrounding points just to the left and right of x, a small distance Δx from the original point x, denoted as $(\frac{1}{2}(y_{x-\Delta x} + y_{x+\Delta x}))$ in (1b). And assume that we know Δx. Then what this discrete version of Poisson's equation tells us is that the difference between the average vertical position at neighboring points and the vertical position halfway between them (multiplied by the constant $-2/\Delta x^2$) is equal to the applied force, a highly local prescription. In this specific problem, the applied force is 0 everywhere, except at one-third from the right end of the string. Note that the laws of physics used here state a simple highly *local* fact: the relation between the dependent variable at one point in space and the dependent variable at neighboring points in space. Specifically, nothing about the specific shape in figure 12.3 is stated in the equation. Additional tools are necessary to deduce the global vertical position field. Problems of this sort, where some dependent variable at a point is related to its symmetric neighborhood and some conditions are prescribed at the beginning and end of the domain are called boundary value problems.

In this relatively simple case, one can guess at the global field shape by examining the meaning of equation (1b). At all points x other than where the force is applied, the right-hand side of (1b) is 0, which means that the position $y_x = (\frac{1}{2}(y_{x-\Delta x} + y_{x+\Delta x}))$, the average in its neighborhood. Therefore, the function needs to be linear at that point, since only a linear function has the property that the value at a point is the average of the surrounding points. We therefore predict that the position of the string will be linear at all points other than the point at which the force is applied. At that point, the force is some positive number, therefore, according to equation (1b), the position of the string at that point must be higher than the average of the surrounding points. This is exactly the shape we predict conceptually and that we see in figure 12.3.

Now consider a slightly different case, where instead of a single force, applied by a single hook to the string, we apply two *exactly equal* forces

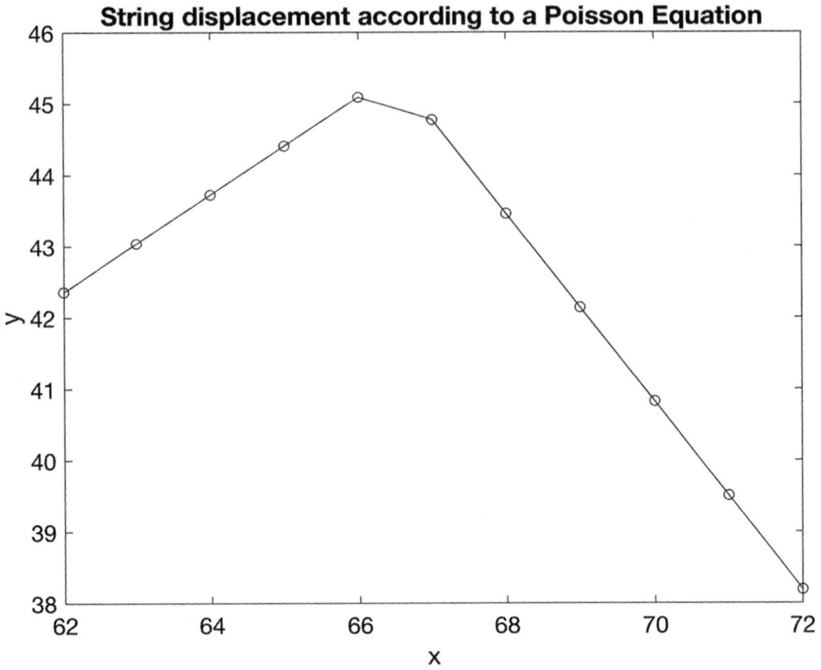

12.4 Clash avoidance in a simple dynamical system.

very close together onto the string, say with two hooks. To make the situation concrete, the string is one hundred units long; the forces are of unit magnitude; and forces are applied at points 66 and 67. What would be the shape of the string in this situation? It may seem that the string would be linearly shaped from the left end all the way to the point at which the first force is applied, point 66 here; then would remain flat to the point at which the second force is applied, point 67; and would then slope linearly downward until the right end. This is not what happens. A close-up of the string where the forces are applied is shown in figure 12.4. As can be seen, one point is actually higher than the other point. We can see therefore that it is possible that two points of the string, subject to two equal forces, exactly contiguous to each other, each of the points abiding by the same local law, show somewhat different behaviors. We can say that the physical law implies that the positions of two contiguous points under equal exactly contiguous forces do not *clash*, that is, they do not acquire exactly equal values.[2] This follows from the fact that the physical law needs to apply everywhere in the string, and consistent application of it from one end to the other allows certain phenomena such as clash avoidance to emerge.

Many mathematical methods have been developed to solve local equations as in (1) to yield global solutions as in figures 12.3 and 12.4, the first of which was the calculus itself. There are two mathematical technologies for determining the global field from the equation that will now be discussed. The first is the relaxation method, which we claim is the one used by Goldsmith and Larson (1990) to solve an equation quite similar to that in (1b), and the second is the GF method, since our analysis of the DCN model in section 12.4 will depend on it.

12.3.2. Relaxation Method

In this method (Southwell 1940), we look at equation (1b) as providing a constraint on the value of the vertical position everywhere in the string, given that the position is 0 at the ends and there is a force of 1 at 1/3 from the right end (for instance). This constraint can be seen through algebraic manipulation of (1b) into 2:

$$y_x = \tfrac{f}{2} + \tfrac{1}{2}(y_{x-\Delta x} + y_{x+\Delta x}) \tag{2}$$

That is, the value at each point is obtainable from the average of the surrounding points and the force, given $y=0$ at the boundaries. The problem is that we cannot know the value of y, unless we know y at surrounding points, but those themselves need to be obtained. The relaxation method works by starting out with random values for y at an initial *computational* time (except for the 0 values at the ends), and then enforcing equation (2) repeatedly to eventually realize the constraint in the equation at some later computational time. If we start with random numbers for y, then certainly, the value for each y will not be related to f and the average of the surrounding y. An initial application of equation (2) takes each y and makes it the average of its surrounding $+f/2$, but at the same time, the surroundings change, making each number not actually be related in the manner sanctioned by equation (2). Repeated application of the constraint will, however (if the problem has a convergent solution), yield the solution as we can see in figure 12.5.

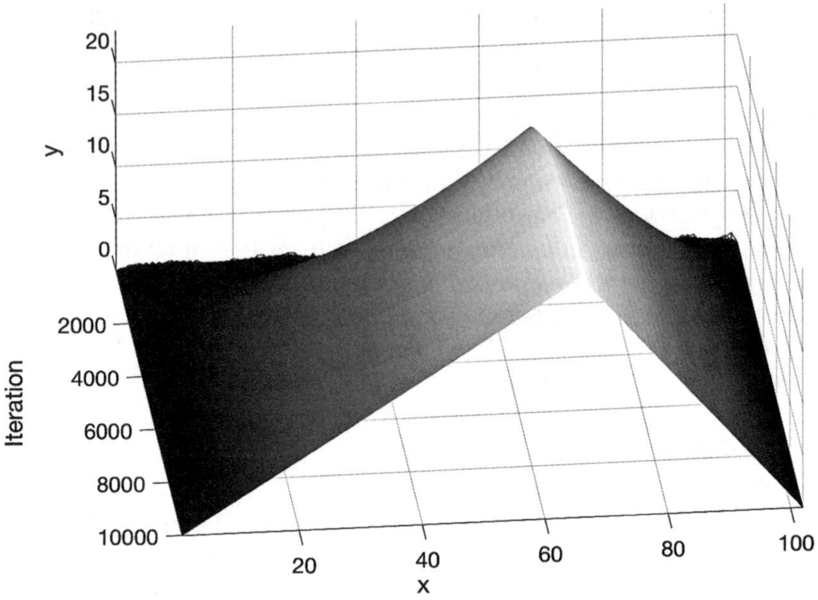

12.5 Solving Poisson's equation via the relaxation method.

The random values for y at the beginning eventually turn into the solution we saw in figure 12.3 at some eventual equilibrium *computational* time. The relaxation method therefore sees equation (2) as the computational algorithm in equation (3), assuming knowledge of the force:

$$y_x^{t+1} = \tfrac{f}{2} + \tfrac{1}{2}\left(y_{x-\Delta x}^t + y_{x+\Delta x}^t\right) \tag{3}$$

This algorithm computes a new set of y values at each time-step, based on the values of y at the previous time-step. It is very important here, however, to note that time here is not physical time, but an auxiliary computational time in which the constraints enforced by the Poisson equation, together with the forces and boundary conditions, eventually determine the shape. In other words, the fact that this is a dynamical equation is not due to the dependence on time, rather it is due to the local relation between the dependent variable for neighboring points in space. The time dependence is artificial and is convenient as it serves this specific method of solution. The similarity between this equation and the DCN model will be explored fully in section 12.4.

12.3.3. GF Method

Another method for using the local description in equations (1) to obtain the solution in figure 12.3 is the GF method, which will be useful for obtaining a full analysis of the model in section 12.4. To understand how this method applies to the Poisson equation, it is best to use equation (1b), the discrete form. If we approximate the string at ten equidistant points with $\Delta x=1$, assuming that points 1 and 10 have $y=0$, and that the force is applied at the sixth point, we can write equation (1b) as eight equations as in equations (4):

$$
\begin{aligned}
2y_2-y_3&=0\\
-y_2+2\,y_3-y_4&=0\\
-y_3+2\,y_4-y_5&=0\\
-y_4+2\,y_5-y_6&=0\\
-y_5+2\,y_6-y_7&=1\\
-y_6+2\,y_7-y_8&=0\\
-y_7+2\,y_8-y_9&=0\\
-y_8+2\,y_9&=0
\end{aligned} \tag{4}
$$

To understand how these equations instantiate the discrete Poisson equation (1b), consider, for instance, the third equation. At point 4 (i.e., $x=4$), when Δx is 1, (1b) relates y_4 to y_3 and y_5, that is, the equation relates the displacement at $x=4$ to the displacements at the two surrounding points. Therefore, for $x=4$, the discrete Poisson's equation $-2\left(\frac{\frac{1}{2}(y_{x-\Delta x}+y_{x\Delta+\Delta x})}{\Delta x^2}-y_x\right)=f$ becomes $-2\left(\frac{\frac{1}{2}(y_3+y_5)}{1}-y_4\right)=0$, which after simplification becomes the third equation in (4). The force, the right-hand side, is 0, since there is no force at the sixth point in this example. The system in (4) is a linear system of equations in nine unknowns and can be solved by any method for solving linear systems of equations. To solve this system means to find values for the variables $y_2 \ldots y_9$ that actually make all the equations true, in other words, the left-hand side and the right-hand side of each equation must be equal. Since each of the dependent variables occurs in multiple equations, the solution values must be consistent across all the equations. Note how each equation specifies a *local* algebraic constraint specifying a particular relation between the values of the dependent variables are two or three consecutive points. The solution, however is *global*, and is achieved by

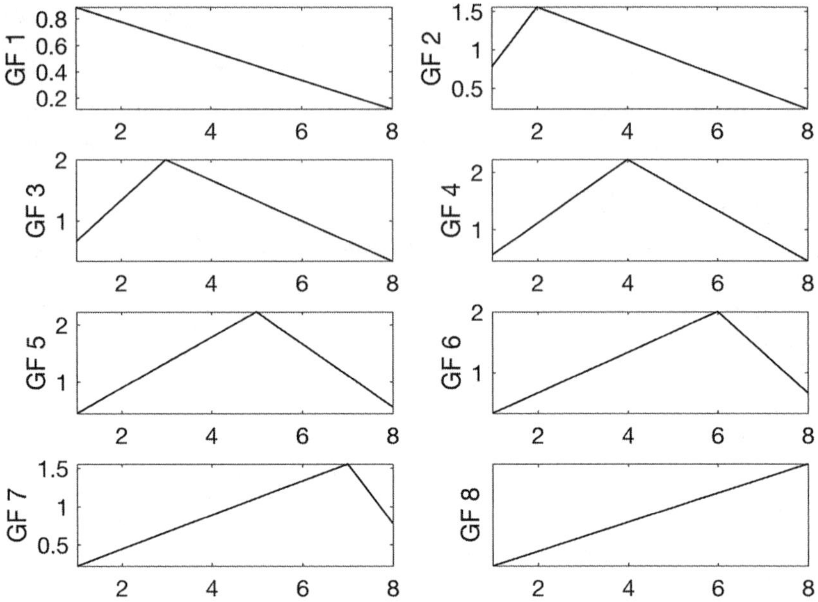

12.6 GFs for one-dimensional Poisson's equation with fixed ends.

making sure that all the constraints are satisfied in parallel, creating one global solution across the entire domain, the GF. The actual solution is obtained mechanically using one of several alternatives, such as row reduction, Cramer's rule, or Gaussian elimination (Strang 2007), but is not of interest here. Note also that there are only eight equations, since the values at $x = 1$ and $x = 10$ are known here to be 0. And it is for this reason that the first and last equations have two terms on the left-hand side, instead of three—since one of the terms in each (y_1 in the first and y_{10} in the last) is 0. The solution $y_2 \ldots y_9$ of the system is called the GF for an impulsive force applied at the sixth location. This solution can be obtained by any method for solving a linear system of algebraic equations. As we progressively shift the 1 on the right-hand side from the first equation to the last, while keeping all the other forces 0, we obtain eight GF solutions for this system, as can be seen in figure 12.6.[3]

The specific situation described here is of the string plucked at point 6, which can be seen as GF6. What is special about these impulse responses, that is, the responses of the string to pulses of force, is that they can be used to build the response to any force function by adding these GFs weighted by the force. For instance, if a constant downward force is applied to the string, so that the forces are all constant, we would mul-

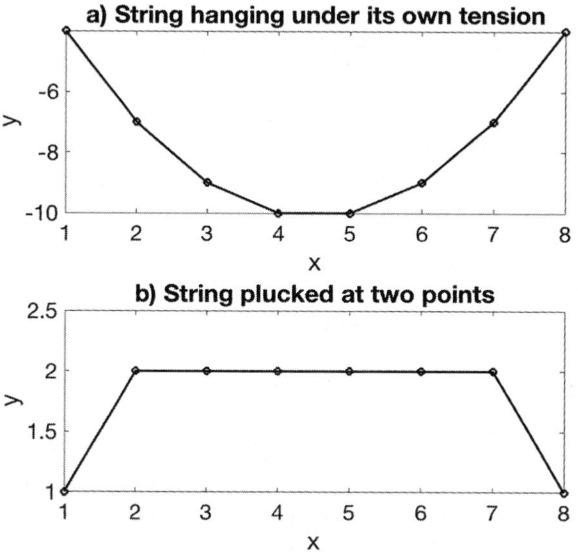

12.7 Complex force solutions. (*a*) String hanging under its own tension. (*b*) String plucked at two points.

tiply each GF by −1 and add them all together. The resulting solution is shown in figure 12.7a, whereas if we pluck the string at points 2 and 7, we would add GF2 and GF7 to obtain figure 12.7b.

Therefore, once we know the GFs for a (linear) differential system (given its boundary conditions), we can obtain complex solutions as a weighted linear combination of the GFs. This is called the convolution theorem. One way of looking at GFs is that they show the global consequences of the local specification in a differential/difference equation, since they show complete global solutions for the simplest local forces (impulses such as $f = [0\ 0\ 0\ 0\ 1\ 0\ 0]$), which can then be recombined to obtain any solution. This will be important in the next section, since it will be shown that for each of the DCN models obtained by changing the signs of the coefficients in the model, we obtain a new set of GFs, which completely determine the responses of the model and give us a preview of each such model's global potential.

12.4. DCN as a Dynamical System

In this section, we will argue that the Goldsmith-Larson DCN is an instance of a boundary value problem, with some differences from the problem of the plucked steady string discussed in section 12.3, but also with many similarities. This will allow us to understand the conceptual claim about the nature of metrical systems made by the model. Equation (5a) shows the DCN model without the time variable (and ignoring $N(i)$, which is not necessary for QI systems), and equation (5b) shows the string boundary value problem with the independent variable labeled as i, instead of x and Δx set to 1:

$$a_i = \alpha\, a_{i+1} + \beta\, a_{i-1} + P(i) \quad (5a)$$

$$y_i = \tfrac{1}{2} y_{i+1} + \tfrac{1}{2} y_{i-1} + f(i) \quad (5b)$$

It is quite obvious that these are basically the same model, except that in DCN, the signs and values of the coefficients are variable. Note that the positional activation $P(i)$ of DCN lines up perfectly with the force in the string dynamical system. One similarity that may not be as obvious is that in both models, the boundary values are set to 0. In the DCN model, computation of the internal node prominences are based on the surrounding node prominences, whereas the left boundary node has only a single neighbor, the one on the right, which means that it is assumed that its left neighbor is set to 0. And the rightmost node has only one neighbor, meaning that it is assumed that the there is a shadow right neighbor set to 0 prominence.[4] Therefore, we can regard the DCN model as a boundary variable problem with 0-boundary conditions and variable coefficients. This identification of the mathematical nature of DCN is important, since there has been some confusion regarding its true mathematical nature due to the time variable that is usually included in its statement. For instance, Prince (1993) in some passages considered the problem as a boundary value problem, but at other times as an initial value problem, specifically a critically damped system. These problems have different fundamental properties. Having said that, it may very well be that in future developments of the model, it could be changed mathematically to an initial value problem, if it turns out that the emergent properties of such systems are better matches to those of stress systems. Moreover, in boundary value problems, there are different ways of setting the boundary conditions. The one used by Goldsmith and Larson (1990) is the fixed-fixed condition (since the prominence value is set to 0 in shadow nodes before and after the visible units), which is usually called Dirichlet conditions. The other two possibilities are setting the change in prominence at both boundaries to be 0 (free-free or Von Neumann conditions), or having one end fixed and the other free (Robin conditions). These latter two possibilities are less restrictive and might provide for a less powerful model.

The time variable usually presented as part of the DCN model can now be seen as a relaxation time that is not connected to the dynamical nature of the model but is more of a computational/algorithmic time used in one particular way of solving the model, the relaxation method. It may seem strange to call a model *dynamical* if time is not an independent variable, but the fundamental nature of dynamical systems does not have to do with the interpretation of the dependent and independent variables but does involve the use of purely local relations to describe a phenomenon using a differential/difference. DCN as presented in equation (5a) is therefore clearly a dynamical system, despite the lack of time as an explicit variable.[5]

12.4.1. GFs Applied to Metrical Systems

Due to the identification of DCN as a boundary value problem, we can now discuss the GFs of the different models.[6] This is complicated by the fact that there is literally an infinite number of models for variable coefficients, even when we abide by the restriction $|\alpha\,\beta| \leq \frac{1}{4}$. We will now see that GF analysis, by showing us the global capability of the different models, shows us that there are only a few qualitatively different models. As an example of a GF analysis, consider the model for generating the Garawa stress pattern in figure 12.2, with $\alpha=-0.8$ and $\beta=0$. If we write out the individual algebraic equations for the model as in equations (4), we can then determine all GF (assuming a seven-node model) by solving seven linear algebraic systems, with a single 1 and seven 0s for the force. But we do not need all of these seven functions. As discussed, the forces act as weights or multipliers on the GFs, and the QI model uses only the *I* and *F* parameters, which therefore multiply/weight GF1 and GF7 only. Therefore the $I=1$ and $F=-0.5$ specification of DCN is now seen to be an instruction to multiply GF1 by 1 and GF7 by -0.5 (where the GFs used are for the $\alpha=-0.8$ and $\beta=0$ model) and to add the two functions to obtain the global prominence function. In figure 12.8, we a present a comparison of the Garawa prominence function computed via the relaxation method (circles) and the GF method (crosses). The results are the same and also the same as those obtained from DCN, confirming the specific identification of the DCN model as a boundary value problem with fixed-fixed conditions, while showing that the GF method works for this specific model.[7]

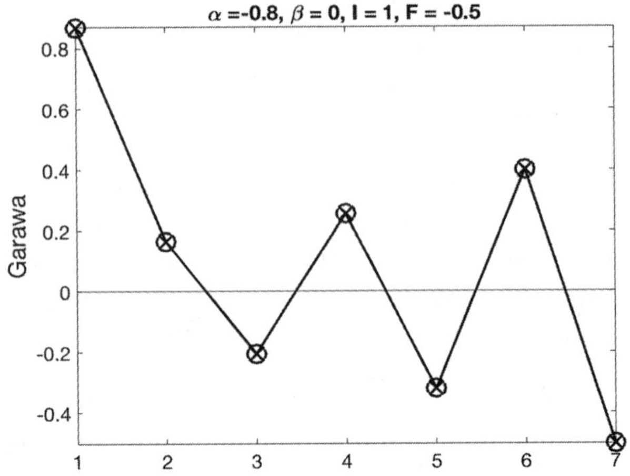

12.8 Comparison of relaxation and GF solutions to DCN equations for Garawa.

Given all this, it is possible to conclude that all we need to consider are the first and last GFs to predict the behavior of a particular model. To explore the shapes of these GFs, we generated 973 systems in which α and β take the values from –1 to 1 in small increments, while satisfying the condition $|\alpha\ \beta| \leq 1/4$. Figure 12.9 shows the first and last GFs of all these systems, in eight categories, with the first sign on top of the panels specifying the sign of α or if it is 0, and the second sign specifying the sign of β or if it is 0. Figure 12.10 gives the same information for words with an even number of syllables. We claim that these shapes give a complete view of the current DCN model. One of the most important mathematical features of these shapes is how consistent they are within each category. This demonstrates the deep qualitative similarity between quantitatively different models, as discussed by Goldsmith and Larson (1990), but seen in a new way.

From the metrical point of view, the beauty of these first and last GFs is that their shapes capture the most important global features of metrical systems: binary rhythm, culminativity, demarcativity, boundedness, and extrametricality. Some GFs are periodic, allowing for binary rhythm, others have a single extremum near the periphery, allowing for unboundedness and demarcativity. Some are peaked at the very periphery while others peak in the neighboring syllable allowing for extrametricality.

It is striking that these patterns represent the complete set of global patterns that can be generated by this dynamical system (which is local

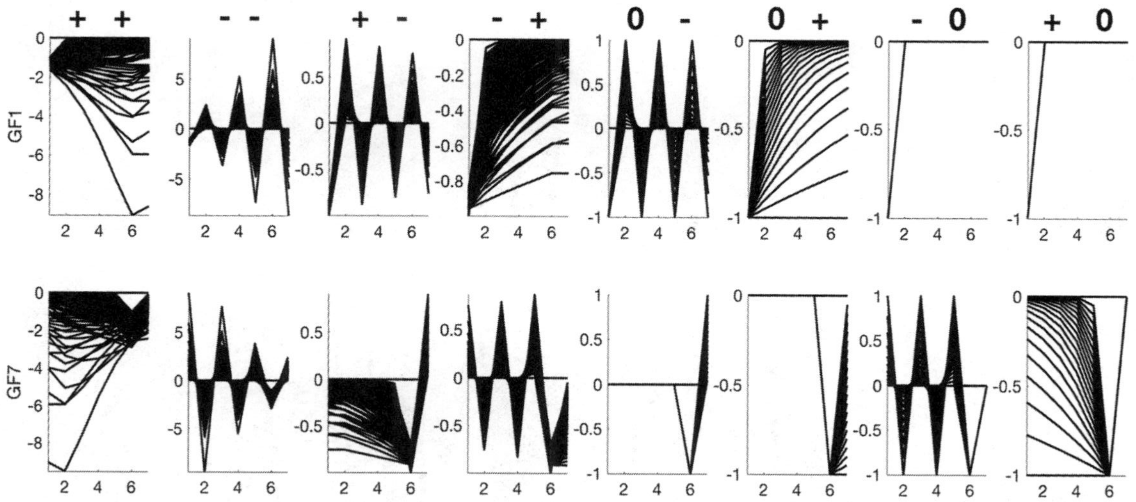

12.9 First and last GFs for DCN systems. Each panel has the sign or value for α, then the sign or value of β. Odd number of syllables.

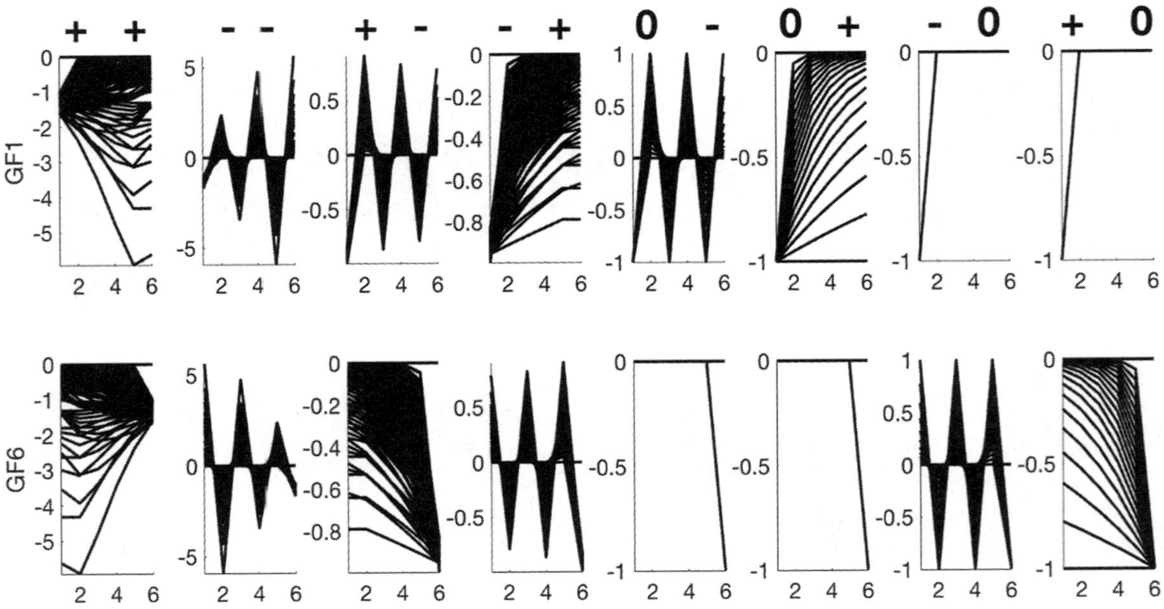

12.10 First and last GFs for DCN systems. Each panel has the sign or value for α, then the sign or value of β. Even number of syllables.

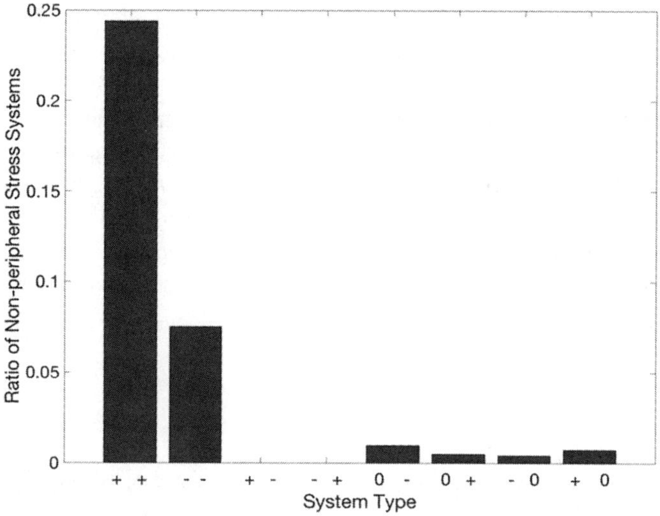

12.11 Comparison of systems as to whether they generate stress on syllables other than first, second, penultimate, or ultimate.

computation). It is rare in cognitive science, we believe, to have a model that bears such a close fit to the patterns of data in some domain, when the model is based on first principles and hypotheses, rather than fitting the model to the data. The relevant principles and hypotheses here are (i) that accent systems can be modeled as boundary value problems with ends fixed to 0 and (ii) that QI accent systems can be modeled by applying forces (prominence) only on the first or last syllables.

The GF approach also allows us to investigate the consequences when we combine them with positive and negative weights on *I* and *F*. In this way, we can check whether the model overgenerates, and we can discover the minimal model that will generate attested simple and complex patterns, while being extensible to quantity-sensitive systems easily. One issue of this sort that we tested is whether it is possible to generate prominence profiles with the maximum not on the first two or last two syllables, thereby violating demarcativity. For each of the 973 systems, using the seven-syllable case, we generated eighty-one weight combinations where *I* and *F* vary from −1 to 1 increments of 0.25. Figure 12.11 shows the proportion (out of 1) of the number of systems not obeying demarcativity. The first type of system, where α and β are both positive, gives the greatest number of violations, and indeed it is the type avoided by Goldsmith (1994) and Larson (1993). Category 2, where α and β are both negative, leads to the second most violations and in general seems to be good at generating rhythm, but not very good at producing unbounded systems, based on the GF periodicity. The other systems perform far better, with categories 3 and 4 showing no violations, and the others showing only very few violations, basically when α and β are almost equal, which leads to the removal of the distinction between primary and secondary stress. In future development of the theory, these latter asymmetrical systems from category 3 onward, are likely to lead to the best minimal model.

12.5. Conclusion

In this chapter, we have presented Goldsmith (1994)'s dynamical theory of metrical structure as an example of a local-computation-to-global-structure model. By analyzing the structure of the model, we found that it is an instance of a boundary value problem. The GF method was also proposed as a solution strategy that makes clear exactly how global structure arises from local constraints from first principles. We say *first principles,* since the GF is an application of Green's theorem, a generalization of the fundamental theorem of calculus. The linguistic hypotheses here are that accent systems can be modeled as a boundary value problem and that QI accent systems apply prominence (forces) only at the ends. We believe that this model could serve as a prototype of dynamical models in different areas in linguistic research. This may seem surprising, since prominence feels like a relatively low level variable, so a theory that works quite well for it may not generalize to other more abstract aspects of language. However, several disciplines in language have started to use dynamical models. For instance, Meidros (2012) and Uriagereka (2012) have developed models of c-command and other aspects of hierarchical structure in syntax based on the Fibonacci equation $F_n = F_{n-1} + F_{n-2}$, a local relation between three numbers that has remarkable global properties. Indeed, we expect more and more work using dynamical systems in various domains in language, since the emergence of global properties from local constraints is so essential all across language. And Goldsmith's dynamical theory of syllable and metrical structure may provide a route to further such unifying theory.

Notes

This work was supported by National Science Foundation grant 1246750 to the University of Southern California.

1. Gordon (2002) presented instances of dual-stress systems and other systems beyond the ones in table 12.1. In future work, we will attempt to show how DCN can account for these systems.
2. There is one exception: if the forces are exactly in the middle of the string. It is also possible according to this specific law for many contiguous points of the string to assume the same vertical position, if the two forces are far from each other.
3. This can also be done by separating the coefficients into a matrix

$$\begin{bmatrix} 2 & -1 & 0 & 0 & \\ -1 & 2 & -1 & 0 & \\ & & & & \cdots \\ 0 & -1 & 2 & -1 & \\ 0 & 0 & -1 & 2 & \\ & & \cdots & & \end{bmatrix},$$

   and then inverting the matrix. The columns of the inverse matrix are the GF (Strang 2007).
4. This was checked by calculating many examples presented in Goldsmith (1994) and Larson (1993) using 0-boundary conditions for a node before the leftmost one and a node after the rightmost one considered part of the network and getting the same exact values plotted in these papers.
5. Time *is* an independent variable in equation (5a), since each syllable occurs at one point in time, but here time acts like space, since it is in space that we provide conditions at both ends. The behavior of time like space may be a very general property of language (Iatridou 2014) to be explored in the future as DCN analyses are extended to other domains in language.
6. Prince (1993) also provided a GF analysis of DCN, in terms of the impulse response, but his analysis is quite different from ours, based on different interpretations of the dynamical nature of the model.
7. Something very interesting that happens with this specific model is that it is a first-order, not second-order model, since the left neighbor plays no role. However, the model has two boundary conditions, which seems improper. There is a great deal of theory, however, developed for such situations under the heading of boundary layer theory, which treats exactly this situation. The physical situations treated are those in which a system is overconstrained, and the extra constraint is satisfied by forming a *boundary layer*, which could be seen here as an extrametrical syllable. This issue and its implications for how the model predicts certain prominent features of metrical systems will be explored in further work.

References

Beckman, Mary. 1993. Parsing prosody. *Language and Cognitive Processes* 11:17–68.

Borer, Hagit. 2013. *Structuring Sense.* Vol. 3: *Taking Form.* Oxford: Oxford University Press.

Browman, Catherine, and Louis Goldstein. 1989. Articulatory gestures as phonological units. *Phonology* 6:201–251.

Collins, Chris. 1996. *Local Economy*. Cambridge, MA: MIT Press.

Dresher, B. Elan, and Jonathan Kaye. 1990. A computational learning model for metrical phonology. *Cognition* 34:137–195.

Goldsmith, John. 1994. A dynamic computational theory of accent systems. In *Perspectives in Phonology*, ed. Jennifer Cole and Charles Kisseberth, 1–28. Stanford, CA: Center for the Study of Language and Information.

———. 2005/2016. Dynamic computational networks. Presentation slides/notes. February 18, 2016. http://people.cs.uchicago.edu/~jagoldsm/slides/2016-dcn.pdf.

Goldsmith, John, and Gary Larson. 1990. Local modeling and syllabification. In *Papers from the 26th Annual Regional Meeting of the Chicago Linguistic Society*, part 2, ed. K. M. Ziolkowski, K. Deaton, and M. Noske, 129–142. Chicago: Chicago Linguistic Society.

Gordon, Matthew. 2002. A factorial typology of quantity-insensitive stress. *Natural Language and Linguistic Theory* 20:491–552.

Halle, Morris, and Jean-Roger Vergnaud. 1987. *An Essay on Stress*. Cambridge, MA: MIT Press.

Hayes, Bruce. 1980. *A Metrical Theory of Stress Rules*. New York: Garland Press.

———. 1995. *Metrical Stress Theory: Principles and Case Studies*. Chicago: University of Chicago Press.

Hyman, Larry. 1977. On the nature of linguistic stress. In *Studies in Stress and Accent*, ed. Larry Hyman, 37–82. Los Angeles: University of Southern California, Department of Linguistics.

Iatridou, Sabine. 2014. About determiners on even descriptions, about time being like space (when we talk), and about one particularly strange construction. *Natural Language Semantics* 22:219–263.

Iskarous, Khalil, Christine Mooshammer, Philip Hoole, Daniel Recasens, Christine Shadle, Elliott Saltzman, and Douglas H. Whalen. 2013. The coarticulation/invariance scale: Mutual information as a measure of coarticulation resistance, motor synergy, and articulatory invariance. *Journal of the Acoustical Society of America* 134:1271–1284.

Kager, René. 2007. Feet and metrical stress. In *The Cambridge Handbook of Phonology*, ed. Paul de Lacy, 195–227. Cambridge: Cambridge University Press.

Larson, Gary. 1993. Dynamic computational networks and the representation of phonological information. PhD dissertation, University of Chicago.

Liberman, Mark. 1975. The intonational system of English. PhD dissertation, Massachusetts Institute of Technology.

Love, A. 1906. *A Treatise on the Mathematical Theory of Elasticity.* Cambridge: Cambridge University Press.

Meidros, D. 2012. Economy of command. PhD dissertation, University of Arizona.

Prince, Alan. 1993. *In Defense of the Number i: Anatomy of a Linear Dynamical Mode of Linguistic Generalizations.* Technical Report 1. Piscataway, NJ: Rutgers University Center for Cognitive Science.

Prince, Alan, and Paul Smolensky. 1993. *Optimality Theory: Constraint Interaction in Generative Grammar.* Technical Report 2. Piscataway, NJ: Rutgers University Center for Cognitive Science.

Saltzman, Elliot, Hosung Nam, Louis Goldstein, and Dany Byrd. 2006. The distinctions between state, parameter and graph dynamics in sensorimotor control and coordination. In *Motor Control and Learning,* ed. M. L. Latash and F. Lestienne, 63–73. New York: Springer.

Southwell, R. V. 1940. *Relaxation Methods in Engineering Science.* Oxford: Oxford University Press.

Strang, Gilbert. 2007. *Computational Science and Engineering.* Wellesley, MA: Wellesley-Cambridge Press.

Trubetzkoy, Nikolay S. 1939. *Grundzüge der Phonologie.* Travaux du Cercle Linguistique de Prague 7. English translation: *Principles of Phonology.* Berkeley: University of California Press, 1969.

Uriagereka, Juan. 2012. Phase periodicity. In *Phases: Developing the Framework,* ed. Gallego Angel. Berlin: Walter de Gruyter.

THIRTEEN

French Liaison in the Light of Corpus Phonology: From Lexical Information to Patterns of Usage Variation

BERNARD LAKS, BASILIO CALDERONE, AND CHIARA CELATA

[Our] view of linguistics . . . is epistemologically empiricist. . . . It is empiricist in the belief that the justification of a scientific theory must drive deep into the quantitative measure of real-world data, both experimental and observational, and it is empiricist in seeing continuity (rather than rupture or discontinuity) between the careful treatment of large-scale data and the desire to develop elegant high-level theories. To put that last point slightly differently, it is not an empiricism that is skeptical of elegant theories, or worried that the elegance of a theory is a sign of its disconnect from reality. But it is an empiricism that insists on measuring just how an elegant a theory is, and measuring how well it is (or isn't) in sync with what we have observed about the world. It is not an empiricism that is afraid of theories that leave observations unexplained, but it is an empiricism that insists that discrepancies between theory and observation are a sign that more work will be needed, and sooner rather than later. NICK CHATER, ALEXANDER CLARK, AMY PERFORS, AND JOHN A. GOLDSMITH, *EMPIRICISM AND LANGUAGE LEARNABILITY*

13.1. Introduction: The Liaison Phenomenon

French liaison is a well-known external *sandhi* phenomenon by which a word apparently ending in a vowel is syllabically linked to the subsequent vowel-initial lexical unit thanks to the surfacing of a consonant: *un petit enfant* [ɛ̃pøtitɑ̃fɑ̃] versus *un petit café* [ɛ̃pøtikafe]. This liaison consonant (LC), which does not surface unless the following word begins by a vowel, has been analyzed as latent, epenthetic, or suppletive and as belonging either to the preceding word (W1) or to the following one (W2) or even to neither of them, according to different authors.

The liaison phenomenon has been documented since the very origin of French grammatical studies (Palsgrave [1530] 2003; Meigret [1542] 1972). Between the sixteenth and the nineteenth centuries at least two hundred descriptions were produced (Thurot 1881–1883) and for nineteenth and twentieth centuries, Morrison (1968) listed more than two hundred additional references. Since the last decades of the twentieth century, the number of studies devoted to liaison has not diminished and another one hundred references can be added, according to Côté (2011) and Barreca (2015).

In the history of liaison descriptions and analyses, the generative and postgenerative period represents a peculiar moment. Schane (1965) proposed that liaison should be reduced to a morphophonological dimension only. Based on less than twenty-five bibliographical references and seventy-three liaison examples taken from prescriptive grammars (Grevisse 1936),[1] Schane proposed a formal system for the analysis of all French phonological processes (including liaison for consonants and elision[2] for vowels) and a large amount of French morphology. Schane's purpose, as was typical for generativism, was not that of a closer analysis or a more complete description of the phenomenon, but rather of building for these seventy-three examples a system of no less than forty-one ordered rules allowing the formal derivation of all existing liaisons, elisions, and truncations in French. As Goldsmith and Laks (2001: 3) pointed out, "rather than focusing on discussions in the professional literature of how phonological data could be organized and subjected to various analytic procedures, the focus of the phonologist's attention became, within the framework of generative phonology, the actual form of the grammar being proposed; the relationship of the observed data to the formal grammar that was under discussion became more indirect, and indeed, it seems to have been a noteworthy terminological innovation in generative phonology that the analyst could and would point, proudly, to the result that the data 'simply fall out' of the analysis" (see also Goldsmith 2015).

As frequently observed, to obtain his formal descriptive system, Schane (1965) drew a parallel between elision, that is, a vocalic process that consists in the loss of an orthographic vowel both in spoken and written language, and liaison, that is, a consonantal process that consists in the nonrealization of an orthographic consonant before a consonant-initial word in speech.[3] Now this parallelism is only apparent, as many French phonologists before him had noticed, especially because all contextual constraints and morphological conditioning factors are so different in the two processes that it is impossible to reduce them to one and the same abstract rule.

The elision is a phonic and graphemic process (unlike the liaison that is not graphemic) and involves a limited number of constructions with obligatory determinant, pronoun, or clitic on the left side. It is a process that is stable and invariant for all the speakers.

For this empirical inadequacy and the absence of any morphosyntactic constraint, Schane's (1965) proposal was criticized (Milner 1967; Selkirk 1972) and then abandoned. However, Schane's "solution ingénieuse [qui ne peut] être retenue" 'smart solution that cannot be maintained' (Dell 1973: 182) had a strong and durable impact on the way subsequent scholars approached the problem of liaison. As a matter of fact, Schane indirectly introduced the view that the central question in dealing with liaison was the process of its instantiation, and secondarily its formalization. Variation in speaker usage and the contextual constraints operating at all levels of the grammar were relegated to the borders of linguistic description, and they could be safely ignored to the benefit of a strictly procedural treatment of the liaison phenomenon. Now for the very large majority of linguists from the sixteenth century onward, the reverse was true: liaison as a process is totally clear and well understood. From this point of view, liaison simply is—as prescriptive grammarians used to say—a process needed to "faire entendre devant un mot commençant par une voyelle une consonne finale normalement muette" 'pronounce a usually silent final consonant before a word beginning with a vowel' (Chevalier et al. 1964). The persistent work of formalization, still manifest in the postgenerative era (Encrevé 1988; Scheer 2015; Scheer, Wauquier, and Encrevé 2015) adds no supplementary linguistic information, with respect to the ordinary definition just mentioned. Rather, what is important is to understand what can and what cannot be a *consonne muette* in French, and under which conditions this consonant can or cannot be realized in speech.

With the exception of the generative and postgenerative period, then, liaison has always been considered as a complex and multiparametric phenomenon, involving at the same time almost all grammatical levels and dimensions of external variation: from prosody and syllabification to orthography, from morphology and syntax to semantics and the lexicon, from diachrony to geography and sociolinguistics (Laks 2005). On top of this, a dimension of inherent variation (Labov 1994), irreducible to all other dimensions of variation, also appears to play a role in determining French liaison, which will also be dealt with in the following sections of this chapter.

The remainder of this chapter is structured as follows. After a brief survey of the generative and postgenerative accounts, section 13.2 argues that liaison cannot be reduced to a phonological process of enchainment, but liaison is rather motivated by the lexical information carried by the liaison consonant. Section 13.3 reviews three previous accounts of the liaison consonant as suppletive, latent, or epenthetic and concludes that none of them is able to capture the specificity of the liaison phenomenon, including the difference between those constructions in which liaison is mandatory and those constructions in which it is optional. In sections 13.4 and 13.5, an empirical analysis based on the principles and practices of corpus phonology is proposed. After a short presentation of the liaison data set available from the Phonologie du Français Contemporain (PFC) corpus and an explanation of its usefulness for the study of linguistic variation (section 13.4), the analysis shows that, although a few construction types account for mandatory liaison, the great majority of the data reflect variable phenomena (section 13.5), including within-item variation (i.e., one and the same word can be produced with or without realized liaison) and variation between items sharing the same phonological and morphosyntactic class. It is additionally shown that age-related individual variation, probably reflecting a change in progress, is precisely attested in the subset of variable liaisons. Section 13.6 summarizes and concludes by emphasizing that quantitative investigations of real-world data, as the one proposed here, not only contribute to an accurate description of languages, but also allow putting forth verifiable hypotheses on the cognitive status of linguistic phenomena.

13.2. Liaison Is Not a Phonological Process

If we look at liaison within the postgenerative autosegmental framework (as in, e.g., Scheer 2015: 100), we find that a word such as *petit* 'small' has a lexical or underlying phonological representation without /t/ before a consonant-initial word (*petit café* [pøtikafe] 'small coffee') and one with /t/ before a vowel-initial word (*petit enfant* [pøtitɑ̃fɑ̃] 'small child'). This is shown in (1a). Example (1b) shows instead the structure of a word such as *pépite* 'nugget' in which the last syllable is closed and which has a final /t/ both before a vowel and before a consonant. In French, a general enchainment process applies by which lexical units are dynamically linked to one another within larger prosodic units, generally called prosodic or phonological words. Enchainment produces the resyllabification of a word-final (W1) consonant as the onset of the following syllable if the second word (W2) begins with a vowel (Delattre 1951; Fouché 1959; Grammont 1914).[4] This process is shown in (2), where the final consonant of *pépite* is resyllabified at the beginning of *ovale* 'oval': it is detached from the last syllable of *pépite* and attached to the initial syllable of *ovale*.

(1a)

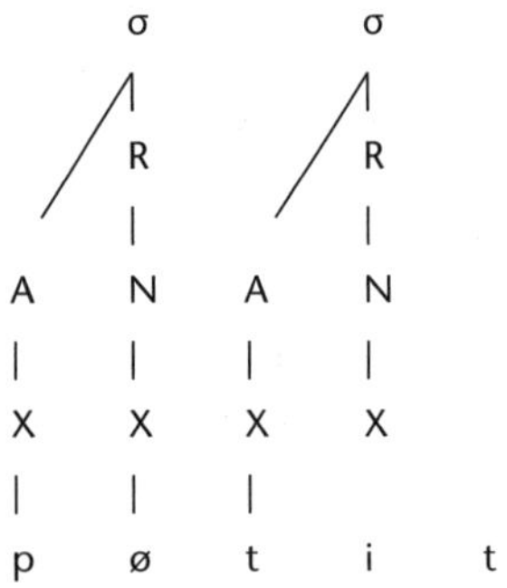

(1b)

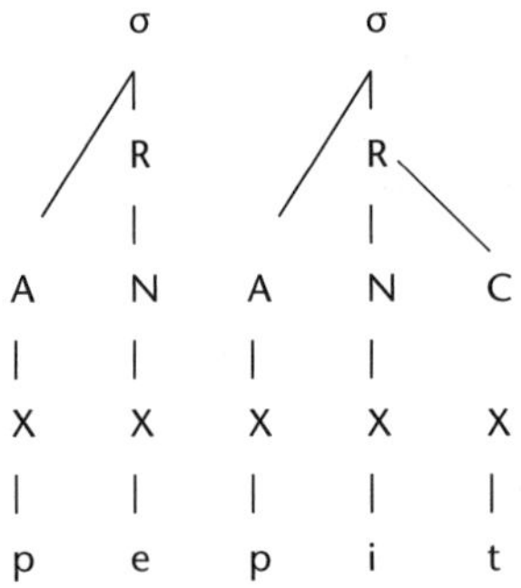

(2)

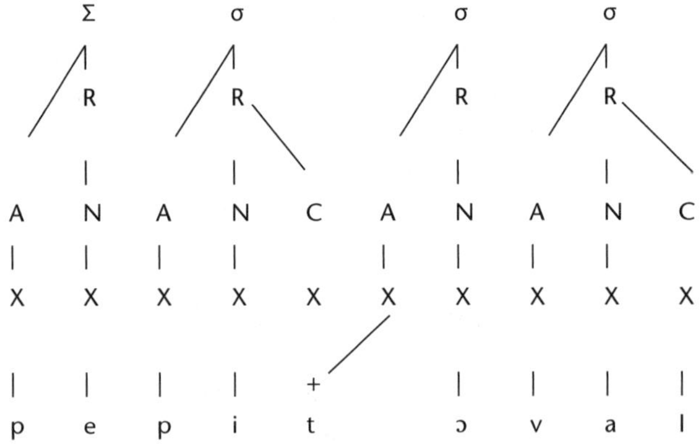

As Encrevé (1988) correctly pointed out, liaison in French is nothing but a particular case of enchainment, in other words, of the just mentioned resyllabification process of final consonants on the vocalic onset of the following word. What is then crucially important is to discover and understand the reason for such specificity. Enchainment by itself works in the same way in (2), with a fixed final consonant, as in (3a), with a LC. The only difference consists in the representation of LC in (3a). As the /t/ in *petit* is not linked to the skeleton, it does not need to be detached; the opposite is true for *pépite*.

(3a)

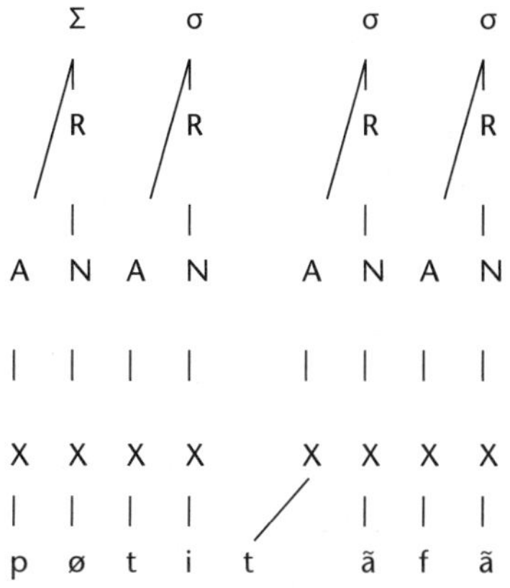

(3b)

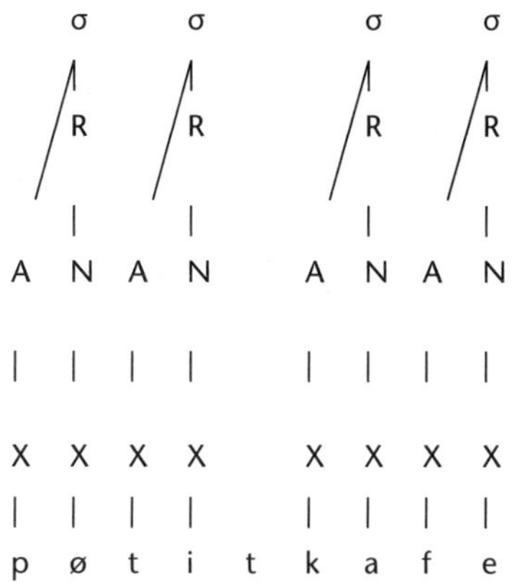

In [pøtikafe] (3b), enchainment cannot apply because the word onset is already associated to a position in the melodic tier; final /t/ remains therefore delinked, that is, unsyllabified and unrealized.

From the point of view of the general mechanism (the "rule"), then, liaison has nothing special. In liaison, enchainment applies, quite simply. The idea that there must be a rule in French to account for liaison, or rather for the nonapplication of liaison under certain circumstances, is an illusion introduced by the generative treatment proposed by Schane (1965). As a matter of fact, in Scheer's (2015) and Encrevé's (1988) accounts, the LC is always present in the lexical entry of W1. The regular case is when it is resyllabified to vowel-initial W2. When its resyllabification is blocked by the presence of an initial consonant in W2, enchainment does not apply. It can be deduced, then, that liaison is always virtually present; wherever consonant-vowel (CV) enchainment is possible, liaison occurs.

Now this view is profoundly false. Compare for instance *nous sommes des‿amis* 'we are friends' where liaison is obligatory, with *nous ne sommes pas/amis* 'we are not friends', where liaison is variable and in certain cases may not apply. In both cases, the segments involved are the same and syllable structure can be the same (unless resyllabification of

/s/ in *pas* is blocked by a different prosodic phrasing), but in *nous sommes des‿amis* the omission of /s/ resyllabification is disallowed: all French speakers, in all speech styles, will always produce liaison of the plural determinant. Not applying liaison here is equivalent to not speaking French. By contrast, not applying liaison after the negative particle *pas* is perfectly possible; in fact, in most styles, most French speakers do not link the /s/ of the negative particle. The question is therefore, why liaison is sometimes obligatory and sometimes variable in a given segmental and syllabic context.

Dell (1973) proposed to use two different labels, obligatory versus optional liaison. Yet, besides the fact that this labeling should be applied to each construction and therefore should again correspond to a lexical marking of each entry, the label of optional does not account for the existence of typical patterns of variation that differ according to the individual construction involved. In ordinary conversation, for instance, monosyllabic adverbs are linked three times more often, on average, than the negative adverb *pas* 'not' (see section 13.5.2 for further discussion). A similar case is illustrated in examples (4a) and (4b). The first corresponds to the construction *un petit‿écrou* 'a small nut', in which liaison is obligatory for all speakers, the second corresponds to *(un morceau de viande) petit/et cru* '(a) small and raw (piece of meat)', in which liaison is unequivocally prohibited. The segmental and syllabic contexts are however the same in the two cases.[5] It is not, therefore, at the phonological level that the asymmetry can be explained. The reasoning that is at issue here is well known. In recent times, it was fully developed by Morin (1986, 2003, 2005a, 2005b) and Morin and Kaye (1982): the constraints regulating French liaison are of a morphosyntactic, syntactic, or semantic nature. They have to be specified according to the individual construction types (see also Bybee 2001a, 2001b).

(4a)

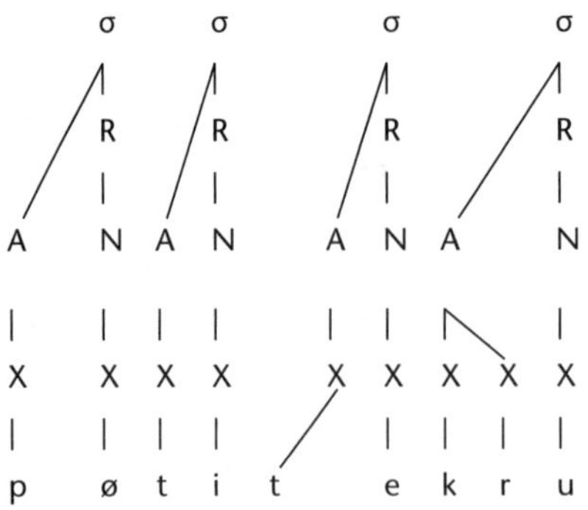

(4b)

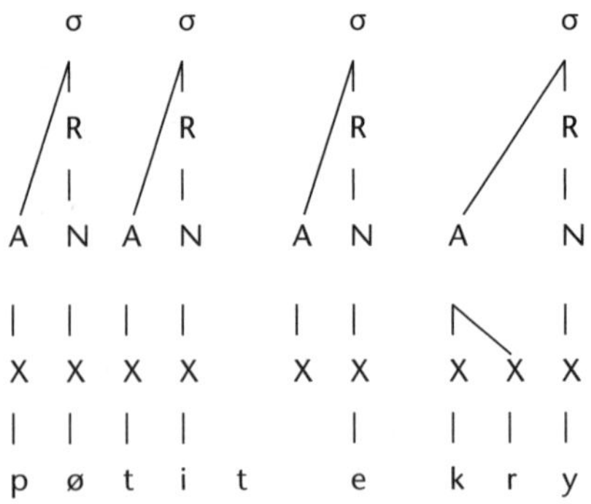

Before concluding, it is worth coming back to (2) and (3) once again. In (2), we have enchainment of a final consonant and in (3a) enchainment of a LC. From the formal point of view, both are to be interpreted as enchainment within phonological words. The question is, therefore, what distinguishes liaison from the other case. The answer comes from the diagrams: it is the representation of the LC. According to Encrevé (1988), LC is syllabically uninterpreted and lacks a position in the skeleton. Liaison formalization thus consists of this double floating. The effect of double floating on the mechanisms of enchainment has no particular specificity; rather, the general principles of enchainment are here at play. Now as Tranel (1995: 801) pointed out, this double floating acts as a diacritic. If *only* LC are marked by double floating,[6] and if *all* LC are, then the formal interpretation—in terms of information structure—must be that of a lexical marking, in other words, LC are marked as such in the lexical entry. After all, this is what Scheer said: "La consonne de liaison fait partie de l'information lexicale du mot qui la porte, et à ce titre son choix est arbitraire" ('the linking consonant is part of the lexical information of the word that carries it, and its choice is arbitrary' [2015: 99]).

This point is of crucial importance. In fact, in generative and postgenerative phonology, the interest is on the process, either derivational or not, that has to be formalized. Any proposed solution starts from the assumed lexical representation, on which the process applies. It is therefore on the assumed lexical representation that all analysis is developed; but this representation is most often only stipulated, never discussed in detail. As a result, the analysis, argumentation, and justification are not directed at the right target. Rather, it is on the postulated lexical information that the critical evaluation of the proposed treatment must focus. In the case of liaison, everything is definitively based on the lexical representation of the LC. Specifying a consonant as an LC already contains all the necessary information: an LC by definition is enchained to the following syllable if W2 begins with a vowel. There is no problem of phonological representation here. Should the final consonant of *petit* in (3a) be represented in the same way as other consonants, that is, linked and even syllabified, that will change absolutely nothing in the information available since it is lexically marked as LC and therefore subject to regular enchainment whenever possible, that is, before a vowel-initial word. The lexical marking of LC provides exactly the information needed; everything else is just redundant.[7]

In conclusion, the critical review of the formal analyses can be briefly summarized: French liaison cannot be said to be a phonological process *stricto sensu*. From the phonological point of view, liaison is the application of the general enchainment and resyllabification process that applies everywhere in the language. The phenomenology of liaison is rather accounted for by the specific lexical marking of some consonants; the analysis should therefore focus on the lexical status of LC and on the constraints regulating, at the level of the specific construction, its realization or nonrealization. As we have shown, this is precisely the position shared by all linguists up to the generative and postgenerative period. This is also the position shared, in most recent times, by numerous scholars attempting an analysis of the patterns of variation and the multiparametric constraints shaping liaison, based on corpus linguistics and the use of the speakers (see, e.g., Côté 2011; Durand et al. 2011; Laks, Calderone, and Celata 2014).

13.3. Status of the LC and the Structure of Lexical Information

In the history of liaison accounts, three analyses have been proposed for the status of the LC. The LC can be analyzed as latent or as epenthetic or the surface forms can be seen as suppletive (see Bonami and Boyé 2003; Bonami, Boyé, and Tseng 2005; Côté 2005, 2011, for bibliographical details). The analysis in terms of suppletion is based on the observation that a certain number of adjectives, pronouns, and determinants show two different forms when they precede a noun, depending on whether the latter begins by a vowel or a consonant. For example, we have *ce panneau* 'this panel' [søpano] but *cet‿anneau* 'this ring' [sɛtano], *beau camarade* 'nice comrade' [bokamarad] but *bel‿ami* 'good friend' [bɛlami], *mauvais compromis* 'bad trade-off' [movɛkõmprɔmi] but *mauvais‿argument* 'bad argument' [movɛzargymã]. The suppletion analysis assumes that the corresponding lexical entries have two different forms, one called "long" and the other called "short." The question of whether the long form corresponds to the feminine form (Durand 1936; Pichon 1938) is not at issue here. What is important is that in the suppletive analysis, lexical information must include which form occurs before a vowel-initial W2, thus which form occurs under the liaison condition. It is therefore not the LC that is lexically marked, but rather the suppletive form itself, since the alternation is more complex than the simple surfacing of a *consonne muette*. As a matter of fact, if we consider the lexical information in itself, both for the quality and the quantity of nonredundant information, the two solutions are almost equivalent. Marking *petit* 'small' either with an LC /t/ or with two suppletive forms [pøti] and [pøtit], the second being the one selected for liaison, does not involve any informational difference. For the enchainment process, whether W2 selects the LC or the long form of W1, the result is the same.

The second analysis, that of LC as latent consonant, is reminiscent of what Pichon (1938: 26) first proposed. A latent consonant is grammatically present but cannot be pronounced. As already mentioned, generative and postgenerative analyses systematically adopted this solution by putting the LC in the lexical form and by trying to formalize the conditions according to which the LC does not appear on the surface. The analysis by latency opens the question of the motivation of the latent consonant. The latent consonant has often been motivated by orthography. Orthographic consonants are stored in what Martinon (1913: 356) ironically called *le conservatoire ou musée des liaisons* 'the repository or museum of liaisons'; in metropolitan French, any LC is necessarily an orthographic consonant. However, the reverse is not equally true, since not all orthographic consonants are LC (/t/ in *et* 'and', /p/ in *champ* 'field', /s/ in *univers* 'universe' are never linked). What is even more important, assuming that latency derives from orthography implies a vision of the relation between spoken and written language that is questionable to say the least (Damourette and Pichon 1911–1927; Laks 2005).[8] In the opinion of Damourette and Pichon, the latent consonant can only be motivated from an internal point of view. A lexical unit can manifest itself in several forms and its alternation is caused by the latent consonant. Thus, for both the quality and the quantity of lexical information, the latency view and the suppletion view are essentially the same. As in the case of suppletion, it is impossible to rely on the derivational root because there are examples of consonants with paradigmatic motivation that do not trigger liaison: compare *petit* 'small', *petitesse* 'smallness', *petitement* 'in a small way', *petit ⁀ ami* 'small friend' with *temps* 'time', *temporaire* 'temporary', *temporal* 'temporal', *temps/épouvantable* 'frightful time'. Marking the latent consonant as LC is therefore a notational variant of the analysis by suppletion.

The third solution consists in analyzing the LC as an epenthetic consonant (see Côté 2011, 2014, for a discussion). It is true that in some varieties of French, notably in Canada, there are purely epenthetic consonants that are neither orthographic, nor paradigmatic, and even less normative. Treating the LC as an epenthetic consonant implies establishing which word the epenthesis applies to. Côté (2011, 2014) explained at length the arguments in favor of W1 and those supporting

W2 as the word to which the epenthetic consonant belongs. When this consonant is a number or person morpheme (e.g., *petits ⁀ amis* 'small friends', *nous⁀avons* 'we have'), the most coherent analysis consists in saying that number is marked at the beginning of the word when the word begins by a vowel and therefore in attributing this marking to W2. Although this analysis is in apparent contradiction with orthography, scholars such as Gougenheim (1938), Morin and Kaye (1982), and Morin (1986) proposed very solid arguments in support of it (Côté 2011). The problem of epenthetic consonant linking is not of primary importance here. If, on the one hand, the LC is linked to W1, from the point of view of informational structure, epenthesis parallels suppletion: determinants and pronouns have two forms, one short before consonants and one long before vowels. But for these grammatical categories, liaison (and therefore enchainment) is mandatory and stable. These are constructions stored as such. If, on the other hand, the LC is linked to W2, nothing changes to the extent that we are always left with a mandatory, enchained liaison and lexically represented constructions. In other words, the proclitics are part of the same construction as the following word and *petits⁀amis* 'small friends' or *nous⁀avons* 'we have' are one word each.[9]

In this section, we have thus examined the lexical status of LC and concluded that liaison is not a phonological process. Rather, liaison derives from the specific lexical marking of some forms that are subject to the phonological process of enchainment before an initial vowel. However, not all lexical units that have the same LC marking behave the same. What still has to be done, thus, is to analyze the patterns of variation that characterize each class of lexical units or even each unit. To perform such an analysis, we have to turn to corpus linguistics, which is the only empirical instrument allowing a solid investigation of what speakers really do.

13.4. The PFC Database and Variation in Usage

In the domain of speech uses, native speaker intuition is particularly erratic and when a speaker categorically claims that he/she pronounces something in a given way, it often happens that he/she is immediately contradicted by the spontaneous use of a different pronunciation variant (Laks 2008). Moreover, if variation is present, individual intuitions completely miss the point. The investigation paradigm must therefore be radically different and rely on corpus linguistics to document actual usages and variation patterns to the extent that they are present within a linguistic community. This is particularly true for liaison, which is a central locus of variation in French.

In order to detect the relevant parameters shaping usage variability in liaison, it is therefore necessary to rely on a large corpus of spoken French, such as the PFC corpus (Durand, Laks, and Lyche 2013; http://www.projet-pfc.net/). At present, PFC includes data from 38 surveys conducted in 35 cities or regions of 8 different francophone countries. The database includes the recordings of 418 different speakers (239 female and 191 male) varying for age, sociocultural background, and educational level.

The data set used in this study included 27,788 liaison sites, of which were 11,761 with realized liaison and 16,027 with nonrealized liaison. These were extracted from free conversations of forty-eight francophone speakers aged ten to ninety (average: forty-eight years old) and recorded in one of the forty-three geographical points of the PFC survey.[10] Of the total 27,788 liaison sites, W1 is monosyllabic in 19,814 cases, while it is disyllabic in 7,969 cases. Monosyllabic left words are not only more frequent, but also more frequently targeted by a realized than by a nonrealized liaison: of the 19,814 left monosyllables, 11,484 have a realized liaison, whereas of the 7,969 disyllables, only 273 have a realized liaison. This ratio thus confirms previous knowledge about the preference for liaison to be triggered by monosyllables (e.g., Durand et al. 2011).

13.5. The Empirical Analysis

13.5.1. Motivation and Hypotheses

The analysis proposed here is a follow-up to our previous work on liaison based on the PFC data set (Laks et al. 2014). In that essay, we showed that the distribution of realized liaison is similar to a power-law distribution inasmuch as a few types of W1_L_W2 word chunks (L indicates liaison) are ranked high for frequency of occurrence and account for approximately half of the total observations. A restricted set of liaison environments has a very high frequency of occurrence in the corpus and this set does not change substantially if we vary the age of the speakers or their educational status. By contrast, a large "periphery" of infrequent uses, and particularly the set of very infrequent environments, accounts for some aspects of style- and speaker-dependent variation. We interpreted these results as consistent with the general usage-based hypothesis: liaison is more frequently realized in those word groups that have strong internal cohesion and high frequency of co-occurrence (see Bybee 2001a and Chevrot, Nardy, and Barbu 2011 for an acquisitional point of view). However, the results also demonstrated that mnesic storage of high-frequency and highly cohesive structures cannot alone explain the complex mechanism regulating the realization of liaison in French, since the remaining 50 percent of realized liaisons was accounted for by a large number of low-frequency structures that partly varied across different subsets defined by external (sociostylistic) factors. Thus the conclusion was that, for the corpus-based lexicalist view to account for the whole process, we need to analyze the properties of those variable environments occupying the "tail" of the function and to differentiate among reasoned subsets of the PFC corpus that can be defined according to sociostylistic parameters.

The present study also capitalizes on the results obtained on a study of a large corpus of political speech recordings covering the 1999–2015 period and on the comparison with similar corpora covering earlier temporal intervals from the beginning of the twentieth century to 1998 (Laks and Peuvergne 2017). Three issues in particular were of interest for the present study: the relationship between realized and nonrealized (or "virtual") liaisons, the distinction between obligatory and variable liaison, and the changes occurring in the production of liaison over the last fifteen years.

As a matter of fact, the global rate of liaison and the relationship between realized and nonrealized liaisons appeared to be remarkably stable in time (66 percent in 1908–1998 political speeches, 57 percent in 1999–2015). However, as for the distinction between obligatory and variable liaison, the picture was very different. Although the global rate of realized liaison appeared quite stable across the generations of French politicians, the behavior of some sets of words exhibiting optional liaison was rapidly changing. Thus, the probability with which optional liaisons occur changes over time.

In the same paper, Laks and Peuvergne (2017) also showed that two different phenomena are at play under the name of liaison.

On the one hand, there is a phenomenon of obligatory linking, which is extremely stable and invariant across decades, as manifested by the analysis in apparent time. This is the case of determiners, monosyllabic prepositions, personal pronouns, and adjectives in prenominal position, which are permanently linked to the following word (the rate of non-realized liaison, around 1–2 percent for these words, can be conceived of as "noise"). This categorical phenomenon is stable not only in time but also in space and style. Indeed, as many linguists and grammarians have suggested, there are word chunks constituted by frozen liaisons (e.g., *nous allons* 'we go'), which function as single words for all French speakers and all speaking situations (Gougenheim et al. 1956; Morin and Kaye 1982; Tranel 1987).

On the other hand, another set of categories whose members oscillate between realization and nonrealization of liaison, and sometimes differ within the same category (e.g., within adverbs, *bien* 'well' realizes liaison in 65 percent of cases, whereas the negative adverb *pas* realizes liaison in only 13.5 percent of cases), must be considered as the locus of a specific variable liaison phenomenon that is crucially sensitive to diachronic, as well as stylistic and geographic, changes. In this perspective, distinguishing between obligatory and variable liaison is crucial not only to account for ongoing changes in French phonology, but it is also of prime importance for our general understanding of the liaison phenomenon itself, of its real status in the concrete uses of speakers, and of its probable representation at the cognitive level.

Based on these premises, we will now discuss our quantitative analysis of the distributional properties of French liaison in the PFC corpus. Our methodology was the following. We started with the entire data set of left words (W1) potentially triggering liaison, as they are coded in the PFC corpus, thus including the contexts with and without overt realization of the LC. Stated differently, for each W1 coded as a potential liaison site in the PFC corpus (i.e., each LC-ending word followed by a vowel-initial word), we took into account not only the number of times in which the liaison was actually produced (realized liaisons, as in Laks et al. 2014), but also the number of times in which the word was produced *without* overt production of the LC (nonrealized liaison). By considering all this information, we obtained a different picture of what is the "core" and what is the "periphery" of the liaison phenomenon. In particular, this methodology enabled us to distinguish between liaisons that are infrequently realized because the corresponding W1 is infrequent in the corpus, and liaisons that are infrequently realized because the corresponding W1 is preferably produced with a nonrealized liaison. In the latter case, the word can in principle have a very high frequency of occurrence in the corpus with a vowel-initial word following it, but if it is produced more often *without* an overt pronunciation of LC, then it will be ranked low (i.e., lower than another word that is preferentially produced with overt realization of the LC).

The difference with respect to Laks et al. (2014), therefore, is that in the current study, we did not simply count the number of realized liaisons for a given word; rather, we determined the ratio between realized and nonrealized liaisons. An additional difference, as already pointed out, is that in the Laks et al. (2014) essay, the object of the analysis was the entire liaison environment (i.e., the W1_L_W2 word chunk), whereas here we focused on the left word (W1) only. Our analysis of W1 was in two steps: W1s were first considered in themselves, as lexemes, and then coded according to their grammatical category (or part of speech [POS]). As for the data set, it was first considered in its entirety, then subdivided into four subsets according to four age groups.

13.5.2. Results: Lexical Information Encoded in the LC, and Age-Related Differences

Figure 13.1 shows the entire data set of W1 that are coded as potential liaison sites in PFC (we excluded words with a frequency of less than twenty occurrences). The figure displays the percentage of realized and nonrealized liaisons. The values are normalized to 100 percent occurrences in each category.[11] There are 120 words altogether, of which 8 have 100 percent realized liaisons and 53 have 100 percent nonrealized liaisons. To the group of W1 with obligatorily realized liaison, one should also add another ten to thirteen words for which the percentage of realized liaison is equal to or higher than 93–95 percent, considering, as we have already said, that 5–8 percent of idiosyncratic productions can reasonably be considered irrelevant exceptions or "noise" due to the dimensions of the data set. We thus ended up with a set of 18–21 left words, out of 120, which categorically trigger overt pronunciation of the LC. The ratio is therefore one of very strong imbalance toward noncategorical liaison.

Our corpus perspective with a focus on W1 thus appears to strongly support the view that, basically, obligatory and variable liaisons are two very different phenomena. As the fine-grained morpholexical, syntactic, and prosodic analysis of those environments in which external sandhi is mandatory has previously suggested (based on structural and formal arguments), the obligatory contexts are the results of a morpholexical fusion of syntactically and morphopragmatically strongly interconnected items. Remember for instance that Martinet (1965) claimed that *je la lui*

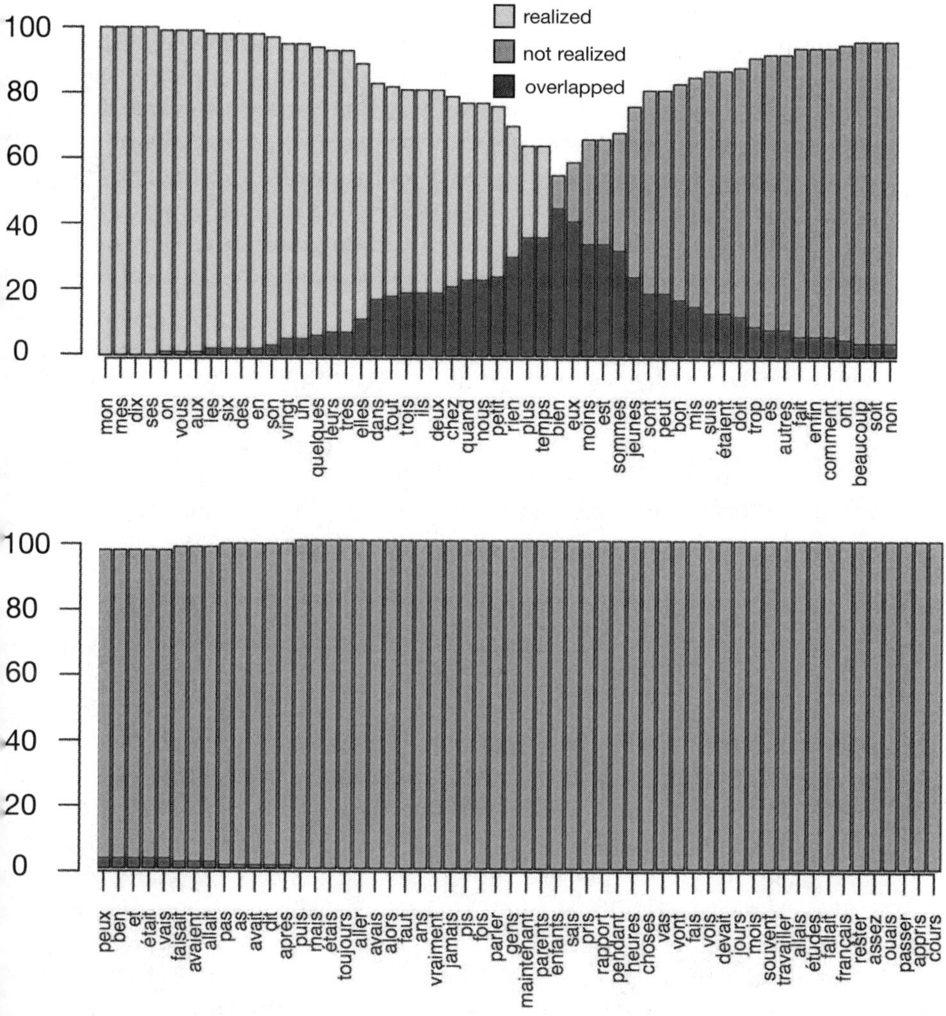

13.1 Percentages of realized and nonrealized liaisons for W1 (frequency > 20) in the PFC corpus.

donne 'I give it to her' is a single word in current French. What we are showing here, from the point of view of concrete linguistic productions and with arguments related to the statistics of the liaison lexicon, is that these suggestions are confirmed. A few items and a few construction types account for obligatory liaison production while many items and construction types trigger liaison variably. Obligatory and variable liaison are thus to be coded as different processes in the grammar.

If, as suggested, categorical liaison is a phenomenon of freezing that applies to strongly fused constructions, then these eighteen to twenty-one items in figure 13.1 that show categorically realized liaison should share some morpholexical characteristics that favor W1-W2 fusion, and then freezing. As much of the literature suggests, this should be the case for clitics (pronouns, articles, etc.), words included in idioms, and pseudo-prepositions functioning as prefixes in fixed expressions. Figure 13.2 shows that this is indeed the case for our data set and confirms previous analyses. Figure 13.2 zooms in on the subset of W1 with at least 4 percent of realized liaisons.

The first twenty words from the bottom of the diagram are possessive adjectives (*nos* 'our [pl.]', *ses* 'his/her [pl.]', *mes* 'my [pl.]', *mon* 'my [m.sg.]', *son* 'his/her [m.sg]', *leurs* 'their [pl.]'), demonstratives (*ces* 'these'), personal pronouns (*on* 'one', *vous* 'you [2nd pl.]'), articles or prepositions + articles (*aux* 'to the [pl.]', *les* 'the [pl.]', *des* '[of] the [pl.]', *un* 'a/an'), the *en* particle ('of it/of which/there', which can act as a pronoun, a preposition, or an adverb), quantifiers/numerals (*huit* 'eight', *dix* 'ten', *six* 'six', *vingt* 'twenty', *quelques* 'some [pl.]'), and the high-frequency adverb *très* 'very'. It is not surprising that they regularly occur with realized liaison, given their grammatically dependent status and their degree of prosodic and syntactic cohesion with the following word. What is more relevant, however, is that, although possessive adjectives are always ranked very high in the diagram (no possessive adjectives actually occur in the diagram except for those with categorically realized liaison), other categories can also appear at lower rankings in the diagram. So for instance, among personal pronouns, *ils* 'they' has 19 percent of nonrealized liaisons, *nous* 'we' has 23 percent; among quantifiers, *deux* 'two' and *trois* 'three' have 19 percent of nonrealized liaisons; the high-frequency adverb *plus* 'more' has 36 percent.

These data therefore suggest that, if one looks at grammatical categories instead of individual items, the truly obligatory liaisons are even more restricted.

In addition, and more importantly, there appears to be no way of capturing the behavioral difference between *on* and *ils*, or between *huit* and *trois*, in purely grammatical or structural terms. The difference, though small, is rather a matter of usage distributions related to the specific occurrences in the specific data set (and finally, to the identity of W2). Ultimately, what the corpus data really suggest is that there is a residual of variation between items, an inherent probability that is likely to be ascribed to the lexical entry itself.

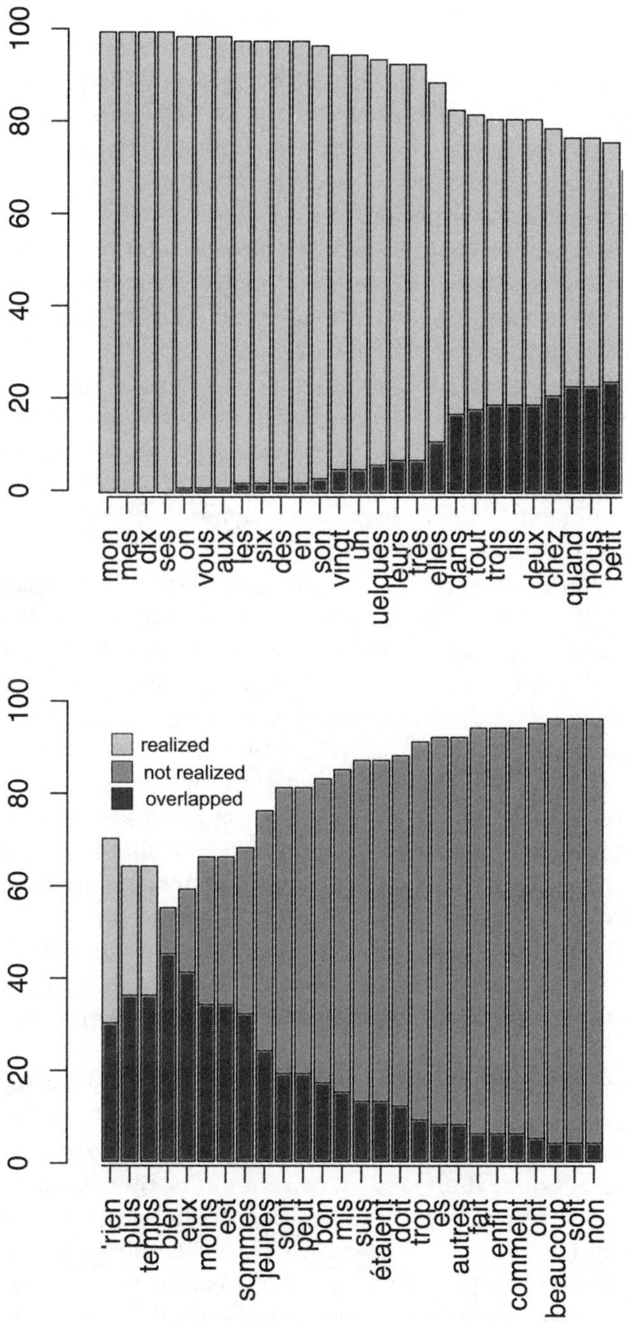

13.2 Zoom-in on the subset of W1 with at least 4 percent of realized liaisons in the PFC corpus.

Besides the small group of items with categorical or quasi-categorical overt realization of the LC, figures 13.1 and 13.2 also show that a large part of the liaison domain is occupied by items with variable realization. These are prepositions, mono- and disyllabic adjectives and nouns, and verbal forms. For nouns and verbs, the syntactic category of W2 is less predictable and consequently the ratio of realized/nonrealized liaison strongly decreases, as expected.

Both figures thus confirm what we have previously found, but from a different perspective: the number of items (or environments, in Laks et al. [2014]) accounting for variable liaison is higher than the number of items accounting for invariable liaison.

According to figure 13.1, the number of items accounting for potential but unrealized liaison is even greater: in trivially quantitative terms, there are at least as many consonant-final W1+vowel-initial W2 that *do not* trigger liaison (because of the lack of necessary morpholexical, syntactic, and pragmatic requisites), as consonant-final W1+vowel-initial W2 that *do* trigger (variable) liaison.

Although this observation may sound irrelevant, it is nevertheless revealing of the very nature of liaison: it is certainly not a phonological phenomenon (contrary to earlier views; see section 13.1), but rather a multicausal pronunciation process rooted in complex statistical dynamics of the language. As suggested by some linguists on more intuitive grounds (e.g., Damourette and Pichon 1911–1927), in variable contexts, nonliaison seems to be the rule and liaison the marked case.

As we anticipated, looking at grammatical categories seems to produce different pictures of the relationship between realized and nonrealized liaisons. To test this, we plotted the same data set of figure 13.2, with the frequency of occurrence of realized and nonrealized liaison, as a function of the words' grammatical categories (figure 13.3). The POS tags correspond to those used in the French TreeTagger (Schmid 1997).[12] As we have already discussed, the values are normalized to 100 percent occurrences in each category.

At the bottom of the diagram, the three categories of possessives, articles, and prepositions+articles are produced with realized liaison in almost 100 percent of their corpus occurrences. As already specified, percentages of nonliaison below 5 percent can be considered "noise" due to the size of the data set. By contrast, at the top of the diagram, verbs, adverbs, and nouns are produced with realized liaison only in a minority of their occurrences (around 10 percent). As already mentioned, this is most likely due to the variety of constructions that are possible with a

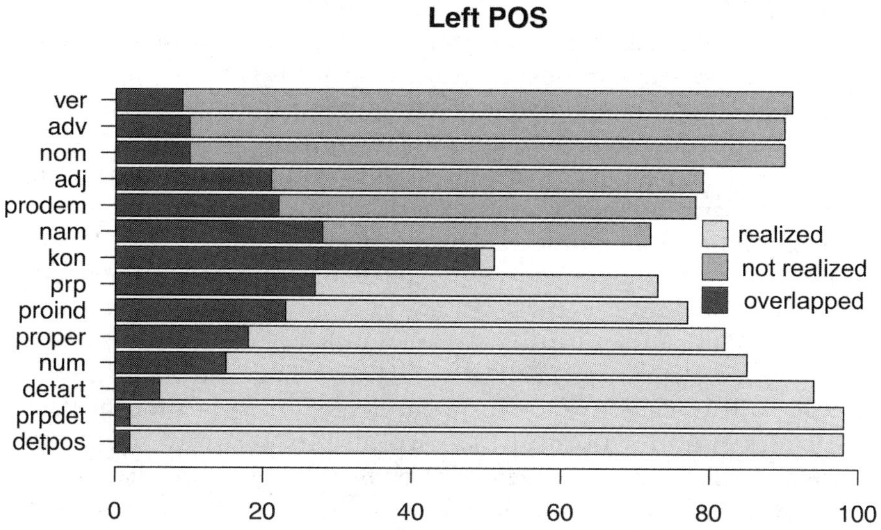

13.3 Percentages of realized and nonrealized liaisons for each grammatical category (POS) of W1 in the PFC corpus.

verb, adverb, or noun followed by a vowel-initial word: those with the necessary degree of syntactic, prosodic, or even pragmatic cohesion between W1 and W2 for the realization of liaison (most of which are frozen expressions) are comparatively few. In the middle of the diagram, the category of conjunctions is the one with the most variable liaison behavior: in our corpus, the choice between realization and nonrealization is apparently random. Adjectives, demonstrative pronouns, and proper names are more often uttered with nonrealized than with realized liaison; by contrast, prepositions, indefinite pronouns, personal pronouns and numerals tend to exhibit realized more often than nonrealized liaison.

By comparing figure 13.3 with figure 13.2, the most striking difference concerns the personal pronouns: as we said, items such as *on* and *vous* were categorically linked and appeared to fall under the label of obligatory liaison, whereas items such as *ils* and *nous* showed variability (figure 13.2). The result is that the category of personal pronouns in itself comprises a high degree of cross-item variation (figure 13.3). A similar pattern emerges for numerals (recall the difference between *huit* and *trois* in figure 13.2) or demonstrative pronouns (recall that *ces* was ranked the highest, i.e., 100 percent realized liaison, in figure 13.2).

Cross-item variation is different from within-item variation (characterizing, e.g., all verbal forms, which are variably produced with or without overt pronunciation of the LC). If we look at liaison from the classical point of view of morphosyntactic classes, the two types of variability produce the same result: a grammatical category that variably realizes liaison. As we have anticipated, however, this is not the whole story. Part of the behavior is linked to the intrinsic probability that an individual item, pertaining to a given grammatical category, has of overtly linking itself to the following word. W1-W2 cohesion is, thus, an issue not only for obligatory liaison (as classical usage-based approaches suggested, e.g., Bybee 2001a), but for variable liaison as well, as initially suggested by some classical analyses (e.g., Martinon 1913; Grammont 1914). This is even more evident if we compare our findings of 2014 with the data depicted in figures 13.2 and 13.3. According to Laks et al. (2014: 40, table 1), the ten most frequent environments with realized liaison (in terms of token frequency in the corpus) are made of a personal pronoun (*on* 'one', *ils* 'they'), an indefinite pronoun (*en* 'of it'), a conjunction (*quand* 'when'), a preposition (*dans* 'in'), and a quantifier (*deux* 'two') as W1 (and a verb, a noun, a pronoun, or a determiner as W2). According to figure 13.2 here, only *on* and *en* fall within the group of obligatory liaisons; the remaining four words show a percentage of nonrealized liaison oscillating between 17 percent (for *dans*) and 23 percent (for *quand*). Moreover, from the point of view of their grammatical category, none of them fall into one of the three grammatical categories that, according to figure 13.3, obligatorily produce liaison (possessives, articles, and prepositions+articles).

These findings lead us to an additional observation. From the point of view of token frequencies, French speakers are exposed to a small set of environments with realized liaison that occur very frequently in the spoken language. For at least some of them, however, W1 can be produced, in different environments, with nonrealized liaison; alternatively, there are other W1s pertaining to the same grammatical category, which can be produced with nonrealized liaison. Then, the conclusion will necessarily be that the liaison phenomenon *in itself* is stored as a variable process. If the most frequent "exemplars" are those that produce stronger mnesic traces, figures 13.2 and 13.3 tell us that at least some of these mnesic traces are automatically associated to variable liaison. If *quand_L_on* is one of the most frequently occurring environments in the corpus (absolute token frequencies), then the mnesic traces associated to this environment will include 23 percent of nonrealized liaisons as well.

As suggested in our previous work (Laks et al. 2014), the contexts with a highly variable rate of liaison realization are the most probable loci of variation across groups of individuals or speaking styles. The analysis of the ratio between realized and nonrealized liaison in terms of grammatical categories, shown in figure 13.3, called for further exploration in this direction.

We therefore subdivided the data set into four subgroups, according to the age of the speakers. This was possible thanks to the large number of speakers included in the PFC corpus. The first group (that of "very young" speakers) comprised speakers between ten and twenty years of age (1,200 liaison contexts, both realized and nonrealized). The second group (that of "young" speakers) comprised speakers between twenty-one and forty years of age (6,000 liaison contexts). The third group (that of "middle-aged" speakers) comprised speakers between forty-one and sixty years of age (5,500 liaison contexts). Finally, the fourth group (that of "old" speakers) comprised speakers between sixty-one and ninety years of age (4,100 liaison contexts). For the four subgroups, the percentages of realized and nonrealized liaisons as a function of W1 grammatical category were plotted (as was previously done for the whole data set). The results are given in figure 13.4.

Figure 13.4 shows that some of the patterns are kept constant across the age groups. Not surprisingly, this is true for the three categories of categorically realized liaison, that is, articles, possessives, and prepositions+articles. The absence of variation for the subset of obligatory liaison is a further confirmation of the categorical status of LC and the frozen nature of the constructions in these particular contexts. Similarly, adverbs, verbs, and nouns are rarely produced with realized liaison in any of the four subgroups, as was to be expected given the variety of constructions in which these words can be included.

For the group of very young speakers, however, the category of demonstrative pronouns is also ranked among the lowest in the percentage of realized liaison; this is in striking opposition with the 42 percent of realized liaisons in the subgroup of old speakers. Recall that in the analysis of the whole data set, one of the indefinite pronouns, *ces*, had 100 percent realized liaison.

Similarly, indefinite pronouns (*tout* 'all/any', *chacun* 'each', *certain* 'some') are produced with a higher percentage of realized liaisons in the oldest group (almost 90 percent, which puts this grammatical category closer to the ones with categorically realized liaison), compared to middle-aged and young speakers (around 75 percent) and to the youngest ones (less than 70 percent).

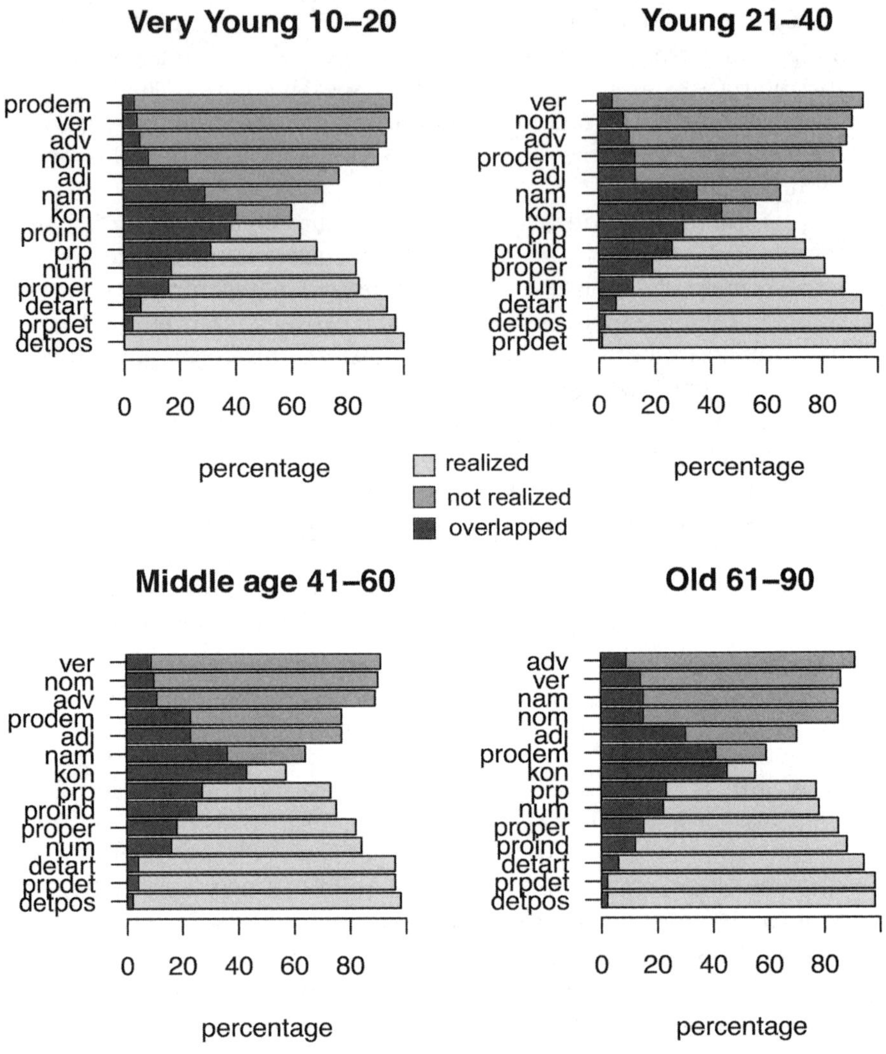

13.4 Percentages of realized and nonrealized liaisons for each grammatical category of the W1 across the age groups.

As for conjunctions, there is a strong opposition between young and very young speakers, on one hand, who tend to produce conjunctions with nonrealized liaison, and middle-aged and old speakers, on the other hand, who tend to produce conjunctions with realized liaison. As Laks and Peuvergne (2017) showed for political speech, the category of conjunctions is of particular interest for liaison because the number of

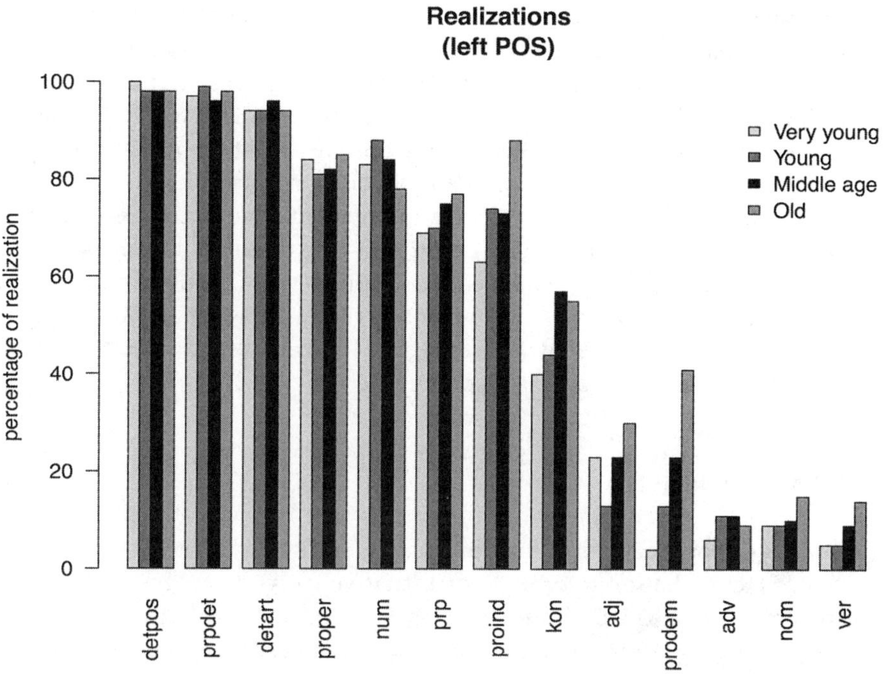

13.5 Percentages of realized liaisons for each grammatical category (POS) of the W1 across the age groups.

items included in it is relatively small (i.e., *et* 'and', *mais* 'but', *quand* 'when'), but individual behavior is highly varied: *quand* 'when' is almost categorical in realizing liaison, whereas *mais* 'but' is much more variable. This fact is even more significant if one considers that all these items necessarily have a very high token frequency in a speech corpus, independently of any social characteristics of the speaker or stylistic factor. From the data in figure 13.4, it appears that the higher the age of the speakers, the more frequently the liaison is realized. It could therefore be hypothesized that the decline in liaison production among the youngest speakers is motivated by a gradual erosion of liaison in some of the conjunctions, which are evidently less resistant to change. This hypothesis needs to be validated by an in-depth analysis of the data relative to this word set. But if it was confirmed, conjunctions, given their bipartite behavior between the youngest and the oldest speakers, could be one of the most significant loci of age-related variation in the production of liaison.

A better visualization of these patterns of age-related variation can be seen in figure 13.5. It plots the percentage of realized liaison for each grammatical category as a function of the age of the speakers. It basically confirms that the most striking differences, with liaison realization decreasing from the oldest to the youngest speakers, are to be seen in the domain of highly variable liaison categories (right half of the diagram). In particular, liaison appears to have dramatically diminished in the production of indefinite and demonstrative pronouns and of conjunctions.

These data on diachronic change in apparent time can be related to the findings in Laks and Peuvergne (2017) concerning political speech. In that paper, an abrupt change in the youngest generations of politicians (particularly female ones) was observed, with a global decrease in the rate of realized liaison. The PFC data illustrated here seem to confirm this evolution in ordinary speech.

13.6. Conclusion

We have proposed a corpus-based analysis of the distributional properties of French liaison in order to quantitatively investigate the variation in the liaison lexicon. We focused on left words (W1) that potentially trigger liaisons. All the potential liaison words retrieved from the PFC corpus were analyzed, thus including the contexts with and without overt realization of the LC. Left words were first considered as lexemes, and then coded according to their grammatical category (POS).

Consistently with the results of Laks et al. (2014), the results showed that a large part of the liaison domain is occupied by lexical items produced with variable realization, whereas a few construction types account for obligatory liaison. This tendency is also confirmed by the grammatical category tagging in which, with the exception of three categories (possessives, articles, and prepositions+articles) showing a robust regularity of liaison realization, the remaining categories present variation in the ratio between realized and nonrealized liaison.

This kind of variation has also been analyzed across age groups (old, middle-aged, young, and very young speakers). Although some of the patterns were stable across the groups (i.e., mandatory liaison with articles, possessives, and prepositions+articles), aspects of age-related variation emerged from the data. In particular, conjunctions and indefinite and demonstrative pronouns were produced with realized liaison by the oldest speakers much more frequently than by the youngest speakers. This suggested that a diachronic process of decline in liaison realization is at place in current French, at least for those item classes characterized by optional liaison.

We believe that these results are of interest for at least three reasons. First, our analyses confirm that obligatory liaison is triggered by no more than twenty left words (W1) and three grammatical categories, thus representing the minority of liaisons in actual usages. The great majority is represented by variable liaison. Variation in liaison realization refers to two different phenomena, that we have called within- and cross-item variation. Within-item variation means that one and the same W1 can be produced with or without realized liaison. For instance, conjunctions such as *mais* 'but' are variably linked to the following vowel-initial word. The reason of this kind of variation is likely to be related to the degree of cohesiveness of the W1-W2 individual construction in which a given W1 is included, that is, in essence, to the nature of W2. Cross-item variation refers to the fact that, within one and the same grammatical category, two W1s that should behave the same given the identity of their morphosyntactic and phonological characteristics, behave differently instead. For instance, within the class of personal pronouns, items such as *on* 'one' and *vous* 'you (pl.)' are produced with 100 percent realized liaison, whereas items such as *ils* 'they' and *nous* 'we' are produced with nonrealized liaison in about 20 percent of the cases. We have proposed that the reason of this kind of variation is to be seen in the intrinsic liaison probability of each individual item, in other words, an inherent property of lexical items that is irreducible to any other plausible dimension of variation.

The second point of interest consists of the fact that speakers of different ages differ in the rate of realized liaison for a subset of categories triggering variable liaison. This is likely to represent the manifestation in apparent time of a diachronic change progressively leading to a decrease in the rate of realized liaison in the speech of the youngest speakers. Future analyses will have to ascertain whether this process is predominantly a change in within-item variation (that is, W1s with variable liaison are increasingly realized with no liaison) or a change in cross-item variation (that is, the number of W1s triggering obligatory liaison decreases and the number of W1s triggering variable liaison increases). It is however worth repeating that change and variation seem to affect (a subset of) categories triggering variable liaison; the nucleus of categories triggering obligatory liaison tends to remain unaffected by change.

As a third and last point, we want to highlight that our corpus analysis allows putting forth hypotheses about the status of liaison in the cognitive representation of the speakers. As a matter of fact, thanks to the comparison with the absolute frequencies of liaison environments of Laks et al. (2014), it has been shown that many of the liaison environments occurring with the highest token frequency in the corpus (e.g., the adverb *quand* 'when' + vowel-initial word) are made of left words that can be produced with nonrealized liaison, thus pertaining to the set of words triggering variable (or optional) liaison. This result demonstrates that the strongest mnesic traces are automatically associated to variable, not obligatory, liaison. We then argue that liaison in itself is likely to be stored as a variable process.

Notes

1. That is, twenty-six examples for truncation and elision, fourteen for fixed final consonants and the numeral adjectives, three for *h aspiré*, two for hiatus, twenty for junctures within the verbal phrase and inversions, and eight for postposed pronouns. An additional twenty-two examples are in the footnotes.
2. Vowel elision is the loss of a vowel before a vowel: *le palais* [løpalɛ] versus *l'hotel* [lotɛl], *la semaine* [lasəmɛn] versus *l'année* [lane].
3. "Elision and liaison can be considered as the same process: . . . a final vowel is deleted or truncated before another word beginning with a vowel, whereas a final consonant is deleted before another word beginning with a consonant. In order to be neutral between the terms elision and absence of liaison, we shall often refer to this one and the same process as truncation" (Schane 1965: 92).
4. Enchainment is very widespread and productive in French and is not limited to CV only. Enchainment also applies in VV, CC, and VC sequences and produces a resyllabification of the sequence to produce a single phonological word as in the classic example *je suis parti si vite que je n'ai pas pris le temps de mettre mon chapeau* 'I left so quickly that I didn't get even the time of wearing my hat', produced as [ʒœsɥipartisivitkœʒœnɛpaprilœtãdœmɛtr mõʃapo].
5. In addition, (4b) is ill formed. According to Scheer and Encrevé's (2015) phonological account, when enchainment does not occur, a glottal stop intervenes, occupying the empty onset, and the floating /t/ is syllabified as W1 coda. This gives a nonenchained liaison: [pøtit?ekry]. This mechanism was initially introduced to account for the nonenchainment observed in the public speech of French politicians. For cases such as (4b), the two authors would simply label liaison, and therefore enchainment, as impossible. But this marking is not phonological in essence. It is rather a lexical label of the specific construction, which is precisely the point that we make in this chapter.
6. To the best of our knowledge, double floating has not been introduced for any other process of any other language outside French liaison.

7. It is worth noticing that Scheer (2015: 100) presented at the beginning the formal and notational framework of the phonology he proposed. Then, he pointed out that double floating is a formal possibility. He finally concluded, concerning liaison: "La prédiction autosegmentale que [le double flottement] existe réellement dans les langues est donc un succès au vu de la liaison en français—un bon point pour notre cadre théorique" 'The autosegmenal prediction that [double floating] really exists in languages is then a success for French liaison—and a good point for our theoretical framework'. This is a clear demonstration of the reversed perspective highlighted by Goldsmith and Laks (2000: 3) and mentioned in section 13.1.
8. Schane (1967: 57) and Dell (1973: 45) supported the partial parallelism between abstract lexical forms and orthographic forms.
9. This was indeed the case in Latin; in French, the orthographic separation oscillated for a long time (Marchello-Nizia 1999).
10. In 99.5 percent of the cases in the PFC corpus, the realized liaison consonant is linked (nonenchainment being represented by an extremely reduced number of occurrences, which justifies treating it as an exception in ordinary speech; see section 13.5.2 and Laks and Peuvergne 2017).
11. The bars represent the ratio between realized and nonrealized liaisons for each item, independently of the frequency of occurrence of the items themselves.
12. According to the French tag set available at http://www.cis.uni-muenchen.de/~schmid/tools/TreeTagger/data/french-tagset.html, ver=verb (e.g., *est* '[it] is'), adv=adverb (e.g., *bien* 'well', *plus* 'more'), nom=noun (e.g., *temps* 'time'), adj=adjective (e.g., *petit* 'small', *neuf* 'new'), prodem=demonstrative pronoun (e.g., *ces* 'these'), nam=proper name (e.g., *Paris, Aveyron*), kon=conjunction (e.g., *mais* 'but', *quand* 'when'), prp=preposition (e.g., *avant* 'before', *dans* 'in', *en* 'in'), proind=indefinite pronoun (e.g., *tout* 'any', *chacun* 'every', *certain* 'some', *en* 'of it'), proper=personal pronoun (e.g., *on* 'one', *nous* 'we'), num=numeral (e.g., *ving-trois* 'twenty-three'), detart=article (e.g., *les* 'the [pl.]'), prpdet=preposition+articles (e.g., *des* 'of the [pl.]', *aux* 'to the [pl.]'), detpos=possessive (e.g., *mon* 'my [m. sg.]', *tes* 'your [pl.]').

References

Barreca, Giulia. 2015. L'acquisition de la liaison chez des apprenants italophones. Des atouts d'un corpus de natifs pour l'étude de la liaison en français langue étrangère (FLE). PhD thesis, Université de Paris Ouest Nanterre.

Bonami, Olivier, and Gilles Boyé. 2003. Supplétion et classes flexionnelles dans la conjugaison du français. *Langages* 152:102–126.

Bonami, Olivier, Gilles Boyé, and Jesse Tseng. 2005. Sur la grammaire des consonnes latentes. *Langages* 158:89–100.

Bybee, Joan. 2001a. Frequency effects on French liaison. In *Frequency and the Emergence of Linguistic Structure*, ed. Joan Bybee and Paul Hopper, 337–359. Amsterdam: John Benjamins.

———. 2001b. *Phonology and Language Use*. Cambridge: Cambridge University Press.

Chater, Nick, Alexander Clark, John Goldsmith, and Amy Perfors. 2015. *Empiricism and Language Learnability*. Oxford: Oxford University Press.

Chevalier, Jean-Claude, Claire Blanche-Benveniste, Michel Arrive, and Jean Peytard. 1964. *Grammaire du français contemporain*. Paris: Larousse.

Chevrot, Jean-Pierre, Aurélie Nardy, and Stéphanie Barbu. 2011. Developmental dynamics of SES-related differences in children's production of obligatory and variable phonological alternations. *Language Sciences* 33, no. 1: 180–191.

Côté, Marie-Hélène. 2005. Le statut lexical des consonnes de liaison. *Langages* 2:66–78.

———. 2011. French liaison. In *The Blackwell Companion to Phonology*, ed. Marc van Oostendorp, Charles Ewen, Elizabeth Hume, and Keren Rice, 2685–2710. Malden, MA: Willey-Blackwell.

———. 2014. Liaison et assibilation en français laurentien. In *La liaison: Approches contemporaines*, ed. Christiane Soum-Favaro, Anne-Lise Coquillon, and Jean-Pierre Chevrot, 9–27. Berlin: Peter Lang.

Damourette, Jacques, and Edouard Pichon. 1911–1927. *Des mots à la pensée: Essai de grammaire de la langue française*. Paris: D'Artrey.

Delattre, Pierre. 1951. *Principes de phonétique française à l'usage des étudiants anglo-américains*. Middlebury, VT: Middlebury College.

Dell, François. 1973. *Les règles et les sons: Introduction à la phonologie générative*. Paris: Hermann.

Durand, Jacques, Bernard Laks, Basilio Calderone, and Atanas Tchobanov. 2011. Que savons-nous de la liaison aujourd'hui? *Langue Française* 169: 103–135.

Durand, Jacques, Bernard Laks, and Chantal Lyche. 2013 French phonology from a corpus perspective: The PFC programme. In *The Oxford Handbook of Corpus Phonology*, ed. Jacques Durand, U. Gut, and Gjeert Kristofersen, 486–497. Oxford: Oxford University Press.

Durand, Marguerite. 1936. *Le genre grammatical en français parlé à Paris et dans la région parisienne*. Paris: Bibliothèque du Français Moderne.

Encrevé, Pierre. 1988. *La liaison avec et sans enchaînements: Phonologie tridimentionnelle et usages du français*. Paris: Le Seuil.

Fouché, Pierre. 1959. *Traité de prononciation française*. Paris: Klincksieck.

Goldsmith John. 2015. Towards a new empiricism for linguistics. In *Empiricism and Language Learnability*, ed. Nick Chater, Alexander Clark, John Goldsmith, and Amy Perfors, 58–105. Oxford: Oxford University Press.

Goldsmith, John, and Bernard Laks, eds. 2000. Editors' introduction. In *On the History of Phonology*. Special issue, *Folia Linguistica* 34, nos. 1–2: 1–10.

Gougenheim, Georges. 1938. *Le système grammatical de la langue française*. Paris: D'Artrey et Rondeix-D'Artrey.

Gougenheim, Georges, Pierre Michéa, Pierre Rivenc, and Aurelien Sauvageot. 1956. *L'élaboration du français élémentaire*. Paris: Didier.

Grammont, Maurice. 1914. *Traité pratique de prononciation française*. Paris: Delagrave.

Grevisse, Maurice. 1936. *Le bon usage*. Paris: Gembloux.

Labov, William. 1994. *Principles of Linguistic Change*. Vol. 1: *Internal Factors*. Oxford: Blackwell.

Laks, Bernard. 2005. La liaison et l'illusion. *Langages* 158:101–126.

———. 2008. Pour une phonologie de corpus. *Journal of French Language Studies* 18:3–32.

Laks, Bernard, Basilio Calderone, and Chiara Celata. 2014. French liaison and the lexical repository. In *Advances in Sociophonetics*, ed. Chiara Celata and Silvia Calamai, 29–54. Amsterdam: John Benjamins.

Laks, Bernard, and Julie Peuvergne. 2017. La liaison en français contemporain dans la parole publique (1999–2015). *Journal of French Language Studies* 27, no. 1: 55–72.

Marchello-Nizia, Christiane. 1999. *Le français en diachronie: douze siècles d'évolution*. Paris: Ophrys.

Martinet, André. 1965. Le mot. *Diogène* 51:39–53.

Martinon, Philippe. 1913. *Comment on prononce le français: Traité complet de prononciation pratique avec les noms propres et les mots étrangers*. Paris: Larousse.

Meigret, Louis. [1542] 1972. *Traité touchant le commun usage de l'écriture françoise*. Lyon: Republications Slatkine Genève.

Milner, Jean-Claude. 1967. French truncation rule. *Quarterly Progress Report of the Research Laboratory of Electronics* 86:273–283.

Morin, Yves-Charles. 1986. On the morphologization of word-final consonant deletion in French. In *Sandhi Phenomena in the Languages of Europe*, ed. Andersen Hennig, 167–210. Berlin: Mouton de Gruyter.

———. 2003. Remarks on prenominal liaison consonants in French. In *Living on the Edge: 28 Papers in Honour of Jonathan Kaye*, ed. S. Ploch, 385–400. Berlin: Mouton de Gruyter.

———. 2005a. Liaison et enchaînement dans les vers aux XVIe et XVIIe siècles. In *De la langue au style*, ed. J.-M. Gouvard, 299–318. Lyon: Presses Universitaires de Lyon.

———. 2005b. La liaison relève-t-elle d'une tendance à éviter les hiatus? Réflexions sur son évolution historique. *Langages* 158:8–23.

Morin, Yves-Charles, and Jonathan Kaye. 1982. The syntactic bases for French liaison. *Journal of Linguistics* 18:291–330.

Morrison, Allen S. 1968. A critical bibliography of studies of liaison in French speech since 1800. PhD dissertation, Columbia University.

Palsgrave, Jehan. [1530] 2003. *L'esclarcissement de la langue françoyse, composé par maistre Jehan Palsgrave, Angloys, natyf de Londres et gradué de Paris*. Paris: Honoré Champion.

Pichon, Edouard. 1938. Genre et questions connexes (sur les pas de Mlle Durand). *Le français moderne* 6:107–126.

Schane, Sanford A. 1965. *The Phonological and Morphological Structure of French.* Cambridge, MA: MIT Press.

———. 1967. L'élision et la liaison en français. *Langages* 8:37–59.

Scheer, Tobias. 2015. *Précis de structure syllabique: Accompagné d'un apparat critique.* Lyon: ENS Editions.

Scheer, Tobias, Sophie Wauquier, and Pierre Encrevé. 2015. Autosegmental news from h aspiré and liaison without enchaînement. Paper presented at the 13èmes Rencontres du Réseau Français de Phonologie (RFP), Bordeaux, June 29–July 2.

Schmid, Helmut. 1997. Probabilistic part-of-speech tagging using decision trees. In *New Methods in Language Processing*, ed. Daniel Jones and Harold Somers, 154–164. London: UCL Press.

Selkirk, Elisabeth O. 1972. *The Phrase Phonology of English and French.* Cambridge, MA: MIT Press.

Thurot, Charles. 1881–1883. *De la prononciation française depuis le commencement du XVIème siècle, d'après les témoignages des grammairiens.* Paris: Bibliothèque Nationale.

Tranel, Bernard. 1987. *The Sounds of French: An Introduction.* Cambridge: Cambridge University Press.

———. 1995. Current issues in French phonology: Liaison and position theories. In *The Handbook of Phonological Theory*, ed. John A. Goldsmith, 798–816. Oxford: Blackwell.

FOURTEEN

A Phonological Approach to the Unsupervised Learning of Root-and-Pattern Morphology

ARIS XANTHOS

14.1. Introduction

The most frequent way of forming words in languages of the world is by concatenating morphs. Consequently, research on the unsupervised learning of morphology—an area on which John Goldsmith's pioneering work has left an indelible imprint—has been mostly concerned with the segmentation of words into morphs, as illustrated by a large majority of the publications reviewed in Hammarström and Borin (2011: 319–321). In contrast, there have been few attempts to design algorithms for learning the word formation mechanism that is prevalent in languages of the Semitic family and that can be illustrated by such pairs as Arabic *jabal* 'mountain' ~ *ajbāl* 'mountains' and *ḥajar* 'stone' ~ *aḥjār* 'stones'.[1] Arabic grammatical tradition views such forms as resulting from the combination of two types of units: *roots* are sequences of consonants (e.g., *jbl*, *ḥjr*) associated with specific—although sometimes quite wide—semantic fields; *patterns* (e.g., *-a-a-*, *a--ā-*) are typically strings of vowels interspersed with insertion points (special symbols serving as placeholders for root consonants) that convey inflectional and derivational meanings. Modern linguistic treatments of Semitic languages have initially attempted to formalize this two-level model (e.g., Harris 1941; Chomsky 1951) before adopting a three-level, autosegmental perspective (McCarthy 1979). In a sense, the structure of these languages has pushed the field of morphological analysis out of its (mostly concatenative) comfort zone, and the same observation holds, decades later, for the unsupervised language learning paradigm. In general, there are many more ways of decomposing a word into two possibly discontinuous components than there are ways of splitting it into stem and suffix, for example. Moreover, the discovery procedures that have become traditional in this context, such as the successor count method of Zellig Harris (1955, 1967) and its variants, typically fail to capture discontinuous phenomena, which call for different learning mechanisms.

In Xanthos (2008), I have described (in French) an algorithm for the unsupervised learning of root-and-pattern morphology whose originality resides in its division of this learning problem into a phonological and a morphological subproblem. Using a purely distributional method, the phonological component of the analysis seeks to partition the symbols of a corpus into two sets that correspond well with the phonetic definition of consonants and vowels. Building around this result, the morphological component attempts to establish the list of roots and patterns in the corpus and to account for their combinations, in a way that has been largely inspired by John Goldsmith's conception of unsupervised learning, as embodied in the Linguistica algorithm (2001, 2006). This algorithm has been implemented in a computer program called Arabica and empirically evaluated from the point of view of its ability to learn the system of Arabic noun plurals.[2] The present contribution extends this work in two main ways. On the one hand, the learning algorithm has been further developed and several heuristics that were only evoked as part of thought experiments in Xanthos (2008) have been fully implemented. On the other hand, the empirical evaluation of the system is conducted in a more rigorous and systematic way, and the output of the algorithm is compared with that of a method recently proposed by Khaliq and Carroll (2013a) (cf. section 14.2).

The remainder of this chapter is organized as follows. Section 14.2 reviews other approaches to the unsupervised learning of root-and-pattern morphology. Section 14.3 provides a detailed description of the Arabica algorithm, including the underlying theory of root-and-pattern morphology. Section 14.4 exposes the revised methodology and new results of the empirical evaluation of the learner. Section 14.5 briefly concludes the contribution.

14.2. Related Work

Most studies addressing the unsupervised learning of root-and-pattern morphology have been concerned with modern written Arabic or classical Arabic (usually in fully vowelized form). To the best of my knowledge, the earliest work in this area is that of Roeck and Al-Fares (2000), whose goal was to cluster words that share the same root. They do so by representing words as bags-of-*n*-grams[3] and measuring the degree of overlap between these representations, taking their inspiration from a technique initially proposed by Adamson and Boreham (1974) for measuring document title similarity. Roeck and Al-Fares proposed several adaptations of the original method in order to deal with the specificities of Arabic morphology, notably the inclusion of hard-coded phonological knowledge and affix inventories. Bati (2002), working on Amharic, also made use of hard-coded phonological categories, with the more ambitious objective of identifying paradigmatic relationships between words. This work explicitly based on the methodology of Goldsmith (2001) is a precursor to the research described in Xanthos (2008) and extended in the present contribution—with the important difference that here the phonological categories are inferred in an unsupervised fashion.

In a series of related publications, Elghamry (2004) and Rodrigues and Ćavar (2005, 2007) explored the possibility of identifying triliteral Arabic roots by setting constraints on the distance between the letters they contain. Letter types are then scored with regard to the frequency with which they are found to satisfy these constraints, and these scores are in turn used to identify the most likely root for each word. The third study in this series attempts to go beyond the identification of roots and provides a paradigmatic account of root-and-pattern morphology. As far as I know, it is also the first attempt to design an integrated system for learning concatenative and nonconcatenative aspects of Arabic word formation.

The ambition of learning both kinds of morphological phenomena within a single framework is shared by two recent contributions. Fullwood and O'Donnell (2013) adopted the three-level representation advocated by McCarthy (1979), but they fuse affixes and patterns into a single type of unit, which they call *residue*. Thus, they decompose a word such as Arabic *ḥarajāt* 'forests' into root *ḥrj*, residue *aaāt*, and template *r-r-r--* (where *r* denotes a root consonant and the dash stands for a residue segment). By contrast, Botha and Blunsom (2013) were able to provide distinct representations for root and pattern intercalation and affix concatenation within a unified formalism, namely that of range concatenation grammars (Boullier 2000). Both studies use the adaptor grammar framework introduced by Johnson, Griffiths, and Goldwater (2007) as their unsupervised learning engine.

Finally, Khaliq and Carroll (2013b) recently extended the line of research pioneered by Roeck and Al-Fares (2000). Incorporating the insights of De Pauw and Wagacha (2007), they used letter subsequences as features for training a maximum entropy classifier to detect morphological relationships between Arabic words and showed that this can be done with considerable accuracy without resorting to hard-coded, language-specific knowledge. Khaliq and Carroll (2013a) proposed a different approach, which they referred to as *contrastive rescoring*. Their algorithm examines each possible decomposition of each word of a corpus into root and pattern, and iteratively scores each hypothetical root in proportion of its tendency to co-occur with frequent (hypothetical) patterns and vice versa. Their experiments show that this conceptually simple method identifies triliteral roots in stemmed, undiacriticized Arabic words with a very high accuracy. Arabica is compared to a variant of their contrastive rescoring algorithm in section 14.4.

14.3. Arabica

In line with the tradition of generative grammar, and like most recent work in the field of unsupervised language learning, Arabica relies on a conception of learning as a form of optimization. The goal of the algorithm is to identify, among a set of morphological descriptions that can account for the observed data, the one that maximizes some evaluation metric. In this section, we will successively discuss (i) the range of morphological descriptions among which an optimal one is sought, which constitutes in effect a formal theory of root-and-pattern morphology, (ii) the objective function used to evaluate candidate descriptions, and (iii) the learning (i.e., search) mechanisms put in action to that effect. It is worth noting that, regarding all aspects that are not specific to root-and-pattern morphology, Arabica is a very straightforward adaptation of the algorithm for concatenative morphology learning described in Goldsmith (2001: 164–168), and familiarity with that work should prove helpful for understanding the following characterization.

14.3.1. A Formal Theory of Root-and-Pattern Morphology

Arabica operates on the basis of a corpus D segmented into words: $D \in W^+$, $W \subset P^+$, where P stands for the set of symbols (letters or phonemes) in the corpus and W for its lexicon (in general, A^+ represents the set of all sequences that can be built by assembling elements of A, and A^* represents the same set with the addition of the empty string). Let $\tilde{P} \subset P \cup \{\text{-}\}$ denote the set consisting of all vowels plus the symbol - (hyphen) that stands for an insertion point. The output of the program is a *model* M uniquely associated with a *description* D^M of the corpus under this model (more on D^M in the next paragraph). The model is a triple (R, T, Π), where R is a set of *roots* (sequences of symbols in P^+), T is a set of *patterns* (sequences of symbols in $\tilde{P}^*$), and Π is a set of *root-and-pattern (RP) structures*. RP structures are analogous to *signatures* in Goldsmith (2001). Each RP structure consist of a list of pointers to elements of R and a list of pointers to elements of T; it encodes the information that any of these roots can be *composed* with any of these patterns (i.e., its consonants can be placed in the pattern's insertion points) in order to form a word.[4] For instance, an RP structure pointing to roots *jbl* and *ḥjr* as well as patterns *-a-a-*, *-i-ā-*, and *a--ā-*, accounts for six words: Arabic *jabal* 'mountain', *jibāl/ajbāl* 'mountains', *ḥajar* 'stone', and *ḥijār/aḥjār* 'stones'.[5] It is further assumed that every model includes a special, so-called *zero* RP structure, which points to a unique pattern (similarly called a *zero* pattern), to which no other RP structure points. This pattern can be thought of as an identity operator that, when composed with any given root, returns the root itself. Words generated in this way by the zero RP structure are said to be *unanalyzed*. It is also important to note that every root in R is pointed to by exactly one RP structure—if only the zero RP structure.

The description D^M of corpus D under model M represents each occurrence of a word $w \in W$ by means of its *analysis* $A(w)$, which is a triple of pointers: to an RP structure and, within it, to a root (pointer) and a pattern (pointer). Thus the original corpus can be reconstructed losslessly based on D^M and M using the following procedure: for each word analysis in D^M, retrieve the RP structure it points to in Π and then the relevant root and pattern pointers within this structure; using these pointers, retrieve the actual root and pattern in their respective sets R and T, compose them, and add the resulting word to the corpus.[6]

14.3.2. Evaluation Metric

Arabica relies on an evaluation metric to guide its search for an optimal model M (and associated corpus description D^M) for a given corpus D. Following a well-established line of research (see, e.g., Brent and Cartwright 1996; Kazakov 1997; Goldsmith 2001, 2006; Creutz and Lagus 2002), this metric is based on the *minimum description length* (MDL) principle (Rissanen 1978). This principle essentially states that when selecting among candidate hypotheses for explaining a set of observations, one should seek to simultaneously minimize the complexity of the hypothesis and the complexity of the description of the observations under this hypothesis. In our case, this translates to look for the model M that minimizes the sum $L(M)+L(D^M)$ of the length of the model and the length of the corpus description under the model.

The main challenge for implementing this seemingly simple program is to provide a sound formal definition for the intuitive notion of length, which typically involves a systematic recourse to elements of probability, coding, and information theory. Spelling every detail of the resulting formalism in the case of Arabica's evaluation metric is beyond the scope of this chapter, and we will limit ourselves to a high-level overview.[7] In general, we seek to evaluate the length of an item (be it a root, a pointer to an RP structure, or an entire model) as the minimal number of bits with which it can be encoded (or compressed) under some optimal coding scheme. In so doing, we resort to the following information-theoretic results:

1. The compressed length of a pointer to an element in a distribution, for example a root $r \in R$, is $-\log P(r)$, that is the inverse log probability of this element—its *plog*, in John Goldsmith's terminology (see, e.g., Goldsmith and Riggle 2012). In some cases, notably when the elements are symbols in P or $\tilde{P}$, we will simplify calculations by approximating this value with $\log m$, where m is the number of distinct items in the distribution in question.[8]
2. The compressed length of a sequence of n elements (e.g., the list R of roots) is the sum of the length of each individual element in the sequence plus a small term $\lambda(n)$, slightly greater than $\log n$, which is the cost for consolidating them into a list (Goldsmith 2001: 166).

For instance, using these principles, the compressed length of a root $r \in R$, which is really a sequence of pointers to symbols in P, can be evaluated as $L(r) := \lambda(|r|) + |r| \log |P|$, where $|\cdot|$ stands for the cardinality of a set and, by extension, the number of items in a sequence. In turn, the compressed length $L(R)$ of the entire list of roots can be calculated as $\lambda(|R|)+\Sigma_{r\in R}L(r)$. By contrast, the compressed length of a *pointer* to a root $r \in R$ in an RP structure is $-\log P(r)$, where the probability of r can be estimated by the corpus count of words that have r in their analysis divided by the total number of words in D. With an additional degree of abstraction, the compressed length of a pointer to a pointer to a root $r \in R$ (as found in the analysis of a word in D^M) is $-\log P(r|\pi)$, the plog of the conditional probability of the root (pointer) within the RP structure π that contains it. The same logic can be applied to the evaluation of the compressed length of all elements of M and D^M.

14.3.3. Learning Process

For anything larger than a toy corpus, the range of possible models compatible with the theory of root-and-pattern morphology exposed in section 14.3.1 is much too large to be searched exhaustively. For this reason, a series of heuristics are used to restrict (drastically) the number of models that are effectively evaluated as part of the learning process. Here again, Arabica takes inspiration from Linguistica, in that it uses a first heuristic to bootstrap the search procedure and identify a suitable starting point, which consecutive heuristics attempt to improve in an incremental fashion, under the guidance of the MDL-based evaluation metric discussed in section 14.3.2.

14.3.3.1. Phonological Bootstrapping

What crucially distinguishes Arabica from other approaches to the unsupervised learning of root-and-pattern morphology is that it uses a phonological approach to bootstrap the morphological learning process. In particular, it applies an unsupervised method for partitioning the symbols of the corpus into consonants and vowels, taking advantage of the tendency for these categories to alternate more often than they cluster in the languages of the world. Several techniques can be used to that effect, as reviewed in Goldmith and Xanthos (2009). The technique that is currently implemented in Arabica is the algorithm of Sukhotin (1962), which is conceptually simple, computationally efficient, and yet reasonably accurate (see Xanthos 2008: 75–89). In a nutshell, it starts with the assumption that all symbols are consonants and iterates over the following steps: (i) find the consonant that occurs most frequently next to a consonant (relative to its frequency next to a vowel); (ii) reclassify this symbol as a vowel. The algorithm terminates when no consonant is found to co-occur more frequently with a consonant than with a vowel.

Once a division of symbols into consonants and vowels has been found, Arabica tentatively decomposes every word in the corpus into a hypothetical root and pattern (e.g., Arabic *sadīm* 'fog'→*sdm*, *-a-ī-*). At this point, it is crucial to take certain precautions: whereas in a Semitic language, the results of this first analysis are likely to be quite accurate, the same does not hold for the vast majority of the world's languages. Therefore, in a truly unsupervised setting (i.e., when the language of the data is not known a priori), it is essential to set further conditions for accepting this initial decomposition into root and pattern. The current implementation of Arabica follows the practice advocated by Goldsmith (2001: 173) and rejects every decomposition unless it enters a *Greenberg square* (Greenberg 1957), which is a set of four words that can be composed (in our case) based on a pair of roots and a pair of patterns. For instance, the presence in the corpus of Arabic *sudum* 'fogs', *ṭarīq* 'road', and *ṭuruq* 'roads' would support the decomposition of *sadīm* into *sdm* and *-a-ī-* and more generally the creation of an RP structure associating roots *sdm* and *ṭrq* with patterns *-a-ī-* and *-u-u-*.[9]

14.3.3.2. Incremental Heuristics

At the end of the bootstrapping step, most words of the corpus are expected to remain unanalyzed, but the identified roots and patterns should be fairly reliable. Arabica then successively applies several heuristics that leverage the inferred structure to increase the data coverage. This is where the MDL-based evaluation metric comes into play: each heuristic identifies a number of possible changes to the current state of the model M and validates only those that decrease the sum of the compressed lengths of M and D^M. The first such heuristic is *extend known RP structures* (EKRPS), which was already implemented in the version of Arabica described in Xanthos (2008). It examines each existing RP structure by decreasing order of robustness[10] and tries to find sets of unanalyzed words in the corpus that can be decomposed into a previously unknown root associated with each of the patterns in this RP structure. This root is then created and added to the RP structure (provided that it leads to a decrease in the evaluation metric, which will be implicit in the remainder of this discussion).

In the version of Arabica that has been rewritten for the purpose of this study, three more incremental heuristics have been implemented.

Extend fragments of known RP structures examines each RP structure by decreasing order of robustness, this time in order to find sets of unanalyzed words that are associated with a subset of this RP structure's patterns (at least two of them), and creates new roots and RP structures for the words in question. For instance, if the model already contains an RP structure associating a set of roots with patterns *-a--*, *-u-ū-*, and *a--u-*, and plural variants *aʿyun* and *ʿuyūn* 'eyes' are still unanalyzed, this heuristic will create a new root *ʿyn* as well as a new RP structure linking it with *-a--* and *-u-ū-*. *Extend known roots to known patterns* attempts to find unanalyzed words that can be decomposed into previously identified roots and patterns and creates new RP structures for them. For example, suppose that there exists an RP structure associating several roots, including *mlḥ*, with patterns *-i-ā-* and *a--ā-*, thus accounting for plural variants *milāḥ* and *amlāḥ* 'salt-PL' among others; further suppose that another RP structure contains pattern *-i--*, and that *milḥ* 'salt' is still unanalyzed. Then this heuristic will create a new RP structure associating *mlḥ* (and possibly other roots) with patterns *-i--*, *-i-ā-*, and *a--ā-*. Finally, *extend known roots* considers each root in RP structures whose robustness is above a given threshold and looks for unanalyzed words that can be decomposed into this root and a new pattern. Then it collects all such patterns in a list and creates new RP structures for those that are more frequent than a given threshold. For instance, if a robust RP structure associates a set of roots, among which *šʿr*, with patterns *-a--* and *-u-ū-* (thus accounting for the collective versus plural opposition in *šaʿr* 'hair-COL' ~ *šuʿūr* 'hair-PL'), and the singulative *šaʿra* 'hair-SGV' is still unanalyzed, the heuristic will create a new pattern *-a--a* and a new RP structure with root *šʿr* and patterns *-a--* and *-u-ū-*, and *-a--a* (provided that there are enough occurrences of the latter in the corpus). The entire series of four incremental heuristics is applied iteratively until no more decrease of the evaluation metric can be observed.

14.4. Empirical Evaluation

The methodology used for evaluating the original implementation of Arabica focused on the detailed inspection of the data and of the output of the algorithm at various stages of the learning process, which made it possible to formulate precise predictions about the expected impact of several incremental heuristics that had not yet been implemented (see Xanthos 2008: 178–199). Now that three more such heuristics are available, it makes sense to effectively evaluate them, and we take advantage of this opportunity for attempting to improve aspects of the evaluation procedure.

14.4.1. Data

The corpus used for this evaluation is the one that has been compiled and used in Xanthos (2008: 178–181).[11] It has been created by looking up the eighty-four nouns of the word list developed by Morris Swadesh (1952) in the dictionary of modern written Arabic of Hans Wehr (1994), and recording from the latter the first singular form (or the noun of unity), the collective form (if any), as well as all plural forms of each noun. An important difference with the setup of Xanthos (2008) is that the corpus has not been stemmed with Linguistica prior to the execution of Arabica, in the perspective of getting a better view of how the presence of concatenative morphology actually affects the process of root-and-pattern morphology learning.[12] The data finally used for the evaluation contains 243 tokens and one fewer type (the form *anhur* being a plural of both *nahār* 'day' and *nahr* 'river').

14.4.2. Method

The experiment reported in Xanthos (2008) assessed mainly one aspect of the algorithm's output: the proportion of words that were analyzed (i.e., associated with a nonzero RP structure), that is a form of *recall*. The algorithm's *precision* was not formally reported, essentially because none of the inferred RP structures was found to associate with the same root words that actually belonged to distinct lexemes. Since the new version of the algorithm runs several supplementary incremental heuristics, we expect a larger proportion of analyzed words and more errors, which makes it desirable to adopt a more systematic way of evaluating precision and recall.

Calculating these measures requires comparing a fixed number of observed responses to a binary decision with the corresponding desired responses (the so-called *gold standard*). In Xanthos (2008), the binary decision in question was to analyze a word or leave it unanalyzed, and the computation of recall implicitly relied on the assumption that all words should be analyzed—a questionable assumption, if only because the corresponding precision can only be 100 percent. In the present experiment, the relevant binary decision is whether a relationship exists between each pair of word types in the corpus (ignoring self-pairings). We consider two distinct kinds of relationships, namely sharing the same root and sharing the same pattern, which leads us to reporting separate precision and recall values for roots and patterns.

Establishing the gold standard for this evaluation is not a trivial task. For roots, the entries of the Swadesh list have been used as the clustering criterion. In most cases, this means that related words share the exact same sequence of consonants, but it also leads to grouping words whose consonants do not exactly correspond (notably because of the various modifications that so-called *weak* consonants *y*, *w*, and *ʿ* undergo) as well as a few cases of suppletion. For patterns, I have initially grouped words based on the patterning of symbols used for transcribing vowels, then modified the resulting clustering based on known morphophonological processes and analogical reasoning. For instance *ʿain* 'eye' is taken to have pattern *-a--* because (i) the symbol *i* is sometimes used as a transliteration of the same semivowel as *y* (ي); (ii) the corresponding plurals *ʿuyūn* and *aʿyun* contain *y*; (iii) treating *y* as a root consonant in the plural forms leads to the frequent patterns *-u-ū-* and *a--u-*; and (iv) these patterns are frequently associated with singular forms whose pattern is *-a--*. Feminine and sound plural suffixes (*-a* and *-āt*) have also been systematically treated as part of the pattern.

14.4.3. Results

The results of the evaluation are summarized in figure 14.1, where precision and recall for root and pattern relationships are reported at various stage of the learning process: after the phonological bootstrapping phase (INIT); after the first incremental heuristics, for comparison with Xanthos (2008) (EKRPS); and after one, two, and three runs of the entire set of incremental heuristics (1 ITER, 2 ITER, 3 ITER).[13] The complete list of inferred RP structures is given in Appendix 14b.

Compared to the version of Arabica described in Xanthos (2008), represented by EKRPS in figure 14.1, the addition of new incremental heuristics and their iterations leads to a substantial increase in recall: +22.4 percent for roots and+27 percent for patterns. Pattern precision remains 100 percent in all cases, but root precision decreases slightly with the application of the new heuristics. The inferred relationships that cause this decrease are between three pairs of entries from the Swadesh list that correspond each to a single entry of the Wehr dictionary (*nahār* 'day'–*nahr* 'river', *baʿl* 'husband–*baʿla* 'wife', and *rijāl* 'men'–*rijl* 'foot'), and it is not always obvious that they should really be counted as errors. In any event, the final results (100 percent precision and 56.2 percent

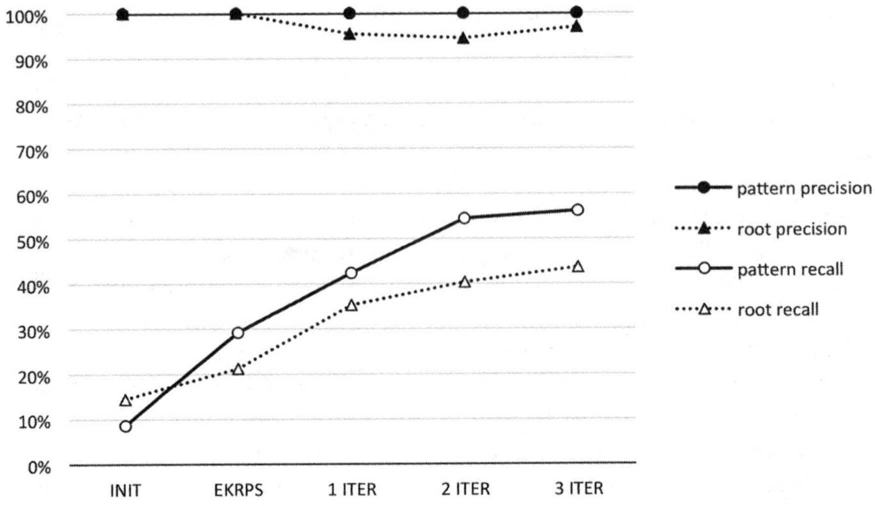

14.1 Precision and recall for root and pattern relationships.

recall for patterns, 97 percent precision and 43.6 percent recall for roots) confirm that a considerable portion of the morphological relationships can be learned at the cost of very few precision errors.

Except for the bootstrapping phase, the algorithm obtains consistently better results on pattern relationships than root relationships, particularly from the point of view of recall. The most likely explanation for this is that patterns are less subject to formal variations than roots. Even without taking the sound plural suffix *-āt* into account, 51 of 146 plural forms of our corpus do not contain exactly the same consonants as the corresponding singular and thus elude our phonological approach. In the rare cases where a pattern undergoes a similar modification, it is usually related to a root modification.

Figure 14.2 shows a comparison between the results of Arabica and those of the contrastive rescoring algorithm of Khaliq and Carroll (2013b) on the same corpus.[14] Arabica fares better with these data on most accounts. The reason why contrastive rescoring proves better at retrieving pattern relationships seems to be that this algorithm initially conceived for dealing with undiacriticized data tends to assign only part of the short vowels to patterns. As a result, some of the patterns it infers cover a very large number of words (e.g., 61 of 242 words are associated with pattern *--ā-*) and fewer pattern relationships end up being overlooked. It should also be noted that contrastive rescoring is able to find root relationships between a number of words that Arabica fails to associate because

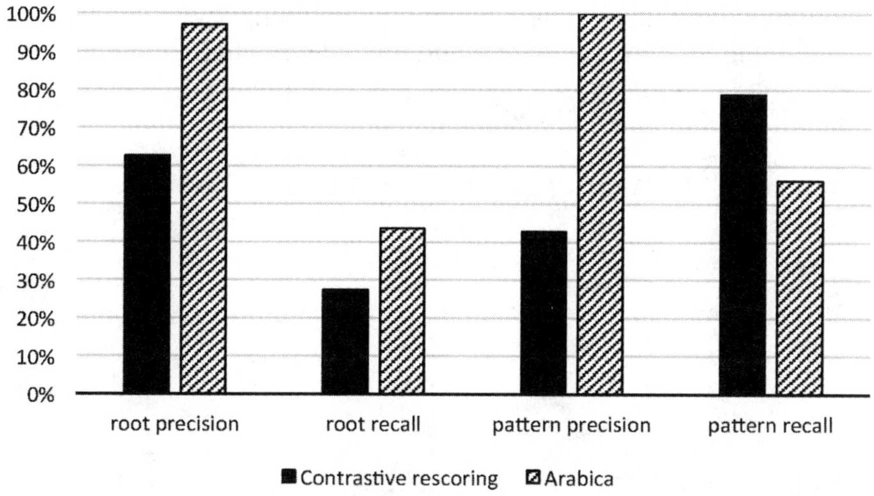

14.2 Comparison of contrastive rescoring (Kahliq and Carroll 2013a) and Arabica.

of root consonant modifications, so that it would be worth exploring the possibility of having the two algorithms cooperate in some way.

14.5. Conclusion

This contribution has offered a brief summary of the phonological approach to the unsupervised learning of root-and-pattern morphology originally described in Xanthos (2008) and largely developed under the direct supervision of John Goldsmith, to whom this volume is dedicated.[15] The original work has been extended here in mainly two ways, namely the development of the learning mechanism and the refinement of the evaluation procedure. In my view, the new results confirm that the conception of unsupervised learning I have learned from working with John Goldsmith remains as relevant as ever: start by identifying a restricted set of highly reliable units, then gradually extend the analysis to less clear-cut cases, guided by a suitable evaluation procedure. While this conception is useful for dealing with a variety of problems, it is crucial in the perspective of applying a phonological approach to the problem of root-and-pattern morphology learning. Presumably, every language in the world lends itself to the induction of phonological categories, but in the vast majority of them, using these categories as the main criterion for learning morphology would lead to disastrous inferences. The challenge is then to design appropriate ways of initially restraining the power of the inference and later making up for it by leveraging the safe bits of information previously acquired.[16]

Appendix 14a: Wehr's Transliteration Scheme

Arabic	Wehr	Arabic	Wehr	Arabic	Wehr
ا	*ā* or *ʾ*	ر	*r*	ق	*q*
ب	*b*	ز	*z*	ك	*k*
ت	*t*	س	*s*	ل	*l*
ث	*ṯ*	ش	*š*	م	*m*
ج	*j*	ص	*ṣ*	ن	*n*
ح	*ḥ*	ض	*ḍ*	ه	*h*
خ	*ḵ*	ط	*ṭ*	و	*w*, *u*, or *ū*
د	*d*	ظ	*ẓ*	ي	*y*, *i*, or *ī*
ذ	*ḏ*	ع	*ʿ*	ة	*a*
ر	*r*	غ	*ḡ*		

Appendix 14b: Inferred RP Structures

The following table indicates, for each RP structure inferred by Arabica during the empirical evaluation, its robustness (see note 10), the roots and patterns it contains, as well as the heuristics responsible for initially creating it.

Robustness	Roots	Patterns	Creator
33	*smk, ḥrj, ṯmr*	*-a-a-, -a-a-a, -i-ā-, a--ā-*	PBS
19	*bṭn, r's, ẓhr*	*-a--, -u-ū-, a--u-*	PBS
18	*bḥr, ḥbl*	*-a--, -i-ā-, -u-ū-, a--u-, a--ā-*	EKRKP-1
15	*qlb, šms, šḥm, ṯlj*	*-a--, -u-ū-*	PBS
9	*jbl, ḥjr*	*-a-a-, -i-ā-, a--ā-*	EKRKP-1
8	*b'l, š'r*	*-a--, -a--a, -u-ū-*	EKR1
5	*dḵn, trb*	*-u-ā-, a--i-a*	PBS
5	*bḍ, ll*	*-ai-, -ai-a*	PBS
4	*ryš, ryḥ*	*-i-ā-, a--ā-*	PBS
4	*sdm, ṭrq*	*-a-ī-, -u-u-*	PBS
4	*kbd, ṭyr*	*-u-ū-, a--ā-*	EFKRPS-2
3	*klb, rml*	*-a--, -i-ā-*	PBS
3	*qšr, 'rq*	*-i--, -u-ū-*	PBS
−3	*'yn*	*-u-ū-, a--u-*	EFKRPS-1
−3	*rqb*	*-a-a-a, -i-ā-*	EFKRPS-1
−3	*wrq*	*-a-a-, -a-a-a*	EFKRPS-1
−3	*šjr*	*-a-a-, -a-a-a, a--ā-*	EFKRPS-1
−3	*'ẓm*	*-a--, -i-ā-, a--u-*	EKRKP-1

Robustness	Roots	Patterns	Creator
–3	*lḥm*	*-a--, -i-ā-, -u-ū-*	EKRKP-1
–3	*nhr*	*-a--, -u-u-, -u-ū-, a--u-, a--ā-*	EKRKP-1
–3	*mlḥ*	*-i--, -i-ā-, a--ā-*	EKRKP-1
–3	*qml*	*-a--, -a--a*	EFKRPS-2
–3	*snn*	*-i--, a--ā-*	EFKRPS-2
–3	*zhr*	*-a--, -a--a, -u-ū-, a--u-, a--ā-*	EKRKP-2
–3	*rjl*	*-i--, -i-ā-, a--u-*	EKRKP-2
–3	*lsn*	*-i-ā-, a--i-a, a--u-*	EKRKP-2
–3	*bḏr*	*-a--, -a--a, -i-ā-, -u-ū-*	EKRKP-2
–3	*jnḥ*	*a--i-a, a--u-*	EFKRPS-3
–3	*ḥrb*	*-a--a, -i-ā-*	EFKRPS-3

Note: EFKRPS, extend fragments of known RP structures; EKR, extend known roots (the numeric suffix of incremental heuristics indicates the iteration); EKRKP, extend known roots to known patterns; EKRPS, extend known RP structures; PBS, Phonological bootstrapping.

Notes

This contribution extends the work carried on during a stay (funded by the Swiss National Science Foundation) at the University of Chicago, in John Goldsmith's Linguistica group. It would simply not have been possible without John's illuminating, diligent and benevolent guidance.

1. Here and throughout the chapter, the modern written variant of Arabic is being used and Arabic forms are transliterated according to the conventions of Wehr (1994) (cf. Appendix 14a).
2. Arabica v1.0 was originally written in Perl. The program has been entirely rewritten in Python for the purpose of this study, and the new implementation, Arabica 2.0 (as well as the legacy code), is available from https://github.com/axanthos/arabica.
3. With $n=2$, for instance, *zalzala* 'earthquake' would be represented by the set of bigrams *za, al, lz, la*.
4. In this context, *pointers* are conceived as a means to avoid the redundancy of writing the same piece of information (e.g., a morph's phonological form) at more than one place in the morphology.
5. More examples of RP structures can be found in Appendix 14b.
6. This means that the model is, under this theory, a purely descriptive (as opposed to predictive) device, in the sense that it makes no attempt to account for previously unseen data.
7. The reader interested in a full specification of the evaluation metric is referred to Xanthos (2008: 163–165).

8. This simplification amounts to using a block code (i.e., a code where each item is written with a fixed number of bits, such as the ASCII 8-bit code) in place of a truly optimal, variable-length binary code in which frequent items are written with a lesser number of bits than rare ones are.
9. An additional precaution is that a root can be posited only if its length is not less than a given threshold (two letters in the current implementation).
10. The *robustness* of a (nonzero) RP structure is defined as the number of symbols that are saved by writing the set of roots and patterns it points to in place of the corresponding set of words. It serves as an approximation of the impact of an individual RP structure on the overall evaluation metric.
11. The complete corpus including forms in Arabic script and Wehr transliteration can be found in an appendix of Xanthos (2008: 235–242). An electronic version using the Buckwalter ASCII transcription (cf. http://www.qamus.org/transliteration.htm) is available from https://github.com/axanthos/arabica.
12. Less importantly, two pairs of nouns that are distinct in the Swadesh list but correspond each to a single entry of Wehr (1994) have been collapsed here (*rijl* 'foot/leg' and *ṯalj* 'ice/snow').
13. For this corpus, no more modifications of the model occur after the third iteration.
14. To be precise, the contrastive rescoring applied here excludes the refinement step discussed in Khaliq and Carroll (2013b: 1014), and the number of iterations has been set to ten for this experiment. These results have been kindly provided by Bilal Khaliq, whom I thank for his help.
15. What may come as a surprise for John is that I have not forgotten his advice to publish this material in English—if I were him, I would have given up any hope of it ever happening long ago.
16. Conforming to this prescription is a true form of asceticism in the name of the unsupervised: with our data, simply removing the Greenberg square condition in the phonological bootstrapping phase (see section 14.3.3) leads to a precision of 88.4 percent and a recall of 72.5 percent for root relationships as well as a precision of 99.8 percent and a recall of 86.4 percent for pattern relationships.

References

Adamson, George W., and Jillian Boreham. 1974. The use of an association measure based on character structure to identify semantically related pairs of words and document titles. *Information Storage and Retrieval* 10, no. 7–8: 253–260.

Bati, Tesfaye Bayu. 2002. Automatic morphological analyzer for Amharic. Master's thesis, Addis Ababa University.

Botha, Jan, and Phil Blunsom. 2013. Adaptor grammars for learning non-concatenative morphology. In *Proceedings of the 2013 Conference on Empirical Methods in Natural Language Processing*, ed. David Yarowsky, Timothy Baldwin, Anna Korhonen, Karen Livescu, and Steven Bethard, 345–356. Stroudsburg, PA: Association for Computational Linguistics. http://aclweb.org/anthology/D13-1034.

Boullier, Pierre. 2000. A cubic time extension of context-free grammars. *Grammars* 3, no. 2–3: 111–131.

Brent, Michael R., and Timothy Cartwright. 1996. Distributional regularity and phonotactic constraints are useful for segmentation. *Cognition* 61:93–125.

Chomsky, Noam. 1951. Morphophonemics of modern Hebrew. Master's thesis, University of Pennsylvania.

Creutz, Mathias, and Krista Lagus. 2002. Unsupervised discovery of morphemes. In *Proceedings of ACL-02 Workshop on Morphological and Phonological Learning*, ed. Mike Maxwell, 21–30. Stroudsburg, PA: Association for Computational Linguistics. http://aclweb.org/anthology/W02-0603.

Elghamry, Khaled. 2004. A constraint-based algorithm for the identification of Arabic roots. In *Proceedings of the Midwest Computational Linguistics Colloquium*. Bloomington: University of Indiana. https://www.researchgate.net/publication/228522853_A_Constraint-based_Algorithm_for_the_Identification_of_Arabic_Roots.

Fullwood, Michelle, and Tim O'Donnell. 2013. Learning non-concatenative morphology. In *Proceedings of the 4th Annual Workshop on Cognitive Modeling and Computational Linguistics (CMCL)*, ed. Vera Demberg and Roger Levy, 21–27. Stroudsburg, PA: Association for Computational Linguistics. http://aclweb.org/anthology/W13-2603.

Goldsmith, John A. 2001. Unsupervised learning of the morphology of a natural language. *Computational Linguistics* 27, no. 2: 153–198. http://www.aclweb.org/anthology/J01-2001.

———. 2006. An algorithm for the unsupervised learning of morphology. *Natural Language Engineering* 12, no. 4: 353–371.

Goldsmith, John A., and Jason Riggle. 2012. Information theoretic approaches to phonological structure: the case of Finnish vowel harmony. *Natural Language and Linguistic Theory* 30, no. 3: 859–896.

Goldsmith, John A., and Aris Xanthos. 2009. Learning phonological categories. *Language* 85, no. 1: 4–38.

Greenberg, Joseph Harold. 1957. *Essays in Linguistics*. Chicago: University of Chicago Press.

Hammarström, Harald, and Lars Borin. 2011. Unsupervised learning of morphology. *Computational Linguistics* 37, no. 2: 309–350. http://www.aclweb.org/anthology/J11-2002.

Harris, Zellig S. 1941. Linguistic structure of Hebrew. *Journal of the American Oriental Society* 61, no. 3: 143–167.

———. 1955. From phoneme to morpheme. *Language* 18, no. 3: 190–222.

———. 1967. Morpheme boundaries within words: Report on a computer test. *Transformations and Discourse Analysis Papers* 73:68–77.

Johnson, Mark, Thomas L. Griffiths, and Sharon Goldwater. 2007. Adaptor grammars: A framework for specifying compositional nonparametric Bayesian models. In *Advances in Neural Information Processing Systems*, vol. 19, ed. Bernhard Schölkopf, John Platt, and Thomas Hoffman, 641–648. Cambridge, MA: MIT Press.

Kazakov, Dimitar. 1997. Unsupervised learning of naïve morphology with genetic algorithms. In *Workshop Notes of the ECML/MLnet Workshop on Empirical Learning of Natural Language Processing Tasks*, ed. Walter Daelemans, Antal van den Bosch, and Ton Weijters, 105–112. Prague.

Khaliq, Bilal, and John Carroll. 2013a. Induction of root and pattern lexicon for unsupervised morphological analysis of Arabic. In *Proceedings of the 6th International Joint Conference on Natural Language Processing*, ed. Ruslan Mitkov and Jong C. Park, 1012–1016. Nagoya, Japan: Asian Federation of Natural Language Processing. http://aclweb.org/anthology/I13-1137.

———. 2013b. Unsupervised induction of Arabic root and pattern lexicons using machine learning. In *Proceedings of the 9th Conference on Recent Advances in Natural Language Processing (RANLP-13)*, ed. Ruslan Mitkov, Galia Angelova, and Kalina Boncheva, 350–356. Hissar, Bulgaria: INCOMA Ltd. Shoumen. http://aclweb.org/anthology/R13-1045.

McCarthy, John J. 1979. Formal problems in Semitic phonology and morphology. PhD dissertation, Massachusetts Institute of Technology.

Pauw, Guy de, and Peter W. Wagacha. 2007. Bootstrapping morphological analysis of Gĩkũyũ using maximum entropy learning. In *Proceedings of the 8th Annual Conference of the International Speech Communication Association (INTERSPEECH 2007)*, Antwerp, Belgium, 1517–1520. Baixas, France: International Speech Communication Association. http://www.isca-speech.org/archive/interspeech_2007/index.html#Biblio.

Rissanen, Jorma. 1978. Modelling by shortest data description. *Automatica* 14:465–471.

Rodrigues, Paul, and Damir Ćavar. 2005. Learning Arabic morphology using information theory. *Proceedings from the Annual Meeting of the Chicago Linguistic Society* 41:49–58.

Rodrigues, Paul, and Damir Ćavar. 2007. Learning Arabic morphology using statistical constraint-satisfaction models. In *Perspectives on Arabic Linguistics: Papers from the 19th Annual Symposium on Arabic Linguistics*, ed. Elabas Benmamoun, 63–75. Amsterdam: John Benjamin.

Roeck, Anne de, and Waleed Al-Fares. 2000. A morphologically sensitive clustering algorithm for identifying Arabic roots. In *Proceedings of the 38th Annual Meeting of the Association for Computational Linguistics*, 199–206.

Stroudsburg, PA: Association for Computational Linguistics. http://aclweb.org/anthology/P00-1026.

Sukhotin, Boris V. 1962. Eksperimental'noe vydelenie klassov bukv s pomoščju EVM. *Problemy strukturnoj lingvistiki* 234:189–206.

Swadesh, Morris. 1952. Lexico-statistic dating of prehistoric ethnic contacts: With special reference to North American Indians and Eskimos. *Proceedings of the American Philosophical Society* 96, no. 4: 452–463.

Wehr, Hans. 1994. *A Dictionary of Modern Written Arabic*. Urbana, IL: Spoken Language Services.

Xanthos, Aris. 2008. *Apprentissage automatique de la morphologie: Le cas des structures racine-schème*. Bern: Peter Lang.

Contributors

Diane Brentari is the Mary K. Werkman Professor of Linguistics and a director of the Center for Gesture Sign Language at the University of Chicago. Her ongoing interests are in sign languages. Currently her work focuses on how phonological and morphological systems emerge in new sign languages and in the protactile variety of sign language used by DeafBlind individuals.

Basilio Calderone is a research engineer at the French National Center for Research (CNRS), working in the University of Toulouse–Jean Jaurès. He obtained his PhD in 2008 from the Scuola Normale Superiore of Pisa, Italy. His current research interests include computational morphology, phonotactics, and lexicon design.

Chiara Celata is researcher of linguistics and speech sciences at Scuola Normale Superiore di Pisa and assistant professor of educational linguistics at the University of Siena. Her current research interests include multilevel articulatory approaches to speech variation, the sociophonetics of the Romance languages, bilingualism, and first-language phonological attrition.

John Coleman is professor of phonetics and director of the Phonetics Laboratory at the University of Oxford, England. His research is in acoustic phonetics, speech processing, computational and quantitative phonology, and modeling of sound change. Before his academic career, he worked in speech technology research for the telecommunications industry.

Louis Goldstein is professor of linguistics at the University of Southern California. Previously he spent twenty-seven years at Yale

University and Haskins Laboratories. He works on articulatory phonology and other dynamical systems approaches to phonology and phonetics, developing models of speech production, and supporting these efforts through new approaches to articulatory data acquisition and analysis.

Larry M. Hyman is professor of linguistics and executive director of the France-Berkeley Fund at the University of California, Berkeley. His long-standing interests are in phonological theory and typology and the comparative and historical study of Niger-Congo languages, particularly Bantu and its closest relatives.

Khalil Iskarous is associate professor of linguistics at the University of Southern California. His interests span phonetics and phonology, which he studies from a dynamical systems perspective.

James Kirby received his PhD in linguistics from the University of Chicago in 2010. Since that time he has been a lecturer (now reader) in the Department of Linguistics and English Language at the University of Edinburgh. His research considers the phonetic and phonological underpinnings of sound change, with particular attention to the emergence of lexical tone and register systems.

D. Robert (Bob) Ladd studied pre-Chomskyan linguistics as an undergraduate at Brown University in the 1960s and has been trying to make sense of phonology ever since. He finished his PhD at Cornell University in 1978, and after a series of one- and two-year jobs in the United States and Europe, he ended up at the University of Edinburgh in1985, where he spent the rest of his career. He officially retired in 2011 and was elected Fellow of the British Academy in 2015.

Bernard Laks is professor of language sciences at Paris Nanterre University. He is a senior member of the Institut Universitaire de France. He has published extensively in phonology, corpus linguistics, and cognitive linguistics. Recently he has done research in the history of linguistics and cognitive sciences, in collaboration with John Goldsmith.

William R. Leben is emeritus professor of linguistics at Stanford University with a PhD in linguistics from the Massachusetts Institute of Technology. His publications include a number of African-language textbooks and articles on tone and phonological theory. With Brett Kessler, he recently published *Introduction to the Languages of the World* (Oxford University Press).

Jackson L. Lee is a PhD candidate in the Department of Linguistics at the University of Chicago. He works mainly on computational linguistics, natural language processing, morphology, and phonology.

Mark Liberman is trustee professor of phonetics in the Department of Linguistics and professor in the Department of Computer and Information Sciences at the University of Pennsylvania. His main research interests lie in phonetics, prosody, and other aspects of speech communication. His early research was instrumental in establishing the linguistic subfield of metrical phonology, and much of his current research is conducted through computational analyses of linguistic corpora.

David Odden was professor of linguistics at Ohio State University and specializes in phonological theory and the structure of African languages. He is particularly known for his empirical studies of Bantu tone systems.

Bridget D. Samuels received her PhD in linguistics from Harvard University and has taught at Harvard, the University of Maryland, and Pomona College. She focuses primarily on the intersection between linguistic theory and biology and is currently based at the Center for Craniofacial Molecular Biology at the University of Southern California.

Morgan Sonderegger is assistant professor of linguistics at McGill University, Canada. He received his PhD in computer science and linguistics from the University of Chicago in 2012. He works on variation in phonology and phonetics, primarily using corpus data and quantitative methods.

Bert Vaux is reader in phonology and morphology at the University of Cambridge. He is primarily interested in phenomena that shed light on the structure and origins of the phonological component of grammar, especially in the realms of psychophonology, historical linguistics, and sociolinguistics.

Caroline Wiltshire is associate professor of linguistics at the University of Florida. John Goldsmith was her advisor for her PhD (University of Chicago, 1992). Her research focus is theoretical phonology, especially syllable phonology, and its interactions with morphology, phonetics, and second language acquisition in languages including Spanish, Tamil, Arabic, and World Englishes.

Aris Xanthos, a linguist by training, is senior lecturer in humanities computing at the University of Lausanne. His current research interests lie mainly in the study and development of innovative methods and interfaces for the analysis of arts and humanities data, with a particular emphasis on their textual and linguistic aspects. He is the author of several open source software products, notably the Textable visual programming environment for text analysis.

Index